NEW DEVELOPMENTS IN LEARNING RESEARCH

NEW DEVELOPMENTS IN LEARNING RESEARCH

SAMUEL N. HOGAN
EDITOR

Nova Science Publishers, Inc.
New York

Copyright © 2006 by Nova Science Publishers, Inc.

All rights reserved. No part of this book may be reproduced, stored in a retrieval system or transmitted in any form or by any means: electronic, electrostatic, magnetic, tape, mechanical photocopying, recording or otherwise without the written permission of the Publisher.

For permission to use material from this book please contact us:
Telephone 631-231-7269; Fax 631-231-8175
Web Site: http://www.novapublishers.com

NOTICE TO THE READER

The Publisher has taken reasonable care in the preparation of this book, but makes no expressed or implied warranty of any kind and assumes no responsibility for any errors or omissions. No liability is assumed for incidental or consequential damages in connection with or arising out of information contained in this book. The Publisher shall not be liable for any special, consequential, or exemplary damages resulting, in whole or in part, from the readers' use of, or reliance upon, this material.

This publication is designed to provide accurate and authoritative information with regard to the subject matter covered herein. It is sold with the clear understanding that the Publisher is not engaged in rendering legal or any other professional services. If legal or any other expert assistance is required, the services of a competent person should be sought. FROM A DECLARATION OF PARTICIPANTS JOINTLY ADOPTED BY A COMMITTEE OF THE AMERICAN BAR ASSOCIATION AND A COMMITTEE OF PUBLISHERS.

LIBRARY OF CONGRESS CATALOGING-IN-PUBLICATION DATA
New developments in learning research / Samuel N. Hogan, editor.
    p. cm.
Includes bibliographical references and index.
ISBN 1-59454-669-X
1. Learning, Psychology of. I. Hogan, Samuel N.
BF318.N49   2006
153.1'5--dc22   2005030407

Published by Nova Science Publishers, Inc. ✢ New York

Contents

Preface		**vii**
Chapter 1	Factors Involved in Complex Learning: A Model of Expert Competence Acquisition *Juan L. Castejón Costa and Raquel Gilar Corbi*	**1**
Chapter 2	Object Exploration: A Non-Aversive Measure of Object Recognition, Spatial Memory, and Context Familiarity *Matthew J. Anderson*	**35**
Chapter 3	One Size Doesn't Fit All: Achieving Accountability Through Application of Learning Patterns *Donna W. Jorgensen*	**49**
Chapter 4	The Influence of Motivation on the Use of Learning Strategies in the Classroom *Ayumi Tanaka and Kiho Tanaka*	**65**
Chapter 5	Written Metacognitive Guidance - A Psychological Tool that Facilitates Learning and Cognitive Achievements *Eva Guterman*	**85**
Chapter 6	Effects of IQ and Knowledge Cohesiveness on Memory Task Performance in Early Elementary School *Joyce M. Alexander, Che-yu Kuo, Kathy E. Johnson, Victoria M. Fleming, James B. Schreiber and Katrina M. Daytner*	**119**
Chapter 7	Foreign Language Learning: The Role of Phonological Memory *Marcella Ferrari and Paola Palladino*	**145**
Chapter 8	Situated Knowing and Learning During Science Laboratory Activities: Models, Methods, and Examples *Wolff-Michael Roth*	**165**
Chapter 9	Teacher Communication Behaviour and Enjoyment of Science Lessons *Harkirat S. Dhindsa*	**191**

Chapter 10	What Makes Desirable Learning Activities? Exploring the Rhetoric and Practice in Hong Kong Kindergartens *Yuen Ling Li*	**217**
Chapter 11	Situational Interest: A Curriculum Component Enhancing Learning in Physical Education *Ang Chen, Catherine D. Ennis, Robert Martin and Haichun Sun*	**235**
Index		**263**

PREFACE

Learning as used here, refers to concerted activity that increases the capacity and willingness of individuals, groups, organizations and communities to acquire and productively apply new knowledge and skills, to grow and mature and to adapt successfully to changes and challenges. Such learning empowers individuals and organizations to make wise choices, solve problems and break new ground. In particular, it is sustainable, it is a lifelong, renewable process for people and for the institutions that serves people. Learning certainly includes academic studies and occupational training through high school and beyond but also encompasses the physical, cognitive, emotional and social development of children in the earliest years of their lives. This book presents new research in this explosive field.

The main purpose of chapter 1 is to define those factors responsible for the acquisition of knowledge and in a complex learning situation. This work focus on the main theories and models elaborated on the acquisition of the knowledge and cognitive skills involved in the initial development of expert competence. It is an empirical work attempting to gather a group of characteristics that help overcome certain difficulties or lacks in the existing studies on the acquisition of expert competence. It includes all or most of the factors involved in the development of expert competence, from the organization of knowledge and practice, to the components of Sternberg's model, intellectual abilities, motivation, knowledge, learning strategies, and variables of the academic or professional context. The work is focused on the initial stages of the development of expert competence, which usually starts with specialisation at university or professional training, as most of the work has been developed on high or low levels of specialisation. A suitable level for this purpose is that of the last years of Master. The work includes the new conceptualisations and operative definitions of general intellectual abilities, including a range of aspects wider than that included in most of the usual tests. The methodological designs and data analysis techniques used for this work allow for the analysis of the independent contribution of each factor involved in the acquisition of expert competence. The aims proposed and the process followed require the use of a correlational and predictive design where different techniques are used, ranging from the correlation analysis and multiple regression to the covariance structures analysis. Concerning the identification of the elements explaining the acquisition of knowledge and cognitive skills, and having employed different data analysis techniques, the results obtained in a sample of college students are convergent. It is the variables related to conceptual organization, practical intelligence, motivation and learning environment, the elements that make a significant contribution in an independent way to explain the variations in the performance.

Berlyne first illustrated that rats spend more time exploring novel objects than ones previously encountered. Since 1950, variations on this task have been used to examine object memory, spatial memory, context familiarity, and numerous related topics. Driven by the task's simplicity and non-aversive characteristics, the use of object exploration tasks has risen dramatically in recent years. Following a historical recount and description of the original procedures, chapter 2 reviews the many areas in which object exploration tasks have been employed (e.g., pharmacological and ontogenetic investigations). A particular emphasis is placed on the behavioral and biological influences on performance in such tasks. Potential directions for future research employing such tasks are discussed.

Chapter 3 reviews a relatively new approach to understanding the brain-mind connections associated with learning. The Let Me Learn Process® Learning Connections Inventory© (which helps students and teachers to identify personal learning combinations of four patterns) will be discussed in detail. The major premise of this chapter is that when teachers and students work together to identify learning patterns and access them appropriately, students will learn to assume responsibility for increased learning and performance. Further, because students will know how to access patterns and create strategies for different kinds of assessment situations, they will perform better on various measures of achievement. Students and teachers will have the accountability that is demanded of them.

Students use a variety of learning strategies in the classroom. To understand students' learning process and provide effective support for them, it is important to examine how and why they use a particular strategy in a given situation. Researchers have reported that students' motivational orientation has significant influence on their use of learning strategies. Among the many perspectives in the research of motivation in chapter 4, the authors focus on self-determination or autonomy, achievement goals, and self-efficacy. They report the results of three studies of Japanese elementary, junior high school, and college students. The relationships between students' perceived autonomy, achievement goals, and deep and surface processing strategies as well as self-handicapping strategy was examined in the first study. In the second study, the relationship between motivation and learning strategies were examined including the role of self-efficacy. Help-seeking strategy was the focus of the third study, and examined in relation to achievement goals. Based on the findings, we suggest a direction for future instructional interventions designed to improve students' learning.

Chapter 5 attempts to provide a theoretical-practical framework that links assessment practice to learning theory by synthesizing three theoretical axes of learning: Schema theory – emphasizing the role of prior knowledge in learning; Metacognitive awareness theory – profiling an expert reader; and the Vygotskian notion of the zone of proximal development – extending and facilitating learners' cognitive abilities and performance by providing a "psychological tool." This theoretical basis resulted in the development of written metacognitive awareness guidance – a "psychological tool" – whose fundamental purpose is to raise learners' metacognitive awareness of their prior knowledge (schemata) before they begin to process authentic reading assessment tasks. Increasing learners' metacognitive awareness by means of well-planned guidance based on their prior knowledge will not only facilitate their learning and improve the outcomes of assessment tasks, but will also increase their chances of internalizing the guidance components and applying them in changing learning situations. The chapter suggests stages in educational assessment to better serve the goal of equity, and to facilitate the kind of assessment that will benefit our students most, the kind of assessment to which our students are entitled.

Chapter 6 summarizes results from two separate studies concerning the role of IQ and knowledge cohesiveness in memory task performance. Results from Study 1 suggest that some degree of domain cohesiveness is necessary to facilitate sophisticated strategy use though IQ exerted additional effects on recall that were not mediated by more sophisticated strategy use. Study 2 examines the role of IQ when children are taught a cohesive organization for a domain. Results suggest that IQ facilitates knowledge acquisition and, over time, facilitates the use of multiple strategies. Implications for theory development and educational applications are discussed.

Chapter 7 reviews recent research on the role of phonological memory skills in typical and disordered foreign language learning. The authors will briefly illustrate a working memory model and its phonological component, focusing on its relationship with foreign language learning. In the last part of the chapter two recent experiments that add significant data in favour of a crucial role of phonological memory in foreign language learning are presented. In the two experiments, the authors examined working memory problems in groups of 7th and 8th grade Italian students who studied English as a second language. Participants were tested on a visuo-spatial working memory task, on passive verbal working memory tasks and more active ones, in order to clarify which component of working memory may be involved in the foreign language learning ability. Phonological awareness was tested comparing experimental and control groups on phonological memory tasks. Results are discussed within the working memory framework.

We teach according to our understanding of how students know and learn. Conducted from a perspective of phenomenological sociology, the research in chapter 8 has shown that many science teaching practices are inconsistent with the state of the art on knowing and learning. An important instructional method lies in hands-on activities; these are said to help students learn science concepts. However, there is no theory that would help us understand the microlevel details of how doing something with the hands is helping to learn and understand general concepts. Correlatively, most science teachers consider laboratory activities as add-ons and fun, but with little benefit for doing better on tests. In recent years, researchers have come to understand cognition as a situated and distributed. Here, the authors present a model of and a methodology for studying situated knowing and learning as they arise from laboratory activities in school science. This allows us to make a direct connection between manual activity and general concepts. They use case studies from an extensive database established during a four-month study of learning during school science laboratory activities to illustrate both model and method. In addition, the case studies presented here illustrate cognitive development of different types at shorter and longer time scales. As students engage science activities, the entities that they are attuned to change in character and kind, which affords changes in their cognitive development. Collective activities, including discussions with a teacher or peer, coordinate and scaffold the complexity of individual cognition.

Teacher communication behavior in a classroom is an important dimension of classroom learning environment that significantly contributes towards a unique learning environment. The aim of chapter 9 was to study secondary students' perceptions of science teacher communication behaviour and its association with enjoyment of science lessons. Data were collected (a) by administering a teacher communication behaviour questionnaire and students' enjoyment of science lesson questionnaire to 1098 students in 53 classes and (b) by direct observation of 20 science classes. Factor analysis, alpha reliability and discriminant validity coefficients for the five scales in the instruments using a student or a class or a school as a unit of analysis supported internal consistency and the distinct nature of the scales, thus the high quality of the data collected. The results of the study revealed that Bruneian science students perceived their teachers to some extent friendly and understanding who exercise dominance in the classrooms controlling the overall classroom interaction without so often challenging their students with higher order questions. The students seldom received praise, non-verbal support, and encouragement from their science teachers despite a large number of the teachers are expatriates with qualifications from and experience in developed countries. The female students perceived their teachers to be statistically significantly more challenging as well as understanding and friendly than the male students. A low level statistically significant difference in favour of Form 5 (Grade 10) students was observed on encouragement when compared to Form 4 students. Low to moderate level statistically significant differences between class means as well as school means revealed that teacher communication behavior varied marginally between the classes and schools. Statistically significant positive simple correlation values between students' perceptions of enjoyment of and factors of teacher communication behaviour in science lessons suggest that teacher communication behaviour directly influence enjoyment of science lesson. The implication of this research is (a) for classroom teachers to optimse their classroom communication behaviour and (b) for teacher educators to redesign their training programs to optimize pre-service teachers' communication behaviour to make science lessons more enjoyable.

There is a good deal of evidence within the psychological literature that desirable learning activity is an interactive event, where the child actively constructs his/her own understandings within a social and physical environment. This kind of learning is sometimes referred to as 'active learning'. Active learning refers to the interactive process between teacher and learner, and it is also applied to include the provision of some aspects of the learning environment. These ideas were introduced to kindergarten teachers when they received their in-service teacher education started in 1981. In a two-year school-based project, sixty teachers in five schools were to develop some videos on models of good practices collaboratively after sharing each others' 'effective' teaching episodes with peer teachers who were experimenting with 'desirable learning activities' in their classrooms. Chapter 10 reports the planning, implementation, assessment, classroom ethos and adult support displayed in the project deliverables (videos) so as to portray the context in which children are expected to learn in Hong Kong kindergartens. Records of dialogues during sharing sessions/case discussion sessions and post-project evaluation meetings, and project deliverables (four to five vignettes from each of the five schools) were collected and analysed. Teaching records (lesson plans), and commentary of videos were sources of data collected for triangulation. The aim was to capture the belief of teachers and a variety of 'desirable learning activities'/learning and teaching episodes so they could be analysed for learning environment and pedagogy. During sharing/case discussion sessions, the principles of 'high child participation' and a joyful and harmonious learning environment were upheld and teachers in general consented their initiation to engage children in learning activities. The project deliverables showed that teachers tended to introduce activities that targeted a 'collaborative and permissive learning environment' but freely chosen play activities or child initiated learning were absent in the vignettes. Items that were found to be 'worked' in peers' classrooms were internalized and absorbed into the teachers' repertoire. The findings of the study suggest that there was some evidence of significance in the use of case discussions/worked examples to shape instruction, though strategies concerning the scrutiny of the pool of knowledge for the development of 'cases' are of concern.

Learning in physical education has become more important than ever in helping young generations of Americans develop and sustain a healthy body and lifestyle. To accomplish this overarching goal, learning in physical education is operationalized in two general types. One is learner acquisition of knowledge and skills necessary for a physically active lifestyle, the other is learner participation in in-class physical activities to receive health benefits. In chapter 11, guided by the Model of Domain Learning and interest-based motivation theory, the authors examined the predictability of situational interest for both in-class physical activity and knowledge acquisition in physical education. The data for this investigation were collected from 83 lessons taught by 30 physical education teachers who and their students (n = 83 classes representing approximately 7,000 pupils) were participating in a physical education curriculum intervention study involving 30 schools. A health-science-based curriculum and a comparison curriculum were randomly assigned to 15 experimental and 15 comparison schools. Both experimental and comparison schools were represented in the current investigation. Situational interest and its sources (Novelty, Challenge, Attention Demand, Exploration, and Instant Enjoyment) were measured using the Situational Interest Scale. In-class physical activity was measured in Vector Magnitude (VM) counts using accelerometers. Knowledge acquisition was assessed using pre- and post-tests on concepts of heart, healthy exercise zone, and exercise benefits. Results show that pupils in the experimental group demonstrated higher achievement than those in the comparison group (in regression residual gain scores, $p = .001$). No differences were found in activity levels ($p > .05$) or most situational interest dimensions ($p > .05$) except Novelty ($p = .025$) and Exploration Intention ($p = .001$); both were rated higher by the experimental group. Regression analysis revealed that Instant Enjoyment was the sole predictor for in-class physical activity ($R^2 = .37$, $\beta = .37$), indicating that "fun" experiences motivated children *to become physically active*. Valid predictors ($R^2 = .55$) for knowledge acquisition included the curriculum ($\beta = -.24$, experimental = 1, comparison = 2), Total Interest ($\beta = .40$), Challenge ($\beta = -.16$), Attention Demand ($\beta = .19$), and Instant Enjoyment ($\beta = .23$). The findings suggest that motivating children *to learn* demands more than "fun". Situational Interest is an integral component of the curriculum that motivates children to be attentive and active and provides manageable challenges and instant enjoyment. The findings imply that the functions of situational interest should be emphasized in developing a coherent curriculum. Situational Interest: A Curriculum Component Enhancing Learning in Physical Education

Chapter 1

FACTORS INVOLVED IN COMPLEX LEARNING: A MODEL OF EXPERT COMPETENCE ACQUISITION

Juan L. Castejón Costa and Raquel Gilar Corbi
University of Alicante
Spain

ABSTRACT

The main purpose of this work is to define those factors responsible for the acquisition of knowledge and in a complex learning situation. This work focus on the main theories and models elaborated on the acquisition of the knowledge and cognitive skills involved in the initial development of expert competence. It is an empirical work attempting to gather a group of characteristics that help overcome certain difficulties or lacks in the existing studies on the acquisition of expert competence. It includes all or most of the factors involved in the development of expert competence, from the organization of knowledge and practice (Ericsson, 1999), to the components of Sternberg's model (1999), intellectual abilities, motivation, knowledge, learning strategies, and variables of the academic or professional context. The work is focused on the initial stages of the development of expert competence, which usually starts with specialisation at university or professional training (Sternberg, 1998), as most of the work has been developed on high or low levels of specialisation. A suitable level for this purpose is that of the last years of Master. The work includes the new conceptualisations and operative definitions of general intellectual abilities, including a range of aspects wider than that included in most of the usual tests (Sternberg, 1985a; Sternberg, Castejón, Prieto, Hautamäki and Grigorenko, 2001). The methodological designs and data analysis techniques used for this work allow for the analysis of the independent contribution of each factor involved in the acquisition of expert competence. The aims proposed and the process followed require the use of a correlational and predictive design where different techniques are used, ranging from the correlation analysis and multiple regression to the covariance structures analysis. Concerning the identification of the elements explaining the acquisition of knowledge and cognitive skills, and having employed different data analysis techniques, the results obtained in a sample of college students are convergent. It is the variables related to conceptual organization, practical intelligence, motivation and learning environment, the elements that make a significant contribution in an independent way to explain the variations in the performance.

INTRODUCTION

The study of knowledge and cognitive skills acquisition involved in the initial development of the expert competence is one of the present subjects of cognitive science, as it is shown by diverse theories and explanatory models which have established recently on development of performance and expert competence (Ericsson, 1999; Ericsson and Charnes, 1994; Sternberg, 1994, 1998, 1999a; Ericsson, 2003; Ericsson, 2005). Sternberg (1998, 1999a) proposes a model of expertise development in which several factors take part and interact. It is a fundamentally descriptive model in which, the key explanatory elements and the relations among them are established. The advantage of a model is its greater possibilities of empirical verification, as opposed to theoretical assumptions, like the assumptions on the role of the environmental factors of experience and the innate factors of capacities, more difficult to verify.

The only initial assumption upon which Sternberg's model on the development of the expertise is based is that the main determining factor for the achievement of expertise is not some previous fixed level of capacity, but a decisive commitment with direct instruction, an active participation, the modelling, and the reward (Sternberg, 1999a).

The elements of Sternberg's model (1999a) of developing expertise are five: the metacognitive skills, the learning skills, the thinking skills, knowledge and motivation. These elements are interactive. They are influenced by each other, both in a direct and in an indirect way. For example, learning leads to knowledge, but knowledge facilitates a greater learning. The metacognitive skills or metacomponents (Sternberg, 1985a) are referred to the knowledge and control of the own cognition. These skills are involved in the resolution of any kind of problems, including everyday life problems, and they are modifiable.

The learning skills, also known in the triarchic theory as components of knowledge acquisition, are essential in the model of expertise development and in the theory of intelligence by Sternberg. The main components of the acquisition of knowledge are selective codification, which allows to distinguish relevant information from irrelevant one; selective combination, which allows to establish relations between the codified information to integrate it in a whole; and selective comparison, which implies relating the new information to the information already stored in the memory (Sternberg, 1985a; Sternberg and Davidson, 1995; Sternberg, Bermejo and Castejón, 1997).

The thinking skills represent the executive components that are the closest to intelligence. To Sternberg there are the three types of thinking skills, the analytical, the creative and the practical one (Sternberg, 1985a, 2000; Sternberg, Prieto and Castejón, 2000; Sternberg, Castejón, Prieto, Hautamäki and Grigorenko, 2001).

Knowledge is another key aspect of Sternberg's model, which distinguishes between the academic, declarative and procedural knowledge and the tacit knowledge, which involves knowing the way the system where you operate works (Sternberg, Forsythe, Hedlund, Horvath, Wagner, Williams, Snook and Grigorenko, 2000).

Motivation, which presents several types, the achievement motivation (McClelland, 1985) and the motivation regarded as competence or self-efficacy, which refers to people's ideas on their own abilities. To Sternberg, experts need to develop a sense of their own efficacy to face the difficult tasks in their domain of expertise. Furthermore, this sort of self-efficacy can be the result of both intrinsic and extrinsic rewards (Sternberg and Lubart, 1997).

Context includes those characteristics that are present in the environment, and which belong mainly to the family and school environment.

A characteristic of the model is, as mentioned before, the interaction among elements. Thus, the novel person advances towards expertise through deliberate practice. But this practice requires an interaction of all the key elements. Motivation is at the centre, leading all the elements. Without it, the elements remain inert. Motivation impels the metacognitive skills, which at the same time activate the thinking and learning skills, which provide feedback to the metacognitive skills, allowing the own level of expertise to increase. The knowledge acquired through the learning and thinking skills also involves a more effective use of these skills in the future. All of these processes are affected by, and can affect as well, the context in which they operate.

Nevertheless, from the perspective of the traditional theories of expert competence (Ericsson and Charness, 1994; Ericsson and Lehmann, 1996; Ericsson and Smith, 1991; Ericsson, 2005), the key elements that take part in the acquisition of competence are, on one hand, the deliberate practice of the task; and on the other hand, the knowledge and memory skills that are developed in direct relation to the former.

The traditional explanatory hypothesis on the acquisition of expert competence grants a very outstanding role, almost exclusive, to deliberate practice (Ericsson and Charness, 1994; Ericsson and Lehmann, 1996) as opposed to other factors like innate predispositions and talent. Nevertheless, from the perspective that considers the acquisition of expert competence as talent, instruction and practice are necessary but not sufficient to reach expert levels of execution. From the book of Galton (1869/1979) on the inheritability of genius, it is considered that performance depends on a mixture of innate predispositions of hereditary type, motivation, and experience and practice. From another similar perspective, like that of Gardner (1983) on Multiple Intelligences, talents are not general, as Galton believed, but specific of a field although they also have a biological basis. In both cases, the hypothesis of the general talent and the specific talents in a domain, predict that individuals must show talent signs from an early age or after a short initial period of exposure to the domain. In agreement with this hypothesis, the initial talent is the true cause of the increase of practice, so that the correlation observed between practice and performance is confused with or influenced by the differences in initial talent.

In Gardner's theory of Multiple Intelligences (1983) it is considered that an important evidence of the strong inherited base of the musical talent, is that most of the outstanding musicians are discovered at an early age, frequently before they are 6 years old, and even at 2 or 3, even if they do not come from musician families. In this sense: "the differences between children [in musical ability] are enormous, and it seems that training has comparatively little effect to reduce these differences"(Gardner, 1983, p. 188). Although, the most outstanding aspect of talent, according to Gardner (1983, 1993, 2001), is not its innate structure, but rather the potential for performance and the ability to quickly learn the relevant material in one of the intelligences. This perspective is congruent with his proposal to evaluate each one of intelligences during the course of the learning of each domain in particular.

The hypothesis that grants an essential role to practice in the acquisition of expert competence (Ericsson, et al., 1993; Ericsson, 1999; Ericsson and Charness, 1994; Ericsson,

2005), on the contrary, emphasizes the value of practice over talent or innate predispositions. Part of the argumentation supporting this hypothesis is based on two facts: a) the lack of relation between the initial execution and the final one in the acquisition of the skills and expert performance; and b) the qualitative changes that take place as a result of extensive practice, which do not seem to be in direct relation to previous stages.

Evidence from studies on the acquisition of skills suggests that performance during the initial, middle and final phase of skill acquisition is correlated with different types of abilities in each phase (Ackerman, 1988; Ackerman and Cianciolo, 2000). The initial performance is correlated to general cognitive abilities, and the final performance is correlated with perceptual-motor abilities. These results, which have been transferred to the acquisition of cognitive abilities in general (Ericsson, Krampe, and Tesch-Römer, 1993; VanLehn, 1996), are interpreted by Ericsson, Krampe and Tesch-Römer (1993) as an evidence supporting their theory, since they consider that practice at the initial phase serves to compensate the differences in the previous cognitive abilities of the individuals, and on that basis, execution depends on the specific knowledge and the skills implied in the accomplishment of the task or tasks in that domain. More specifically, the amount and organization of knowledge on a domain acquired as a result of the experience and the practice in that domain, as well as the acquired skills of short term working memory, which enables the individual to avoid the general capacities of processing -of innate nature-, are the factors responsible for the acquisition of expert competence. Both the structure of knowledge and the memory skills are acquired only or almost exclusively as a result of experience and practice.

The theoretical debate between the supporters of the general or specific talent theory and the supporters of the deliberate practice theory finds continuity in the controversy maintained by Gardner on one hand, and Sternberg on the other, with the authors of the deliberate practice theory.

Gardner (1995) launches a question in a title of one of his works: "Why would anyone become an expert?". He uses the question as the starting point to comment the work of Ericsson and Charness (1994) on the importance of deliberate practice for the success of high levels of performance. Gardner agrees with this fact, but he opposes to the assumption that individual differences in talent or innate ability are much less important than practice. Ericsson and Charness (1994) consider that children and young people show their preferences for certain domains, but they attribute these individual differences to interest, motivation and personality, rather than to talent. The main question for Gardner is if, once a child has started to work on a domain, he/she shows substantial quantitative and qualitative differences in the way they approach it and make progress in it, as it is the case. Ericsson and Charness suggest that every child works on the different domains in the same way and that the main differentiating variable is the amount of deliberate practice that they carry out in each particular domain. This conclusion seems to Gardner incorrect for two reasons. One, the existing evidence on the existence of several different aptitudes, both from the psychometric point of view of intelligence tests, and from that of other types of experimental studies. The other reason is centred in the topic of which children are actually committed in deliberate practice during long periods of time, that Garden explains by the success in the accomplishment of certain activities, just like the failure in others leads to the abandonment of its practice, depending on the particular profile of strong points and weak points shown in both scopes. This variable, significant from the perspective of Gardner, is ignored in the explanation of Ericsson and his colleagues. In short, for Gardner, "exceptional performance can come about only when one beholds a happy confluence of biological proclivities and situational supports" (Gardner, 1995, p. 803).

In Ericsson and Charness' (1995) reply to Gardner (1995), the authors claim that Gardner does not challenge their conclusions that specific talent in a domain does not have an effect for the acquisition of performance and expert competence. They share the idea that the execution in a domain and the general or specific abilities in that domain arise gradually during development, and are based on the integration of the individual with the environment. But contrarily to Gardner's view, they regard the differences in capacities as a result of the history of relevant activities that each individual has performed, as a consequence of which the capacities associated with them have been developed. Within this explanatory frame, interest, personality and motivation, are the factors that predispose the individual to commit themselves in extended activities. Ericsson and Charness (1995) add that the same type of acquired mechanisms of memory determine individual differences in domains ranging from music, to daily activities or the comprehension of texts, although these memory skills are only developed in association with the activities practiced in a particular domain.

The question about the clear prevalence of factors like predisposition or talent as opposed to environmental factors like practice, reminds us of the old debate between the relation inheritance-environment, especially on this level of theoretical generality. Although it is true that the factors that predispose to practice in a domain, either capacities or personality, seem to have biological roots, as Gardner affirms, it also seems to exist evidence that practice causes structural changes of neurological nature, as Gautier, Tarr, Anderson, Skudlarski and Gore (1999) results. These researchers found out, by using images of magnetic resonance, that the expertise in the recognition of objects leads to a specialization of the fusiform areas of the brain.

Sternberg (1996a, 1998) has opposed to the hypothesis that deliberate practice is the fundamental and almost only aspect in the acquisition of expert competence and performance, supporting his critics both on theoretical and methodological aspects. To Sternberg, the initial error from which the theory of deliberate practice sets is the elementary confusion between correlation and causation. Although he indicates another number of aspects that are not considered by the theory (Sternberg, 1996a). These aspects are:

1. Ignoring contradictory findings, such as the findings of genetics or those of empirical studies that show a negative relation between the amount of hours of practice and performance.
2. Rendering views nondisconfirmable. When negative effects of practice are obtained they say that this practice was not deliberate and when positive effects are obtained, this is attributed to practice. There is a lack of operative and conceptual definitions of practice.
3. Confounding of correlation with causation, because the existence of correlation between high levels of expertise and high levels of deliberate practice does not explain anything about the common causal mechanisms of both. This does not mean, as Sternberg indicates, that practice is not important, but that it is possible to find alternative interpretations of this correlation that locate the true causal factors in ability and motivation.
4. Nonexistence of control groups in the research on the development of expert competence, which prevents it from obtaining causal relations between the variables

of practice and competence. Without control groups we cannot know how many people have had many hours of deliberate practice like that of experts, and yet have not reached the levels of efficacy of experts. Although, as Sternberg is aware of, it is difficult to obtain control groups in the area of expertise acquisition, we consider that it is necessary to be able to establish causal relations between variables through the establishment of control groups, or at least through longitudinal studies that allow to infer the causal relation between variables.
5. Ignoring of dropout effects. It is necessary to know how many people leave an activity field after they have already begun, since most of the people who wish to become an expert in a field do not seem to achieve this aim. The abandonment of the activity implies a correlation between deliberate practice and expertise. In other words, greater talent can lead to more deliberate practice and vice versa. The methodological question is that in retrospective studies carried out with people who are already experts, the hours of practice can be confused with other variables like talent or motivation.
6. Choosing domains to maximize fit of data to theory, such as chess, sport, etc., where practice plays an important role. Nevertheless, there are cases in which early signs of talent are observed, such as in the fields of the mathematics and poetry.
7. Finally, they do not take into account the effects of the well-known statistical phenomenon of regression to the average, and to illustrate this point Sternberg gives a clear and direct example: many of the children of expert people in a field do not reach the expected achievements in that field, although their parents, - and here Sternberg himself is included- use all their knowledge, support and persistence to attain this. Whereas children of families of low socio-cultural level do obtain it.

To Sternberg (1996a) the supporters of the theory of deliberate practice make the same mistakes as behaviourism and neo behaviourism when considering this factor as the only important variable in the acquisition of excellent achievement. The truth for Sternberg is that deliberate practice is only part of the question. On the one hand abilities and motivation can play a causal role for practice. On the other hand, deliberate practice and expertise can interact in a bidirectional way so that deliberate practice leads to expertise, and the satisfaction that expert competence brings leads to more deliberate practice.

The role of knowledge in the explanation of expert competence, and its relation to other components such as cognitive and thinking skills, has been object of theoretical controversy in the theories and models of expertise. Sternberg (1994, 1995) disagrees with the perspective maintained by theorists of expertise, who claim that the decisive factor in the development of expert competence is the way knowledge is integrated and differentiated in the structure of the knowledge-base of the individual. This perspective considers that a greater organization of knowledge in memory influences or causes learning and reasoning processes. Apart from the theorists of expertise, this is also supported by many researchers in the field of development and learning (Chi, 1985; Chi and Ceci, 1987; Glaser, 1984, 1991; Glaser and Bassok, 1989).

From the perspective of Sternberg (1994), the organization of knowledge is only important in the sense that it allows to analyze the new information in a more effective way. In the synthetic theory of expertise (Sternberg, 1994, 1995) it is considered that the general capacities and processes are those that influence the organization of knowledge, and this organization is the one that favours expert competence. The establishment of inferences goes beyond the amount and organization of knowledge, it requires the effective use of this knowledge. A true expert is not only an individual having knowledge, but also someone who knows how to use knowledge in order to analyze new information while it is being acquired. From this point of view, it is not information *per se* what matters, but the efficacy of its organization to facilitate the analysis of new information. An expert is not somebody who stores facts, but somebody who knows how to effectively operate the facts stored. This perspective does not grant a fundamental role to memory either, like theorists of expertise do, but rather to the cognitive processes that make possible the use of the knowledge that we have stored. Sternberg claims that an expert lawyer is expected to use his knowledge-base to analyze the information presented to the court, and it is his superiority in performing this analysis, which grants him credibility as an expert.

Sternberg (1985b) discusses Glaser's ideas (1984) on the importance of knowledge, both for its understanding as for its use, in an article titled "All's well that ends well, but it's a sad tale that begins at the end: A reply to Glaser ". In this paper he is in disagreement with the idea expressed by Glaser that the acquisition of expert competence must be understood fundamentally, although not exclusively, in terms of the specific knowledge in a certain domain. To Sternberg, the research carried out by Glaser and others has been useful in showing the qualitative differences in the organization of knowledge within specific domains, differences that are produced while learning in several specific fields takes place. Nevertheless, to Sternberg, the processes of several degrees of generality are essential for the acquisition and use of the specific knowledge in a domain, in the same way that the specific knowledge of a domain is essential for the acquisition and use of more specific knowledge. Both, processes and knowledge must be broadly and jointly considered in any theory of expertise, learning and instruction. It is time to analyze the way they interact (Sternberg, 1985b).

Sternberg (1998, 1999a), maintains this interactive position on the relation between general processes and knowledge, when he declares specifically that "the declarative and procedural knowledge acquired through the extension of the learning and thinking skills also results in these skills being used more effectively in the future" (Sternberg, 1999a, p. 365).

The interactive position present in Sternberg's Model of Developing Expertise (1999a, 1999b) is very similar to Ceci's theory (1996) on cognitive complexity. Complex cognitive performance, as that shown by experts, is the result of the interaction between elaborated knowledge structures and cognitive processes. The way in which knowledge is organized influences the way in which we remember, interpret and reason, and vice versa. The relation between general cognitive processes and knowledge structures is reciprocal. Efficient general cognitive processes provide structure and complexity to the existing knowledge in a domain, and, at the same time, this structure helps to improve the efficacy of the cognitive processes that operate on it.

From our point of view, the question lying behind the different positions is if there is an ability to organize knowledge that depends on general cognitive abilities, such as intelligence, if it is independent from the latter or if it acts in a joint way with it. This last case would be the closest to the interactive hypothesis; part of the ability to organize knowledge would depend on intelligence, and part would make a specific contribution to the explanation of expert performance. The level of contribution of each of them would help us consider their relative importance. When the question is formulated in these terms, a solution is found from the empirical and methodological point of view.

From the methodological point of view, longitudinal and multivariate studies of causal type are required, such as those which make use of the statistical techniques of analysis of covariance structures in order to establish the interrelations that take place among these variables, and to infer causal relations among them.

The empirical works that have approached this question in a more or less direct way, and used appropriate methodological techniques (Minnaert and Janssen, 1996; Veeman, Elshout and Meijer, 1997; Veeman and Elshout, 1999) have normally shown that the degree of previous knowledge and the methods of work used, metacognitive and learning skills, make a contribution to the explanation of complex learning which is independent of general intellectual abilities. Nevertheless, the work of Veeman and colleagues are carried out with very few participants and they are restricted to the logic-mathematic domain. Whereas the work of Minnaert and Janssen (1996) uses a higher number of participants and it is made in the field of social sciences, but it includes few variables and it only considers the amount of the specific previous knowledge in the domain, rather than the qualitative organization of that knowledge.

Therefore, it is necessary to carry out empirical studies that have as an objective to check the different theoretical hypotheses on the development of expert competence. These works should have a number of characteristics:

a) To include all or most of the factors implied in the development of expert competence, from knowledge organization and practice (Ericsson, 1999; Ericsson, Krampe and Tesch-Römer, 1993), to the components of Sternberg's model (1999b), intellectual abilities, motivation, knowledge, learning strategies and variables of the academic or professional context.

b) To be focused in the initial stages of expert competence development, which normally begins with specialization at the academic level of university or professional training (Sternberg, 1998; Jackson and Ward, 2004), since most of these works has been performed in superior or inferior levels of specialization. An appropriate level for this objective can be the last courses of college degrees.

c) To attend the new conceptualisations and operative definitions of general intellectual abilities, which include more aspects than the ones implied in most of the existent tests (Sternberg, 1985a; Sternberg, Castejón, Prieto, Hautamäki and Grigorenko, 2001), and to establish the relations between the different aspects of intelligence and performance.

d) To increase the number of participants, and to apply them to areas of content different from those requiring logical-mathematical reasoning.

e) To extend the empirical studies on development of expertise to environments much more significant and realistic than the solution of problems in the laboratory.

f) To define the characteristics of deliberate practice in real learning environments and its effects on the acquisition of knowledge, such as the learning of larger pieces of significant information.

g) To use methodological designs and data analysis techniques that allow to analyze the complex interrelations that occur among the different factors implied in the acquisition of expert competence: knowledge with intellectual abilities, motivation with strategies and intelligence, knowledge and strategies, etc. It implies the use of diverse methodological approaches and powerful statistical models.

A STRUCTURAL MODEL OF EXPERT COMPETENCE

Taking into account the previous considerations, a model is proposed trying to include the most important factors that have become part of the explanatory theories and models on the development of expert competence and performance (Ericsson, 1999; Ericsson and Charness, 1994; Ericsson, Krampe and Tesch-Römer, 1993; Sternberg, 1994, 1998, 1999a).

The components of the model are basically four elements: general intellectual abilities, knowledge organization, motivation and context. These elements are both general and specific of a certain domain, although due to the specificity of some of the components of the model, it is not assumed that the results obtained through it can be transferred, in principle, to different domains. Other elements included in Sternberg's model (1999a) such as metacognitive skills are operatively integrated under the aspect of intellectual abilities, whereas learning skills would be placed nearer the study and learning strategies which are implemented during the phase of study and deliberate practice.

1. General intellectual abilities. General intellectual abilities represent the different aspects of intelligence (Sternberg, 1985a; Sternberg, Castejón, Prieto, Hautamäki and Grigorenko, 2001) better than one only general component - factor g-. These aspects of intellectual ability are analytical intelligence, practical intelligence and creative intelligence. Intellectual abilities are one of the explanatory elements of expert competence (Sternberg, 1999a) getting to exert a direct influence on the ability of knowledge organization (Sternberg, 1994, 1995).
2. Knowledge organization. The possession of a great quantity of well organized knowledge on some or all aspects of a specific academic or professional domain is the key element that would explain expert competence for the theorists of expertise (Ericsson, 1999; Ericsson and Charness, 1994; Glaser, 1996). The amount of knowledge is not which accounts for expert competence, but rather the quality of knowledge (coherent, organized).
3. Motivation. Motivation is for some authors the essential element, necessary to initiate the process of competence acquisition (Sternberg, 1999b). Although there are many explanatory hypotheses on human motivation, it seems that these can be grouped into two great approaches. In the first one, motivation is mainly understood as a biological impulse towards execution and performance, having its theoretical roots in the neobehaviourism paradigm (Pelechano, 1973a), and in achievement motivation (McLelland, 1985). The other approach sees motivation as the result of internal mechanisms of cognitive type and gathers different theories, such as the theory of attribution (Weiner, 1986, 1990) or the theory of self-efficacy (Bandura, 1977, 1996). In the context of the research on expert competence development, Ericsson and collaborators (Erricsson and Charness, 1994; Ericsson, Krampe and Tesch-Römer, 1993) have highlighted the importance of the motivational factors of personality and emotional type that predispose for the hard work and continued effort

that the practice of a task requires. Therefore, these individual differences in emotionality and general level of activity would influence motivation to obtain competence. In Sternberg's model (1999a) on expert competence development, motivation understood as self-competence perception plays a relevant role. The expert would need to develop a general awareness of his own efficacy to solve the tasks in his domain of knowledge.

4. Context. Context is referred to the familiar, academic or professional environments that influence, in a direct or indirect way, facilitating or making more difficult the performance of the diverse factors that take part in the acquisition of expertise. The traditional theory of expertise (Ericsson and Charness, 1994; Ericsson, 1998, 1999) grants great importance to the familiar environment as a support of the activities children are involved in during their first years, activities which are later decisive for the achievement of expert competence. It is also considered that the school environment, and in particular certain instructional strategies – direct instruction, consideration of previous knowledge, feedback and knowledge of results and concurrent and varied practice-, directly influence the type of learning activities the student carries out and the practice performed in the task. Part of the deliberate practice is bound to the academic environment and to the formal situation of instruction. More recently, the theorists of situated learning have highlighted the importance of an instruction deep-seated in context, cooperative learning and the design of powerful learning environments for the acquisition of expert competence (Goldman, Petrosino and CTGV, 1999). On the other hand, Sternberg and collaborators (Sternberg, Grigorenko, Ferrari, and Clinkenbeard, 1999; Sternberg, Torff and Grigorenko, 1998) have highlighted the necessity to fit instructional methods to students' abilities and preferences, both at the level of primary school and college.

The model is general and applies to diverse domains of content, although it also considers the differences between different domains. These differences are placed in the different explanatory weight that the components of the model have in each domain.

A fundamental characteristic of the model is the interaction among its components, as can be observed in figure 1. In this figure the four components of the model implied in the acquisition of expert competence and the relations among them are shown. It is assumed that all components directly influence the acquisition of the expert competence. In addition, an interrelation among these components occurs: some components directly influence others, while simultaneously some exert an indirect influence on the knowledge and abilities that define the expert performance through another mediating component.

Intellectual abilities are an exogenous variable in the structural model, since they are not influenced by any other variable. Obviously, the fact that they are not influenced by any variable constitutes a didactic and methodological simplification, as it can be assumed that these abilities are also the result of the knowledge and abilities acquired and consolidated with time, in close relation to innate factors and predispositions. Nevertheless, to make the model more operative, it is considered that abilities constitute an exogenous factor in the model.

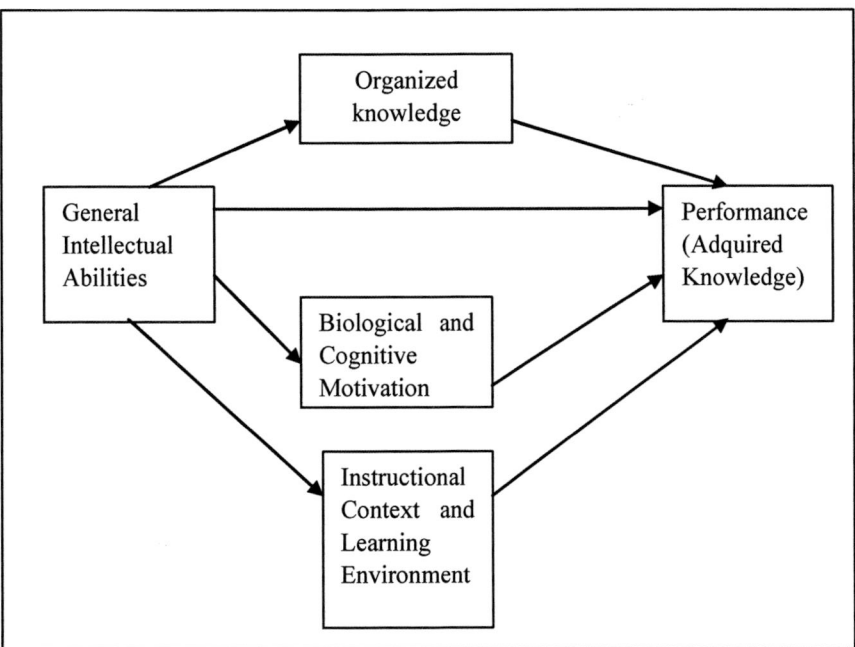

Figure 1. Structural model of the expert competence acquisition components.

The term "abilities" itself suggests the existence of diverse aspects of intellectual ability which only maintain a moderate relation to each other, as well as a differential relation with the other elements of the model, as opposed to the existence of an only general ability represented by a common factor "g", (Gardner, 1983, 1993; Sternberg, 1985a, Sternberg et al., 2001).

In the proposed model, intellectual abilities interact with other variables to explain competence. Thus, it is assumed that intellectual abilities exert a direct influence on the ability to organize knowledge, as well as on the final results of performance, in line with Sternberg (1994, 1999a). Intellectual abilities can also be related to motivation, if we suppose that a part of motivation is due to a greater intellectual ability. On the other hand, it is expected that intellectual ability influences the perception students have about the instruction received.

Organized knowledge exerts a direct influence on competence acquisition that is supposed to be independent of the influence intellectual abilities exert. In this way, the role that knowledge plays in the development of expert competence is acknowledged (Charness and Schultetus, 1999; Day, Arthur and Gettman, 2001; Ericsson and Lehmannn, 1996; Glaser, 1984, 1996; Patel, Kaufman and Arocha, 2000), independently of the intellectual abilities. However, the fact that intellectual abilities also exert some degree of direct influence on knowledge and some indirect influence through it on the acquisition of the knowledge and abilities which are a part of expert competence, is in agreement with the synthetic theory of expertise (Sternberg, 1994, 1999a) and the theory of cognitive complexity by Ceci (1996) on the acquisition of competence, which emphasize the interactive character of both elements.

Motivation covaries with intellectual abilities, and it has a direct influence on competence. Motivation is a complex mechanism in which biological and cognitive factors are implied (Covington, 2000). These factors determine the general impulse towards the activity, the sense of self-efficacy and the motivation towards achievement.

The instructional context, represented by teaching methods and the global learning environment, also exerts a direct influence on the acquisition of knowledge and abilities that define expert competence, in the learning situation in which the model is formulated. Certain instructional procedures seem to be related more directly than others to the acquisition of expert competence (Ericsson, 1998; Ericsson and Charness, 1994; Ericsson, Krampe and Tesch-Römer, 1993), or the fitting of the student's characteristics and certain instructional methods lead to a greater performance (Sternberg, Grigorenko, Ferrari, and Clinkenbeard, 1999). On the other hand, Goldman, Petrosino and CTGV (1999) have highlighted the importance a rich learning environment has for the acquisition of expert competence.

METHOD

Participants

The participants in this research are 124 post graduate students who are on their first year of Master in School Psychology of the University of Alicante (Spain). It is a group of students who have acceded to the studies of School Psychology after selection process. This fact explains that most students have prior psychological and/or educative knowledge in this field. It is then a sample of individuals who are studying an academic and/or professional specialization in education.

When 11 out of 124 participants had missing value in some variables, the non-respondents' characteristics were studied in order to verify if the lack of response was significant. Any significant statistical difference from participants that were included in the overall sample regarding the sex (p= .47), group (p= .15), and achievement (p= .24) variables was not found.

Instruments and Variables

Diverse materials and instruments were used for this work, some of which were elaborated during the development of the research. The material and tests used, divided according to their function, are listed below.

a) Instructional material. It consists of a series of issues that form the essential core Instructional Psychology. The content of such issues are comprises in a manual of *Instructional Psychology* published by one of the authors of this work (Castejón, 2001).
b) Tests of evaluation of the psychological characteristics

Test STAT (Sternberg Triarchic Abilities Test), level H, is an instrument designed to measure the three abilities of triarchic intelligence, (Sternberg, 1985; 2000). STAT is an instrument of evaluation of triarchic intelligence, with different levels used at different ranks of age (Sternberg, 1991; 1993). Level H, used in this implementation, is intended to be appropriate for high school students and for college students. The test measures three aspects of abilities, the analytical one, the practical one and the creative one, in three models of presentation of problems: verbal, numerical and figurative.

The test comprises of 36 items divided into nine scales, of four items in each, divided as well in the 3 categories: analytical, practical and creative. Each of the three subscales for each aspect of intelligence contains items of the verbal, quantitative or figural kind, of which items of that subscale are formulated.

Preliminary validation of STAT-Level H (Sternberg and Clinkenbeard, 1995; Sternberg, Grigorenko, Ferrari, and Clinkenbeard, 1999) has shown it to be appropriate for the intended purpose. The factorial analysis made on an American sample revealed 3 independent factors - analytical, creative and practical-. The analysis was based on both multiple choice and essay items. The first results obtained in adapting this instrument in Spain indicate that the test has a suitable psychometric characteristics of reliability and validity, and that the distributions scores in the sample approximate the normal distribution (Sternberg, Prieto and Castejón, 2000). The reliability index of internal consistency of each one of the 3 subtests goes from .65 to .75. These values, although moderate, reflect the fact that each subscale is composed by elements of the 3 modalities of content. Research on the structural validity of the test, like those carried out on samples of international participants (Sternberg, Castejón, Prieto, Hautamäki, y Grigorenko, 2001) in order to evaluate the crossed validity made as much with national samples Sternberg, Prieto and Castejón 2000), as the ones carried out in samples of international participants (Sternberg, Castejón, Prieto, Hautamäki, and Grigorenko, 2001), with the purpose of examining the crossed validity of the instrument, reveals that the model which achieves the best fit to the data is the model based on the triarchic conception of intelligence.

The instrument used for the evaluation of motivation, through inventory, is the MAE (Motivation and Anxiety of Execution) by Pelechano (1973,b). MAE questionnaire is elaborated from the research developed by the school of achievement motivation and performance, devoted to the analysis of the determinants of the manifest execution, within the neobehaviourism paradigm (Pelechano, 1973,a). Therefore, the questionnaire includes aspects regarding the work or study behaviour, supposed to be directly related to performance, such as the proportion of effort invested, the level of self-demand of the individual, etc. In this sense, it complements the instruments that consider the cognitive aspects of motivation. Although the MAE questionnaire was initially elaborated to evaluate work motivation, it has been repeatedly used (Pelechano, 1989) to evaluate study motivation in samples of students in upper courses, mainly of secondary education and college students. In these cases participants are warned that the term work has the sense of work of study. The questionnaire comprises of 72 items, with 2 alternatives of answer "yes" and "no", divided into six factors: Tendency to Work/Study Overload (M1), Work/Study Indifference and Separation between the Private Life and Work/Study one (M2), Self-demand at work/study (M3), Positive Motivation towards Action (M4), Anxiety Inhibiting Performance (A1) and Anxiety Facilitating Performance (A2). Our research considers the factors relative to motivation. M1, M3 and M4 factors have positive sense and they are considered to be positively related to performance, whereas M2 factor has negative motivational sense. The Tendency to Work Overload factor (M1) is formed by 11 elements that try to evaluate the objective and subjective aspects relative to the self-tendency to work overload in relation to the others. The factor of

Work/Study Indifference and Separation between the Private Life and the Work/Study World (M2) reflects a certain indifference towards the world of work or study, as well as a separation between this one and the private world. The Self-demand at work/study factor (M3) reflects a tendency to constantly better oneself at work and/or at studying and to evaluate positively the world of work or study, where there are important interests for the individual. The factor of Positive Motivation towards Action, Positive ambition (M4) is formed by elements that include aspects referred to the necessity of achievement in general. This is the less specific motivational factor. The structural validity -factorial composition- of the questionnaire and the reliability of the different factors is appropriate, both in samples of adults and in samples of students of secondary education (Pelechano, 1973b; 1989).

The evaluation of learning strategies is carried out by using the Study Process Questionnaire (SPQ), originally elaborated by Biggs (1987,b) with samples of college students. This questionnaire is made up of 42 items which include some aspects both of motivation and of the processes and strategies of studying and learning followed by students of upper levels, secondary and university education. The inventory is based on the theory of the approaches of learning by Biggs (1987,a) in which the strategies appear closely related to the reasons that stand behind them. When it is considered that learning in educative situations results from the interaction of three key elements, the intention or the reason of the learner, the process or strategy used the achievements obtained. The main purpose of the questionnaire is to evaluate the degree in which students applies one learning approach or the way to approach the study tasks adopted by students in their learning process. The 42 items are divided into 6 scales, 3 of motivational type (superficial motive, deep motive and achievement motive) and 3 scales relative to strategies (superficial, deep and achievement strategy), which are divided as well, combining the corresponding motives and strategies in three large approaches, superficial, deep and achievement approaches. Therefore, this gives rise to 9 variables, 3 referred to motives (superficial, deep and achievement), 3 to strategies (superficial, deep and achievement) and 3 to approaches (superficial, deep and achievement). The version of the CPE questionnaire used in our research is the adaptation made by Hernández (1996) on a large sample of students of college students in Spanish Universities.

The evaluation of styles of teaching and learning is carried out through an inventory elaborated during the development of the research, whose main characteristics are described below. The "Questionnaire on preferences for teaching-learning styles" has its main theoretical foundations in the theories on the development of the expert competence (Ericsson, 1998; Ericsson and Charness, 1994; Ericsson, Krampe, and Tesch-Römer, 1993; Ericsson and Lehman, 1996; Goldman, Petrosino and the Cognition and Technology Group of Vanderbilt, 1999), in instructional and professional environments. The formulation of the elements that form the scale was made by the members of the work team who are part of the research project this research belongs to, coordinated by its director, and after having analysed the corresponding bibliography that constitutes its theoretical support. The original questionnaire consists of 25 items which include 5 aspects which are theoretically different from the instructional process: independent work, group discussion, teacher lecture, cooperative work and practical work, each being operativised with 5 items as well. Participants must answer each statement in a Likert type scale with 5 graduations of answer, ranging from no agreement to total agreement. Unlike what was expected, the results of the questionnaire's structural validation showed the existence of a single factor that explained the 78,80% variance, defined as "global perception of the learning environment", which reflect participants' greater or lesser preference for the use of a combination of methodological approaches to the instructional process. The scale's reliability, established by means of Carmines' Θ theta coefficient (Carmines and Zeller, 1979) was very high, equaling 0.93.

c) Instrument for the evaluation of knowledge organization. The evaluation of the structure of knowledge acquired during the learning process is through the *pathfinder*, a procedure widely used for the measurement of the organization of knowledge, established by Schvaneveldt (1990), and which has shown its validity in several research, both experimental and field research (Cooke et al., 2000; Dorsey, et al., 1999; Kraiger et al., 1995; Ruiz et al., 1998; Schvaneveldt, et al., 1985). Pathfinder calculates several indexes that offer diverse information about the conceptual structure and organization of concepts. Those that are more used are the measurement of coherence (COH) and similarity (SIM) of the proximity matrices of each individual or group. The computer program PCKNOT (Knowledge Network Organizing Tool) for PC's, Version 4,3, published in 1999 by InterLink, Inc., was used for the calculation of both indexes.

In our research a matrix of relations among 20 concepts relative to the subject of study was presented to students twice, before and after the explanation and the stage of study. These twenty concepts are selected as essential concepts of the subject to learn. The task of the individual was to define the relation degree between each pair of concepts, in a scale of 5 points, out of the $[n*(n-1)]/2 = [20*19]/2 = 190$ possible pairs. Two indexes were calculated for each individual taking part in the research, the coherence index and the index of similarity to the expert, at two different moments, before and after the learning task. The similarity index required a referential structure to compare that of students with. Such expert structure was provided by two members of the research equipment, who also evaluated the relation between all possible pairs of concepts in an independent way.

Two different approaches of the validation of these measures were used; the calculation of the difference between the values of each index before and after the instructional process, on the one hand. And on the other hand, the correlation between the indexes and between them and the final performance obtained in the test of knowledge, before and after learning.

The change of the coherence index from the beginning to the end of results to be statistically significant ($t_{(123)} = 2.37$, $p = .02$). In the similarity index a highly significant change takes place ($t_{(123)} = -7.22$, $p = .000$) from the beginning to the end of the instruction, as expected. On the other hand, the coherence index nor the similarity index do not show any significant correlations with performance before the instructional process, ($r = .15$) and ($r = .11$), while they do have significant relations with performance after the same process ($r = .25$; $p<.01$) and ($r = .36$; $p<.001$), respectively. These results indicate the validity of these indexes, especially the similarity index, as measurement of the conceptual organization. Therefore, both the coherence index and the index of conceptual similarity obtained after the instructional process are taken as indicators of the conceptual organization.

d) Evaluation of performance

The evaluation of learning of participants was done through two procedures: an objective test of performance and an examination similar to an essay. For the construction of the objective test the basic procedure for the construction of tests referred to criterion was followed (Popham, 1978). From the universe of measurement defined by the set of contents included in the study material, 20 items corresponding to two sectors of the domain were elaborated, the conceptual part and the procedural part. The format of the items consisted of 20 statements with four answer alternatives, which participants had to answer by choosing the correct alternative. The total score of the test was fixed through the popular formula $P = A-E/(n-1)$, where mistakes in the answers are penalized. The reliability of internal consistency of the total test was of 0.70. The essay examination consisted of 10 questions referred to conceptual and procedural aspects in the field of Instructional Psychology.

Procedure

The general procedure was carried out in different phases and included diverse aspects. All phases were developed throughout the normal time schedule of the subject as part of its practical exercises, where participants received information about the test applied to them and, in some cases, about the results which they obtained, providing them with the corrections through a template elaborated for such purpose.

At the first stage they were applied the test of evaluation of intellectual abilities, STAT, and the test of general motivation. STAT was applied during a session of approximately one hour, although participants may have more time, since it is a test of power. The test of motivation, MAE, was applied during a second session, where the instructions were given in the first place, and participants were offered the correction keys after making the test, so that each one could know the results obtained. The application of both tests took place before the development of the instructional phase, at the end of the month of October.

At the second phase, during the months from November to January, the instructional program was developed. In the first place, and previously to the beginning of the teacher lectures, the task of evaluation of concepts was applied, where participants were requested to set relations between concepts according to the degree of similarity or dissimilarity existing between them; for this purpose they had to consider the total set of concepts to evaluate. Next, the professor carried out the presentation of the material to learn. The instructional method followed is a mixture of professor explanation, class discussion and individual work of learning. Each session began with the explanation by the professor, both to offer a general vision of the subject and to facilitate the understanding of concrete concepts and their application to practice. Next, diverse aspects of the contents presented were commented and discussed, trying to get all members of the class group participate.

As the instructional process was being developed, and once its fifty percent was completed, the test of evaluation of study and learning strategies was applied, the Study Process Questionnaire, SPQ, for the purpose of having a measurement of the study processes and the learning strategies normally followed by students, obtained by inventory.

Simultaneously to the conclusion of the instructional phase, the questionnaire of teaching-learning styles was applied, where students had to express their preferences for different styles and general instructional procedures followed by professors.

At the end of the instructional phase, participants in the research had to carry out the task of evaluation of concepts again, in post-test phase, at the same session in which the test of evaluation of knowledge was made, and once this one had ended. The final evaluation of acquired learning was made at the session following the conclusion of the instructional phase, through the test of knowledge.

Design and Analysis of Data

Both the proposed objectives and the method used require the use of a co-relational and predictive design in which different techniques of correlation analysis and multiple regression are used, making use of different methods, such as the regression method "step-by-step" and the analysis of covariance structures. Several statistics programs have been used for data analysis, like SPSS-Version 12 and EQS-Version 4.02, (Bentler, 1993) used for structural analysis.

RESULTS

Correlational Analysis

In this section the results of the correlations between the used variables are analysed. The results of the Pearson linear correlation coefficients appear in Table 1 along with the descriptive statistics, averages and standard deviations, corresponding to each one of the variables.

In the first place, it is observed that the three measures of intelligence show moderate correlations to each other, since the common variance is of 26% in most cases. The correlation coefficient value between analytical intelligence and practical intelligence is of $r=.29$; the correlation between analytical intelligence and creative intelligence is of $r=.51$ and the correlation between practical intelligence and creative intelligence is of $r=.48$, all correlations being statistically significant at the level $p=.001$.

On the other hand, the variables related to strategies, motives and approaches to learning keep many significant relations to each other, as expected.

Some significant correlations of the nine variables related to strategies, motives and approaches to learning with the rest of variables also appear. The superficial strategy has a significant correlation ($r=.27$) with the Work/Study Indifference -a type of negative motivation-, a negative correlation ($r=-.26$) with the Self-demand at work/study, and a positive correlation ($r=.21$) with the positive motivation towards action. The deep strategy only presents a significant correlation with the Self-demand at work/study ($r=.30$). As regards motives, the superficial motive has a significant correlation ($r=.22$) with the Work/Study Indifference, whereas the motive of achievement shows positive correlations with the motivational variable of work overload ($r=.25$) and with the positive motivation towards action (r=.44), which is to be found within the expected correlations. From the three approaches to study and learning, it is the deep approach which maintains positive relations with the self-demand at work/study (r = .27), the achievement approach has a positive correlation with the motivational variable of tendency towards work overload (r=.26) and with the positive motivation towards action (r=.28), whereas the superficial approach presents a significant correlation with Work/Study Indifference (r=.30). It is important to emphasize that all these correlations fit in with the theoretical framework that defines the features of each one of the variables.

It is worth highlighting that none of the six strategic variables, evaluated through inventory, shows any correlation with any of the aspects of the performance.

As for motivational variables, the only motivational variable that has significant relations with the academic performance is the Self-demand at work/study, which has a positive correlation with the final performance (r=.46).

The variable relative to the preferences expressed by participants also shows significant relations with the achieved performance (r=.59), taking into account the teaching methods used by the professor and their own learning methods, herein denominated learning environment.

The variables which keep significant correlations with the performance measures which define the different aspects of knowledge acquisition at the end of the instructional process are practical intelligence (r=.44), creative intelligence (r=.23), coherence (r=.25) and similarity measures (r=.36) taken at the end of the learning process, the motivational variable of Self-demand at work/study (r=.46), and the preference for a rich and broad global environment of learning (r=.59).

However, the bi-varied correlations between performance and the mentioned variables are not sufficient to fix their efficacy to forecast and/or to explain the performance, since these variables may well be redundant. The technique of multiple regression allows to fix the independent contribution of each variable to the prediction/explanation of the criterion, after having separated the part of common variance with other forecasting variables. This is the reason why a set of multiple regression analysis between the rest of variables and the performance measure, acting as criterion, is carried out.

Multiple Regression Analysis

In order to set the predictive value of the considered variables on performance, a multiple regression analysis is carried out, following the stepwise method, in which the final qualification achieved is regarded as variable criterion.

Stepwise Regression Analysis

The step-by-step regression method is useful to select, from a wide set, those variables that make a relatively independent contribution to the prediction of the criterion.

Table 1. Correlation Matrix

	V1	V2	V3	V4	V5	V6	V7	V8	V9	V10	V11	V12	V13	V14	V15	V16	V17	V18	V19	V20	V21	V22
V1	1.00																					
V2	.29**	1.00																				
V3	.51**	.48**	1.00																			
V4	.02	.08	.00	1.00																		
V5	-.18	.19	.07	.09	1.00																	
V6	-.29	.12	-.14	.20	.23*	1.00																
V7	-.29**	.14	-.00	.00	.30*	.31**	1.00															
V8	.02	-.05	-.04	-.05	-.09	-.05	.05	1.00														
V9	.04	-.01	.00	-.06	-.02	.07	-.09	-.17	1.00													
V10	.06	-.11	-.09	-.03	-.02	.03	-.15	.52**	1.00													
V11	.02	-.13	-.17	-.13	.03	-.08	.32**	.18	.12	1.00												
V12	-.02	.01	-.06	.09	-.06	.21*	.17	.13	.49**	.46**	.15	1.00										
V13	.04	-.04	.04	-.06	-.06	.07	.18	.38**	.03	.14	.27*	.33**	1.00									
V14	.03	-.11	-.14	-.12	-.14	-.01	-.03	.78**	.02	-.01	.83**	.17	.40**	1.00								
V15	.01	.01	-.04	.02	-.05	.17	.06	-.01	.84**	.56**	.19	.88**	.22*	.11	1.00							
V16	.07	-.10	-.05	-.10	-.06	.04	.14	.15	.36**	.75**	.26*	.52**	.76**	.26*	.52**	1.00						
V17	.08	.00	.01	-.01	.03	.00	-.04	.10	.14	-.07	.13	.25*	-.07	.14	.26*	1.00						
V18	-.09	-.07	-.10	.05	.11	.16	.07	.27*	-.14	-.10	.22*	-.08	.09	.30**	-.13	-.00	-.09	1.00				
V19	-.01	.23*	.16	.06	.15	.11	.19	-.26*	.30**	-.20	-.02	.17	.04	-.16	.27*	.16	.14	-.27*	1.00			
V20	.07	-.15	.01	-.03	-.04	-.05	.06	.21*	-.08	-.02	.10	.13	.44**	.19	.03	.28**	.39**	.14	-.03	1.00		
V21	-.05	.35**	.17	.16	.20	.05	.28**	-.09	-.01	-.07	-.18	.03	.01	-.17	.01	-.04	-.01	.03	.25	-.12	1.00	
V22	.01	.44**	.23*	.15	.25*	.11	.36**	-.09	.01	-.05	-.12	.04	.06	-.13	.03	.01	.08	-.16	.46**	-.02	.59**	1.00

Media 7.45 7.80 6.93 .49 .43 .24 .29 20.06 22.99 19.00 23.19 22.15 19.12 43.26 45.15 38.12 4.04 4.10 10.81 5.86 63.75 6.83
DS 1.84 2.05 2.59 .23 .20 .06 .08 3.29 3.74 4.75 3.73 4.27 4.82 5.71 6.93 7.25 2.68 1.79 2.28 1.96 15.05 1.46

*p= 6 <.01; **p= 6 <.001. N= 124. V1= analytical intelligence; V2= practical intelligence; V3= creative intelligence; V4= conceptual coherence pre-instruction; V5= conceptual coherence post-instruction; V6= conceptual similarity pre-instruction; V7= conceptual similarity post-instruction; V8= superficial strategy; V9= deep strategy; V10= achievement strategy; V11= superficial motive; V12= deep motive; V13= achievement motive; V14= superficial approach; V15= deep approach; V16= achievement approach; V17= work overload; V18= work indifference; V19= work self-demand; V20= positive motivation; V21= preference for global learning environment ; V22= performance.

Table 2 shows the results of the stepwise method, used to predict the final performance. This analysis is based on the total number of students who take part in the research, 124, once the results of the regression analysis are practically the same when it only consider the cases with values in all the variables, that when the 11 cases with missing values in some variables are included, using the meansubstitution method.

The variable that makes a greater contribution to the explanation of the variance of the criterion is the preference for a rich and broad global learning environment (β= .39, p=.0000). The motivational variable of Self-demand at work/study (β= .28, p =. 0001), the practical intelligence (β= .22, p =. 0018), and the variable relative to the organisation of knowledge with conceptual similarity (β= .16, p =. 0187) also contribute considerably to the explanation of knowledge acquisition.

Therefore, the variables that acquire greater predictive relevance are related to the perception of a diverse and rich learning environment by participants, to the self-demand at work/study, intelligence -practical-, and to the knowledge organisation.

Table 2. Results from the regression analysis carried out through the stepwise method, establishing performance (acquired knowledge) as criterion.

R= .72 R^2 = .52   F= 31.63   Sig. F= .0000.

Variables in the equation

Variable	B	β	"t"	Sign. "t"
V4	.04	.39	5.56	.0000
V3	.18	.28	4.13	.0001
V1	.16	.22	3.20	.0018
V2	2.77	.16	2.38	.0187

N= 124.
V1 = Practical intelligence; V2 = Conceptual similarity (organized knowledge); V3 = Self-Demand at work/study (motivation); V4 = Learning environment; V5 = performance (acquired knowledge).

Examination of the Assumptions of the Multiple Regression Analysis.

In order to examine if our data adapt to the suppositions of the multiple regression analysis, it is verified if they satisfy the requirements of normality, linearity and homogeneity of the variance, and independence of errors.

The supposition of normality of the multivariate distribution of the variables was verified by comparison of the distribution observed of residual with the expected one under the supposition of normality, resulting that the standardized scores of the residual ones distributed throughout an straight line diagonal, overlapping itself with the points of that straight line, which is indicating of the normality of the joint distribution of the variables.

The supposition of linearity and homogeneity of the variance were verified by observation of the scatter diagram in which the residuals were projected against the predicted values. The scatter plot diagram showed that the residuals are distributed at random around the centre of the diagram. Furthermore, no value is placed outside the expected results (outlier).

A test of the supposition of the error independence is the test of Durbin-Watson. The value of the statistical D of Durbin-Watson for our data was of 1.95, which allows us to consider that this supposition is also verified.

Although the results of the regression analysis seem quite consistent, it is necessary to take into account that the step-by-step method tries to explain a criterion as a whole, without considering the relation between the predicting variables. Therefore, it makes more sense to use the method within a predictive context than within a theoretical context that intends to account for the relations that take place between the predicting variables and between such variables and the criterion. In order to attain this conclusion, it is necessary to use a technique that allows to analyze the ways of influence of certain variables on others and of such variables on the criterion.

Causal Analysis Through the Technique of Structural Equations

The contrast of a theoretical model that allows to establish the particular relation existing among the predicting variables, and between such variables and the criterion, demands the formulation of a structural model which considers both, the direct and indirect effects between the variables. The estimation of the parameters of the model is carried out from the definition of a system of structural equations which reflects the relations established in the theoretical model, and through the use of the statistical technique of the analysis of covariance structures (Bentler and Dudgeon, 1996; Jöreskog, 1978; MacCallum and Austin, 2000).

Figure 1 shows the structural representation corresponding to the initial theoretical model of the relations between the considered variables. The references adopted by such initial theoretical model are, on the one hand, the theoretical model of the acquisition of the expert competence, and on the other, the results of the multiple regression analysis, which allow to identify the four variables included in this model as predicting variables. As we can appreciate, the variables have been renumbered, since only the previously selected variables are included in this analysis.

According to the structural scheme represented in Figure 1 there is an exogenous variable -which does not receive any influence of other variables-, V1 (practical intelligence), three endogenous variables, V2 (conceptual similarity), V3 (motivation) and V4 (perception of the instructional environment), and a criterion variable, V5, which is the total score attained in the corresponding test of knowledge, in this case operativised in the total qualifications obtained. All the variables are observed, no latent factor is included. The exogenous variables have variance (*), whereas the endogenous variables are affected by the prediction errors (E).

According to the structural model, intelligence (V1) is considered to affect performance (V5), both in a direct and indirect way through the organization of knowledge (V2). On the other hand, motivation (V3) directly affects performance -acquired knowledge- (V5), but it is influenced by intelligence as well. The V4 variable, perception of the instructional environment, has a direct effect on total performance (V5) and is also affected by intelligence.

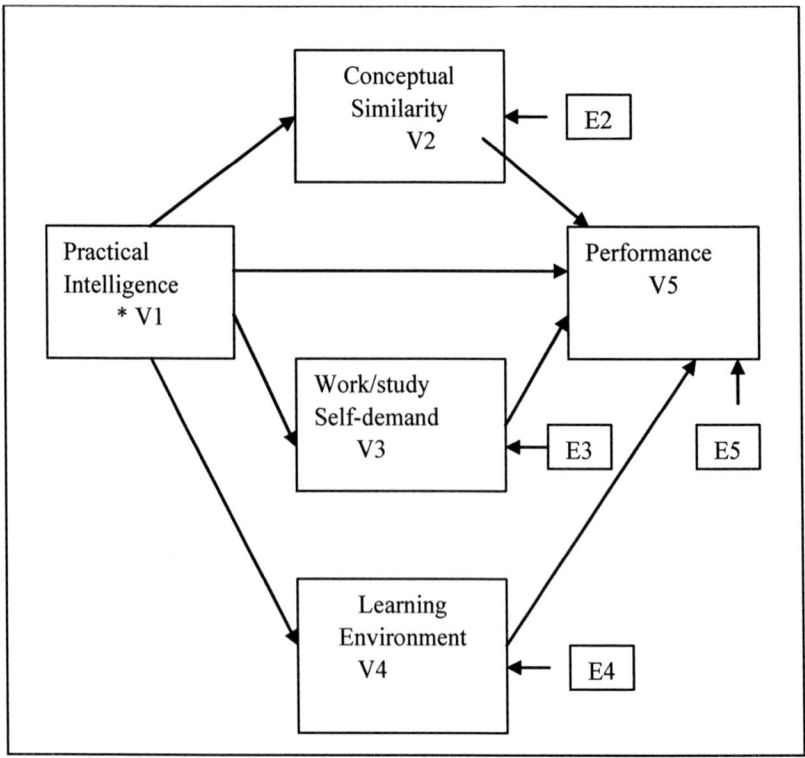

Figure 2. Initial structural model of the relations between the components of acquisition of knowledge and abilities present in expert competence.

The results obtained by using the maximum likelihood –LM- method, showed an unacceptable adjustment to the data. The overall chi-square fit index was, $\chi^2 = 14.41$, based on 3 degrees of freedom, with a probability value for the chi-square statistic, p = 0.0024. Furthermore, the comparative fit index, CFI, was 0.904.

The structural coefficients, in the proposed model output, revealed that some hypothesized effects were negligible, suggesting that a revised model might result in a better-fitting model. The Wald test for dropping parameters, suggested the elimination of the path: V1 (practical intelligence) to V2 (conceptual similarity). After having eliminated this relation, the resulting model still suffered from a substantial departure from empirical data. Simultaneously the Lagrangian Multiplier Test - LM Test- for adding parameters suggested the inclusion of the paths: V2 (conceptual similarity) to V4 (learning environment) and V2 (conceptual similarity) to V3 (Self-demand at work/study).

After having consecutively introduced these modifications in the model of structural equations the degree of fit of the model to the data was considered again, revealing a value of $\chi^2 = 5.40$ based on 2 degree of freedom, an associated probability value for the chi-square statistics p = .067, -not significantly different from empirical data-, and a comparative fit index CFI = 971. That is, the inclusion of the V4,V2 and V3,V2 parameters led to a better fit of the model to the data. Furthermore, the W and LM tests did not suggest the elimination or the introduction of a parameter of the model, respectively. Figure 2 represents the model that better fits to the empirical data collected in our work, with the values of the considered parameters.

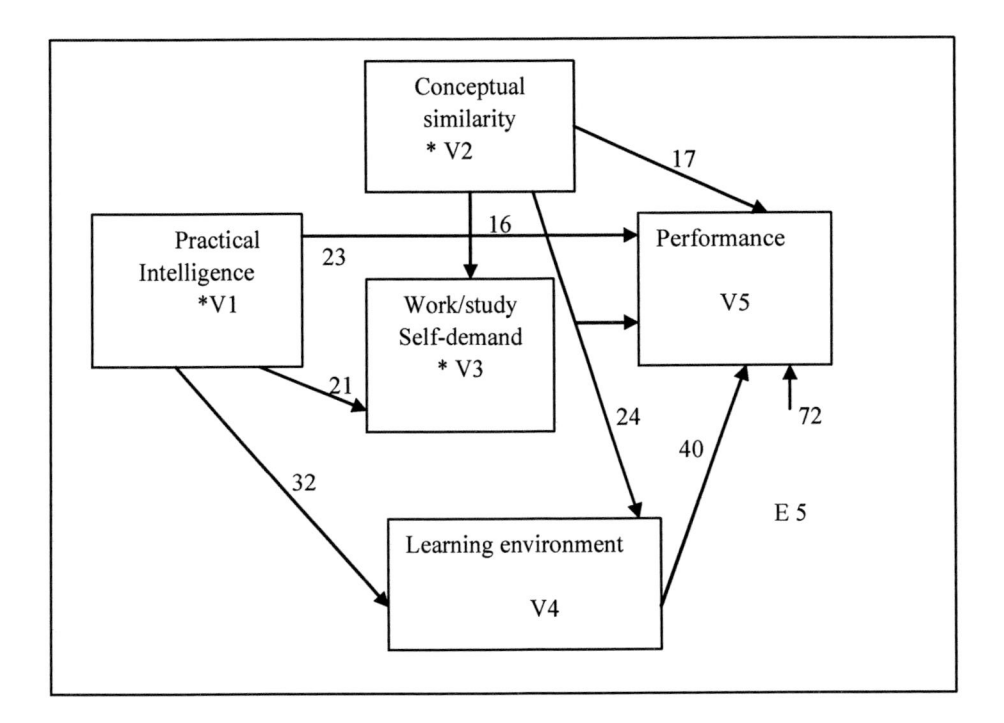

Figure 3. Model of better adjustment to the data about the components of acquisition of knowledge and abilities present in expert competence.

As we may see in the figure, the most important direct effect on performance is that of the learning environment variable. The value of the regression coefficient is of 0.40. Direct effects of the motivational variable Self-demand at work/study, of intelligence and of the conceptual organization -similarity- also take place.

All the considered variables have a direct effect on the performance; in addition to the learning environment (β= .40), motivation (β= .28), practical intelligence (β= .23), and the conceptual organization (β= .17), just as it is measured by the conceptual similarity with the expert.

In order to more thoroughly gauge the effects of the variables included in the model, the correlation between the predictors and the variable criterion were decomposed into the sum of their direct, indirect and total effects. Table 3 shows the values of the standardized direct, indirect, total, and unexplained effects of each of the variable included in the model.

The indirect effect of practical intelligence, through Self-demand at work/study and of the learning environment is of .188 (z = 3.81, p = .0023). That is, the indirect effect of intelligence on the acquisition of knowledge, through motivation and through the perception of the learning environment, is statistically significant.

Therefore, the total effect of the intellectual ability on the acquisition of knowledge (β= .417) is the strongest one of the total effects on final performance. Practical intelligence directly and indirectly influences acquired knowledge through motivation and through the perception of the learning environment by students.

Table 3. Direct, indirect, total, and unexplained effects

		Effect on			
Effect of		V2	V3	V4	V5
V1	Direct	-	0.210*	0.317**	0.229**
	Indirect	-	-	-	0.188**
	Total	-	0.210*	0.317**	0.417**
	Unexplained	-	0.021	0.030	0.028
V2	Direct		0.165*	0.239**	0.166*
	Indirect		-	-	0.144**
	Total		0.165*	0.239**	0.310**
	Unexplained		0.028	0.041	0.045
V3	Direct			-	0.285**
	Indirect			-	-
	Total			-	0.285**
	Unexplained				0.174
V4	Direct				0.404***
	Indirect				-
	Total				0.404***
	Unexplained				0.183

*$p< 0.05$; **$p<.01$; ***$p<.001$.
V1 = Practical intelligence; V2 = Conceptual similarity (organized knowledge); V3 = Work/study self-demand (motivation); V4 = Learning environment; V5 = Performance

Another significant indirect effect is that of the conceptual similarity on performance with a value of .144 ($z= 3.11$, $p=.0047$). This effect also takes place through learning environment, and less through self-demand at work/study. The total effect of the conceptual similarity, on acquired knowledge is of .310.

CONCLUSION

In the first place, in relation to the identification of the explanatory elements of the acquisition of knowledge and cognitive abilities, it is observed that the results of the different techniques of data analysis lead to quite convergent results.

The variables that show a significant correlation of order zero with the performance during the instructional process of a complex significant material, carried out in a real instructional situation, focus on the aspects of intellectual ability, knowledge organization, motivation, and the instructional context in which this process is carried out.

The multiple regression analysis, which considers the presence of overlapping of variance among variables, obtains similar results. The variables related to conceptual organization, practical intelligence, motivation, and the perception of the learning environment are those that contribute in a significant way to explain the variation in the learning results regarding knowledge and abilities acquisition. These aspects are indeed those that are present to a greater or lesser extent in the theories, models and explanatory hypotheses of the acquisition of the knowledge and the abilities that take part in the development of expert competence (Ericsson, 1999; Ericsson and Smith, 1991; Ericsson and Charness, 1994; Ericsson and Lehman, 1996; Sternberg, 1994, 1998, 1999a).

The results concerning *intellectual ability* show that the different dimensions of intelligence evaluated show moderate correlations to each other, as well as different relations with the other variables, which is consistent with other results obtained by Sternberg, Castejón, Prieto, Hautamäki and Grigorenko, (2001), Sternberg, Prieto and Castejón, (2000), on the relative independence of the three aspects of triarchic intelligence - analytical intelligence, practical intelligence and creative intelligence. The type of intelligence that appears to be more related to knowledge acquisition is the practical intelligence.

The *quality of the organization of knowledge*, operatively defined by the variables of coherence and conceptual similarity, is another aspect that also appears to be related in a significant way to the acquisition of knowledge and abilities.

The results of the experimental validation of the evaluation procedure of cognitive structures, show the consistency of these measurements, which behave as it is theoretically expected, especially the similarity index, as in the case of Pinkerton (1998). On one hand, a change takes place from the beginning to the end of the instructional process in the sense of a greater similarity between the students' conceptual structure and that of the professor. On the other hand, the correlation between the measurement of the student's conceptual organization and the results of learning obtained at the end of the process is significant. These findings sustain the validity of this procedure for the evaluation of cognitive structures in diverse fields (Acton, Johnson and Goldsmith, 1994; Gillan and Schvaneveldt, 1999; Gonzalvo, Canes and Low, 1994; Kraiger, Rooms and Cannon-Bowers, 1995; Schvaneveldt, Durso, Goldsmith, Breen and Cooke, 1985; Vinogradov and Kirkland, 2003)

It is also remarkable that the measurements of conceptual organization taken at the beginning of the knowledge acquisition process are not related to learning results. This suggests that the change or the conceptual reorganization that takes place during the learning process is produced in a more or less "radical" way, in the sense pointed by Chi, Slotta and Leeuw (1994), Well (1997), Tsai (2003), and Thagard (1992).

Of special interest is the relation between knowledge organization and the general intellectual ability understood as intelligence in the traditional psychometric sense.

The results of our work clearly show that both intelligence and knowledge organization make a contribution to the explanation of acquired knowledge and abilities. The results of the multiple regression analysis demonstrate that both conceptual organization, and particularly the measurement of conceptual similarity, and practical intelligence contribute in a significant way to the prediction/explanation of performance.

The study of the precise relation between intellectual ability and the degree of knowledge organization the structural model offers, shows more clearly that both variables exert an independent influence on knowledge acquisition. The results of the statistical analysis of the structural equations model show that intelligence has a direct influence on knowledge acquisition and an indirect influence through motivation and the perception of the learning environment.

These results are coincident with the results obtained in some studies that have considered the question of the independence of knowledge of general intellectual ability. In one of the few studies on the subject which also uses appropriate methodology to respond to this question, Minnaert and Janssen (1996) found out that the specific previous knowledge of a domain had more effect to explain the acquired final knowledge in a subject of a university course, than general intellectual abilities, which also exerted a significant effect on learning skills.

Organized knowledge directly influences the acquisition of competence, effect which is independent of that exerted by intelligence in a direct way. The qualitative organization of knowledge explains the acquisition of new knowledge and cognitive skills, beyond, and independently, of the direct influence of intellectual abilities. In this way, the role played by knowledge in the development of expert competence is recognized (Charness and Schultetus, 1999; Ericsson and Charness, 1994; Ericsson and Lehmann, 1996; Glaser, 1984, 1996; Patel, Kaufman and Arocha, 2000), independently of intellectual abilities.

The theories on expert competence establish that the critical factor in the acquisition of knowledge and skills is the way in which knowledge is organized in the cognitive structure of individuals (Ericsson and Lehman, 1996; Ericsson and Charness, 1994; Charness and Schultetus, 1999). Nevertheless, from Sternberg's perspective (1994), knowledge organization is only important inasmuch as it allows to analyze new information in a more effective way. The establishment of inferences goes beyond the amount and organization of knowledge, it requires the effective use of this knowledge. From this point of view, it is not information *per se* what matters, but the efficacy of its organization to facilitate the analysis of new information.

Sternberg (1985b) is in disagreement with the idea expressed by Glaser (1984), that the acquisition of expert competence must be understood fundamentally, although not exclusively, in terms of the specific knowledge in a certain domain. To Sternberg, both aspects, general processes and specific knowledge, must be jointly considered in any theory of expertise, learning and instruction. The important thing is to establish the way in which they interact (Sternberg, 1985b).

In Sternberg's model (1998, 1999a) on the acquisition of expert competence, an interactive view on the relation between general processes and knowledge is kept, when it is specifically stated that: "the declarative and procedural knowledge acquired through the extension of the learning and thinking skills also results in these skills being used more effectively in the future" (Sternberg, 1999a, p. 365). The interactive position present in Sternberg's Model of Developing Expertise (1999a, 1999a) is very similar to Ceci's theory (1996) on cognitive complexity, where a reciprocal relation between general cognitive processes and knowledge structures is established. Efficient general cognitive processes provide structure and complexity to the existing knowledge in a domain, and, at the same time, this structure helps to improve the efficacy of the cognitive processes that operate on it.

The results obtained in our work clearly sustain the hypothesis that quality - organization of knowledge a person has, is an important factor in the acquisition of expert competence. And the fact that this organization is independent of intelligence. However, the question of what determines the specific character of knowledge organization remains unanswered. It seems to be an ability of qualitative knowledge organization that is different from intelligence, at least from the intelligence understood according to the traditional psychometric definition.

On the other hand, the use of strategies does not have a direct influence on knowledge acquisition, since none of the factors of the Study Process Questionnaire (SPQ), shows a significant relation with learning results. This can be due to different reasons. On one hand the strategies evaluated are fundamentally learning strategies, aimed to understand knowledge, rather than thinking strategies related to deep understanding and a conceptual reorganization of material. In this respect, Sternberg in his model of expert competence acquisition (1998, 1999a), distinguishes between learning skills, metacognitive skills and thinking skills, being the latter those which seem to have a more important role (Sternberg, 1998; Veeman, Wilhelm and Beishuizen, 2004). On the other hand, it is most probable that the ability to organize knowledge qualitatively and the strategies aimed at the acquisition of knowledge are independent mechanisms. This would be in agreement with the unconscious nature of knowledge organization abilities.

Motivation is another factor that affects knowledge and skills acquisition in a direct way. Motivation is, in the different theories on expert competence acquisition, the motor that impels to get involved in deliberate practice (Ericsson, Krampe and Tesch-Römer, 1993; Ericsson and Lehman, 1996) and the indispensable element to initially activate the factors that take part in competence acquisition (Sternberg, 1998,b; 1999a).

However, motivation is a complex mechanism in which biological and cognitive factors are implied (Covington, 2000). These factors determine the general impulse towards activity, the sense of self-efficacy and the achievement motivation. Perhaps for that reason, it has been suggested that possibly different types of motivation take part in the acquisition of expert competence (Sternberg, 1999a).

Our results indicate that the motivational aspect that is systematically related to learning and knowledge acquisition is M3 factor of self-demand at work and study, used in our work. This questionnaire has as a theoretical reference the research of the achievement motivation school, dedicated to the study of the determining elements of manifest execution, and located within the neobehaviourism paradigm. The factor of self-demand at work reflects a tendency to continuously improve at work and/or in study and to positively evaluate the world of work/study, where important interests for the individual can be found. This is, therefore, a motivational aspect linked to achievement motivation, where motivation is understood as a continued effort to achieve goals and improve performance.

This is a motivational aspect associated with biological and temperamental factors, related more to the general impulse towards the activity and performance than to cognitive aspects of motivation. This motivational aspect has been considered indeed as the most important aspect in the development of expert competence (Ericsson and Charness, 1994; Ericsson, Krampe and Tesch-Römer, 1993), although also motivational aspects of self-demand can be implied, as it seems that experts need to develop a sense of their own self-efficacy to face difficult tasks in their expertise domain (Sternberg, 1999a). However, the effect that conceptual organization exerts on the motivational factor in our study, also suggests the presence of cognitive components in the particular aspects of involved motivation.

Although motivation exerts a specific effect on the acquisition of the knowledge and abilities implied in expert competence, our results indicate that it is just another element that, although important, is not the most significant in the process of competence acquisition. Other aspects such as general intellectual abilities, and the ability to qualitatively organize knowledge have a greater effect than the factors related to motivation. These results would therefore sustain to a greater extent the position of Gardner (1995) and Sternberg (1996a, 1998) against considering motivation and practice as the fundamental and almost unique elements in the development of expert competence, as supported by Ericsson and Charness (1994, 1995). The results support the existence of a series of elements that in interaction determine the acquisition of competence, as it is established in the most recent models (Ceci, 1996; Sternberg, 1999a,b; Sternberg, Grigorenko and Ferrari, 2002).

An outstanding element of such model is *context* in which competence is developed. Instructional context in this case, defined by the learning environment, appears in our work/study related, in a systematic and very significant way, to learning results and it makes a very important direct contribution to the explanation of those results.

Before examining the learning context influence and its instructional implications on the acquisition of knowledge, we will talk about a previous result relative to the dimensionalization of the instructional context. According to the initially proposed model and to the results from other recent research about the adjustment between the characteristics of students and the methods of teaching (Sternberg, Grigorenko, Ferrari and Clinkenbeard, 1999; Sternberg, Torff and Grigorenko, 1998), the hypothesis that the preferences of students for certain strategies or teaching styles of their teacher could be related to the results obtained by them from learning.

Nevertheless, the results about the validation of the "Questionnaire on preferences for teaching-learning styles" revealed the existence of a unique factor, around which all items of the questionnaire largely load. Contrary to all expectations, participants in the research did not show any preferences for teaching-learning styles or others, but showed their preference for a combination of styles and methods of teaching and learning which included individual work, group discussion, lectures, cooperative work and practice. This factor is denominated global learning environment, since it contains the different teaching and learning methods that are present in the instructional context.

The results of our research reveal that this factor has a very important direct and significant influence on the acquisition of knowledge, and that this perception is influenced as well by intellectual ability and conceptual organization. On the one hand, the preference for a rich learning environment is positively related to the acquisition of knowledge. On the other hand, the perception of a better learning environment is defined, partially, by a larger intellectual ability and larger skills of conceptual organization. In any case, although a larger intellectual ability and ability to organize information influence the preference for a richer and rich learning environment, such a learning environment is responsible for the acquisition of better knowledge, to a great extent.

The instructional implication for the development of expert competence is quite clear, rich learning environments should be encouraged in order to stimulate the acquisition of this competence. Goldman, Petrosino and CTGV (1999) have set a series of principles for the explicit design of powerful learning environment based on the socio-cultural theory of situated learning and on knowledge about the characteristics of expert competence. The four outstanding principles are: a) instruction must be organized around significant learning and with appropriate purposes for students; b) instruction must provide foundations for the achievement of significant learning, obtained through two ways, the solution of authentic tasks and instructional methods encouraging the establishment of consistent and richly interconnected knowledge-basis; c) instruction must provide opportunities for practice with feedback, revision and reflection; and d) instruction must be designed and developed in such a way that encourages cooperation, distribution of expertise and learning communities.

Sternberg (1998, 1999b) suggests the design of an instruction in which the principles of the theories of intelligence are applied. Thus, Sternberg, Torff and Grigorenko (1998) found that the triarchic instruction, which tries to power the analytical, creative and practical abilities, improves performance, since it allows students to codify the information to be learned and memorized in three different ways, and in consequence they will have more possibilities of getting back and use such information. Identical results were obtained in subsequent research (Sternberg, Grigorenko, Ferrari and Clinkenbeard, 1999; Grigorenko, Jarvin and Sternberg, 2000), where it is concluded that all students must receive a variety of methods so that each one individually benefits from those methods that best fit their characteristics.

Our data support this hypothesis, since the results from the analysis of reliability and validity of the questionnaire on preferences for teaching-learning styles reveal that students do not show clear preferences for certain instructional styles and methods, and that they do not generally consider certain teaching methods to be better than others, but that rather a combination or mixture of these styles and methods should be developed in class so that students can achieve better results.

In short, in our research we have identified a group of variables which are directly involved in the acquisition of knowledge and cognitive skills which are part of the initial development of expert competence, according to the synthetic theory of expertise (Sternberg, 1996b; 1999), in which different elements are combined. The extension of this research to other participants, other contents and another instructional context may help verify the results obtained and avoid its possible limitations.

REFERENCES

Ackerman, P.L. (1988). Determinants of individual differences during skill acquisition: Cognitive abilities and information processing. *Journal of Experimental Psychology: General, 117*, 288-318.

Ackerman, P.L. and Cianciolo, A.T. (2000). Cognitive, perceptual-speed, and psychomotor determinants of individual differences during skill acquisition. *Journal of Experimental Psychology: Applied, 6*(4), 259-290.

Acton, W.H., Johnson, P.J., and Goldmisth, T.E. (1994). Structural knowledge assessment: comparison of referent structures. *Journal of Educational Psychology, 86*, 303-311.

Bandura, A. (1977). Self-efficacy: Toward a unifying theory of behaviour change. *Psychological Review, 84*, 181-215.

Bandura, A. (1996). *Self-efficacy: The exercise of control*. New York: Freeman.

Bentler, P.M. (1993). *EQS: Structural Equations Program Manual*. Los Angeles, CA: BMDP Statistical Software, Inc.

Bentler, P.M., and Dudgeon, P. (1996). Covariance structure analysis: statistical practice, theory and directions. *Annual Review of Psychology, 47*, 563-592.

Biggs, J.B. (1987,a). *Student approaches to learning and studying*. Hawthorn, Victoria: Australian Council for Educational Research.

Biggs, J.B. (1987b). *Study Process Questionnaire: SPQ*. Hawthorn, Victoria: Australian Council for Educational Research.

Carmines, E.G., and Zeller, R.A. (1979). *Reliability and validity assessment*. London: Sage Pub.

Castejón, J.L. (2001). *Introducción a la psicología de la instrucción* [Introduction to Intructional Psychology]. Alicante: Ediciones Club Universitario.

Ceci, S. (1996). *On intelligence. A bioecological treatadise on intellectual development. (Expanded edition)*. Cambridge, MA: Harvard University Press.

Cooke, N.J., Salas, E., Cannon-Bowers, J.A., and Stout, R.J. (2000). Measuring team knowledge. *Human Factors, 42*(1), 151-173.

Covington, M.V. (2000). Goal theory, motivation, and school achievement: An integrative review. *Annual Review of Psychology, 51*, 171-200.

Charness, N., and Schultetus, R.S. (1999). Knowledge and expertise. In F.T. Durso (Ed.), *Handbook of applied cognition* (pp. 57-82). New York: Wiley.

Chi, M.T.H. (1985). Changing conception of sources of memory development. *Human Development, 28*, 50-56.

Chi, M.T.H., and Ceci, S. (1987). Content knowledge: its role, representation, and restructuring in memory development. *Advances in Child Development and Behavior, 20*, 91-146.

Chi, M.T.H., and Slotta, J.D. (1993). The ontological coherence of intuitive physics. *Cognition and Instruction, 10*, 249-260.

Day, E, A, Arthur, W and Gettman, D. (2001). Knowledge structures and the acquisition of a complex skill. *Journal of Applied Psychology, 86*(5), 1002-1033.

Dorsey, D.W., Campbell, G.E., Foster, L.L., and Miles, D.E. (1999). Assessing knowledge structures: relations with experience and posttraining performance. *Human Performance, 12*(1), 31-57.

Ericsson, K.A. (1998). The scientific study of expert performance: General implications for optimal learning and creativity. *High Ability Studies, 9*, 75-100.

Ericsson, K.A. (1999). Creative expertise as superior reproductible performance: Innovative and flexible aspects of expert performance. *Psychological Inquiry, 10*(4), 329-361.

Ericsson, K.A. (2001). Expertise in interpreting: An expert-performance perspective. *Interpreting, 5*(2), 187-220.

Ericsson, K.A. (2002). Attaining excellence through deliberate practice: Insights from the study of expert performance. In R. Fox and C. Desforges (Eds.), *Theaching and learning: The essential readings* (pp.4-37). Malden: Blackwell Publishers.

Ericsson, K.A. (2003). The search for general abilities and basic capacities: Theoretical implications from the modifiability and complexity of mechanisms mediating expert performance. In R.J. Sternberg (Ed.), *The psychology of abilities, competences, and expertise* (pp. 93-125). New York: Cambridge University Press.

Ericsson, K.A. (2003). The search for general abilities and basic capacities: Theoretical implications from the modifiability and complexity of mechanisms mediating expert performance. In R.J. Sternberg (Ed.), *The psychology of abilities, competences, and expertise* (pp.93-125). New York: Cambridge University Press.

Ericsson, K.A. (2005). Superior decision making as an integral quality of expert performance: Insights into the mediating mechanisms and their acquisition through deliberate practice. In

R. Lipshitz and H. Montgomery (Eds.), *How professionals make decisions* (pp.135-167). Nahwah: Laurence Erlbaum Associates.

Ericsson, K.A., Krampe, R.T., and Tesch-Römer, C. (1993). The role of deliberate practice in the acquisition of expert performance. *Psychological Review, 100*, 363-406.

Ericsson, K.A., and Charness, N. (1994). Expert performance: Its structure and acquisition. *American Psychologist, 49*, 725-747.

Ericsson, K.A., and Charness, N. (1995). Expert performance: Its structure and acquisition: Reply to Gardner (Abilities evidence for talent or characteristics acquired through engagement in relevant activities? *American Psychologist, 50*(9), 803-804.

Ericsson, K.A., and Lehmann, A.C. (1996). Expert and exceptional performance: Evidence on maximal adaptations on task constraints. *Annual Review of Psychology, 47*, 273-305.

Ericsson, K.A., and Smith, J. (1991). Prospects and limits of the empirical study of expertise: an introduction. In K.A. Ericsson and J. Smith (Eds.), *Toward a general theory of expertise. Prospects and limits* (pp. 1-38). New York: Cambridge University Press.

Galton, F. (1979). *Hereditary genius: An inquiry into its laws and consequences*. London: Julian Friedman Publishers (original Publication 1869).

Gardner, H (2003) Three distinct meanings of intelligence. In R.J. Sternberg J. Lautrey and T.I. Lubart (Eds.) *Models of Intelligence: International perspectives* (pp. 43-54) Washington, DC, US: APA

Gardner, H. (1983). *Frames of mind: The theory of multiple intelligences*. New York: Basics Books.

Gardner, H. (1993). *Creating minds*. New York: Basic.

Gardner, H. (1995). Expert performance: Its structure and acquisition: Comment (Why would anyone become an expert?). *American Psychologist, 50*(9), 802-803.

Gauthier, I., Tarr, M.J., Anderson, A.W., Skudlarski, P. and Gore, J.C. (1999). Activation of middle fusiform "face area" increases with expertise in recognizing novel objects. *Nature-Neuroscience, 2*(6), 568-573.

Gillan, D.J., and Schvaneveldt, R.W. (1999). Applying cognitive psychology: Bridging the gulf between basic research and cognitive artifacts. In F.T. Durso (Ed.), *Handbook of applied cognition* (pp. 3-33). New York: Wiley.

Glaser, R. (1984). Education and thinking. The role of knowledge. *American Psychologist, 39*(2), 93-104.

Glaser, R. (1996). Changing the agency for learning: Acquiring expert performance. En K.A. Ericsson (Ed.), *The road to excellence: The acquisition of expert performance in the arts and sciences, sports, and games* (pp. 303-311). Hillsdale, NJ: LEA.

Glasser, R. and Bassok, M. (1989) Learning theory and the study of instruction. *Annual review of Psychology, 40*, 631-666.

Goldman, S.R., Petrosino, A.J., and Cognition and Technology Group at Vanderbilt (1999). Design principles for instruction in content domains: Lessons from research on expertise and learning. In F.T. Durso, R.S. Nickerson, R.W. Schvaneveldt, S.T. Dumais, D.S. Lindsay and M.T.H. Chi (Eds.), *Handbook of Applied Cognition* (pp. 595-627). New York: John Wiley and Sons.

Gonzalvo, P., Cañas, J., and Bajo, M.T. (1994). Structural representations in knowledge acquisition. *Journal of Educational Psychology, 86*, 601-616.

Grigorenko, E., Jarvin, L. and Sternberg, R. J. (2002). School-based test of triarchic theory of intelligence: Three setting, three samples, three syllabi. *Contemporary Educational Psychology*, *27*(2), 167-208.

Hernández, F. (1996). *Cuestionario de Procesos de Estudio* [Study Process Questionnaire]. Murcia: Departamento de Métodos de Investigación y Diagnóstico en Educación, University of Murcia.

Jackson and Ward (2004). A fresh perspective on progress files: A way of representing complex learning and achievement in higher education. *Assessment and evaluation in higher education*, *29*(4), 423-449.

Jöreskog, K.G. (1978). Structural analysis of covariance and correlation matrices. *Psychometrika*, *43*, 443-447.

Kraiger, K., Salas, E., and Cannon-Bowers, J.A. (1995). Measuring knowledge organization as a method for assesssing learning during training. *Human Factors*, *37*, 804-816.

MacCallum, R.C., and Austin, J.T. (2000). Applications of structural equation modeling in psychological research. *Annual Review of Psychology*, *51*, 201-226.

McClelland, D.C. (1985). *Human motivation*. New York: Scott Foresman.

Minnaert, A., and Janssen, P.J. (1996). How general are the effects of domain-specific prior knowledge on study expertise as compared to general thinking skills?. In M. Birenbaum and F. Dochy (Eds.), *Alternatives in assessment of achievements, learning processes and prior knowledge* (pp. 265-282). London: Kluwer Academic Publishers.

Patel, V.L, Kaufman, D.R., and Arocha, J.F. (2000). Conceptual change in the biomedical and health sciences domain. In R. Glaser (Ed.), *Advances in instructional psychology: Educational design and cognitive scienc: Vol 5* (pp. 329-392). Mawhah, NJ: LEA.

Pelechano, V. (1973a). *Personalidad y parámetros. Tres escuelas y un modelo* [Personality and parameters. Three theories and a model]. Barcelona: Vicens Vives.

Pelechano, V. (1973b). *Manual del cuestionario MAE* [Cuestionnaire MAE Manual]. Madrid: Fraser.

Pelechano, V. (1989). Informe de Investigación [Research Report]. *Análisis y Modificación de Conducta*, *15*, (45/46).

Pinkerton, K.D. (1998). Network similarity (NETSIM) as a method of assessing structural knowledge for large groups. *Journal of Interactive Learning Research*, *9*(3-4), 249-269.

Popham, W. (1978). *Criterion referenced measurement*. Englewood Cliffs, NJ: Prentice Hall.

Ruiz, J.C., Algarabel, S., Dasí, C., and Pitarque, A. (1998). El papel de los diagramas en la organización del conocimiento: Evidencia desde el pathfinder y el escalamiento multidimensional [The role of diagrams in knowledge organization: Evidence from the pathfinder and the multidimensional scaling]. *Psicológica*, *19*, 367-386.

Schvaneveldt, R.W. (1990). *Pathfinder associative networks. Studies in knowledge organization*. Norwood, NJ: Ablex Publishing Co.

Schvaneveldt, R.W., Durso, F.T., Goldsmith, T.E, Breen, T.J., Cooke, N., Tucker, R.G., and De Maio, J.C. (1985). Measuring the structure of expertise. *International Journal of Man-Machine Studies*, *23*, 699-728.

Sternberg, R.J. (1985,a). *Beyond IQ. A triarchic theory of human intelligence*. New York: Cambridge University Press

Sternberg, R.J. (1985,b). All's well that ends well, but it's a sad tale that begins at the end: A reply to Glaser. *American Psychologist*, *May*, 571-572.

Sternberg, R.J. (1991). Theory-based testing of intellectual abilities: rationale for the triarchic abilities test. In H.A. Rowe (Ed.), *Intelligence: reconceptualization and measurement* (pp. 183-202). Hillsdale, NJ: LEA.

Sternberg, R.J. (1993). *Sternberg Triarchic Abilities Test (Level H)*. Non published test Manual.

Sternberg, R.J. (1994). Cognitive conceptions of expertise. *International Journal of Expert Systems*, 7(1), 1-12.

Sternberg, R.J. (1995). Expertise in complex problem solving: A comparison of alternative conceptions. In P.A. French and J. Funke (Eds.), *Complex problem solving* (pp. 296-321). Hillsdale, NJ: LEA.

Sternberg, R.J. (1996 b). *Successful intelligence*. New York: Cambridge University Press.

Sternberg, R.J. (1996,a). Costs of expertise. In K.A. Ericsson (Ed.), *The road to excellence: The acquisition of expert performance in the arts and sciences, sports, and games* (pp. 347-354). Hillsdale, NJ: LEA.

Sternberg, R.J. (1998). Abilities are forms of developing expertise. *Educational Researcher*, 27(3), 11-20.

Sternberg, R.J. (1999a). Intelligence as developing expertise. *Contemporary Educational Psychology*, 24, 359-375.

Sternberg, R.J. (1999b). Ability and expertise. It's time to replace the current model of intelligence. *American Educator*, Spring, 10-13 and 50-51.

Sternberg, R.J. (2000). The concept of intelligence. In R.J. Sternberg (Ed.), *Handbook of intelligence* (pp. 3-15). New York: Cambridge University Press.

Sternberg, R.J. (2003). *The psychology of abilities, competencies, and expertise*. New York: Cambridge University Press.

Sternberg, R.J., Bermejo, M.R., and Castejón, J.L (1997). Factores intelectuales y personales en la cognición creativa definida por el insight [Intellectual and personal factors in the creative cognition defined by insight]. *Boletín de Psicología*, 57, 41-58.

Sternberg, R.J., Castejón, J.L., Prieto, M.D., Hautamäki, J., and Grigorenko, E. (2001). Confirmatory factor analysis of the Sternberg Triarchic Abilities Test (Multiple Choice Items) in Three International Samples: An empirical test of the Triarchic Theory. *European Journal of Psychological Assessment*, 17, 1-16.

Sternberg, R.J., and Clinkendbeard, P. (1995). A triarchic view of identyfying, teaching and assessing gifted children. *Roeper Review*, 17(4), 255-260.

Sternberg, R.J., and Davidson, R. (1995). *The nature of insight*. Cambridge, MA: MIT Press.

Sternberg, R.J, Forsythe, G.B., Hedlung, J., Horvath, J.A., Wagner, R.K., Williams, W.M., Snook, A., and Grigorenko, E.L. (2000). *Practical intelligence in everyday life*. New York: Cambridge University Press.

Sternberg, R.J., Grigorenko, E., Ferrari, M., and Clinkenbeard, P. (1999). An triarchic analysis of an aptitude-treatment interaction. *European Journal of Psychological Assessment*, 15, 1-11.

Sternberg, R.J., Grigorenko, E. and Ferrari, M.. (2022). Fostering Intellectual Excelence Throught Developing Expertise In M. Ferrari (Ed.), *The pursuit of excellence through Education* (pp. 57-85). Mahwah, N.J.: LEA.

Sternberg, R.J., and Lubart, T.I. (1997). *La creatividad en una cultura conformista* [Defying the crow. Cultivating creativity in a culture of conformity]. Barcelona: Paidós

Sternberg, R.J., Prieto, M.D., and Castejón, J.L. (2000). Análisis factorial confirmatorio del Sternberg Triarchic Abilities Test (nivel H) en una muestra española: resultados preliminares

[Confirmatory factor análisis of the Sternberg Triarchic Abilities Test (Level H) in a spanish sample: Preliminary results. *Psicothema, 12*(4), 642-647.

Sternberg, R.J., Torff, B., and Grigorenko, E.L. (1998). Teaching triarchically improves school achievement. *Journal of Educational Psychology, 90*(3), 374-384.

Thagard, P. (1992). *The structure conceptual revolutions*. Cambridge, MA: MIT Press.

Tsai, C. (2003). Using a conflict map as a instructional tool to change student alternative conceptions in simple series electric-circuits. *International journal of science education, 25*(3), 307-327.

Van Lehn, K. (1996). Cognitive skill acquisition. *Annual Review of Psychology, 47*, 513-539.

Veeman, M., Elshout, J.J., and Meijer, J. (1997). The generality vs domain-specificity of metacognitive skills in novice learning across domains. *Learning and Instruction, 7*(2), 187-209.

Veeman, M., and Elshout, J.J. (1999). Changes in the relation between cognitive and metacognitive skills during the acquisition of expertise. *European Journal of Psychology of Education, 14*(4), 509-523.

Veeman, M.V., Wilhelm, P., and Beishuizen, J.J. (2004). The relation between intellectual and metacognitive skills from a developmental perspective. *Learning and Instruction, 14*(1), 89-109.

Vinogradov, S., Kirkland, J., Poole, J.H., Drexler, M., Ober, B.A. and Shenaut, G.K. (2003). Both processing speed and semantic memory organization predict verbal fluency in schizophrenia. *Schizophrenia Research, 59*(2-3), 269-75.

Weiner, B. (1986). *An attributional theoery of motivation and emotion*. New York: Springer-Verlag.

Weiner, B. (1990). Searching for the roots of applied attribution theory. In S. Graham and V.S. Folkes (Eds.), *Attribution theory: Aplications to achievement, mental health, and interpersonal conflict* (pp. 1-13). Hillsdale, NJ: LEA.

In: New Developments in Learning Research
Editor: Samuel N. Hogan, pp. 35-47

ISBN 1-59454-669-X
© 2006 Nova Science Publishers, Inc.

Chapter 2

OBJECT EXPLORATION: A NON-AVERSIVE MEASURE OF OBJECT RECOGNITION, SPATIAL MEMORY, AND CONTEXT FAMILIARITY

Matthew J. Anderson
Saint Joseph's College of Maine

ABSTRACT

Berlyne (1950) first illustrated that rats spend more time exploring novel objects than ones previously encountered. Since 1950, variations on this task have been used to examine object memory, spatial memory, context familiarity, and numerous related topics. Driven by the task's simplicity and non-aversive characteristics, the use of object exploration tasks has risen dramatically in recent years. Following a historical recount and description of the original procedures, this chapter reviews the many areas in which object exploration tasks have been employed (e.g., pharmacological and ontogenetic investigations). A particular emphasis is placed on the behavioral and biological influences on performance in such tasks. Potential directions for future research employing such tasks are discussed.

INTRODUCTION

In 1950, Berlyne brought to the field's attention the factors of novelty and curiosity as determinants of exploratory behavior. The importance of these factors as a potential tool for the investigation of learning and memory had previously been ignored. In this pivotal study, rats were initially placed in an empty experimental box for twenty minutes. This was done to pre-expose the animal to the testing conditions and habituate any curiosity the animal had about the box itself. Later, the animals were returned to the box, which now contained three identical stimuli, and exploration of the stimuli were recorded. After five minutes in the box, animals were returned to their home cages for a ten-minute interval before undergoing a second training session, identical to the first. Next, after another ten-minute rest period, animals were returned to the box where they now encountered two of the initial objects, and a third novel object that had previously not been explored. Upon completion of the training/testing sessions, Berlyne compared the time spent exploring the novel and initial objects and found that the animals spent significantly more time exploring objects with which they had had no previous experience. Thus, this is essentially a task dependent upon habituation. The animal habituates to the original object and later spends more time exploring the novel object.

Berlyne perhaps might have understated when he said, "…the everyday activities of both men and animals seem to attest the importance of novelty as well as familiarity in features of the environment, and novelty may, in fact, hold the key to our understanding some of the more complex levels of motivation in the human being." (Berlyne, 1950, p. 68). Not only did this research bring to light the importance of novelty and curiosity, it also gave researchers a new task that relied solely on the animal's natural behavioral repertoire, and avoided any form of noxious stimulation or ill-defined reinforcement.

Prompted by the simplicity of the procedures, many variations of Berlyne's task have appeared in the psychological literature. Indeed, the use of such object exploration tasks has risen dramatically in recent years in countless examinations of a variety of topics. This chapter attempts to provide a general descript of the methods of such tasks, review the findings obtained with such tasks, and perhaps identify some directions for future research.

NOVEL OBJECT RECOGNITION: MEMORY FOR TRAINING STIMULI

The use of a novel object recognition task (NOR) appeared in 1988 in a study by Ennanceur and Delacour. These researchers conducted a series of investigations reconfirming Berlyne's original findings that rats will spend more time exploring novel objects than familiar ones when given equal access to both. Moreover, they greatly expanded on the original design by using object recognition to assess retention across time. Their findings revealed that the animal's ability to discriminate between novel and familiar objects fades quickly, returning to baseline performance within 24 hours. This study brought the task into the modern literature, and reminded researchers of the many benefits and potential uses of this task.

Besheer and Bevins (2000) examined the effects of context pre-exposure and different object presentation techniques. Their findings confirmed Berlyne's idea that environmental familiarization increased interaction with the objects, and demonstrated that a minimum of three minutes interaction time, both at training with initial objects, and testing with novel and familiar objects, is needed to produce significant interaction differences with a one hour train to test interval. Additionally, Besheer and Bevins (2000) draw attention to the fact that decreases in initial object interaction and habituation (Lukaszewska and Radulska, 1994), failures to discriminate the objects at test, and impairments in an animals ability to familiarize with the training environment (Sheldon, 1969) must all be ruled out as possible explanations before claims of initial training (sample) object memory deficit can be made.

It is apparent from the work of Ennaceur and Delacour (1988) and others (Ennaceur, Cavoy, Costa, and Delacour, 1989; Puma, Baudoin, and Bizot, 1998; Puma, Deschaux, Molimard, and Bizot, 1999) that memory for the original training stimuli is forgotten rather quickly, by 24-hours. We conducted a series of experiments in order to examine the permanence of such forgetting. Anderson Karash, Ashton, and Riccio (2003), employing a retention interval (24 hrs) where adult rats typically show forgetting, have demonstrated that 30-seconds of re-exposure to the original training stimuli (training objects and training context) 15-min prior to test effectively enhanced performance in the NOR task, reinstating the memory of the original object and novel object preference. Importantly, in two control experiments it was shown that the 30-second reminder independent of training is not sufficient to produce enhanced test performance, and that the additional 30-sec of object exposure is effective in enhancing performance only if it occurs shortly prior to test. Animals receiving the additional 30-sec immediately following training did not experience such beneficial effects. Thus we concluded that 30-sec pre-test training-stimulus exposures act as reminders in the NOR task, enhancing test performance in a similar fashion to the pre-test cueing treatments commonly employed in more traditional tasks of learning and memory (e.g., Campbell and Jaynes, 1966; Hamberg and Spear, 1978; Rovee-Collier, Sullivan, Enright, Lucas, and Fagan, 1980; Richardson, Wang, and Campbell, 1993), and that these effects are not likely due to the reminder itself producing additional learning (Anderson, et al., 2003). Such evidence suggests that loss of memory for the training objects in the NOR task is the result of a retrieval failure and not some form of decay (Spear, 1973).

Psychologists have long recognized that a mismatch of stimulating conditions from encoding to retrieval can result in retrieval decrement (e.g., Carr, 1925; McGeoch, 1942; Spear, 1973; Tulving and Thomson, 1973). The cues known to influence behavior in such a way include both external, environmental stimuli (e.g., Godden and Baddeley, 1975; Smith, 1979), as well as stimuli occurring within the actual organism such as drug state (e.g., Overton, 1964), circadian rhythm state (e.g., Holloway and Wansley, 1973), hormonal levels (Ebner, Richardson, and Riccio, 1981), hunger level (Davidson, 1987), and perhaps even mood state (e.g., Weingartner, Miller, and Murphy, 1977; Bower, Monteiro, and Gilligan, 1978). Indeed, even mismatches in available odor (e.g., Cann and Ross, 1989; Schab, 1990; Herz, 1997; Pointer and Bond, 1998) and flavor (Anderson, Berry, Morse, and Diotte, 2005) cues from time of training to that of test have been shown to hinder performance. Perhaps not surprisingly, altering the context from time of training to that of test has also been shown to disrupt performance in a novel object recognition task.

Employing an automated variation of the novel object recognition task in which two identical objects are placed in the arms of a Y-maze at initial exposure and one object is switched at test (Dellu, Mayo, Cherkaoui, Le Moal, and Simon, 1992), Dellu, Fauchey, Moal, and Simon (1997) demonstrated that altering the environmental context (visual cues, illumination, and odors) between training and test severely disrupted object recognition at 2-hour test. While it is evident from such results that a mismatch of cues from encoding to retrieval can result in retrieval decrement, it should be noted that for any information to actually affect the retrieval of a memory, these cues must be encoded along with the target information at time of training (Thomson and Tulving, 1970; Postman, 1972). Later we shall see how some researchers have employed object exploration tasks to specifically measure memory for the context itself.

NOVEL OBJECT RECOGNITION: TYPICAL PROCEDURES

In modern NOR studies of learning and memory, (e.g., Anderson, et al., 2003) subjects typically undergo a minimum of two days of 3-minute handling sessions prior to the beginning of the study in order to reduce any anxiety that may interfere with overall activity levels. Handling is followed by a minimum of two days of training/testing context pre-exposure during which each subject is individually placed in the empty chamber for something like 3-min/day. This is done to habituate subjects to the training and testing chamber and ensures that the animals will spend a sufficient amount of time exploring the objects. Approximately 24-hrs after the last pre-exposure session, each animal is returned to the chamber for its training session.

Training sessions typically consist of placing the animal in the box for 3-min with a matching set of 2 identical objects. As at least two object sets are needed to conduct an NOR experiment, it is important that the object set encountered by each subject is counterbalanced within each group. It is also essential that initial preferences for each object are similar. This should be established prior to the start of an experiment. After the 3-min training exposure, the animal is removed and returned to its home cage, and the chamber is cleaned in order to dilute any potential scent trail that the animal may have left behind. In order to eliminate olfactory information and ensure that the animal will rely on visual and other cues (Astur, Klein, Mumby, Protz, Sutherland, and Martin, 2002), cleaning and drying both the apparatus and the objects seems vital. After the passing of the desired retention-interval, each animal is returned to the testing chamber. This time the subject encounters one of the initial objects and an object with which it has had no previous experience. The items serving as novel objects, as well as the side on which the novel object appeared, should again be counterbalanced within each group. After 3-min, each animal is returned to its home cage. This process can be seen in figure 1.

All training and test sessions are typically videotaped, and scored for exploration of each object by several independent scorers blind to the experimental conditions. Exploration can be defined several ways. We have defined exploration as the animal having contact or having its snout within an inch of the object (e.g., Anderson, et al., 2003; Anderson, Barnes, Briggs, Ashton, Moody, Joynes, and Riccio, 2004a). Others have limited the definition of exploration specifically to directed contact (e.g., Besheer and Bevins, 2000). Occasionally an exclusion criterion is established, excluding animals from the experiment if their total exploration of both objects at training is not a satisfactory amount. This is done to ensure that animals are actually receiving object training and to eliminate some of the variability that is inherent to the task (Anderson, et al., 2004a). Others have employed automated variations of the task in order to further reduce variability and potential bias at scoring (e.g., Dellu, et al., 1992).

While scoring test sessions, explorations of the novel and initial objects for each animal are again recorded and one can choose between several measures of novelty preference. One can either calculate an absolute mean preference for novelty score for each group (seconds spent exploring the novel object minus seconds spent exploring initial object), or a relative percent preference score that takes into consideration each individual animal's total exploration ([time with novel object / total exploration of both objects] X 100). It is perhaps most advisable to examine both measures of novelty (e.g., Anderson, Karash, and Riccio,

2004b). Exclusion criteria based on minimum amounts of exploration at test may also be established to ensure the accurate measurement of object preferences.

Chamber Pre-exposure

Training/Initial Exposure

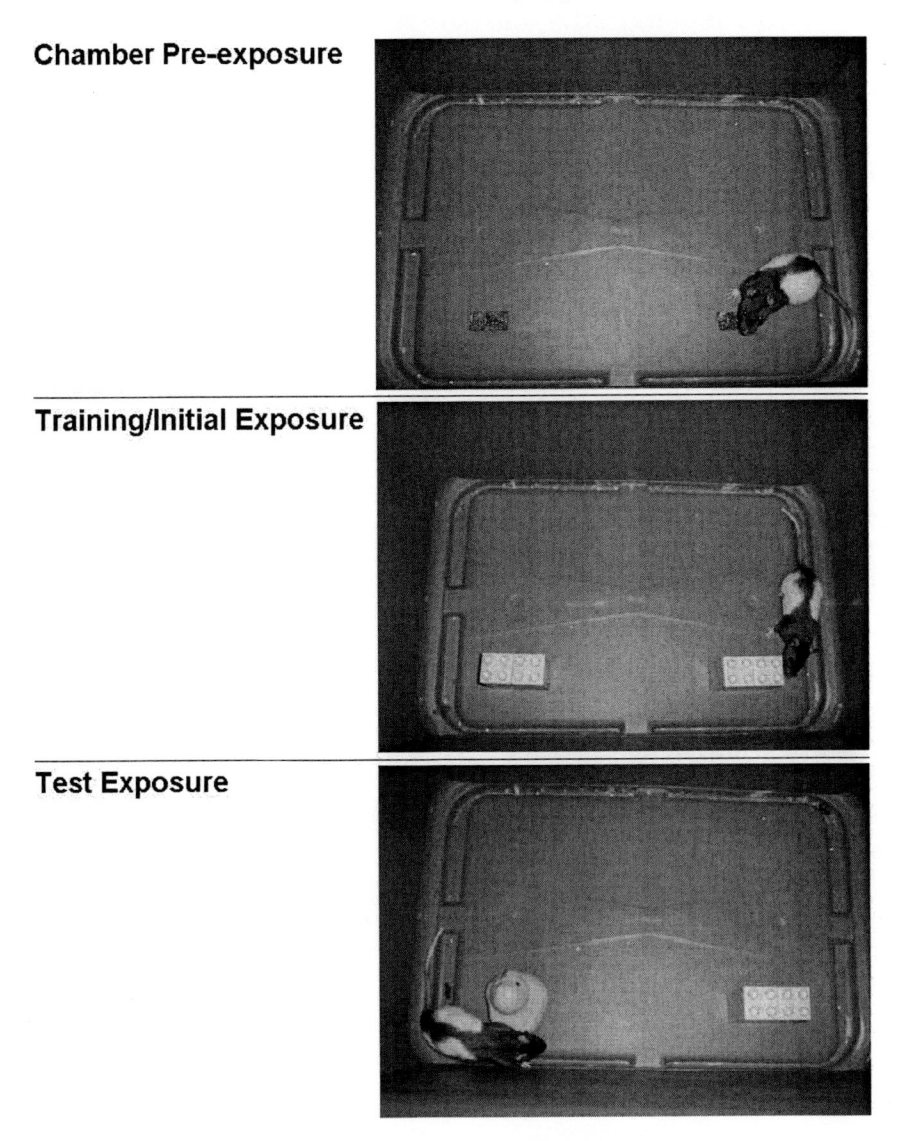

Test Exposure

Figure 1. Depicted are the steps in a typical novel object recognition experiment.

ONTOGENY AND OBJECT RECOGNITION

Psychologists have long recognized that development exerts a significant impact on memory capabilities across an organism's lifespan. In particular, the memory capabilities of both infantile (e.g., Campbell and Campbell, 1962) and senescent animals (e.g., Barnes, Nadel, Honig, 1980) seem to be significantly impaired when compared to healthy young adults. Surprisingly, while infantile amnesia has been demonstrated, the results of studies examining object recognition/memory impairments in senescent rats have been rather inconsistent.

While several studies have demonstrated negative effects of aging on object recognition (e.g., Dellu, et. al, 1992; Liu, Smith, Appleton, Darlington, and Bilkey, 2004; Scali, Casamenti, Pazzagli, Bartolini, and Pepeu, 1994; Scali, Giovannini, Prosperi, Bartolini, and Pepeu, 1997; Scali, Giovannini, Bartolini, Prosperi, Hinz, Schmidt, and Pepeu, 1997), an alarmingly high number have obtained negative results, demonstrating no differences in the object recognition capabilities of young adult and senescent rats (e.g., Cavoy and Delacour, 1993; Lukaszewska and Radulska, 1994). Given the numerous reports of memory problems with aging in other tasks, it seems likely that the negative results reported are the product of procedural technicalities. Additional research into this discrepancy is needed.

Anderson and colleagues (2004a) investigated infantile amnesia or ontogenetic forgetting in a novel object recognition task. 18-day-old Long-Evans rat pups and adults were trained and tested at two retention intervals (1-minute, or 120-minutes). By employing exclusion criteria which demanded minimum amounts of object exploration at training and test, it was found that the performance of 18-day-old pups, but not that of adults was significantly impaired at 120 minutes when compared to 1 minute. This suggests that the ontogeny of the learning and memory as measured by NOR tasks follows a developmental trend similar to that of other forms of learning, with older animals remembering more, and thus performing better than younger animals. Interestingly, while employing pre-test cuing treatments similar to those of Anderson and colleagues (2003), we have demonstrated that the ontogenetic forgetting in the NOR task is not irreversible (Anderson, et al., 2004b).

Many researchers with human subjects have used a similar visual exploration and habituation paradigm to investigate learning and memory for visual stimuli (e.g., Fantz, 1964). In a typical study, the infant is allowed to examine one stimulus visually (training) and then later is presented the original stimulus and some novel stimulus (testing). The amount of attention paid to each of the stimuli is measured. Results show that infants attend more to the novel stimulus than the familiar one. Subsequently, retention can be measured by including a delay between training and testing. As the retention interval increases, attention times between the novel and familiar stimuli become similar, indicating that the memory for the training stimulus has been forgotten. Findings have shown that older infants are capable of remembering the visual training stimulus over longer intervals than younger ones (e.g., Fagan, 1973). It seems likely that NOR could serve as an animal equivalent model to the human visual exploration procedures, allowing for the investigation of many variables deemed to dangerous for human subjects.

BIOLOGY AND OBJECT RECOGNITION

One should be aware that rat strain differences have been demonstrated in this task. Andrews, Jansen, Linders, Pricen, and Broekkamp (1995) employed a simplified procedure consisting of a one time pre-exposure to the training/testing context followed a day later by two test exposures to the objects in the context. No handling was involved prior to the experiment. Their results illustrated that Long-Evans rats far out-perform Wistar and Sprague-Dawley derived animals who show no significant preferences for novelty at even the shortest delays (Andrew, et al., 1995). Interestingly, we have shown the strain difference between the Long-Evans and Sprague-Dawleys to wane with increased amounts of handling (approximately 3 minutes for 2 consecutive days) and context pre-exposure (3 minutes for 2 consecutive days) prior to training and test at a 1-minute retention interval (Yellen, Williams, Asthon, Anderson, and Riccio, 2002; previously unpublished data). The mean preference for novelty scores (time spent exploring novel object minus time spent with original object) for Sprague-Dawley and Long-Evans rats following the extended handling and context pre-exposure can be seen in figure 2. It is unclear whether Wistar derived animals would experience similar beneficial effects of increased handling and context familiarization.

Preference for Novel Object at 1-min Retention Interval

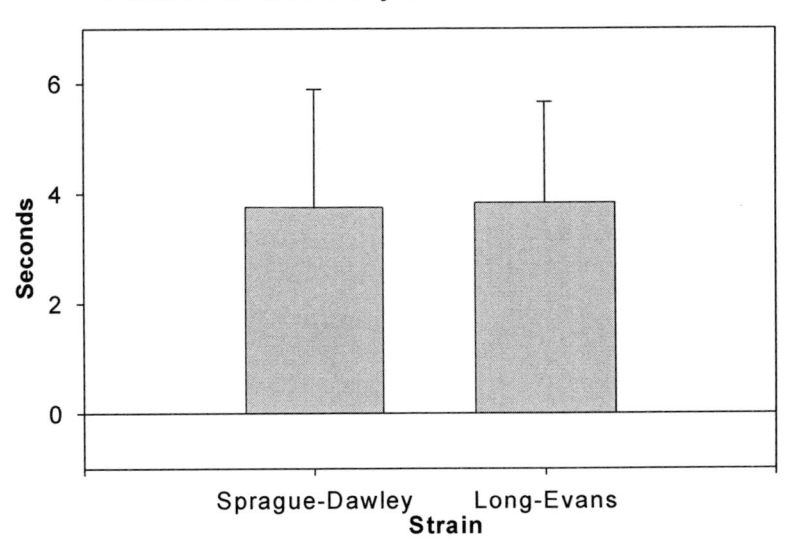

Figure 2. Depicted in the figure are the mean preference for novelty scores (time spent exploring novel object minus time spent with original object) for Sprague-Dawley and Long-Evans rats following extended handling and context pre-exposure. Error bars represent *SEM*.

The strain differences observed by Andrews and colleagues (1995) may perhaps be related to general temperaments and stress responses of the various strains. Indeed, stress has been shown to induce object memory decrement in male but not female rats (for review see Bowman, Beck, and Luine, 2003). The extent of the stress-dependent memory decrement appears to be greatly influenced by food deprivation (Beck and Luine, 1999) and the housing conditions of the animals (Beck and Luine, 2002). Interestingly, stress induced behavioral sex differences are accompanied by differences in neurotransmitter levels in brain areas critical to memory such as the frontal cortex, hippocampus, and amygdala (Beck and Luine, 1999, 2002; Luine, Beck, Bowman, and Kneavel, 2001).

Countless reports have highlighted the importance of temporal lobe structures to mnemonic processes, particularly the hippocampus (e.g., Kim, Rison, and Fanselow, 1993; Phillips and LeDoux, 1992). Surprisingly, only severe hippocampal damage (75-100% of total hippocampal volume) is capable of hindering object recognition memory (Broadbent, Squire, and Clark, 2004). Other regions of the temporal lobe, particularly the perirhinal cortex, appear to be more vital to object recognition memory. For example, Bussey, Muir, and Aggleton (1998) demonstrated that NMDA-induced excitotoxic lesions to the perirhinal and postrhinal cortices, significantly disrupted object recognition. Ennaceur and Aggleton (1997) demonstrated a disruption of novel object recognition in rats with neurotoxic lesions to either the perirhinal cortex or to both the perirhinal cortex and the fornix. Interestingly, those animals with damage to just the perirhinal cortex region showed an amelioration of their deficit by extended exposure to the initial stimuli and lengthened post operative recovery periods. Additionally, Mumby, Glenn, Nesbitt, and Kyriazis (2002) have found evidence of both retrograde and anterograde amnesia in an object recognition task following perirhinal cortex damage. Lesions to the amygdala have also been shown to impair object recognition (Winnicka and Braszko, 1997).

OBJECT RECOGNITION TASKS IN PSYCHOPHARMACOLOGICAL STUDIES

Nowhere has the use of object recognition tasks been more pervasive than in psychopharmacological investigations, particularly those studies investigating the effects of various drug agents on learning and memory capabilities. This is perhaps most attributable to the task's simplistic design and ease of implementation. For example, de Lima, Laranja, Bromberg, Roesler, and Schroder (2005) investigated the effects of MK-801, an NMDA receptor channel blocker, in such a task. Results illustrated that Wistar rats administered this substance either prior to, or immediately following initial object training displayed both impaired short-term (1.5-hours) and long-term (24-hours) retention of the initial object. The task has also been used to examine the effects of possible memory enhancing nootropic drugs. Ennaceur and colleagues (1989) demonstrated that certain doses of Piracetam (400 mg/kg) and Pramiracetam (30 mg/kg) administered 30 minutes before the acquisition trial resulted in significant enhancement of object recognition memory at a 24-hour retention interval. Deschaux, Bizot, and colleagues have obtained similar effects with administration of apamin (Deschaux, Bizot, and Goyffon, 1997), and nicotine (Puma, et al., 1999).

THE OBJECT PLACEMENT TEST: OBJECT EXPLORATION AS A MEASURE OF SPATIAL MEMORY

While the object exploration tasks discussed to this point have concentrated only on object recognition memory, through a relatively minor procedural change such tasks can be adapted to examine spatial memory. For example, Beck and Luine (2002) employed a procedure in which rats were given a 3 minute training session with two identical objects, in the exact manner as described above. At various intervals following training, rats were returned to the training/test chamber for a test session in which one of the two original objects is moved to a new location within the apparatus. At short retention intervals (2.5 hours), rats remember the original spatial arrangement and spend significantly more time exploring the moved object than the one remaining unmoved. As with object recognition memory, such spatial memory is lost rather quickly and appears to be forgotten by 4 hours. Interestingly, while stress has been shown to disrupt spatial memory for male rats, it can facilitate spatial memory enhancement in females (for review see Bowman, et al., 2003).

The object placement test has not been employed to the extent of the object recognition task. As of yet, an abundance of issues remain uninvestigated with this task. For instance, are pre-test cuing reminders capable of alleviating the forgetting of such spatial memories? Also, are there ontogenetic differences in object spatial memory capabilities? As a variety of studies employing other tasks have demonstrated spatial memory impairments with aging (e.g., Cavoy and Delacour, 1993), it seems likely that spatial memory may be more significantly impaired than object recognition in senescence. Does object recognition and object spatial memory emerge at the same ontogenetic time point? Future research is needed to address such issues.

OBJECT EXPLORATION AS A MEASURE OF ENVIRONMENTAL FAMILIARIZATION

The majority of studies reviewed to this point have examined an animal's preference for a novel object or place in comparison to previously experienced stimuli and spatial arrangements. Bevins and colleagues, capitalizing on the finding that increased context familiarity enhances object exploration at test (Sheldon, 1969; Besheer and Bevins, 2000), have promoted simple, single object exploration as a measure of environmental familiarization and context memory. Indeed, they have illustrated that the stronger a rat's memory for the training environment is, the greater the amount of time it will spend in exploring an object (Herrman, Wilkinson, Palmatier, and Bevins, 2004). They have employed object interaction as a measure of context familiarity in order to examine the effects of nicotine on such environmental familiarization (Bevins, Koznarova, and Armiger, 2001). Bevins and colleagues (2001) illustrated that while an acute dose of nicotine could interfere with environmental familiarization and decrease object exploration, chronic pre-exposure to the same nicotine dose had no such effect. While this variation of object exploration task has not yet received a level of attention comparable to that of novel object recognition, further implementation of this simple and non-aversive measure of environmental familiarization and context memory is warranted and likely to be highly beneficial.

CONCLUSION

Object exploration tasks have many advantages over more traditional measures. For instance, object exploration tasks typically involve non-aversive procedures. It can be argued, in fact, that those variants depending upon an animal's preference for novelty are likely to be appetitive or rewarding experiences for the subjects (Bardo, Donohew, and Harington, 1996; Rebec, Grabner, Johnson, Pierce, and Bardo, 1997). Indeed, novel objects have even been shown to increase place preferences for the distinct environment in which the object is located (e.g., Bevins and Bardo, 1999; Bevins, Besheer, Palmatier, Jensen, Pickett, and Eurek, 2002). Thus, a major advantage of such tasks is that they are positive experiences for the subjects and avoid the use of noxious stimuli. Additionally, it has been argued from an ethological standpoint that these exploration tasks, depending solely upon behaviors naturally found in the subject's behavioral repertoire, are much less artificial than more traditional tasks requiring lever presses or avoidance of electrical foot-shock (Dellu, et al., 1992). Object exploration tasks have indeed proven to be useful measures of object recognition and memory, spatial memory, and environmental familiarization. Due to the simplicity of these tasks and the many advantages of their use, continued employment of such procedures is encouraged.

REFERENCES

Anderson, M. J., Barnes, G. W., Briggs, J. F., Ashton, K. M., Moody, E. W., Joynes, R. L., and Riccio, D. C. (2004a). The effects of ontogeny on the performance of rats in a novel object recognition task. *Psychological Reports, 94,* 437-443.

Anderson, M. J., Berry, C., Morse, D., and Diotte, M. (2005). Flavor as Context: Altered Flavor Cues Disrupt Memory Accuracy. *Journal of Behavioral and Neuroscience Research, 3,* 1-5.

Anderson, M. J., Karash, D. L., Ashton, K. M., and Riccio, D. C. (2003). The effects of a target-stimulus reminder on performance in a novel object recognition task. *Learning and Motivation, 34,* 341-353.

Anderson, M. J., Karash, D. L., and Riccio, D. C. (2004b). The alleviation of ontogenetic forgetting in a novel object recognition task. *Journal of Behavioral and Neuroscience Research, 2,* 1-5.

Andrews, J. S., Jansen, J. H. M., Linders, S., Princen, A., and Broekkamp, C. L. E. (1995). Performance of four different rat strains in the autoshaping, two-object discrimination, and swim maze test of learning and memory. *Physiology and Behavior, 57,* 785-790.

Astur, R. S., Klein, R. L., Mumby, D. G., Protz, D. K., Sutherland, R. J., and Martin, G. M. (2002). A role for olfaction in object recognition by normal and hippocampal-damaged rats. *Neurobiology of Learning and Memory, 78,* 186-191.

Bardo, M. T., Donohew, R. L., and Harrington, N. G. (1996). Psychobiology of novelty seeking and drug seeking behavior. *Behavoural Brain Research, 77,* 23-43

Barnes, C. A., Nadel, L., Honig, W. K. (1980). Spatial memory deficit in senescent rats. *Canadian Journal of Psychology, 34,* 29-39.

Beck, K. D., and Luine, V. N. (1999). Food deprivation modulates chronic stress effects on object recognition in male rats: role of monoamines and amino acids. *Brain Research, 830,* 56-71.

Beck, K. D., Luine, V. N. (2002). Sex differences in behavioral and neurochemical profiles after chronic stress: Role of housing conditions. *Physiology and Behavior, 75,* 661-673.

Berlyne, D. E. (1950). Novelty and curiosity as determinants of exploratory behaviour. *British Journal of Psychology, 41,* 68-80.

Besheer, J., and Bevins, R. A. (2000). The role of environmental familiarization in novel-object preference. *Behavioural Processes*, 50, 19-29.

Bevins, R. A., and Bardo, M. T. (1999). Conditioned increase in place preference by access to novel objects: Antagonism by MK-801. *Behavioural Brain Research, 77,* 23-43.

Bevins, R. A., Besheer, J., Palmatier, M. I., Jensen, H. C., Pickett, K. S., and Eurek, S. (2002). Novel-object place conditioning: behavioral and dopaminergic processes in expression of novelty reward. *Behavioura Brain Research, 129,* 41-50.

Bevins, R. A., Koznarova, J., and Armiger, T. J. (2001). Environmental familiarization in rats: Differential effects of acute and chronic nicotine. *Neurobiology of Learning and Memory, 75,* 63-76.

Broadbent, N. J., Squire, L. R., and Clark, R. E. (2004). Spatial memory, recognition memory, and the hippocampus. *PNAS, 101,* 14515-14520.

Bower, G. H., Monteiro, K. P., and Gilligan, S. G. (1978). Emotional mood as a context for learning and recall. *Journal of Verbal Learning and Verbal Behavior, 17,* 573-578.

Bowman, R. E., Beck, K. D., and Luine, V. N. (2003). Chronic stress effects on memory: sex differences in performance and monoaminergic activity. *Hormones and Behavior, 43,* 48-59.

Bussey, T. J., Muir, J. L., and Aggleton, J. P. (1999). Functionally dissociating aspects of event memory: the effects of combined perirhinal and postrhinal cortex lesions on object and place memory in the rat. *The Journal of Neuroscience, 19,* 495-502.

Campbell, B. A., and Campbell, E. H. (1962). Retention and extinction of learned fear in infant and adult rats. *Journal of Comparative and Physiological Psychology, 55,* 1-8.

Campbell, B. A., and Jaynes, J. (1966). Reinstatement. *Psychological Review, 73,* 478-480.

Cann, A., and Ross, D. A. (1989). Olfactory stimuli as context cues in human memory. *American Journal of Psychology, 102,* 91-102.

Carr, H. A. (1925). *Psychology: A Study of Mental Activity.* New York: Longmans, Green and Co.

Cavoy, A., and Delacour, J. (1993). Spatial but not object recognition is impaired by aging in rats. *Physiology and Behavior, 53,* 527-530.

Davidson, T. L. (1987). Learning about deprivation intensity stimuli. *Behavioral Neuroscience, 101,* 198-208.

de Lima, M. N. M., Laranja, D. C., Bromberg, E., Roesler, R., Schroder, N. (2005). Pre- or post-training administration of the NMDA receptor blocker MK-801 impairs object recognition memory in rats. *Behavioural Brain Research, 156,* 139-143.

Dellu, F., Fauchey, V., Le Moal, M., and Simon, H. (1997). Extension of a new two-trial memory task in the rat : Influence of environmental context on recognition processes. *Neurobiology of Learning and Memory, 67,* 112-120.

Dellu, F., Mayo, W., Cherkaoui, J., Le Moal, M., and Simon, H. (1992). A two-trial memory task with automated recording : Study in young and aged rats. *Brain Research, 588,* 132-139.

Deschaux, O., Bizot, J. C., and Goyffon, M. (1997). Apamin improves learning in an object recognition task in rats. *Neuroscience Letters, 222,* 159-162.

Ebner, D. L., Richardson, R., and Riccio, D. C. (1981). Ovarian hormones and retention of learned fear in rats. *Behavioral and Neural Biology, 33,* 45-58.

Ennaceur, A., and Aggleton, J. P. (1997). The effects of neurotoxic lesions of the perirhinal cortex combined to fornix transection on object recognition in the rat. *Behavioural Brain Research, 88,* 181-193.

Ennaceur, A., Cavoy, A., Costa, J., and Delacour, J. (1989). A new one-trial test for neurobiological studies of memory in rats. II : Effects of piracetam and pramiracetam. *Behavioural Brain Research, 33,* 197-207.

Ennaceur, A., and Delacour, J. (1988). A new one-trial test for neurobiological studies of memory in rats. 1: Behavioral data. *Behavioural Brain Research, 31,* 47-59.

Fagan, J. F. (1973). Infants' delayed recognition memory and forgetting. *Journal of Experimental Child Psychology, 16,* 424-450.

Fantz, R. L. (1964). Visual experience in infants: Decreased attention familiar patterns relative to novel ones. *Science, 146,* 668-670.

Godden, D. R., and Baddeley, A. D. (1975). Context-dependent memory in two natural environments: On land and underwater. *British Journal of Psychology, 66,* 325-331.

Hamberg, J. M., and Spear, N. E. (1978). Alleviation of forgetting of discrimination learning. *Learning and Motivation, 9,* 466-76.

Herrman, L. E., Wilkinson, J. L., Palmatier, M. I., and Bevins, R. A. (2004). Factors affecting environmental familiarization in rats. Poster presented at the annual meeting of the Midwestern Psychological Association, Chicago, Il (May).

Herz, R. S. (1997) The effects of cue distinctiveness on odor-based context-dependent memory. *Memory and Cognition, 25,* 375-380.

Holloway, F. A., and Wansley, R. (1973). Multiphasic retention deficits at periodic intervals after passive-avoidance learning. *Science, 180,* 208-210.

Kim, J. J., Rison, R. A., and Fanselow, M. S. (1993). Effects of amygdala, hippocampus, and periaqueductal gray lesions on short- and long-term contextual fear. *Behavioral Neuroscience, 107,* 1093-1098.

Liu, P, Smith, P. F., Appleton, I., Darlington, C. L., and Bilkey, D. K. (2004). Potential involvement of NOS and arginase in age-related behavioural impairments. *Experimental Gerontology, 39,* 1207-1222.

Luine, V., Beck, K., Bowman, R., and Kneavel, M. (2001). Sex differences in chronic stress effects on cognitive function and brain neurochemistry. In Handa, R. J., Hayaski, S., Terasawas, E., and Kawata, M. (Eds.), *Neuroplasticity, Development and Steroid Hormone Action*, CRC Press, Boca Ratan, Fl.

Lukaszewska, I., and Radulska, A. (1994). Object recognition is not impaired in old rats. *Acta Neurobiologiae Experimentalis, 54,* 143-150.

McGeoch, J. A. (1942*). The Psychology of Human Learning: An Introduction*. New York: Longmans, Green and Co.

Mumby, D. G., Glenn, M. J., Nesbitt, C., and Kyriazis, D. A. (2002). Dissociation in retrograde memory for object discriminations and object recognition in rats with perirhinal cortex damage. *Behavioural Brain Research, 132,* 215-226.

Overton, D. A. (1964). State-dependent or "dissociated" learning produced with pentobarbital. *Journal of Comparative and Physiological Psychology, 57,* 3-12.

Phillips, R. G., and LeDoux, J. E. (1992). Differential contribution of amygdala and hippocampus to cued and contextual fear conditioning. *Behavioral Neuroscience, 106,* 274-285.

Pointer, S. C., and Bond, N. W. (1998). Context-dependent memory: Colour versus odor. *Chemical Senses, 23,* 359-362.

Postman, L. (1972). A pragmatic view of organization theory. In E. Tulving and W. Donaldson (Eds.), *Organization of Memory.* (pp. 3-48). New York: Academic Press.

Puma, C., Baudoin, C., Bizot, J.-C., (1998). Effects of intraseptal infusions of *N*-methyl-D-aspartate receptor ligands on memory in an object recognition task in rats. *Neuroscience Letters, 244,* 97-100.

Puma, C., Deschaux, O., Molimard, R., and Bizot, J.-C. (1999). Nicotine improves memory in an object recognition task in rats, *European Neuropsychopharmacology, 9,* 323-327.

Rebec, G. V., Grabner, C. P., Johnson, M., Peirce, R. C., and Bardo, M. T. (1997). Transient increases in catecholaminergic activity in medial prefrontal cortex and nucleus accumbens shell during novelty. *Neuroscience, 76,* 707-714.

Richardson, R., Wang, P., and Campbell, B. A. (1993). Reactivation of nonassociative memory. *Developmental Psychobiology, 26,* 1-23.

Rovee-Collier, C. K., Sullivan, M. W., Enright, M., Lucas, D., and Fagan, J. W. (1980). Reactivation of infant memory. *Science, 208,* 1159-1161.

Scali, C., Casamenti, F., Pazzagli, M., Bartolini, L., and Pepeu, G. (1994). Nerve growth factor increases extracellular acetylcholine levels in the parietal cortex and hippocampus of aged rats and restores object recognition. *Neuroscience Letters, 170,* 117-120.

Scali, C., Giovannini, M. G>, Prosperi, C., Bartolini, L., and Pepeu, G. (1997). Tacrine administration enhances extracellular acetylcholine in vivo and restores the cognitive impairment in aged rats. *Pharmacological Research, 36,* 463-469.

Scali, C., Giovannini, M. G., Bartolini, L., Prosperi, C., Hinz, V., Schmidt, B., and Pepeu, G. (1997). Effect of metrifonate on extracellular brain acetylcholine and object recognition in aged rats. *European Journal of Pharmacology, 325,* 173-180.

Schab, F. R. (1990). Odors and the remembrance of things past. *Journal of Experimental Psychology: Learning, Memory, and Cognition, 16,* 648-655.

Sheldon, A. B. (1969). Preference for familiar versus novel stimuli as a function of the familiarity of the environment. *Journal of Comparative and Physiological Psychology, 67,* 173-180.

Smith, S. M. (1979). Remembering in and out of context. *Journal of Experimental Psychology: Human Learning and Memory, 5,* 460-471.

Spear, N. E. (1973). Retrieval of memory in animals. *Psychological Review, 80,* (3), 163-194.

Thomson, D. M., and Tulving, E. (1970). Associative encoding and retrieval: Weak and strong cues. *Journal of Experimental Psychology, 86,* 255-262.

Tulving, E., and Thomson, D. M. (1973). Encoding specificity and retrieval processes in episodic memory. *Psychological Review, 80,* 352-373.

Weingartner, H., Miller, H., and Murphy, D. L. (1977). Mood-state dependent retrieval of verbal associations. *Journal of Abnormal Psychology, 86,* 276-284.

Winnicka, M. M., and Braszko, J. J. (1997). 6-OHDA lesions to the central amygdala abolish angiotensins facilitation of object recognition in rats. *General Pharmacology, 29,* 239-243.

Yellen, K., Williams, J., Ashton, K. M., Anderson, M. J., and Riccio, D. C. (2002). Strain differences in novel object recognition. Poster presented at the 31st Annual Western Pennsylvania Undergraduate Psychology Conference, Mercyhurst College, Erie, PA (April).

Yellen, K., Williams, J., Ashton, K. M., Anderson, M. J., and Riccio, D. C. (2002). Strain differences in novel object recognition. Previously unpublished data.

In: New Developments in Learning Research
Editor: Samuel N. Hogan, pp. 49-64

ISBN 1-59454-669-X
© 2006 Nova Science Publishers, Inc.

Chapter 3

ONE SIZE DOESN'T FIT ALL: ACHIEVING ACCOUNTABILITY THROUGH APPLICATION OF LEARNING PATTERNS

Donna W. Jorgensen
Rowan University

ABSTRACT

This chapter reviews a relatively new approach to understanding the brain-mind connections associated with learning. The Let Me Learn Process® Learning Connections Inventory© (which helps students and teachers to identify personal learning combinations of four patterns) will be discussed in detail. The major premise of this chapter is that when teachers and students work together to identify learning patterns and access them appropriately, students will learn to assume responsibility for increased learning and performance. Further, because students will know how to access patterns and create strategies for different kinds of assessment situations, they will perform better on various measures of achievement. Students and teachers will have the accountability that is demanded of them.

INTRODUCTION

In increasingly diverse educational settings, standardization is becoming the norm. In the era of No Child Left Behind legislation, the focus is on identifying student achievement not through individual learning but through scores on standardized tests. This continues to be true even though "educational researchers have found that such tests have proven to be of dubious value in predicting one's ability to perform on practical tasks that really matter" (Sacks, 1999, p. 2). Even though one size doesn't fit all, accountability is more and more determined by the ubiquitous standardized test. Knowing this does not change the fact that students are often judged more by their test scores than by their actual learning. Students can learn to decode tasks and apply appropriate patterns to complete them, however.

One size fits all is a phrase I have come to loathe. It is frustrating enough when it is applied to clothing because we all know that people come in a variety of shapes and sizes, but worse when it is unconscionably applied to teaching and learning. This phrase is an indication that we do not fully acknowledge the individuality of each and every learner. One size does not fit all, or even most, when it comes to our attire. Why is it that assessment of student learning, which we are all held accountable for in our nation's classrooms, seems more likely to be of the one size fits all design than it is to be differentiated to meet the needs of today's diverse classrooms? In order to meet the diverse needs of today's and tomorrow's students, every teacher and teacher candidate must be taught how to work with students to achieve intentional teaching and intentional application of learning strategies.

DIFFERENTIATING INSTRUCTION

Even though for a very long time we have heard that children learn differently from each other, and attempts have been made to explain the differences, standardization is the rule rather than the exception when it comes to measuring student learning. Learning in schools generally revolves around reading text and taking tests. In its own way, it is very patterned. Outside of school, learning looks very different. In the "real" world, people are expected to take in and process information, make decisions and produce results, all in ways very different from regurgitation of information on tests or single measures of the learning of all individuals. Tomlinson (1999) makes two statements that should be our mantra as we work with teachers and teacher candidates in assisting them to be prepared for the challenges of diverse classrooms. Where differentiated instruction is in place, she says, "teachers engage students in instruction through different learning modalities [and] teachers are diagnosticians, prescribing the best possible instruction for each student" (p. 2).

It is not simply about what students learn; it is about how they learn. Knowing the goals of an individual lesson as well as those of the overall goals of a unit and the curricular goals of a course is a first step towards differentiating instruction. Intentional teaching requires us to know about both our students and our curricular goals. While we may have the goal of having all students arrive at the same destination, perhaps proficiency on a high stakes standardized test, getting there should be different—one size does not fit all. Pettig (2000) says "differentiated instruction requires from us persistent honing of our teaching skills plus the courage to significantly change our classroom practices. . . .we can slowly shift from the one-size-fits-all paradigm and adopt a differentiated instructional approach" (p. 18). The key to differentiating instruction is determining the learning patterns of individual students. When teachers and students understand what goes on in their brains and minds when learning happens, they will be empowered to take charge of their own learning. Differentiated instruction is a response to differentiated learning and differentiated learning is the product of each person's unique learning patterns combination. Students and teachers share the responsibility for creating the environment in which learning happens. Learners are unique, but they must function in academic worlds where their success or failure is measured by some form of standardized test. If every student processed information and demonstrated knowledge in the same way, this would not be problematical, but this is not the case.

Each and every student brings a contextualized way of looking at learning to every situation. It is possible to assist students to make brain-mind connections so that they use their learning potential with intention. Strategic teaching and strategic learning begin with strategic thinking. Nowhere is strategic thinking more important than on the kinds of standardized tests that are currently mandated under No Child Left Behind legislation. If students are to be prepared for the kind of strategic thinking they need to do for the tests, they need to possess a certain amount of metacognition: self knowledge about how they prefer to demonstrate what they know as well as the ability to access an appropriate pattern to complete an assigned task. Strategic thinking begins with the identification of patterns.

If we want to build a new highway, we look at traffic patterns. If we want to build a new building, we look at use patterns. It follows that if we want to build new learning, we must look at learning patterns. Each of us has a personal, interactive learning cluster through which we make connections and carry on those internal conversations that lead to our demonstration of what we know. When we understand our learning connections patterns, we can develop appropriate strategies for demonstrating knowledge.

Schools and standardized tests demand the use of particular patterns, and if we lack the awareness either of what the patterns are or how to access them at the appropriate time, we are likely to be identified as either unlearned or not proficient. One size does not fit all; it does not even fit most. Every child must be given the opportunity to meet his maximum potential. One thing teachers can do is to identify the particular learning patterns of the students in their classrooms. This can be done very simply and in a cost-effective manner through the use of the Learning Connections Inventory© designed and used in the Let Me Learn Process®.

LOOKING AT LEARNING

Since the 1980s, psychologists and education practitioners have identified a variety of ways to look at how humans learn. Among them are things like multiple intelligences, learning styles, and personality measures. Most teachers will have heard of learning styles and modalities. They will often identify themselves and their students as visual, auditory, or kinesthetic learners. I am never confident that these are not simply terms they have heard and apply without any real understanding. After all, unless we are blind or deaf, we are all visual or auditory learners at some point in our educational journey. If we were not, we would quickly fall behind. It is learning how best to use our visual and auditory skills that helps us to become more successful learners. Many teachers and their students will also identify themselves as left-brained or right-brained or posit that they have some strongly developed intelligence from Gardner's multiple intelligences theory®. This knowledge is an excellent foundation, but each is only a single point of view or piece of the puzzle that is the brain-mind connection we identify as learning. There is a program designed to help teachers and students to identify their unique learning combinations and to design instruction and assessment to enhance learning of every student. As a response to her concern that learning styles and personality measures and learning modalities are only part of the picture of learning, Dr. Christine Johnston developed the Let Me Learn Process® (LML) as a way to help all learners identify their unique learning pattern combinations and to recognize what this means in the way they approach learning and assessment tasks.

Teachers and students examine their beliefs and assumptions about learning. Using the language of LML, [students] approach learning with meta-awareness; they become intentional learners. Essentially, the LML process, by engaging the learner in reflective practice. . .enables teachers and students to improve their performance." (Osterman and Kottkamp, 2004, p. 145)

With the Let Me Learn Process®, students and teachers will share a vocabulary to talk about learning and to plan for productive outcomes.

Learning becomes a partnership with teachers and students sharing goals and outcomes. The ultimate goal in understanding the LML Process is the focus on "taking responsibility for making learning work" (Johnston, 2005, p. 3). Using the Learning Connections Inventory© (LCI), and the Let Me Learn Process® help teachers and students to determine the degree to which a person uses four different learning processes (patterns) as they act and interact within a learner's mind. "Both students and teachers grow in their understanding of how to align strategies with the requirements needed for successful accomplishment of various tasks" (Osterman and Kottkamp, 2004, p. 173). Helping students to recognize those patterns they prefer to use in demonstrating their learning will help those students to develop their metacognition about which combination of patterns will enable them to successfully meet the challenges of the *No Child Left Behind* era in school and in the real world beyond.

ORIGINS OF LET ME LEARN PROCESS®

Dr. Christine Johnston sought a way to help students identify the ways they demonstrate learning and to help them be more accountable in knowing exactly what particular learning tasks demanded of them. In using the Let Me Learn Process®, says Johnston, we will be pledging ourselves to "making a difference each day, all year, one learner at a time" (2000, p. vii).

Because this understanding of the diverse learning patterns of our students is integral to our teaching, Johnston wanted a user-friendly, cost-effective method of assisting teachers and students to identify patterns of learning choice. Over a period of nine years with over 9000 6-18 year old students and 5000 adult professionals, Johnston developed and refined the Learning Connections Inventory© (LCI) for use with children at the elementary and secondary levels. Further testing and use led to the development of a professional version for use with adults in education and additional forms for use with adult professionals in other fields. A further modification was designed for use with families to help them understand their interactions. In every instance the inventory includes 28 Likert scaled items and 3 open-ended questions. It generally takes about one half hour to complete and self-score although there is no time limit. Because inventories do not have to be sent away for scoring, results are immediate. Written responses to the open-ended questions help students and teachers to identify cue words and phrases typical in each of the four Let Me Learn patterns. These answers validate the Likert determined patterns or identify areas to investigate further. Ideally, these responses would be validated by a trained Let Me Learn consultant or teacher, however user's manuals and guides for use are available so that every teacher can use the

LCI. Because this is not a test, students readily accept that the only key is to be completely honest in responding. This is about the chance to tell teachers how they like to learn and to show what they know. Frequently students have "aha" moments when they recognize why they have such an aversion to some assignments but love others.

The LCI is a self-report instrument. It doesn't test a quality; it doesn't determine the capacity to learn; it doesn't measure what a learner knows. The inventory reports what learners selected as descriptions of their learning behaviors. It inventories. It takes stock. It identifies the what and how much of each schema. It is as accurate as the person who reports it is willing to make it. It doesn't diagnose what is wrong. It doesn't prescribe how to increase an area of deficiency. It simply tallies what is there. It invites learners to express their thoughts on what frustrates them about assignments, how they prefer to show what they know, and how they would have students show what they learned if they were the teachers. The LCI, by its very format, invites learners to report the patterns of their learning process. . . .By interpreting the results of the LCI in light of who the learner is, rather than interpreting the learner on the basis of normed results, the learner and the teacher can use the LCI to carry on substantive conversations about how the learner learns. (Johnston, 1996, pp. 69-70)

Johnston describes what goes on in the brain-mind connection when we are learning as a combination of the cognitive, affective and conative. While these first two terms are readily understood, the conative is a piece that is often overlooked. Simply, it is the doing part of the whole that goes along with the thinking/knowing cognitive process and the feeling, affective process. It is important to have students honestly explore these three elements when they approach a task. We find it easy to express what we feel about assignments; in fact spontaneous outbursts from our students will often tell us exactly what they are feeling. It is also not terribly difficult to get students to talk about what they think, but it is sometimes harder to get them to concretely state what they do to complete a task. The most important thing to remember is that the Let Me Learn Process® helps students to accept responsibility for their own learning. It "emphasizes the importance of taking responsibility for making learning work. In over 10 years of research, involving 40,000 learners, [it] has shown that students can use information about their own learning processes to focus their effort, make informed career choices, and overcome years of underachievement" (Johnston, 2004, pp. 2-3).

LET ME LEARN PROCESS®

The Let Me Learn Process® captures the brain and mind interactions as they work to create a system of learning. In each learning situation, a stimulus enters the brain and from there, neuro impulses are converted into symbolic representations that the mind can process. This processing allows a learner to make connections with information already stored or to store information as new. Four operational patterns are at work in this processing. The patterns work synchronously and in a very personal way in each of us. The mental processes of cognition, conation and affectation are present in each of the four patterns and they interact in each operational pattern to enable us to respond to a stimulus.

Using the internal talk of the patterns (metacognition), these mental operations begin to mull, connect, rehearse, express, assess, and reflect on whether they are interacting and responding appropriately to the learning event with which they are confronted. Each time we accept stimulus into our system, our bodies, brains, and minds are under stress to read the situation and react or respond in a manner that at the very least keeps us safe and at the very most brings us success in the completion of the task we have undertaken. (Johnston, 2005, p. 13)

Developing awareness of this internal "talk" among the patterns will enable us to use our patterns with intention. When we can use patterns with intention, we can raise the probability that we will be successful with an assigned task. Intentional use of patterns is critical in the standardized testing area. It is relatively easy to identify which patterns are needed to complete certain types of assessment tasks. Using the learning patterns, students are able to decode assignments. A student who is able to correctly decode the message of the assignment has a distinct advantage in being able to complete it successfully. Key words repeat themselves within each of the patterns and students become able to quickly identify the words, connect them with the correct pattern, identify the skill or strategy necessary to complete the task and access that pattern in themselves. They can be taught to circle cue words and code them for pattern needed and then to draw on their own strategy cards to complete a task. Johnston (2005) contends that students can be taught to invest in their own success and to put forth intentional effort to complete a given task. In this way students themselves are held accountable for the results of an assessment. They know exactly what they must do to complete a task and they know which personal strategies they must access, with intention, to make it easier.

Students will ask themselves what a task requires of them and will identify what the task requires of each of their patterns. Additionally, they will begin to recognize and respond to the difference between natural use of a pattern and intentional use of a pattern that would not normally be a pattern of first use. They employ a FIT technique. They will Forge, Intensify or Tether patterns as necessary. In order to fully understand how FIT works, we should take a deeper look at each of the patterns.

Let Me Learn identifies four patterns and the LCI identifies for us our personal learning connections combination. The four patterns are sequential, precise, technical, and confluent. What each of these terms means in terms of what a learner thinks, feels, and does in the act of learning will be explained a bit later. "Each pattern exists in all of us to some degree and contributes to our unique learning combinations" (Johnston, 2000, p. 35). "Once I know my combination of learning patterns, I can use them with greater intention. I can analyze work responsibilities, learning tasks, and project assignments always asking myself, 'What processes am I being asked to use? How will I direct my learning processes so that what I do and how I do it matches the expectations of my instructor, my supervisor, or my teammates?'" (Johnston, 2005, p. 16).

Each of the four patterns may be a use first, as needed or avoid pattern as demonstrated by the score on the Likert scaled items of the LCI. When a pattern comes up as a use first pattern (scores between 25 and 35), this means that a learner will gravitate to that pattern to demonstrate learning. It may or may not be the most appropriate pattern for a particular task, but it is the pattern of choice for the student. An as needed pattern (scores between 18 and 24) is one that students can access when appropriate given a little guidance and support even though it might not be the pattern of first choice. The as needed pattern could lie dormant until needed and students could need a little help to find a trigger for "waking up" the pattern at the appropriate time. An avoid pattern (scores between 7 and 17) is just that—one that a learner will avoid using even when it is obviously the best one to use in a given learning situation. It is crucial that students and teachers learn to note the signals that they are using an inappropriate pattern and correct themselves. The program requires students to become responsible for their own learning and the choices they make. School tends to value patterns of sequence and precision and students (and teachers!) who have these as use first patterns will often be very comfortable in educational environments and will be higher achievers. It should be noted that teachers teach to their own use first patterns and where there is a strong match between teachers and students, overall grades for a class will generally be higher (Nickels, 2002).

Sequential processors are seekers of clear directions, practiced planners, and thoroughly neat workers (Johnston, 1996). They become frustrated with unclear or incomplete directions or changes in requirements once an assignment is underway. They have little patience with teachers who are disorganized or move too fast. They want examples to follow. They need time to go over material that is assigned in class and they require sufficient time (in accordance with their own interpretation) to complete a task thoroughly. They generally want their work to be neat and tidy. Often they will make lists and will either number or bullet items.

Precise processors are information specialists, into-details researchers, answer specialists, and report writers. They want to know all the answers and will constantly request clarification. They want to be "right" and need reassurance that they are. They hate confusion and want lots of details in explanations. Frequently they will ask that directions be repeated numerous times. They become frustrated when they do not have sufficient information to complete a task or cannot find the information they need in their texts. They have a strong capacity for trivia and will often take very detailed notes. They are the students who will, if permitted to do so, answer every question the teacher asks. They like to write answers in the form of tests, quizzes, and reports. They may prefer written manifestations of their knowledge to oral presentation. They need time when they are working on written assignments.

Technical processors place relevance as paramount. They are hands-on builders, independent private thinkers and reality seekers. They love activity and may want to move around while they are learning. They much prefer hands-on work to doing book work, either reading or writing. They like the challenge of a real world project and want to be left alone to complete the project. They want to live and experience what they are learning about, not read about it. They tend to keep things to themselves and do not particularly care if they show the teacher what they know so long as they know themselves. These are the learners who might do homework but never turn it in because they have satisfied their own need to prove to themselves that they can do it. The technical processor thrives on field trips into the real world to see the relevance of what he is learning. If information is extraneous, the technical processor will discard it. Any task needs real world validation for the technical processor to invest his time in learning it. They keep both physical and mental distance while they complete tasks. They do not like to be part of a group unless the group members allow them to go off and complete some portion of the task alone.

	How I think	How I do things	How I feel	What I might say
Sequential	I organize information I mentally categorize data I break tasks down into steps	I make lists I organize I plan first, then act	I thrive on consistency and dependability I need things to be tidy and organized I feel frustrated when the game plan keeps changing I feel frustrated when I'm rushed	Could I see an example? I need more time to double-check my work Could we review those directions? A place for everything and everything in its place What are my priorities?
Precise	I research information I as lots of questions I always want to know more	I challenge statements and ideas that I doubt I prove I am right I document my research and findings I write things down I write long e-mail messages and leave long voice mail messages	I thrive on knowledge I feel good when I am correct I feel frustrated when incorrect information is accepted as valid I feel frustrated when people do not share information with me	I need more information Let me write up the answer to that Wanna play trivia? I'm currently reading three different books Did you get my e-mail on that? Did you know that... Actually....
Technical	I seek concrete relevance—what does this mean in the real world? I only want as much information as I need—nothing extraneous	I get my hands on I tinker I solve the problem I do	I enjoy knowing how things work I feel good that I am self sufficient I feel frustrated when the task has no real world relevance I enjoy knowing things, but I do not feel the need to share that knowledge	I can do it myself Let me show you how... I don't want to read a book about it, I want to do it How will I ever use this in the real world? How can I fix this? I could use a little space....
Confluent	I read between the lines I think outside the box I brainstorm I make obscure connections between things that are seemingly unrelated	I take risks I am not afraid to fail I talk about things—a lot I might start things and not finish them I will start a task first—then ask for directions	I enjoy improvisation I feel comfortable with failure I do not enjoy having my ideas criticized I feel frustrated by people who are not open to new ideas I enjoy a challenge I feel frustrated by repeating a task over and over	What do you mean, "that's the way we've always done it"?! The rules don't apply to me Let me tell you about... I have an idea... I have another idea...

Figure 1: When I Have a Use First Pattern. ©Learning Connections Resources and Let Me Learn, Inc. (2004) Used by permission of author.

	How I think	How I do things	How I feel	What I might say
Sequential	These directions make no sense! I did this before. Why repeat it? Why can't I just jump in?	Avoid direction; avoid practice Can't get the pieces in order Ignore table of contents, indexes, and syllabi Leave the task incomplete	Jumbled Scattered Out of synch Untethered/unfettered Unanchored	Do I have to do it again? Why do I have to follow directions? Does it matter what we do first? Has anybody seen. . .?
Precise	Do I have to read all this? How am I going to remember all of this? Who cares about all this 'stuff'?	Don't have specific answers Avoid debate Skim instead of read Take few notes	Overwhelmed when confronted with details Fearful of looking stupid Angry at not having the 'one right answer'!	Don't expect me to know names and dates! Stop asking me so many questions! Does it matter? I'm not stupid!
Technical	Why should I care how this works? Somebody has to help me figure this out. Why do I have to make something; why can't I just talk or write about it?	Avoid using tools or instruments Talk about it instead of doing it Rely on the directions to lead me to the solution	Inept Fearful of breaking the object, tool, or instrument Uncomfortable with tools; very comfortable with my words and thoughts	If it is broken, throw it away! I'm an educated person; I should be able to do this! I don't care *how* it runs; I just want it *to run*!
Confluent	Where is this headed? Where is the focus? What do you mean, imagine?	Don't take social risks Complete one task at a time Avoid improvising Seek parameters	Unsettled Chaotic No more changes or surprises, please!	Let's stay focused! Where did that idea come from? Now what? This is out of control!

Figure 2: When I Avoid a Pattern. ©Learning Connections Resources and Let Me Learn, Inc. (2004) Used by permission of author.

Confluent processors are those who truly march to the different drummer. They are labeled as creative imaginers and unique presenters. Sometimes they seem to be a million miles away from where everyone else is during a lesson. They don't like to be "trapped" in the teacher's ideas or ways of doing things. They might not even listen to directions because they already have their own idea about how something should be done. They like variety in interpretation of assignments and feel confined by having to do something in one certain way. They often chafe at rules and regulations. They like learning to be fun and even artistic and crafty. They love to stand up and talk and might prefer to do a dramatic presentation, participate in a debate or give some kind of oral presentation. They frequently like to write stories, but they write the same way they would speak. This is the pattern of the imagination. Figure 1 shows some of the things we might expect to evidence themselves when each of these is a use first pattern and Figure 2 shows what we might expect when each of these patterns is an avoid pattern.

Once the LCIs have been scored, it is important to look for certain types of learners in your classrooms. One particular type is called the strong-willed learner. A strong-willed learner is one who has three or four use first patterns (scores 25 or above). This is the learner who will often let you know that he would prefer to work alone because he knows he can do any of the parts of a project better than anyone else. Having more than one strong-willed learner in a group can be a disaster. It is equally probable that disaster will follow if you put all the strong-willed learners in a single group; you are likely to get as many products as you had group members because each will be unable to compromise with the others.

Another type of learner is the Bridge. This learner has all scores between 19 and 24 and therefore has all as needed and no use first scores. The bridge learner frequently feels that he is not especially good at anything and may simply fade into the background. What the bridge learner needs to understand is the marvelous contribution he/she has to make to group work. While working alone means that this learner can access whatever pattern is needed to complete a task, this skill can be a tremendous asset to a group. It is the bridge learner who is the facilitator who sees the whole picture and is able to keep the plan on target. It is rare to find more than one bridge learner in a class, so if there appear to be several in a class, it is essential to go back over the LCI to determine whether the student had difficulty committing to a choice in the Likert continuum or has conflicting written responses. If you do find a bridge learner, however, encourage this student to come out of the shadows.

Finally, we identify the dynamic learner who has one or two patterns at a use first level and then any other combination of as needed or avoid patterns. This is the learner we most often meet and the learner who could have difficulty knowing which pattern to use at a particular time for a particular task. Sometimes the patterns get in the way of each other and students need a strategy for accessing the appropriate pattern at the appropriate time. Because of the dynamic quality of this learner, there could be difficulty making correct choices.

IN THE PEDAGOGY CLASS

If our goal as educators is to foster student learning, it is crucial that we have a working idea of how different students, and we ourselves, learn. In a beginning pedagogy course, I start the semester by asking my students to answer a basic question: What does learning look like? Many are surprised by this even though they already have strong reasons for wanting to be teachers. I pose the question in this way because our accountability depends on our ability to recognize that learning is indeed happening. For many, this will be the first time anyone has asked them to figure out how they are going to know if what they are doing in the classroom is actually leading to student learning! For the most part, they have not considered this very crucial piece of what it means to be an effective educator. Before I permit any oral response to the question, I pass out a drawing of an "empty" head with its brain, crayons and colored pencils, and I request that my students fill "their" brain with a personal interpretation of what learning looks like for them. We then do "show and tell" and record on transparencies for later reference, the statements and key words each contributes to explain what learning looks like. This phase of the instruction I end with Henry David Thoreau's famous quote: "If a man does not keep pace with his companions, perhaps he hears a different drummer. Let him step to the music which he hears, however measured or far away." If I have heard it said once, I have heard it a hundred times in recent years: kids learn differently. If we do not accept that and work with those differences, we are doomed to fail in creating classroom environments where all students have an equal chance to succeed at learning. This is a powerful first lesson in helping students to identify the reason for us to be educators. They see immediately the magnitude of the challenge they are accepting.

Once my pedagogy students have completed their "show and tell" about their brains, they complete and score the LCI. They look back at the statements they made when they described their brains and the find similar statements in their LCI, open-ended written responses. We then connect these to their pattern scores by discussing exactly what each pattern means and what we might hear from students who manifest these patterns as either use first or avoid patterns. (Refer to Figures 1 and 2)

Because I want students to appreciate how these patterns translate into teaching/learning situations, I have them make hats that will demonstrate their personal learning connections combination. It does not take long for their use-first patterns to manifest themselves. I provide activity boxes containing scissors, paste, rulers, crayons, colored pencils, compasses, protractors, construction paper, staplers, and paper clips. I generally stock six of these boxes for an average size class—they must share. This can be a problem for the highly technical student who prefers to work alone and it is common to see a highly technical processor gather what he/she needs and retreat to a separate corner and complete the task with little or no interaction with the group. It is also quite common to see a highly sequential learner plan and organize while the confluent processors just let their imaginations take over and they "just do it," frequently without any reference to the written or oral instructions. The use first precise processors will need assurance that what they are doing is "right," and they will often seek clarification of directions.

Following construction of their hats, they reflect in writing about the process of completion of the task. Once again they share and are confronted with the differences in approach and performance of a task. They begin to see and hear the key pattern language as it emerges. Throughout this discussion, it is typical to hear such things as "I'm not creative, so I just..." or "First, I...; then I...; finally I..." and "I had too many ideas and couldn't settle on one so I didn't really finish" or "I didn't have enough time." These are all obvious correlations with their use first patterns. Seated in a circle and wearing their hats, the candidates begin to recognize the very real diversity present in the class and begin to recognize the implications of their patterns for them as future teachers.

The next step is to make the first connections to teaching and learning, so the next question is posed: If these are *my* learning choices, how will that translate into what I value as a teacher and in the way I teach? The candidates begin to recognize the importance of being able to have a conversation with students about how they learn. They begin to recognize that they are most likely to craft lessons that value manifestations of learning that come out of their own patterns. It is here that I have the first clue about how I will need to approach a class. If my class is predominantly use first sequential students, they are going to want a well-ordered syllabus and they are going to expect me to stick to it. I quickly learn which of my students will find keeping logs and reflective journals onerous because they simply do not like to write. Others will write pages more than required or necessary.

WITH STUDENTS IN THE CLASSROOM

Think about the students in your classes who can regularly drive you crazy. Is it possible that this is not something they have set out to do simply to make your life miserable, but rather that it is a manifestation of clashing patterns? Might knowing the learning pattern combinations of your class(es) make you more aware as an instructional planner of ways that you could differentiate instruction to ensure maximum opportunity for success for each and every student in your class(es)?

Nickels (2002) a high school teacher from the Midwestern United States wondered whether there might be a correlation between student learning patterns, his learning patterns and the students' grades. In his small study he discovered that his own LCI scores were high in sequential processing and precise processing. His students with low sequential and precise preferences had lower grades in his classes. As students' patterns more closely matched his, their grades rose. This is indeed food for thought for the beginning teacher to take into the field with them. We can look at certain cue words that teachers use in the creation of assignments. These cue words often reveal the teacher's use first patterns, but more importantly they help students to identify which patterns must be accessed for successful completion of a given task, including those tasks that are a part of standardized assessments. Figure 3 shows typical cue words for each pattern.

Once students have experienced the LCI and discussed its implications for both teaching and learning, they take with them the knowledge about differences in learning pattern combinations. They can make educated guesses about the use first patterns of many of the students they see each week, not to mention the use first patterns of their mentor teachers in the field. This is where they begin to learn about lesson planning and how the learning patterns of both teacher and students will have an impact on instructional decisions. Teacher candidates and teachers begin intentional usage of pattern language and assist students to decode assignments. They begin to recognize whether the language they have used in the creation of the assignment actually matches what they expect of students in their responses. There are times that the language of a use first pattern of a teacher shows a value the teacher did not intend in an assignment.

SEQUENTIAL CUE WORDS		PRECISE CUE WORDS	
Alphabetize	Order	Accurately	Explain
Arrange	Organize	Calibrate	Facts
Classify	Outline	Certainty	Identify
Develop	Plan	Describe	Label
Distribute	Put in order	Detail	Measure
Group	Sequence	Document	Observe
In a series	Show a sample	Exact	Specific
List	Show an array	Examine	Write

TECHNICAL CUE WORDS		CONFLUENT CUE WORDS	
Assemble	Erect	Brainstorm	Improvise
Autonomy	Experience	Carefree	Incredible
Build	Figure out	Create	Independence
Concrete	Illustrate	Different	Invent
Construct	Just do it	Dream-up	Risk
Demonstrate	Make	Far fetched	Take a chance
Draw	Problem-solve	Ideas	Unique
Engineer	Tools	Imagine	Unusual

Figure 3: Let Me Learn Pattern Cue Words. Copyright Let Me Learn, Inc. 2002 Used by permission of author.

Knowing the characteristics of their learners enables teachers to design instruction around their dominant patterns—giving every student the opportunity to work in their use-first patterns often, but not exclusively, challenging learners to identify the pattern needed for success and to use it. It is really about holding the student accountable for his own learning, but he cannot be held accountable if we do not work with him to define his patterns and create plans for forging those patterns he is less comfortable with. The Let Me Learn Process® does not ask teachers to create a multitude of different lesson plans for every day's instruction; rather it requires us to offer opportunities to students to use their patterns judiciously and to assist students to create personal learning plans for identifying when a particular pattern is needed and to access that pattern successfully. This is the point at which teachers and learners work on FIT. If they are going to be able to attack a learning task, they will need to learn to *forge* those patterns that are avoid patterns but are necessary for given tasks, *intensify* the as needed patterns so that they become more immediately accessible and natural, and *tether* those use first patterns that might get in the way of accurate and successful completion of the task.

Traditional classroom assignments have a great deal of reading and writing, including many skill and drill worksheets. These are necessary, but can be roadblocks for certain kinds of learners. For those learners who are not precise processors, the sheer magnitude of reading and writing required, especially in secondary classrooms, can be daunting if not completely overwhelming. Let me assure you that I wholeheartedly endorse writing and reading across the curriculum, but I also know that certain students will tune out, shut down, and eventually drop out (mentally if not physically) because they have little opportunity to show what they know in the ways most productive for them. Often we will find that there is little choice in the manner in which assignments are completed and we will see that what is valued by any given teacher tends to correspond with that teacher's use first patterns.

If we are going to help students to take advantage of their use first patterns and to aid them in developing their as needed and avoid patterns, we must engage in intentional teaching. This means that we must know our own patterns and be self-critical and self-analytical about the assignments we create. Sitting still in a library, researching, reading and ultimately writing a research paper may be so antithetical to a student's patterns that he will accept a failing grade rather than subject himself to this torture. Students can learn to forge the precision necessary to complete the assignment. That is not to say that because students prefer other ways of working and showing what they know, they should always be permitted alternative assignments. We do, however, need to recognize that the vast majority of assignments teachers give favor the sequential and precise processors and this is especially true when those are the use first patterns of the teacher. We must intentionally look at options when we are crafting assignments. We must ask ourselves whether there is a way students can show us what they know other than our first instinctive choice. Then we must permit these alternate possibilities. This can be very hard to do because it does mean creating multiple rubrics and ensuring that all the possibilities are of equal difficulty and value.

Students could make a movie, write and perform a piece of music, create an advertising campaign, design a game. They will still need to do research to ensure accuracy, but the end products of different students will look very different. They may certainly find doing the research less tedious if they know that the end product is going to be something other than that dreaded written research paper. I have students who have created movie style posters for plays, novels, and events in history or science. Other students have written picture or alphabet books to teach a concept to others, particularly younger students or their parents! Students can perform skits or construct models to demonstrate understanding of a concept or theory. Candidates are encouraged to keep open minds about the many options available to them to aid in assessment of student learning.

One of the key methods being used in today's classroom is cooperative or collaborative learning. In this type of group work, all members of the group have roles and tasks to perform. Let Me Learn patterns can make grouping much more fair and productive. Having a precise processor who loves to do research and write working with a technical processor who loves to build, along with a confluent processor who sees the imaginative possibilities and a sequential processor to keep everyone else on task and on target for deadlines can make collaborative work far more productive. It can minimize the complaints about students who do not carry their share of the burden or the complaint about the one person in the group who takes charge and wants to do everything. Creative teaming of students, using their use-first patterns, can enable a teacher to ensure that all students will contribute to a project, each accessing pattern strengths.

Standardized measures of assessment are those that are used to define the accountability of teachers and schools. If students can be taught to decode the tasks and to intentionally apply the needed patterns, success is virtually assured for those students who have the necessary knowledge. Teaching our students to forge, intensify, and tether their patterns to match assessment requirements will enable their success. When a student with an avoid pattern in sequence or precision is confronted by typical standardized tests, he will need immediately to forge these patterns. He will need to make conscious choices in decoding the task and in applying strategies for successful completion. Helping students to decode and forge patterns throughout a school year will give them the skill and confidence to do the same thing during standardized testing situations. When patterns are at as needed levels, there will be the necessity to intensify them. It is not that students do not have these patterns available, but rather that they need to consciously identify the need for them and intensify their use. Sometimes students are at a disadvantage because their use first patterns are not the patterns of need on standardized assessments. When this happens, students must be able to tether the tendency to use the inappropriate patterns because they are patterns of first choice and to forge or intensify the correct patterns. When students can do this, they are intentionally taking charge of their own learning. They are in charge of displaying what they know through intentional choice.

CONCLUSION

I firmly believe that every teacher wants students be successful both in and out of the classroom. Teachers do not go to school each morning with the intention of leaving children behind. If they do not recognize their own learning patterns and those of their students, teachers can unintentionally do exactly that. The Let Me Learn Process® offers teachers and students a way to understand each other and learning. It enables teachers to differentiate instruction and it provides students with ways to access the appropriate patterns to ensure that they will be more successful in every learning situation. Once students become comfortable with their own patterns and how to forge (bring out the weaker but needed) patterns, intensify (turn up the heat), or tether (hold back a strong but not necessarily correct) patterns, both teachers and students will find that the learning environment is more positive and more productive.

NOTE

All materials including the Learning Connections Inventory may be obtained from Learning Connections Resources, LLC, Turnersville, NJ 08012-8861 www.LCRinfo.com and www.letmelearn.org

REFERENCES

Johnston, C. and Dainton, G. (1997). *Learning Connections Inventory.* Thousand Oaks, CA: Corwin Press, Sage Publications.
Johnston, C. (1996). *Unlocking the will to learn.* Thousand Oaks, CA: Corwin Press, Sage Publications.

Johnston, C. (2000). *Let Me Learn: A personal guide to implementing the LML process K-12.* Brooklyn, CT: KGM Print Services.

Johnston, C. (2005). *Learning to use my potential.* Turnersville, NJ: Learning Connections Resources.

Nickels, J. (2002). Using the learning combination inventory to connect teaching methods with student learning strategies: An action research project presented to the Shawnee Mission Board of Education. Unpublished.

Osterman, K. and Kottkamp, R. (2004). *Reflective practice for educators.* Thousand Oaks, CA: Corwin Press.

Pettig, K. L. (2000). On the road to differentiated instruction. *Educational Leadership, 58*(1).

Sacks, P. (1999). *Standardized minds: The high price of America's testing culture and what we can do to change it.* Cambridge, MA: Perseus Books.

Tomlinson, C. A. (1999). Mapping a route toward differentiated instruction. *Educational Leadership, 57*(1).

Tomlinson, C. A. (1999). The differentiated classroom: Responding to the needs of all learners. Alexandria, VA: ASCD.

Chapter 4

THE INFLUENCE OF MOTIVATION ON THE USE OF LEARNING STRATEGIES IN THE CLASSROOM

Ayumi Tanaka and Kiho Tanaka
Doshisha University, Kyoto, Japan

ABSTRACT

Students use a variety of learning strategies in the classroom. To understand students' learning process and provide effective support for them, it is important to examine how and why they use a particular strategy in a given situation. Researchers have reported that students' motivational orientation has significant influence on their use of learning strategies. Among the many perspectives in the research of motivation, we focus on self-determination or autonomy, achievement goals, and self-efficacy. We report the results of three studies of Japanese elementary, junior high school, and college students. The relationships between students' perceived autonomy, achievement goals, and deep and surface processing strategies as well as self-handicapping strategy was examined in the first study (Yamauchi and Tanaka, 1998). In the second study, the relationship between motivation and learning strategies were examined including the role of self-efficacy (Tanaka and Yamauchi, 2000a). Help-seeking strategy was the focus of the third study, and examined in relation to achievement goals (Tanaka, Murakami, Okuno, and Yamauchi, 2002). Based on the findings, we suggest a direction for future instructional interventions designed to improve students' learning.

1. INTRODUCTION

The acquisition, use, and control of learning strategies are essential for effective learning by students. Learning strategies include any thoughts, behaviors, beliefs, or emotions that facilitate the acquisition, understanding, or later transfer of new knowledge and skills (Weinstein, Husman, and Dierking, 2000). Knowing about and using learning strategies is a major factor for discriminating between low-achieving individuals and those who experience success (Pintrich and DeGroot, 1990). Researchers have noted that students must also develop the motivation to use these strategies (McKeachie, Pintrich, and Lin, 1985). In this chapter we examine the influence of motivation on the use of learning strategies, in order to illuminate the mechanism of learning in the classroom. We start with a brief review of the research on learning strategies and motivation.

Types of Learning Strategies

Learning strategies of students have often been categorized as either deep or surface processing strategies (Murayama, 2003). A *deep processing strategy* is aiming at understanding of information, and includes elaboration and organizational strategies (Weinstein and Mayer, 1986). Elaboration strategies are used to make information meaningful and to build connections between the information given in the learning material and the learner's existing knowledge. Organizational strategies are used to construct internal connections among the pieces of information given in the learning material (Weinstein and Mayer, 1986). In contrast, a *surface processing strategy* is aimed at rote memorization of information, and includes repetitive rehearsal strategies. Rehearsal strategies are used to select and encode information in a verbatim manner (Weinstein and Mayer, 1986). In general, students who more frequently use deep processing strategies are more likely to do better in their studies in terms of grades on assignments, exams, papers, and the overall course grade (Pintrich and DeGroot, 1990; Zimmerman and Martinez-Pons, 1990).

Changing Views of Learning Strategy

Advances in research on cognitive psychology in the 1970s provided us with the view that the learner is as an active, self-determined individual rather than a passive receptacle for knowledge. This has lead to the concept of planned and self-directed "cognitive strategies," and these have been recognized as a mutable factor in promoting academic achievement by students (Weinstein, Husman, and Dierking, 2000).

Many studies have investigated strategies that students learned largely on their own, rather than those that they had learned from planned, direct instruction. Several researchers also investigated spontaneous strategy development in children (e.g., Bjorklund and Zeman, 1983). Although it did seem that strategies could develop spontaneously, their development was dependent on students' exposure to effective models of the use of specific strategies and to environments that provided opportunities for practice. However, even when students are exposed to effective strategy use, not all students take advantage of the information provided to them (Bielaczyc, Pirolli, and Brown, 1995). Knowing what strategies to use and knowing how to use them are not enough. What are the precursors of effective strategy use? How can we do to help teachers facilitate the use of effective strategies in their classroom teaching?

Self-Regulated Learning and Motivation

Many researchers are developing integrated approaches to examine strategic and self-regulated learning (e.g., Boekaerts, 1997). *Self-regulation* refers to self-generated thoughts, feelings and actions that are planned and cyclically adapted to the attainment of personal goals (Zimmerman, 2000). This definition does not emphasize only metacognition such as knowledge states and deductive reasoning when, for example, choosing cognitive strategies, but involves self-beliefs and personal motivation. That is, what we believe we are like and what we believe we may become help to provide the impetus for regulating behavior (Pintrich and Garcia, 1994).

Self-regulatory skills are of little value if a person cannot motivate themselves to use them. Students must want to use a certain strategy and must maintain that desire throughout the learning task. Recently, more and more researchers have been focusing on the role of students' motivation as central to learning and teaching contexts. This chapter features three of the most important theoretical concepts in recent research on motivation: self-determination, achievement goal, and self-efficacy. In the following, we briefly describe each theoretical issue.

Self-Determination Theory

S*elf-determination theory* (Deci and Ryan, 1985, 1991) is one of the most comprehensive and empirically supported theories of motivation available today (Pintrich and Schunk, 2002). It assumes that humans have inherent tendencies to be intrinsically motivated, to assimilate their social and physical worlds, and to integrate external regulations into self-regulations (Ryan and Deci, 2000). According to self-determination theory, *intrinsic motivation* is conceptualized as a prototypical form of autonomous or self-determined behavior, with a full sense of choice, and with the experience of doing what one wishes. Further, without the feeling of coercion or compulsion, one spontaneously engages in an activity that interests oneself.

Although intrinsic motivation is an important type of motivation, self-determination theory states that it is not the only type of motivation or even the only type of self-determined motivation (Deci and Ryan, 1985). The term *extrinsic motivation* refers to the performance of an activity to attain some separable outcome and, thus, is different from intrinsic motivation, which refers to doing an activity for the inherent satisfaction of the activity itself. Unlike some perspectives that view extrinsically motivated behavior as invariantly nonautonomous, self-determination theory proposes that behaviors referred to as extrinsically motivated in the previous studies can become autonomous through the process of internalization and integration (Ryan and Connell, 1989). Internalization refers to taking in the values or regulation of the behavior and integration refers to assimilating regulation further into the self.

The most controlled type of extrinsic motivation is called *external regulation*. This type of regulation is the typical extrinsic motivation, by which one's behavior is regulated by contingencies overtly external to the individual. A person in this state experiences externally regulated behavior as controlled, and perceives an external locus of causality. This type of extrinsic motivation is similar to that which has been the focus of operant theorists. When a person starts to internalize and integrate behavior, the motivational state shifts to *introjected regulation*, which can be seen in behaviors associated with or enforced by the expectations of self-approval or of avoiding guilt and anxiety. This type of behavior, even though it is internally driven, has an external locus of causality. This concept is similar to self-involvement, when one is motivated to demonstrate their ability, to avoid failure, or to maintain self-worth. As the behavior advances in internalization and integration, the motivational state becomes *identified regulation*, which is the behavior that occurs with the individual's perception of the importance of the activities. Therefore, an individual perceives an internal locus of control. The most self-determined form of extrinsic motivation is *integrated regulation*, which results when identifications have been evaluated and brought into congruence with the personally endorsed values, goals, and needs that are already part of self.

Intrinsic and extrinsic motivations are both motivated toward activity engagements. Deci and Ryan (1985), however, suggested the existence of activities that are not motivated, and this is called *amotivation*. When people are amotivated, either they do not act at all or they act passively. Amotivation results from feeling either that they are unable to achieve desired outcomes because of lack of contingency (Rotter, 1966; Seligman, 1975) or a lack of perceived competence (Bandura, 1977; Deci, 1975), or because they do not value the activity or the outcomes it would yield (Ryan, 1995).

Deci and his colleagues (e.g., Deci and Ryan, 1985, 1987; Ryan and Connell, 1989; Ryan, Connell, and Deci, 1985) have reported that highly autonomous students maintain effort and activities, and search for optimal strategies, even in difficult situations. In contrast, for students with low autonomy, performance poses the threat of fear, pressure, and stress, and they try to avoid such situations by adopting self-defensive strategies. Furthermore, it is reported that goals of the performance type decrease intrinsic motivation and disturb autonomous engagement toward activity (Dweck, 1986; Nicholls, 1984; Plant and Ryan, 1985; Ryan, 1982; Ryan, Koestner, and Deci, 1991). Ryan and Connell (1989) have suggested that even though both introjected and identified regulation were correlated with high effort, introjected regulation was related to high anxiety at school and maladaptive coping styles toward failure, whereas identified regulation was correlated with enjoyment at school and positive coping style toward failure.

Achievement Goal Theory

Research on *achievement goals* has also been one of the most active areas of motivation research in classroom contexts over the last 15 years (Pintrich, 2003). An achievement goal concerns the purposes of achievement behavior. It defines an integrated pattern of beliefs, attributions, and affects that produces the intentions of behavior, represented by different ways of approaching, engaging in, and responding to achievement activities (Ames, 1992). Although theoretical perspectives and labels differ, two contrasting achievement goal constructs have received the most attention in the research literature (cf. Ames and Ames, 1984; Dweck, 1986; Nicholls, Patashnick, and Nolen, 1985): the goal of developing and improveing ability (referred to in this study as *mastery goals*) and the goal of demonstrating and proving ability (referred to in this study as *performance goals*).

The contrast between mastery and performance goals is basically similar to that between intrinsic motivation and extrinsic motivation (specifically, the introjected regulation mentioned above). However, in achievement goal theory, intrinsic and extrinsic motivation are not defined in reference to basic needs to be self-determining or autonomous, but rather in terms of focus on the task and a goal of mastery and understanding, or a focus on the self and performance relative to others (Linnenbrink and Pintrich, 2000).

Self-efficacy

Self-efficacy is defined as personal judgments of one's capabilities to organize and execute courses of action necessary to attain a designated performance in specific tasks (Bandura, 1986). Self-efficacy affects choice of activities, effort, and persistence. It is said that the judgment of self-efficacy is needed when the situation is stressful, relatively novel, and the coping strategies are ambiguous, as in most learning situations. Self-efficacy basically refers to task-specific expectations, which is the point on which it largely differs from the concepts of self-confidence, self-cognition of ability, or perceived competence (Pintrich and Schunk, 2002).

Social cognitive theory suggests that students' self-efficacy plays a prominent role in regulating the cognitive, affective, and motivational factors that operate in concert in the development of students' capabilities to manage their own learning and academic achievements (Bandura, 1993). Students with higher mean self-efficacy will think actively, choose challenging tasks, be persistent in working on the tasks for longer times, make an effort, develop positive feelings, and achieve high performance. In contrast, students with lower self-efficacy will think passively, avoid effort, develop negative feelings, perform less well, and experience stress (e.g., Bandura, 1993; Bandura and Schunk, 1981; Schunk, 1984). In the studies of self-regulated learning, Zimmerman and Martinez-Pons (1990) investigated self-efficacy beliefs and the use of various learning strategies for self-regulated learning. Their results indicate a substantial relation between self-efficacy and strategy use across children in grades 5, 8, and 9.

* * *

Next, we report the empirical evidence from three studies that reveal how these types of motivation influence the use of learning strategies (Study1: Yamauchi and Tanaka, 1998; Study 2: Tanaka and Yamauchi, 2000a; Study 3: Tanaka, Murakami, Okuno, and Yamauchi, 2002).

2. STUDY 1: STUDENTS' AUTONOMY, ACHIEVEMENT GOAL, AND THE USE OF LEARNING STRATEGIES

In this study, we examined the relations among autonomy, achievement goals and the use of learning strategies, using data from Japanese children (Yamauchi and Tanaka, 1998). The influence over the use of self-handicapping strategy, in addition to the use of deep and surface processing strategies, was also investigated in this study. *Self-handicapping* is a strategic behavior that aims at protecting the self from esteem-threatening situations. According to Snyder (1990, p.119), it can be defined as follows: "self-handicapping is a process of preserving the personal theory of self, wherein the person, experiencing uncertainty about success in an anticipated important performance arena, utilizes seeming impediments in order to (1) decrease the linkage to that impending performance should it prove to be poor (i.e., discounting), and (2) increase the linkage should performance to prove to be good (augmentation)." Although self-handicapping may occur in the service of self-presentational concerns, the enactment of self-handicapping strategies may be motivated by anticipated threats to self-esteem or uncertainty about one's abilities (Rhodewalt, 1990; Tice, 1991). Studies suggest that self-handicapping results in negative effects on subsequent performance (Rhodewalt and Fairfield, 1991; Zuckerman, Kieffer, and Knee, 1998).

It was expected that autonomous types of motivation would correlate with deep processing strategy, whereas nonautonomous types of motivation would correlate with surface processing strategy. Self-handicapping strategy was expected to relate with introjected regulation, as both of them are strongly concerned with the concept of ability.

Children (N=356) were sampled from the fifth and sixth grades of six elementary schools in Japan. Two self-reporting questionnaires were administered: one was designed to measure children's autonomy for schoolwork (Ryan and Connell, 1989) and the other to assess children's goals and learning strategies (Niemivirta, 1996), which we refer to as self-regulated learning.

The correlation coefficients among four types of motivation (Table1) demonstrated a definite simplex structure. The results support the hypothesis of autonomy that motivational regulation lying along an extrinsic-intrinsic continuum, as suggested by self-determination theorists.

Table 1 Correlation between motivation and self-regulated learning

Subscale	External	Introjected	Identified	Intrinsic
Motivation				
External Regulation	-			
Introjected Regulation	.62 ***	-		
Identified Regulation	.26 ***	.50 ***	-	
Intrinsic Regulation	.08	.35 ***	.68 ***	-
Self-regulated Learning				
Value	-.02	.24 ***	.49 ***	.58 ***
Goal Orientation				
Mastery Goal	.15 **	.37 ***	.58 ***	.62 ***
Performance Goal	.28 ***	.50 ***	.33 ***	.16 ***
Work-avoidance Goal	.19 ***	-.02	-.37 ***	-.42 ***
Learning Strategies				
Deep Processing Strategy	-.04	.27 ***	.54 ***	.56 ***
Surface Processing Strategy	.38 ***	.40 ***	.16 **	.13 *
Self-handicapping	.21 ***	.06	-.27 ***	-.26 ***

From Yamauchi, H., & Tanaka, K. (1998). Relations of autonomy, self-referenced beliefs, and self-regulated learning among Japanese children. *Psychological Reports, 82*, 803-816. Copyright 1998 by the Psychological Reports. Reprinted by Permission.

Correlations between scores on autonomy and self-regulated learning as shown in Table 1 indicate an interesting relationship. Better self-regulated learning, reflected in scores on mastery goals, deep processing strategy, and value of learning is positively correlated with the motivation of intrinsic regulation. In contrast, work-avoidance goal and self-handicapping are negatively correlated with scores on intrinsic motivation and positively correlated with external regulation. This result is consistent with the conclusions of Rigby, Deci, Patrick, and Ryan (1992), who reviewed several studies to examine the relationship of autonomy and learning outcome, and concluded that higher-quality conceptual learning is promoted by relatively self-determined forms of motivation.

To explore the nature of these relationships further, we used canonical analysis to identify associations of autonomy and self-regulated learning. The likelihood ratios for all canonical correlations, canonical R^2, and multivariate redundancy indexes were used as criteria for the number of variables to retain. The canonical structures for the first two variates and canonical R^2 are presented in Table 2. Only those loadings greater than or equal to 0.30 are shown.

Table 2 Canonical structure between motivation and self-regulated learning

Subscale	C1	C2
Motivation		
External Regulation		.82
Introjected Regulation	.50	.85
Identified Regulation	.88	
Intrinsic Regulation	.91	
Self-regulated Learning		
Value	.78	
Goal Orientation		
Mastery Goal	.84	
Performance Goal	.37	.75
Work-avoidance Goal	-.58	.46
Learning Strategies		
Deep Processing Strategy	.81	
Surface Processing Strategy		.75
Self-handicapping	-.39	.47
Canonical R^2	.60	.29

From Yamauchi, H., & Tanaka, K. (1998). Relations of autonomy, self-referenced beliefs, and self-regulated learning among Japanese children. *Psychological Reports, 82,* 803-816. Copyright 1998 by the Psychological Reports. Reprinted by Permission

For the autonomy domain, intrinsic and identified regulations show salient loadings. In the domain of self-regulated learning, value, mastery goal, and deep processing strategy have noticeable loadings on the first canonical variate. Therefore, the first canonical variate in the autonomy domain can be interpreted as representing relatively more self-determined forms of motivation, and in the domain of self-regulated learning can be defined as self-regulated learning of higher quality. On the second canonical variate, introjected and external regulations for the autonomy domain, performance goal, and surface processing strategy for self-regulated learning show salient loadings. Therefore, the second canonical variate in the autonomy domain can be defined as the more external or controlled types of motivation, while in the domain of self-regulated learning, this variate can be interpreted as the ego-oriented or ego-defensive learning strategies. Thus the results from the first canonical variate identified the relationships between the self-regulated learning of higher quality and the more self-determined types of motivation, which are reported and discussed in many other studies (see Deci and Ryan, 2002; Tanaka and Yamauchi, 2000b).

3. STUDY 2: STUDENTS' AUTONOMY AND THE USE OF LEARNING STRATEGIES: THE MEDIATING ROLE OF SELF-EFFICACY

This study went a step beyond study 1. We investigated the relationship of autonomy, self-efficacy, and learning strategies, using the data from 112 undergraduate Japanese students (Tanaka and Yamauchi, 2000b). Based on the perspective view of self-determination theory, we aimed to approach students' learning process from the synthesis of both intrinsic motivation and self-efficacy. We assumed that students' motivational states would direct their learning strategies; however, judgments of their self-efficacy would be needed to direct their learning strategies in some motivational states. Accordingly, some influence of motivational states on learning strategies would be mediated through the effects of self-efficacy beliefs. More specifically, students who are intrinsically motivated would engage in activity for the inherent satisfaction of the activity itself. Thus we hypothesized that these students would adapt learning strategies of understanding or gaining knowledge without reference to their self-efficacy beliefs. On the other hand, students who are extrinsically motivated have not internalized or integrated their behaviors completely into the self, so learning situations would be accompanied by stress. Therefore, we hypothesized that these students' self-efficacy beliefs would direct their actual actions. Finally, students who are amotivated toward learning have neither figured out the goals nor the values of the activity, nor motivated themselves toward the activity, so they feel helpless. It was therefore assumed that these students, whatever their scores on self-efficacy are, would adopt avoidance strategies.

We employed three measures of learning-related beliefs: one designed to assess students' degree of autonomy for the learning situation in university courses (Vallerand, Pelletier, Blais, Briere, Senecal, and Vallieres, 1992, 1993; Yamauchi and Tanaka, 1998), one to assess students' perceived self-efficacy related to self-regulated learning (Bandura, 1991; Pintrich and DeGroot, 1990), and one to assess students' self-regulated learning (Zimmerman and Martinez-Pons, 1986; Pintrich and DeGroot, 1990; Yamauchi and Tanaka, 1998). We dealt with two types of self-efficacy: *self-efficacy for academic achievement*, that is, students' conviction that they could understand their learning materials and achieve good grades or scores, and *self-efficacy for controlling behavior*, that is, students' perceived capability to carry out a variety of self-regulatory behaviors associated with studying.

A path model was proposed to assess relations among the learning processes that led to self-regulated learning. We conducted structural equation modeling, using the item scores as manifest variables. A reciprocal relationship between autonomy and self-efficacy was tested in the model. Covariances were considered for five latent independent variables, which were subscales in the motivation scale. We also postulated covariance between error variables of these two latent dependent variables. Figure 1 shows a completely standardized solution with significant effects between the latent variables.

The analyses identified diverse paths by which motivational states influence learning strategies. As predicted, the motivational types lying at either end of the continuum of self-determination were directly related to the learning strategies. Intrinsic motivation was correlated positively with deep processing strategies and negatively with self-handicapping, whereas amotivation showed positive correlation with surface processing strategies. Intrinsic motivation tends to lead to an active use of cognitive and metacognitive learning strategies and passive use of self-handicapping, without being influenced by the perception of self-efficacy. Because intrinsically motivated students are engaged in learning for internal satisfaction, they will pursue the task of understanding content and gaining knowledge. Therefore, whether perceived self-efficacy is high or low, they adopt learning strategies conducive to achieving their aim. In contrast, amotivation tends to facilitate surface learning strategies. The amotivated student is not able to figure out either the learning goals or their value, and is not interested in learning. In school, however, students must complete a task to pass the course. Students with amotivation, therefore, adopt learning strategies such as memorizing or rehearsal, whether they understand the content or not.

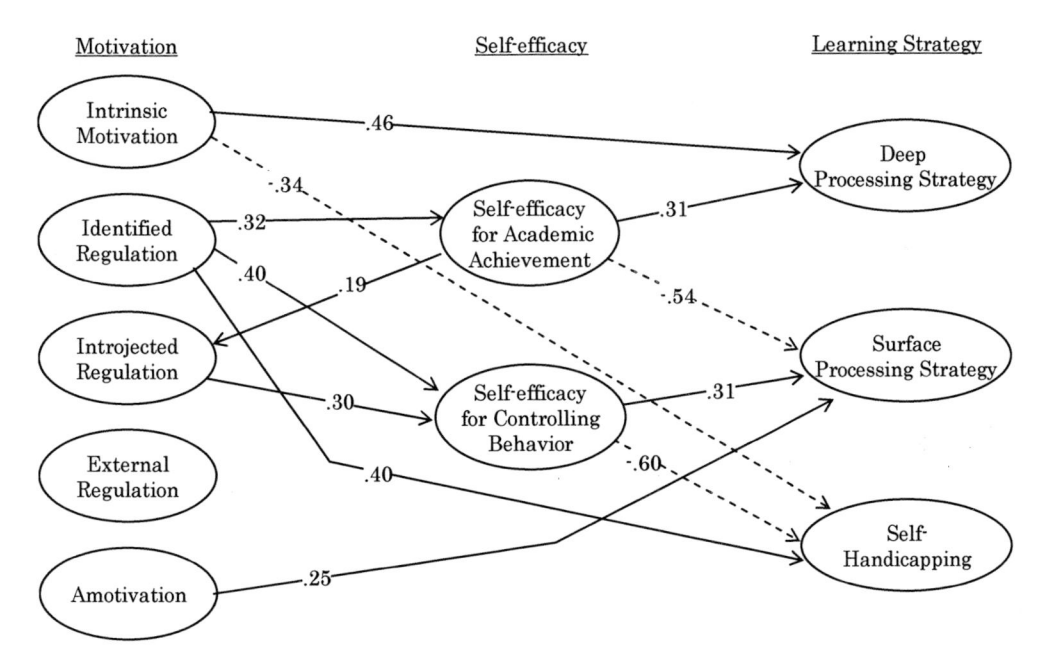

Figure 1. Structural equation modeling of motivational states, self-efficacy, and learning strategies (broken ines represent negative causal coefficients)

There were no relations with external regulation and self-efficacy or learning strategies. Students in this motivational state have not internalized or integrated their activities, so the learning situation is stressful for them. They initiate learning activities only under external pressures whether they perceive learning related efficacy or not. It is suggested that people need to feel competent with respect to behaviors valued by a significant other if they are to engage in and accept responsibility for those behaviors (Deci and Ryan, 2002). If people do not feel competent to perform a target behavior, they are unlikely to internalize regulation of the behavior; in fact, they will likely find an excuse not to do the behavior at all, even in the presence of the significant other.

An unexpected positive link was found between identified regulation and self-handicapping strategies. While many studies suggest that self-handicapping results in negative effects on subsequent performance (e.g., Rhodewalt, 1994; Zuckerman, Kieffer, and Knee, 1998), a few studies have shown positive effects of self-handicapping. Snyder concluded that "the successful handicap may enable the protagonist to focus on relevant task cues and not the potentially interfering self-relevant emotions and cognitions" (Snyder, 1990, p.139). Similarly, Deppe and Harackiewicz (1996) reported that self-handicapping allowed the participants to concentrate on the activity instead of focusing on performance concerns, thereby leading to higher task involvement and enjoyment. From these perspectives, there might be a positive role for the use of self-handicapping strategies by students with identified regulation. However, further research is needed to clarify this relationship.

There was an interesting relation between introjected regulation and self-efficacy. Introjected regulation had a positive effect from self-efficacy for academic achievement, and positive effect on self-efficacy for controlling behaviors. This suggests that the learning activities of students with the introjected type of motivation will be stimulated by the feelings of self-confidence engendered when they regulate their own learning activities. This process, however, occurs only when these students believe that they can master the course work. Students with introjected regulation are fearful of failure because they are engaging in activity as a result of internal pressure and are aiming to gain approval from others. They, therefore, need to perceive their own ability to achieve the goal before they engage in the activity.

4. STUDY 3: ACHIEVEMENT GOALS AND HELP-SEEKING

Help-seeking behavior is a different type of strategy from previously mentioned learning strategies, because it requires interaction with others as a resource to cope with difficulty in the learning process (Newman, 1991; Zimmerman and Martinez-Pons, 1988). It has been found to be a valuable self-regulatory strategy that contributes to student learning (Karabenick and Sharma, 1994; Zimmerman and Martinez-Pons, 1988). Help-seeking behaviors can be captured by two components: adaptive help-seeking and the avoidance of help-seeking. Adaptive help-seeking involves a student asking for hints about the solution to a problem, examples of similar problems, or clarification of the problem (Ryan and Pintrich, 1997). Such help-seeking strategies are adaptive in that the help requested is limited to help needed by the individual to solve the problem independently (Karabenick and Knapp, 1991; Karabenick and Sharma, 1994; Ryan and Pintrich, 1997). In contrast, avoidance of help-seeking refers to instances when a student needs help but does not seek it. When students do not garner help when it is needed they put themselves at a disadvantage for learning and performance (Ryan and Pintrich, 1997).

Approach and Avoidance Achievement Goal, Attitudes Toward Help-Seeking, and Help-Seeking Behavior

One characteristic that has been found important for help-seeking behavior is students' achievement goals, because they may generate different motives for help-seeking. An extensive literature supports the proposition that mastery goals promote a host of positive processes and outcomes, and that performance goals lead to less positive patterns of motivation and self-regulation. However, the empirical picture for the proposition that performance goals elicit negative processes and outcomes is less clear than the literature suggests (e.g., Archer, 1994; Meece, Blumenfeld, and Hoyle, 1988; Pintrich and Garcia, 1991; Wolters, Yu, and Pintrich, 1996). Recently some researchers have shown that the distinction between two dimensions of performance goals enhances the predictive utility of the mastery-performance goal framework. One dimension is to demonstrate superior ability, and the other dimension is to avoid the demonstration of the lack of ability. Elliot and Harackiewicz (1996) labeled these goals performance-approach and performance-avoidance goals, and Skaalvik (1997) used the terms of self-enhancing and self-defeating ego orientation to label the same constructs. These researchers have shown that performance-approach goals, as well as mastery goals, are related to numerous positive processes and outcomes, including high performance outcomes, persistence while studying, effort while studying, and intrinsic motivation, and that performance-avoidance goals are related to maladaptive processes and outcomes, including anxiety, disorganized studying, poor performance, and reduced intrinsic motivation (Elliot and Church, 1997; Elliot and McGregor, 1999; Elliot, McGregor, and Gable, 1999; Middleton and Midgley, 1997; Skaalvik, 1997).

Butler and Neuman (1995) investigated help-seeking by children engaged in problem solving in one of two goal conditions (mastery or performance), and found that children requested more help in the mastery goal condition than in the performance goal condition. Ryan and Pintrich (1997) reported that mastery goals are directly related to the self-reported adaptive help-seeking, whereas they did not find direct relationship between the self-reported help-seeking behavior and performance goals, which were referred to as "relative ability goals" in their study. Newman (1998) reported that mastery goals had a positive influence and performance goals had a negative influence on the frequency of requested help and on actual problem solving. Given these consistent findings, mastery goals are expected to be positively related to adaptive help-seeking. It is expected that somewhat mixed results regarding performance goals will be clarified by the approach and avoidance distinction of performance goal constructs.

Other studies have shown that the relationship between motivational factors and help-seeking behavior is mediated by positive and negative attitudes toward help-seeking. Newman (1990) found that negative attitudes toward help-seeking mediated the relation between perceptions of cognitive competence and intentions to seek help when needed. That is, perceived cognitive competence was negatively related to perceived threats toward help-seeking, which, in turn, was negatively related to intentions of help-seeking. Ryan and Pintrich (1997) found that perceptions of the benefits and threats toward help-seeking mediated the effects of achievement goals on the adaptive help-seeking and the avoidance of help-seeking. In their findings, mastery goals were related to perceived benefits of help-seeking, which were positively related to the adaptive help-seeking behavior and negatively related to the avoidance of help-seeking. Performance goals were found to be related to perceptions of threats, which influenced avoidance of help-seeking. Given these evidences, it seemed likely that one way that achievement goals and help-seeking behavior may be related is through attitudes toward help-seeking.

Direct and Indirect Influence Achievement Goals on Help-Seeking Behavior for Japanese Junior High School Students

We investigated the direct and indirect influence of achievement goals on students' reported likelihood of help-seeking behavior and the mediational role of attitudes towards help-seeking between achievement goals and help-seeking behavior (Tanaka, Murakami, Okuno, and Yamauchi, 2002). It was expected that mastery goals were related to adaptive help-seeking behavior through the perceived benefits of help-seeking. There does not seem to be any research that investigated the relationships among each of the two dimensions of performance goals, attitudes toward help-seeking, and help-seeking behavior. Thus, it was expected that differentiating approach-avoidance dimensions of performance goals would lead to better understanding of the process of help-seeking.

For the sample of 7th and 9th grade Japanese junior high school students ($N=131$), the items from the measures developed by Elliot and Church (1997), Middleton and Midgley (1997), and Skaalvik (1997) were used for the assessment of their achievement goals. For the measurements of attitudes towards help-seeking (perceived benefit and perceived threat) and help-seeking behavior (adaptive help-seeking and avoidance of help-seeking), items from Karabenick and Knapp (1991), Newman (1990), Newman and Goldin (1990), and Ryan and Pintrich (1997) were used.

We constructed the path models in two steps. First, each of the attitudes toward help-seeking variables (perception of benefits and perceived threats) was separately regressed on the three achievement goals. Next, each of the help-seeking behaviors (adaptive help-seeking and avoidance of help-seeking) was separately regressed on the achievement goals and attitudes toward help-seeking. Significant paths of the fully estimated path models are shown in Figure 2.

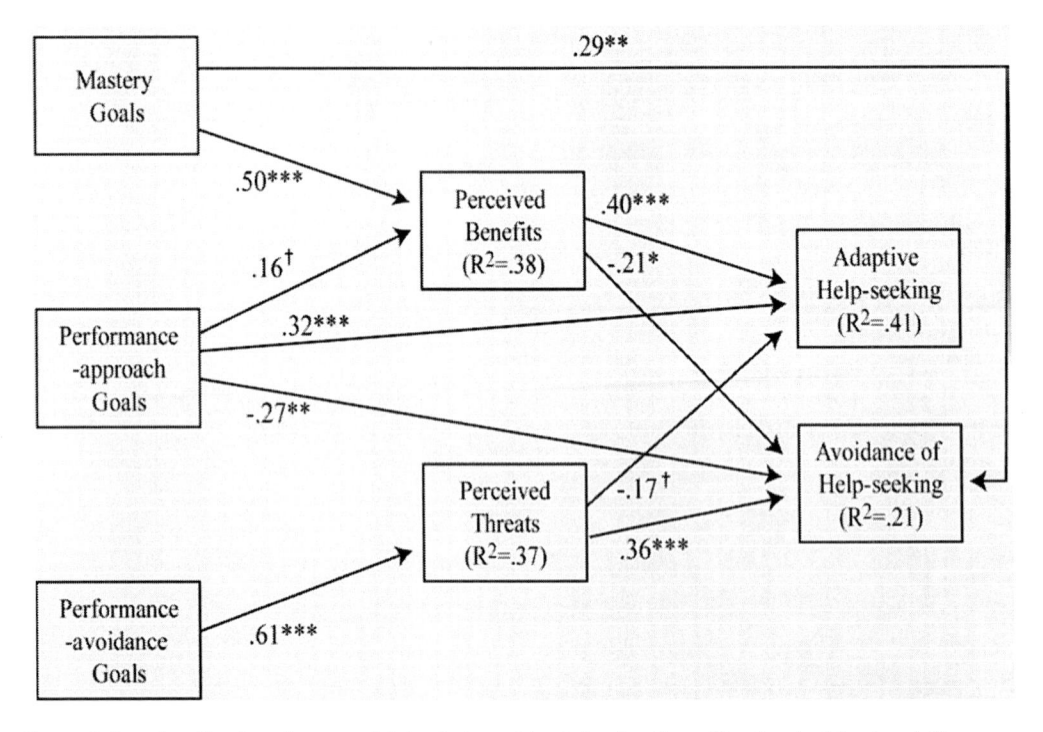

Figure 2. Results of path analyses explaining help-seeking behavior. From Tanaka, A., Murakami, Y., Okuno, T., & Yamauchi, H. (2002). Achievement goals, attitudes toward help-seeking, and help-seeking behavior in the classroom. *Learning and Individual Differences, 13,* 23-35. Copyright 2001 by Elsevier Science Inc. Reprinted by Permission.

Consistent with the study of Ryan and Pintrich (1997), students who were concerned with developing their competence and mastery skills were likely to recognize that help-seeking was a useful strategy that could help them learn, and in turn, those notions were strongly related to self-reported adaptive help-seeking. Interestingly, when perceived benefits were controlled, mastery goals were related to the avoidance of help-seeking. The literature on help-seeking has focused on two main reasons why students may be reluctant to seek help. First, students may be reluctant to ask for help because they perceive help-seeking as evidence of incompetence and thus as threatening to their perceptions of ability (Butler and Neuman, 1995; Nadler, 1987). Second, help-seeking may be considered a dependent behavior that conflicts with personal needs for autonomy (Deci and Ryan, 1987) or independent mastery and self-reliance (Butler and Neuman, 1995; van der Meij, 1988). The relationship between mastery goals and avoidance of help-seeking in the present study may be explained by the second reason. For students who perceived the benefits of help-seeking to the same extent, the stronger their mastery goals, the more they may have regarded help-seeking behavior as dependent.

Additional work using a more sophisticated measure of help-seeking behavior, which draws a distinction between different types of reasons for the avoidance of help-seeking, may be needed.

Performance-approach goals are defined by the goal of demonstrating superior abilities and outperforming other students. Our results showed a direct positive relationship between performance-approach goals and adaptive help-seeking, and a direct negative relationship between these goals and the avoidance of help-seeking. These results showed us the differences between performance-approach goals and mastery goals. Students adopting performance-approach goals may experience no conflict with needs for autonomy and independent mastery when they seek help, because they may value achievement outcomes rather than content or process of learning. In order to expedite successful task completion and demonstrate their ability to other people, students who adapt performance-approach goals should be more likely to ask for help easily. Although these goals may not lead to the outcomes associated with deep level processing and elaboration, such as long-term retention of the material (Elliot and McGregor, 1999), performance-approach goals should be productive in some context, for example, relating to high levels of performance in terms of grades and test scores (Elliot and Church, 1997; Elliot and McGregor, 1999; Harackiewicz, Barron, Carter, Lehto, and Elliot, 1997). The positive focus inherent in performance-approach goals could encourage students to increase their efforts and accomplishments.

In contrast, performance-avoidance goals were strongly related to the perceived threats of help-seeking, which in turn, were related to the avoidance of help-seeking. Performance-avoidance goals are defined by the goal of avoiding the demonstration of incompetence or being negatively judged by others, and regulation of these goals orients individuals toward a negative possibility. The pursuit of performance-avoidance goals is portrayed as fundamentally aversive and threat-based and is posited to elicit negative, affective, cognitive, and behavioral processes that lead to a host of negative outcomes (Elliot, 1999). Students who adopt these goals are vulnerable to worries and concerns about others' reactions if they asked for help, which leads to their avoidance of help-seeking. This process may be one of the detrimental mechanisms that are responsible for the link between performance-avoidance goals and low-level academic performance. Students who ask questions and obtain assistance when it is required not only alleviate immediate academic difficulties but also acquire knowledge and skills that can in turn be used for self-help (Newman, 1990). Teacher practices that encourage students to focus on positive possibilities or to use self-referenced standards could foster positive feelings about help-seeking and lead to actual help-seeking.

5. Conclusion

Across the three studies, we can see consistent motivational profiles of the use of learning strategies and approaches to learning. It seems to be a fairly reliable finding that autonomous and mastery-oriented motivations are more likely to lead to the usage of optimal strategies and effective learning processes (Pintrich and Garcia, 1994). Pintrich (2003) assumed that a focus on learning makes some costs such as the extra time associated with deep processing strategies seem worthwhile, or that these costs are not perceived as being costs under a mastery goal orientation. It may also be that the self-generated interest in the content they study with these motivations may lead to sufficient attention and concentration because the student is less concerned about the outcome and feedback from others. In addition, positive affects such as satisfaction should be provided by progressive mastery, in contrast to the suspension of any sense of success until a final outcome goal is attained.

Our study 2 provides evidence that the relationship between intrinsic motivation and learning strategies is independent of self-efficacy. It is particularly important for learning by students who suffer from lack of academic competence. Whereas self-efficacy or academic competence is a significant component predicting active engagement and superior performance in learning (Pintrich, 2003), it is clear that not all students perceive themselves as being academically competent as long as they are in the classroom, where normative ability is accurately perceived (Nicholls, Cheung, Lauer, and Patashnick, 1989). For the students who must have low competence compared with others, it may be more effective for adaptive learning to provide intrinsic interest in a task and help to shift their focus from a normative standard to self-improvement, rather than to direct approaches to their competence.

The results regarding self-handicapping and the perception of threat associated with help-seeking assist us to understand the motivational nature of self-protective and consequently less productive learning. Elliot and Church (2003) found that self-handicapping was positively predicted by fear of failure and negatively predicted by need for achievement. It seems inevitable that extrinsic or performance orientation is linked to fear of the negative implication of failure. Under these types of motivation, failure is posited to be regarded as the cause of lowered self-esteem and evaluation from others (Dweck and Leggett, 1988), and thus it must either be avoided or an excuse must be found. In contrast, the more students are intrinsically motivated or oriented toward mastery goal in addition to their efficacy in controlling their behavior, the less they use these self-protective strategies. Under these motivations, failure is interpreted as a part of learning (Dweck and Leggett, 1988) so that there is no need for avoiding it or preparing execution. As a result, proactive increases in performance discrepancies would occur, as goals would be raised and more challenging tasks would be sought. The primary implication is that self-protective strategies can be reduced not only by high student efficacy in managing the effort to learn, but also by an instructional effort that facilitate intrinsic interest toward the task and helps to shift the focus onto the task itself.

It is important to note that students need to know the strengths and weaknesses, or costs of using different motivations and strategies. Some are applicable in certain situations and not in others. There is no motivation or strategy which can satisfy all of a student's learning needs. For instance, the normative and diagnostic competence emphasized under introjected regulation or performance-approach goals should have an important informational function in learning processes (see Elliot and Moller, 2003). Even the performance-avoidance goal that has been demonstrated to be the most detrimental regulation may facilitate performance under some circumstances (e.g., Tanaka, 2004). It has also been suggested that a surface processing strategy can be used for both basic and complex or content learning tasks (Weinstein, Husman, and Dierking, 2000). Therefore, students should first obtain conditional knowledge about when any given strategy might or might not be effective. These issues should be investigated for building a more solid foundation for the development of applications at diverse educational settings.

Finally, it should be noted that the primary focus of this chapter is the student's side of the learning process. However, it is also important to examine what works in teaching, such as the nature of the content being taught, methods of teaching and assessment, and the institutional climate and procedures (Kember, Biggs, and Leung, 2004). For example, Murayama (2003) investigated how test format influenced students' use of learning strategies. He found that those who took essay tests used more deep processing strategies and fewer surface processing strategies, and took more notes than those who took the cloze procedure tests. He also made the striking finding that these effects were not seen in students with high mastery goal orientation. The individual students, teaching context, and learning outcomes form a system and affect each other (Kember, Biggs, and Leung, 2004). The interactions and cyclical relations between students' motivation, the teaching context, the use of learning strategies, and learning outcomes have yet to be fully explored. This will be an important area for future research to improve our understanding of learning and establish better practice in the classroom.

REFERENCES

Ames, C. (1992). Classrooms: Goals, structures, and student motivation. *Journal of Educational Psychology, 84,* 261-271.

Ames, C., and Ames, R. (1984). Systems of student and teacher motivation: Toward a qualitative definition. *Journal of Educational Psychology, 76,* 535-556.

Archer, J. (1994). Achievement goals as a measure of motivation in university students. *Contemporary Educational Psychology, 19,* 430-446.

Bandura, A. (1977). Self-efficacy: Toward a unifying theory of behavioral change. *Psychological Review, 84,* 191-215.

Bandura, A. (1991). *Guide for constructing Self-Efficacy Scales.* Unpublished manuscript.

Bandura, A. (1986). *Social foundations of thought and action: A social cognitive theory.* Englewood Cliffs, NJ: Prentice-Hall.

Bandura, A. (1993). Perceived self-efficacy in cognitive development and functioning. *Educational Psychologist, 28,* 117-148.

Bandura, A., and Schunk, D. H. (1981). Cultivation competence, self-efficacy, and intrinsic interest through proximal self-motivation. *Journal of Personality and Social Psychology, 41,* 586-598.

Bielaczyc, K., Pirolli, P. L., and Brown, A. L. (1995). Training in self-explanation and self-regulation strategies: Investigating the effects of knowledge acquisition activities on problem solving. *Cognition and Instruction, 13,* 221-252.

Bjorklund, D. F., and Zeman, B. R. (1983). The development of organizational strategies in children's recall of familiar information: Using social organization to recall the names of classmateds. *International Journal of Behavioral Development, 6,* 341-353.

Boekaerts, M. (1997). Self-regulated learning: A new concept embraced by researchers, policy makers, educators, teachers, and students. *Learning and Instruction, 7,* 161-186.

Butler, R., and Neuman, O. (1995). Effects of task and ego achievement goals on help-seeking behaviors and attitudes. *Journal of Educational Psychology, 87,* 261-271.

Deci, E. L. (1975). *Intrinsic motivation.* New York: Plenum.

Deci, E. L., and Ryan, R. M. (1985). *Intrinsic motivation and self-determination in human behavior.* New York: Plenum Press.

Deci, E. L., and Ryan, R. M. (1987). The support of autonomy and the control of behavior. *Journal of Personality and Social Psychology, 53,* 1024-1037.

Deci, E. L., and Ryan, R. M. (1991). A motivational approach to self: Integration in personality. In R. Dienstbier (Ed.), *Nebraska Symposium on Motivation* (Vol. 36, pp. 237-288). Lincoln: University of Nebraska Press.

Deci, E. L., and Ryan, R. M. (2002). *Handbook of self-determination research.* Rochester, NY: University of Rochester Press.

Deppe, R. K., and Harackiewicz, J. M. (1996). Self-handicapping and intrinsic motivation: Buffering intrinsic motivation from the threat of failure. *Journal of Personality and Social Psychology, 70,* 868-876.

Dweck, C. S. (1986). Motivational processes affecting learning. *American Psychologist, 41,* 1040-1048.

Dweck, C. S., and Leggett, E. L. (1988). A social-cognitive approach to motivation and personality. *Psychological Review, 95,* 256-273.

Elliot, A. J. (1999). Approach and Avoidance motivation and achievement goals. *Educational Psychologist, 34,* 169-189.

Elliot, A. J., and Church, M. A. (1997). A hierarchical model of approach and avoidance achievement motivation. *Journal of Personality and Social Psychology, 72,* 218-232.

Elliot, A. J., and Church, M. A. (2003). A motivational analysis of defensice pessimism and self-handicapping. *Journal of Personality, 71,* 369-396.

Elliot, A. J., and Harackiewicz, J. M. (1996). Approach and avoidance achievement goals and intrinsic motivation: A mediational analysis. *Journal of Personality and Social Psychology, 70,* 461-475.

Elliot, A. J., and McGregor, H. (1999). Test anxiety and the hierarchical model of approach and avoidance achievement motivation. *Journal of Personality and Social Psychology, 76,* 628-644.

Elliot, A. J., and McGregor, H., and Gable, S. (1999). Achievement goals, study strategies, and exam performance: A mediational analysis. *Journal of Educational Psychology, 91,* 549-563.

Elliot, A. J., and Moller, A. C. (2003). Performance-approach goals: Good or bad forms of regulation? *International Journal of Educational Research, 39,* 339-356.

Harackiewicz, J. M., Barron, K.E., Carter, S. M., Lehto, A. T., and Elliot, A. J. (1997). Predictors and consequences of achievement goals in the college classroom: Maintaining interest and making the grade. *Journal of Personality and Social Psychology, 73,* 1284-1295.

Karabenick, S. A., and Knapp, J. R. (1991). Relationship of academic help seeking to the use of learning strategies and other achiement behavior in college students. *Journal of Educational Psychology, 83,* 221-230.

Karabenick, S. A., and Sharma, R. (1994). Seeking academic assistance as a strategic learning resource. In P. Pintrich, D. Brown, and C. Weinstein (Eds.), *Student motivation. cognition, and learning* (pp. 189-211). Hillsdale, NJ: Erlbaum.

Kember, D., Biggs, J., and Leung, D. Y. (2004). Examining the multidimensionality of approaches to learning through the development of revised version of the Learning Process Questionnaire. *British Journal of Educational Psychology, 74,* 261-280.

Linnenbrink, E. A., and Pintrich, P. R. (2000). Multiple pathways to learning and achievement: The role of goal orientation in fostering adaptive motivation, affect, and cognition. In C. Sansone and J. M. Harackiewicz (Eds.), *Intrinsic and extrinsic motivation: The search for optimal motivation and performance* (pp. 195-227). San Diego: Academic Press.

McKeachie, W. J., Pintrich, P. R., and Lin, Y. –G. (1985). Teaching learning strategies. *Educational Psychologist, 82,* 189-200.

Meece, J. L., Blumenfeld, P. C., and Hoyle, R. H. (1988). Students' goal orientations and cognitive engagement in classroom activities. *Journal of Educational Psychology, 80,* 514-523.

Middleton, M., and Midgley, C. (1997). Avoiding the demonstration of lack of ability: An underexplored aspect of goal theory. *Journal of Educational Psychology, 89,* 710-718.

Murayama, K. (2003). Test format and learning strategy use. *Japanese Journal of Educational Psychology, 51,* 1-12.

Nadler, A. (1987). Determinants of help-seeking behavior: The effects of helper's similarity, task centrality and recipients' self-seteem. *European Journal of Social Psychology, 17,* 57-67.

Newman, R. S. (1990). Children's help-seeking in the classroom: The role of motivational factors and attitudes. *Journal of Educational Psychology, 82,* 71-80.

Newman, R. S. (1991). Goals and self-regulatory learning: What motivates children to seek academic help. In M. L. Maehr, and P. R. Pintrich (Eds.), *Advances in motivation and achievement: Goals and self-regulatory processes* (Vol. 7, pp. 151-183).

Newman, R. S. (1998). Studens' help seeking during problem solving: Influences of personal and contextual achievement goals. *Journal of Educational Psychology, 90,* 644-658.

Newman, R. S., and Goldin, L. (1990). Children's reactance to seek help with schoolwork. *Journal of Educational Psychology, 82,* 92-100.

Nicholls, J. G. (1984). Achievement motivation: Conceptions of ability, subjective experience, task choice, and performance. *Psychological Review, 91,* 328-346.

Nicholls, J. G., Cheung, P. C., Lauer, J., and Patashnick, M. (1989). Individual differences in academic motivation: Perceived ability, goals, beliefs, and values. *Learning and Individual Differences, 1,* 63-84.

Nicholls, J. G., Patashnick, M., and Nolen, S. B. (1985). Adolescents' theories of education. *Journal of Educational Psychology, 77,* 683-692.

Niemivirta, M. (1996). *Motivational-cognitive components in self-regulated learning.* Paper presented at the 5th International Conference on Motivation, March, 1996, Landau, Germany.

Pintrich, P. R. (2003). A motivational science perspective on the role of student motivation in learning and teaching contexts. *Journal of Educational Psychology, 95,* 667-686.

Pintrich, P. R., and DeGroot, E. V. (1990). Motivational and self-regulated leanrning components of classroom academic performance. *Journal of Educational Psychology, 82,* 33-40.

Pintrich, P. R., and Garcia, T. (1991). Student goal orientation and self-regulation in the college classroom. In M. L. Maehr and P. R. Pintrich (Eds.), *Advances in motivation and achievement* (Vol. 7, pp. 371-402). Greenwich, CT: JAI Press.

Pintrich, P. R., and Garcia, T. (1994). Self-regulated learning in college students: Knowledge, strategies, and motivatoin. In P. R. Pintich, D. R. Brown, and C. E. Weinstein (Eds.), *Student motivation, cognition, and learning* (pp. 113-133). Hillsdale, NJ: Lawrence Erlbaum Associates.

Pintrich, P. R., and Schunk, D. H. (2002). *Motivation in education: Theory, research, and practice.* Englewood Cliffs, NJ: Merrill.

Plant, R., and Ryan, R. M. (1985). Intrinsic motivation and the effects of self-consciousness, self-awareness, and ego-involvement: An investigation of internally controlling styles. *Journal of Personality, 53,* 435-449.

Rhodewalt, F. (1990). Self-handicappers: Individual differences in the preference for anticipatory self-protective acts. In R. L. Higgins, C. R. Snyder, and S. Berglas (Eds.), *Self-handicapping. The paradox that isn't* (pp. 69-106). New York: Plenum Press.

Rhodewalt, F. (1994). Conceptions of ability, achievement goals, and individual differences in self-handicapping behavior: On the application of implicit theories. *Journal of Personality, 62,* 67-85.

Rhodewalt, F., and Fairfield, M. (1991). Claimed self-handicaps and the self-handicapper: The relation of reduction in intended effort to performance. *Journal of Research in Personality, 25,* 402-417.

Rigby, C. S., Deci, E. L., Patrick, B. D., and Ryan, R. M. (1992). Beyond the intrinsic-extrinsic dichotomy: Self-determination in motivation and learning. *Motivation and Emotion, 16,* 165-185.

Rotter, J. 1966. Generalized expectancies for internal versus external control of reinforcement. *Psychological Monographs, 80,* 1-28.

Ryan, A. M., and Pintrich, P. R. (1997). "Should I ask for help?" The role of motivation and attitudes in adolescents' help seeking in math class. *Journal of Educational Psychology, 89,* 329-341.

Ryan, R. M. (1982). Control and information in the intrapersonal sphere: An extension of cognitive evaluation theory. *Journal of Personality and Social Psychology, 43,* 450-461.

Ryan, R. M. (1995). Psychological needs and the facilitation of integrative processes. *Journal of Personality, 63,* 397-427.

Ryan, R. M., and Connell, J. P. (1989). Perceived locus of causality and internalization: Examining reasons for acting in two domains. *Journal of Personality and Social Psychology, 57,* 749-761.

Ryan, R. M., Connell, J. P., and Deci, E. L. (1985). A motivational analysis of self-determination and self-regulation in education. In C. Ames and R. Ames (Eds.), *Research on motivation in education: The classroom milieu* (pp.13-51). New York: Academic Press.

Ryan, R. M., and Deci, E. J. (2000). When rewards compete with nature: The undermining of intrinsic motivation and self-regulation. In C. Sansone and J. M. Harackiewicz (Eds.), *Intrinsic and extrinsic motivation: The search for optimal motivation and performance* (pp. 13-54). San Diego: Academic Press.

Ryan, R. M., Koestner, R., and Deci, E. L. (1991). Ego-involved persistence: When free-choice behavior is not intrinsically motivated. *Motivation and Emotion, 15,* 185-205.

Seligman, M. E. P. (1975). *Helplessness.* San Francisco: Freeman.

Skaalvik, E. M. (1997). Self-enhancing and self-defeating ego orientation: Relations with task and avoidance orientation, achievement, self-perceptions, and anxiety. *Journal of Educational Psychology, 89,* 71-81.

Schunk, D. H. (1984). Self-efficacy perspective on achievement behavior. *Educational Psychologist, 19,* 48-58.

Snyder, C. R. (1990). Self-handicapping processes and sequelae: On the taking of a psychological dive. In R. L. Higgins, C. R. Snyder, and S. Berglas (Eds.), *Self-handicapping. The paradox that isn't* (pp. 107-150). New York: Plenum Press.

Tanaka, A. (in press). Examination of performance-avoidance goals in Japanese. *Developmental Reports of Social Motivation* (In Japanese with English abstract).

Tanaka, A., Murakami, Y., Okuno, T., and Yamauchi, H. (2002). Achievement goals, attitudes toward help-seeking, and help-seeking behavior in the classroom. *Learning and Individual Differences, 13,* 23-35.

Tanaka, K., and Yamauchi, H. (2000a). *The relation of self-efficacy on motivaiton and learning strategies.* Paper presented at 64th Japanese Psychological Conference, November, 2000, Kyoto, Japan.

Tanaka, K., and Yamauchi, H. (2000b). Influence of autonomy on perceived control beliefs and self-regulated learning in Japanese undergraduate students. *North American Journal of Psychology. 2,* 255-272.

Tice, D. M. (1991). Esteem protection or enhancement? Self-handicapping motives and attributions differ by trait self-esteem. *Journal of Personality and Social Psycholgy, 60,* 711-725.

Vallerand, R. J., Pelletier, L. G., Blais, M. R., Briere, N. M., Senecal, C., and Vallieres, E. F. (1992). The Academic Motivation Scale: a measure of intrinsic, extrinsic, and amotivation in education. *Educational and Psychological Measurement, 52,* 1006-1017.

Vallerand, R. J., Pelletier, L. G., Blais, M. R., Briere, N. M., Senecal, C., and Vallieres, E. F. (1993). On the assessment of intrinsic, extrinsic, and amotivation in education: Evidence on the concurrent and construct validity of the concurrent and construct validity of the Academic Motivation Scale. *Educational and Psychological Measurement, 53,* 159-172.

van der Meij, H. (1988). Constraints on question-asking in classrooms. *Journal of Educational Psychology, 80,* 401-405.

Weinstein, C. E., Husman, J., and Dierking, D. R. (2000). Self-regulation interventions with a focus on learning strateies. In M. Boekaerts, P. R. Pintrich, and M. Zeidner (Eds.), *Handbook of self-regulation* (pp. 727-747). San Diego, CA: Academic Press.

Weinstein, C. E., and Mayer, R. E. (1986). The teaching of learning strategies. In M. Wittrock (Ed.), *Handbook of research on teaching* (pp.315-327) New York: Macmillan.

Wolters, C. A., Yu, S. L., and Pintrich, P. R. (1996). The relation between goal orientation and students' motivational beliefs and self-regulated learning. Learning and Individual

Differences, 8, 211-238. Paris, S.G., Lipson, M. Y., and Wixson, K. K. (1983). Becoming a strategic reader. *Contemporary Educational Psychology, 8,* 293-316.

Yamauchi, H., and Tanaka, K. (1998). Relations of autonomy, self-referenced beliefs, and self-regulated learning among Japanese children. *Psychological Reports, 82,* 803-816.

Zimmerman, B. J. (1994) Investigation self-regulatory processes and perceptions of self-efficacy in writing by college students. In P. R. Pintrich, D. R. Brown, and C. E. Weinstein (Eds.), Student motivation, cognition, and learning. Hillsdale, NJ: Erlbaum. Pp. 239-256.

Zimmerman, B. J. (2000). Attaining self-regulation: A social cognitive perspective. In M. Boekaerts, P. R. Pintrich, and M. Zeidner (Eds.), *Handbook of self-regulation* (pp. 727-747). San Diego, CA: Academic Press.

Zimmerman, B. J., and Martinez-Pons, M. (1986) Development of a structured interview for assessing student use of self-regulated learning strategies. *American Educational Research Journal, 23,* 614-628.

Zimmerman, B. J., and Martinez-Pons, M. (1988). Construct validation of a strategy model of student self-regulated learning. *Journal of Educational Psychology, 80,* 284-290.

Zimmerman, B. J., and Martinez-Pons, M. (1990). Student differences in self-regulated learning: Relating grade, sex, and giftedness to self efficacy and strategy use. *Journal of Educational Psychology, 82,* 51-59.

Zuckerman, M., Kieffer, S. C., and Knee, C. R. (1998). Consequences of self-handicapping: Effects on coping, academic performance and adjustment. *Journal of Personality and Social Psychology, 74,* 1619-1628.

In: New Developments in Learning Research
Editor: Samuel N. Hogan, pp. 85-118
ISBN 1-59454-669-X
© 2006 Nova Science Publishers, Inc.

Chapter 5

WRITTEN METACOGNITIVE GUIDANCE - A PSYCHOLOGICAL TOOL THAT FACILITATES LEARNING AND COGNITIVE ACHIEVEMENTS

Eva Guterman
National Institute of Child Health and Human Development,
National Institutes of Health, Department of Health and Human Services

ABSTRACT

This chapter attempts to provide a theoretical-practical framework that links assessment practice to learning theory by synthesizing three theoretical axes of learning: Schema theory – emphasizing the role of prior knowledge in learning; Metacognitive awareness theory – profiling an expert reader; and the Vygotskian notion of the zone of proximal development – extending and facilitating learners' cognitive abilities and performance by providing a "psychological tool" (Vygotsky, 1978). This theoretical basis resulted in the development of written metacognitive awareness guidance – a "psychological tool" – whose fundamental purpose is to raise learners' metacognitive awareness of their prior knowledge (schemata) before they begin to process authentic reading assessment tasks. Increasing learners' metacognitive awareness by means of well-planned guidance based on their prior knowledge will not only facilitate their learning and improve the outcomes of assessment tasks, but will also increase their chances of internalizing the guidance components and applying them in changing learning situations. The chapter suggests stages in educational assessment to better serve the goal of equity, and to facilitate the kind of assessment that will benefit our students most, the kind of assessment to which our students are entitled.

"We ... are striving to discover not how the child came to be what he is, but how he can become what he is not yet " – Vygotsky, 1978

INTRODUCTION

Research in cognitive psychology has increased our understanding of the nature of competent performance and the principles of knowledge organization that underlie learners' abilities to learn, comprehend, construct meaning, solve problems, read and write. New ideas about ways to facilitate learning – and about who is most capable of learning – can powerfully affect the quality of people's lives. It has always been a concern that formal educational environments are better at identifying talent than at developing it (see, e.g., Bloom, 1964). Many people who had difficulty in school might have prospered if these new ideas about effective instructional practices had been available. Furthermore, given the new teaching practices, even those who did well in traditional educational environments might have developed skills, knowledge, and attitudes that could have significantly enhanced their achievements.

Overall, the new science of learning is providing knowledge that can significantly improve people's ability to become active, motivated, self-regulated learners. Thus, authentic and meaningful classroom activities that are relevant to real-life situations are likely to engender students' cognitive activity and conceptual change (transfer). Scaffolding, dual instruction (verbal persuasion and modeling), and teaching appropriate cognitive strategies are believed to have a positive impact on increasing students' efficacy.

Many advances in cognitive science have already been applied to classroom teaching and learning. Much less effort has been devoted to applying these advances to how learning can adequately be measured. The challenge of the research described here is to provide a theoretical-practical framework that links assessment practice to learning theory. It suggests stages in educational assessment to better serve the goal of equity, to facilitate the kind of assessment that will benefit our students most, the kind of assessment to which our students are entitled.

This chapter attempts to provide such a conceptual framework by synthesizing three theoretical axes of learning: Schema theory – emphasizing the role of prior knowledge in learning; Metacognitive awareness theory – profiling an expert reader; and the Vygotskian notion of the zone of proximal development – extending and facilitating learners' cognitive abilities and performance by providing a "psychological tool" (Vygotsky, 1978). This theoretical basis resulted in the development of written metacognitive awareness guidance – a "psychological tool" – whose fundamental purpose is to raise learners' metacognitive awareness of their prior knowledge (schemata) before they begin to process authentic reading assessment tasks. Increasing learners' metacognitive awareness by means of well-planned guidance based on their prior knowledge will not only facilitate their learning and improve the outcomes of assessment tasks, but will also increase their chances of internalizing the guidance components and applying them in changing learning situations.

SCHEMA THEORY – THE ROLE OF PRIOR KNOWLEDGE IN LEARNING

Cognitive psychology views the learner as an information processing system, assuming that incoming information is processed at various levels and finally stored in long term memory as knowledge. Schema theory is basically a theory about knowledge, about how knowledge is represented and about how that representation facilitates the use of knowledge in particular ways. According to schema theory, all knowledge is packed into units. These units are called schemata (the plural of schema). Schemata reflect the prior knowledge, experiences, conceptual understandings, attitudes, values, skills, and procedures a reader brings to a reading situation. Embedded in these packets of knowledge is, in addition to the knowledge itself, information about how this knowledge is to be used. Schemata have been called the 'building blocks of cognition' (Rumelhart, 1980) and a 'cognitive map of the world' (Neisser, 1976) because they represent the abstract structure of knowledge and the elaborate networks of concepts, skills, and procedures which we use to make sense of new stimuli, events, and situations. This abstract term is used by cognitive psychologists to describe how humans organize and construct meaning. Instructionally, schema theory addresses:

- The essential role of prior knowledge in learners' performance
- The contribution derived from activating the learner's prior knowledge
- The significance of fostering the learner's ability to focus attention on information relevant to performance
- The significance of fostering the learner's ability to build connections among relevant pieces of information
- The significance of fostering the learner's ability to build connections between existing knowledge and new knowledge

Schema provides a framework that allows readers to organize text information more efficiently and effectively and to integrate new information into old, which facilitates retention. Schema allows readers to make inferences about what happened or is likely to happen in the text, thus helping learners to predict upcoming information or to fill in gaps in the material. Schema helps readers to elaborate upon the material. Elaboration, a cognitive activity that involves speculation, judgment, and evaluation, is a powerful aspect of reasoning with print. Schema theory provides powerful support for the importance of prior knowledge in reading comprehension, meaning construction, and learning. According to schema theory, readers understand what they read only as it relates to what they already know, e.g., their existing knowledge about a particular topic influences the extent to which they understand what they will read about that topic.

In general terms, schema engagement relates to: (1) the reader's initial contact with a text, (2) the reader's ability to relate his or her own background of experience to the information represented within the text, and (3) the reader's ability to focus and refine his or her understanding of the text material. Over the years, researchers have demonstrated that readers use their prior knowledge to integrate new information, and that prior knowledge can be used to disambiguate text, indicating that prior knowledge is a major influence on reading comprehension (Bransford and Johnson, 1972; Johnston, 1984; Langer and Nicholich, 1981; Pearson, Hansen, and Gordon, 1979). Other researchers have found that many poor (less successful) readers have difficulty using prior knowledge (Holmes, 1983; Lipson, 1982; Marr and Gormely, 1982). Research has emphasized that not only does lack of knowledge about a topic impede comprehension, but the extent of knowledge influences the quality of understanding a reader can construct. Voss and his colleagues (Means and Voss, 1985;

Spilich, Vesonder, Chiesi, and Voss, 1979) and Chi and her colleagues (Chi, 1978; Chi, Feltovitch, and Glaser, 1981; Chi, Glaser, and Reese, 1982; Chi and Koeske, 1983) showed the advantage in comprehension for high knowledge versus low knowledge individuals. In their review, Pearson, Hansen and Gordon (1979) suggested that increasing a child's store of conceptual knowledge may do more to increase reading comprehension than skill training. They tested the comprehension of second grade children having high and low levels of knowledge about spiders, on a text that dealt with spiders. The children differed on spider knowledge, but not on IQ or achievement test scores. Both explicit and implicit questions were asked to assess comprehension. The high-knowledge group performed significantly better overall, mainly due to their ability to answer the implicit questions. This suggests that comprehension requiring integration of text and world knowledge may be especially facilitated by strong knowledge of the content topic. An important point to be drawn from this and other studies (such as Spilich et al., 1979) is that all the subjects had some knowledge about the content subject being investigated. Clearly, it is the extent and quality of that knowledge that determines how well a text is comprehended.

Because a text is rarely fully explicit, readers must draw from their existing knowledge in order to understand it. Authors expect readers to 'fill in' and 'connect' information in certain predictable way. Decisions about what to fill in and how to connect parts of text are made on the basis of prior knowledge: specific prior knowledge (text-specific and topic-specific) and general world knowledge. Thus the reader's contribution to the act of comprehension is significant, and, in fact, the meaning constructed from the same text can vary greatly among readers because of differences in the level of knowledge available to understand the text, or because some readers may have knowledge that they do not fully utilize. Variations in interpretation often arise because readers have different conceptions about the topic than the author supposed (R. C. Anderson, 1983). In view of this, one can suggest three reasons to explain why readers fail to correctly understand a text:

1. The reader may not have the appropriate schemata. In such a case, s/he simply cannot understand the concept being communicated.
2. The reader may have the appropriate schemata, but the clues provided by the author may be insufficient. Here again, the reader will not understand the text but, with appropriate additional clues, may come to understand it.
3. The reader constructs his or her own meaning. The conception of meaning, which is uniquely determined by each reader and is viewed as dynamic, fluid, socially and culturally located, is illusive.

One clear implication of this, is that some learners may appear to have poor comprehension and understanding skills, not because they have some inherent comprehension or understanding 'deficits', but because they lack or fail to activate the prior knowledge (background knowledge) that was presupposed by the message or the text. Clearly, there are many different levels at which a learner may lack the background knowledge necessary to understand the text.

ACTIVATING AND BUILDING SCHEMATA

A logical extension of the view that new knowledge must be constructed from existing knowledge is the need to identify learners' existing knowledge and beliefs about any of the topics, issues, subjects or concepts and the need to build on them. If the students' initial knowledge, ideas and beliefs are ignored, the understanding that they develop may be very different from what was intended to be learned and or assessed.

A common misconception regarding constructivist theories of knowing (that existing knowledge is used to build new knowledge) is that teachers should never tell students anything directly but, instead, should always allow learners to construct knowledge for themselves. This perspective confuses a theory of pedagogy (teaching) with a theory of knowing. Constructivists assume that all knowledge is constructed from previous knowledge, irrespective of how one is taught (e.g., Cobb, 1994) – even listening to a lecture involves active attempts to construct new knowledge. It is true that sometimes simply lecturing doesn't work. Nevertheless, there are times, usually after learner have first grappled with issues on their own, that "teaching by telling" can work extremely well (e.g., Schwartz and Bransford, 1998). However, students still may need to be helped to act upon and interact with the main ideas of a reading selection *before* they encounter them in print. The value of pre-reading preparation lies in helping comprehenders recognize what they know and what they need to find out more about. This involves building and activating schemata. Two pivotal questions that readers must ask themselves as they approach a reading task are "What do I already know about the subject?" and "What do I need to know?". Readers must learn how to take inventory of their own store of knowledge and experience. Helping students reflect in this manner is crucial from an instructional point of view. For one thing, it's a great confidence booster to know that you know something about a subject to be encountered in print. One of the challenges of teaching is convincing children that they know more about the text than they often give themselves credit for (Vacca, Vacca, and Gove, 1995). On the other hand, "What do I already know?" also helps students recognize what they don't know, but will learn more about from reading. Thus, with respect to reading comprehension, schema theory encourages us to ask: "What is it that children may already know? And how can I use what they know to help them deal with the new ideas that I would like them to know?" rather than, "What is it that children do not know? And how can I get it into their heads?".

When faced with a text, students may lack an available schema for comprehending the material. Here is where background-building activities will help develop a frame of reference to enable students to handle incoming information in text. Although students may have a schema for reading, they may fail to bring it to bear as they read. Novice readers are often unaware that prior knowledge is of consequence to what they need to know. Tierney and Pearson (1994) drew up a set of pedagogical questions (paraphrased below) driven by a schema theoretic perspective. They suggested using them as guidelines for an instructional decision-making process to improve students' reading comprehension and learning from text.

- Does the reader possess the relevant schemata needed for approaching a text?
- Is the reader's schema (purpose, background knowledge, attention, focus, interest) activated prior to, during, and after reading? Is the reader's relevant background experience activated during reading?

- When reading for different purposes, does the reader exhibit flexible processes in terms of activating, focusing, maintaining, and refining an interpretation?
- Is the reader aware of the strategies available for coping with different texts and purposes for reading?
- To what extent is the reader's understanding adequate for coping with the text? When a reader's understanding diverges from the author's intention, does the reader justify his or her idiosyncratic interpretation? Does the reader recognize his or her perspective and the perspective of others?
- Is the reader aware of his or her level of understanding of a text read for different purposes?
- Does the reader recognize new learning and its potential application?

By the time children begin school, most have built a considerable knowledge store that is relevant to reading and constructing new knowledge from reading. They have experiences of reading (print and pictures), listening to various informative-communicative media (books, newspapers, TV, computer) and participate actively in oral talks, discussions, negotiations in their everyday play. If children's knowledge is tapped and built on as teachers attempt to teach them, it is likely that children will acquire a more coherent and thorough understanding than if they are taught as isolated abstractions. Without specific guidance from teachers, students may fail to connect everyday knowledge to subjects taught in school.

The reading process requires retrieval of information about the topic and about the format employed in the written discourse. For example, to read and understand a technical article, one must not only understand the meaning of the words, phrases, and sentences used, but also the conventions specific to technical articles such as the meaning of various types of headings, abbreviations, and so on.

READERS CONSTRUCT THEIR OWN MEANING

In accordance with schema theory, meaning is not a product, but a process that takes place between the individual and the environment and, in our case, between the reader and the text, between old schemata and new. Meaning is determined through the process of transaction between reader and text ('top down' processing), between text and reader ('bottom up' processing), between reader/text and context, and among textual elements on and across various levels. The term 'transactions' is used to suggest the dynamic change that takes place in readers whenever they decide to actively engage in reading, in constructing meaning, understanding, learning – making sense of what is being read. The figure below is a simplified illustration of transaction elements involved in the meaning-making process:

A key point in schema theory, then, is that reading comprehension is akin to the progressive refinement of a scenario or model that a reader develops for a text (Collins, Brown, and Larkin, 1977). That is, reading comprehension proceeds and inferencing occurs via the refinement of the reader's own model. The reader's schemata will be involved in the construction of a scenario which accounts for elements and relationships within the text and in the world as the reader sees it. If the reader's model seems tenable, then those schemata that comprise the model will be involved in the further text processing.

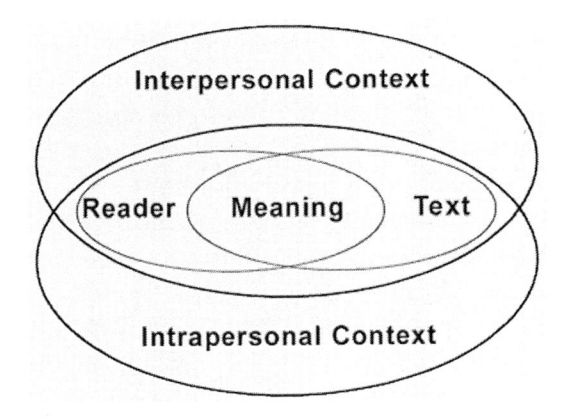

Figure 1: Transactions in the Meaning-Making Process

If the reader's model seems untenable, then schemata will drive the re-examination, reconstruction, or restructuring of elements in the text to build a new model.

Clearly, therefore, a reader's background knowledge, including his or her purposes, has an overriding influence upon the reader's development of meaning; and reading comprehension involves activating, focusing, maintaining and refining ideas towards developing interpretations (models) that are plausible, interconnected and complete. Different readers may develop different interpretations of the same text. In fact, as Norris and Phillips (1987) suggest, the essence of critical reading is raising alternative interpretations, weeding out interpretations to the extent that available information will allow, and then remaining with multiple possibilities. In their view, literary thinking is a complex reasoning process that involves analyzing, synthesizing, reformulating, linking, and generalizing ideas. This is an important point when considering assessment. In evaluating students, we can no linger simply judge whether or not the reader's conclusions are similar to the teacher's or to those of the writer of the test. Instead, what is more important is the quality of the reader's argument or justification.

METACOGNITIVE AWARENESS - A PROFILE OF AN EXPERT READER

Metacognition is another important aspect of a learner's ability to learn (Bereiter and Scardamalia, 1989; Brown, 1978; Flavell and Wellman, 1977). The concept of metacognition, or thinking about thinking, is a key contribution of the cognitive revolution. Vygotsky (1962) describes two phases in the development of knowledge: initially, automatic unconscious acquisition, followed by a gradual increase in the active conscious control over knowledge. The distinction between the two is essentially the difference between cognitive and metacognitive aspects of performance.

Cognition refers to the intellectual functioning of the human mind and is characterized by automatic information processing which requires little mental effort or conscious attention on the part of the learner, and little direct control and attention. It is a rapid, unconscious process.

Metacognition refers to one's knowledge, awareness, and control over this cognitive process. It is characterized by controlled information processing, requiring the learner to be aware of, and to invest mental effort, direct control, and attention in learning.

Cognition implies having the skills. Metacognition refers to awareness of, and conscious control over, those skills. The distinction is similar to one made by Brown (1978; 1980) between 'knowing', 'knowing how to know', and 'knowing about knowing'. Miller, Golanter and Pribram (1960) proposed a relation between 'plans' and 'metaplans' that is also similar to the distinction between cognition and metacognition. They suggested that learning occurs only when the person has some kind of a plan. Furthermore, a plan will not be achieved without "intent to learn ... without executing a metaplan for constructing that which will guide recall" (1960, p. 129). These metaplans generate alternative plans. Once a plan is available, a control process, referred to as a Test-Operate-Test-Exit (TOTE) unit, guides behavior. This TOTE unit continually monitors the progress of the plan currently activated. It is believed that TOTE units and metaplans roughly correspond to the mechanisms of knowledge and control used by mature readers, and that plans correspond to specific strategies which can be activated by higher order cognitive control processes.

METACOGNITIVE COMPONENTS

Flavell (1979) divides metacognitive activity into two categories:

- activities concerned with conscious reflection on one's cognitive abilities and processes
- activities concerned with self-regulation mechanisms during ongoing attempts to learn, read, write or solve problems.

The first category of metacognitive activity involves metacognitive knowledge, consisting primarily of knowledge or beliefs about what factors or variables act and interact, in ways that affect the course and outcome of cognitive enterprises. In this first category of metacognitive knowledge, Flavell delineates three major subcategories:

1. *Personal knowledge* - encompasses everything the student/learner knows and believes about him/herself and other students as a cognitive processor; a person's knowledge about his or her own cognitive resources and the compatibility between the person as a learner and the learning situation.
2. *Task knowledge* - concerns the information available to the student/learner during a cognitive enterprise; the knowledge and awareness of the knowledge about the components of the learning task (abundant or meager, familiar or unfamiliar, well- or poorly-organized, interesting or dull, trustworthy or untrustworthy, etc.). Metacognitive task knowledge is familiarity with these variations, awareness of them in the process of learning, understanding what they imply, and knowing how the cognitive enterprise can best be managed, and how successful the learner is likely to be in achieving his/her goal.
3. *Strategy knowledge* - involves knowledge of whatever strategies are likely to be effective in achieving sub-goals and goals in any sort of cognitive activity undertaken. Flavell (1979) considers this knowledge to represent a very significant,

influential factor in the success or failure of the learner in every task, problem, or other cognitive activity.

The second category of metacognition, that of self-regulation, involves content-free strategies or procedural knowledge. It is used by an active learner during the on-going attempt to learn. These metacognitive activities include checking the outcome of an attempt to learn, planning one's next move, monitoring the effectiveness of an attempted action, and testing, revising and evaluating one's strategies for learning.

Brown (1978) refers to this category as an "executive control system" – a system capable of performing intelligent evaluations of its own operation. He suggested to distinguish between three major activities:

Planning - Activities undertaken prior to problem-solving; tasks which predict outcomes, schedule strategies, and determine various forms of trial and error, etc.

Monitoring - Activities during learning: testing, revising, rescheduling one's strategies for learning.

Checking - Activities evaluating the outcome of any strategic action against the criteria of efficiency and effectiveness.

Haller, Child and Walberg (1988) summarized the essence of metacognition by describing three clusters of activities:

Awareness - one's recognition of implicit or explicit information.
Monitoring - self-questioning and paraphrasing to stimulate understanding.
Regulating - composing and contracting more plausible solutions in problem-solving.

Flavell (1979) relates to one more type of metacognitive awareness which reveals important aspects of effective learning - *metacognitive experiences*. Metacognitive experiences refer to where you are in an enterprise and what sort of progress you are making, or are likely to make: you believe/feel that you have almost memorized those instructions, you are suddenly stymied in your attempt to understand something you are reading; you have just begun to solve what you sense will be an easy problem, and so forth. Metacognitive experiences are best described as items of metacognitive knowledge that have entered consciousness.

Metacognitive experiences can have a very important effect on cognitive goals or tasks, on metacognitive knowledge, and on cognitive actions or strategies. First, they can lead one to establish new goals and to revise or abandon old ones. Experiences of puzzlement or failure, for example, can have any of these effects. Second, metacognitive experiences can affect one's metacognitive knowledge base by adding to it, deleting from it, or revising it. One can observe relationships among goals, means, metacognitive experiences, and task outcomes.

A metacognitive experience occurs when a learner has an 'aha!' feeling about cognition. T. H. Anderson (1980) describes metacognitive experience in reading as 'clicks' (awareness of cognitive success, usually of understanding and remembering) and 'clunks' (awareness of cognitive failure, usually of information confusion or forgetting). The 'aha!' that something is wrong with a reading enterprise is as good as the 'aha!' that all is well. Only when readers detect problems can they adjust processing strategies, perhaps by re-reading a confusing portion of text, slowing down their pace, or consulting an external source for a key definition.

According to a model of metacognitive components proposed by Flavell and other metacognitive theoreticians (see Figure 2), the monitoring of cognitive enterprises proceeds through the actions of, and interactions among, metacognitive knowledge, goals/tasks, and action/strategies. This model implies a dynamic interplay of interaction or combination among three types of metacognitive variables in any situation of learning and/or processing information.

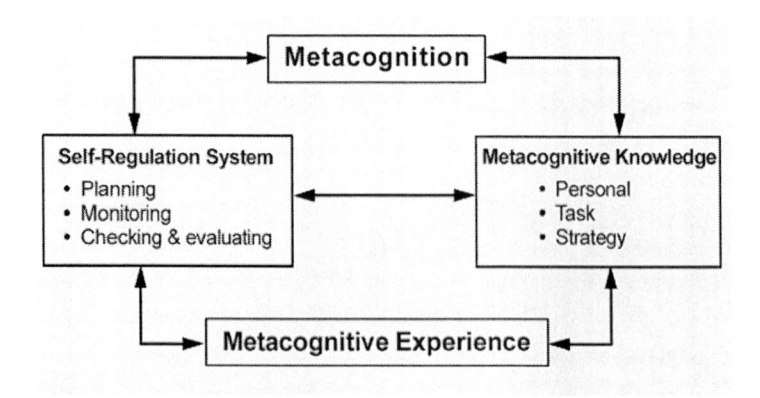

Figure 2: Model of Metacognitive Components (An interactive and integrative model)

Metacognitive awareness of (a) the basic strategies of reading and studying; (b) simple rules of text construction; (c) differing demands of a variety of tasks; and (d) the importance of using any background knowledge, are all prerequisites to self-regulation. Basically this metacognitive awareness is the ability to monitor and check one's own cognitive activities while reading/studying/understanding and creating new knowledge (Baker and Brown, 1984a, 1984b; Brown, Bransford, Ferrara, and Campione, 1983).

Researchers investigating reading comprehension monitoring among skilled and unskilled readers have long recognized the importance of metacognitive awareness in reading comprehension because it distinguishes between these two types of readers. Paris and Jacobs (1984) provided an illustration of the differences between skilled readers and poor or novice readers: *Skilled readers* often engage in deliberate activities that require planful thinking, flexible strategies, and periodic self-monitoring. They think about the topic, look forward and backward in the passage, and check their own understanding as they read. *Novice readers* or poor readers do not recruit and use these skills. Indeed, novice readers often seem oblivious to these strategies and the need to use them (Paris and Jacobs, 1984, p. 2083).

According to Snow, Burns, and Griffin (1998), skilled readers are good comprehenders. They differ from unskilled readers in "their use of general world knowledge to comprehend text literally as well as to draw valid inferences from texts, in their comprehension of words, and in their use of comprehension monitoring and repair strategies" (p. 62). Pressley and Afflerbach (1995) pointed out that skilled readers approach the reading task with a number of general tendencies. For example, they tend to be aware of what they are reading; they seem to know why they are reading; and they have a set of tentative plans or strategies for handling potential problems and for monitoring their comprehension of textual information. Unskilled readers, on the other hand, are quite limited in their metacognitive knowledge about reading (Paris and Winograd, 1990). They do relatively little monitoring of memory, comprehension, or other cognitive tasks (Flavell, 1979; Markman, 1979) and tend to focus on reading as a decoding process rather than as a meaning-getting process (Baker and Brown, 1984b). In addition, they are less likely than skilled readers to detect contradictions or resolve inconsistencies in understanding text (Snow et al., 1998). Finally, they seem not to realize that they do not understand (Garner and Reis, 1981) and as a result, fail to exercise control of their reading processes (Wagner and Sternberg, 1987).

Pearson, Roehler, Dole, and Duffy (1992) synthesize research about reading comprehension processes into a set of seven strategies that consistently surface as a part of the repertoire of the successful reader. Successful meta-readers are those who:

- Search for connections between what they know and the new information they encounter in the texts they read
- Monitor the adequacy of their models of text meaning
- Take steps to repair faulty comprehension once they realize they have failed to understand something
- Learn early on to distinguish important from less important ideas in texts they read
- Are adept at synthesizing information within and across texts and reading experiences
- Draw inferences during and after reading to achieve a full integrated understanding of what they read
- Sometimes consciously, and almost always unconsciously, ask questions of themselves, the authors they encounter, and the texts they read

Meta-readers monitor their state of learning; they plan strategies, adjust effort appropriately, and evaluate the success of their on-going attempt to understand. A fundamental aspect of a meta-reader's metacognition is the ability to monitor the current state of the on-going attempt to read/learn/understand and to create new knowledge. This ability depends on the reader's knowledge of four major factors: text, task, strategy, and learner characteristics. All of these influence the degree to which a meta-reader will be able to coordinate plans and engage in active monitoring, which in turn will lead to successful reading and studying outcomes. Research has provided insight into what successful meta-readers specifically do *before*, *during* and *after* reading.

Before reading, successful readers consider what the text is going to be about, what they already know about the topic and the text, and what specifically they are looking for as they read. *During reading*, meta-readers ask themselves many questions: Does the meaning they are developing make sense? What might come next? Are they using the right background information? What might they do to understand better? *After reading*, meta-readers decide if they have successfully read the text, whether they should go back and examine specific parts of the text, or whether they should reread for different purposes using a different strategy.

Whenever students are engaged in a process of generating questions throughout reading, they are involved in active comprehension. Nolte and Singer (1985) explain that teachers can show students how to generate their own questions for a story by adhering to a 'phase-in, phase-out' strategy. Phase-in, phase-out refers to gradually shifting the burden of responsibility for question-asking from the teacher to the students. A good deal of this strategy involves modeling question-asking behavior and making students aware of the value of questions before, during, and after reading. Self-questioning as a monitoring strategy helps students to set a purpose for reading and to direct the reading behavior. Asking questions involves readers in the process of predicting, verifying, judging and extending thinking about the text materials, and builds critical awareness of the reader's role and responsibility while interacting with the text.

Palincsar and Brown (1984) provide additional strong evidence for the effectiveness of student-generated questions. In a series of studies, they trained junior high school students in four important learning strategies: summarizing, questioning, clarifying, and predicting. Careful modeling in the form of a teacher-student pair was established to train students how to ask good questions. The researchers reported impressive effects for their instructional intervention program.

Figures 3 and 4 sum up the discussion of the metacognitive components of reading and studying, and the role of successful (meta) readers (based on Brown, 1980, 1982a, 1982b; Pearson, 1993; Pearson et al., 1992).

---

1. The reader consciously intends to control the reading act (a metacognitive experience) - create a focus
2. The reader establishes the goal of the reading act - a purpose, reason(s) for doing it
3. The reader mentally reviews prior knowledge of author, topic and skills; considers reading rate
4. The reader makes predictions/hypothesis about:
   a. content and text structure
   b. type of responses indicated by the questions (such as compose/construct, detail)
5. The reader begins to construct an idea about text content and its relation to prior knowledge
6. The reader recalls prior knowledge of reading - learning strategies.
7. The reader focuses on his/her own metacognitive knowledge (a metacognitive experience)
   a. knowledge of her/his cognitive processes
   b. knowledge of the demands imposed by different reading goals and different types of reading material
8. The reader strategically plans the regulation and monitoring of the reading act
   a. Consideration of metacognitive skills and strategies:
      Reading, skimming, summarizing
      Paraphrasing, predicting
      Looking for important ideas
      Testing one's understanding
      Discovering what is still unknown
      Designing a possible structure or method for approaching the topic
      Considering application to other situations- further concept into long term memory
      Identifying the pattern of text
      Sequencing
      Looking for relationships
      Reading ahead for clarification
      Mentally executing the directions
      Relating new knowledge to prior knowledge
   b. Selection of metacognitive skills and strategies
   c. Implementation of the skills and strategies
9. Periodic assessment of reading success (a metacognitive experience)
   a. Evaluate comprehension
   b. Identify important information
   c. Engage in review of other fix-up strategies
   d. Evaluate process
   e. Monitor need for further action

Figure 3: Metacognition and the Reading Process

Meta-components	Meta-reader
Plan	What am I doing? Why I am doing it? Why is it important? What kind of text is this? What do I already know? What do I expect to learn? What do I need to do when I am done?

Strategy	How/Where does this fit in with I already know?
	What questions do I have?
	Sets purpose according to:
	  a. prior knowledge
	  b. author's intent
	  c. task demands
	  d. lesson objective

Monitor	Do I need a specific plan to understand or learn about this?
	How effective have I been in this process?
	Do I need to do more?
	Uses prior knowledge to:
	  a. predict
	  b. make inferences
	  c. note new learned information
	  d. ask questions
	Detects unclear text fix up
	Elaborates/Summarizes

Evaluate	How can I use this information in other areas of my life? What did I learn? Was I able to meet the demand of the task? How do my responses differ from others? When should I read like this again?

Figure 4: The Role of the Meta-reader

As can be concluded from the above, both pre-existing knowledge (schema theory) and metacognitive awareness of one's prior knowledge are foundations of the comprehension process. Being aware of the different kinds of prior knowledge, and the need to use this knowledge in the process of constructing meaning and creating knowledge from written text, are essential parts of the reading process and lie at the heart of all mindful activity of the learner. Basically, we can say that prior knowledge makes the difference between success and failure in any cognitive task. In other words, successful meta-readers use existing knowledge to make sense of text; they monitor their comprehension throughout the reading process and they ask questions.

METACOGNITIVE AWARENESS AND TRANSFER

Metacognitive skills possess an enormous potential for 'transfer' – learning something in one situation and then applying it to another, significantly different, one. Salomon and Perkins (1989) distinguish between two fundamentally different mechanisms of transfer: 'low road' and 'high road'. 'Low road' transfer depends on the reflexive activation of well-practiced patterns. It is automatic and mindless. In contrast, 'high road' transfer depends on the conscious, aware abstraction of principles from one context, to their application in another. Thus, transfer can be improved by helping students become more aware of themselves as learners who actively monitor their learning strategies and resources and assess their readiness for particular tests and performances. After a series of experiments, Brown (1994) and Campione and Brown (1990) concluded that transfer is more likely when (a) the knowledge to be transferred figures in a cause/effect relationship; (b) there is emphasis during learning on flexibility and the possibility of multiple application; (c) some effort is made to separate the principle from the initial learning context.

Metacognitive approaches to instruction have been shown to increase the degree of transfer without the need for explicit prompting of students. The following examples illustrate research on teaching metacognitive skills across domains of reading, writing, and mathematics. Reciprocal teaching to increase reading comprehension (Palincsar and Brown, 1984) is designed to help students acquire specific knowledge and also to learn a set of strategies for explicating, elaborating, and monitoring necessary for independent learning. The three major components of reciprocal teaching are instruction and practice of strategies that enable students to monitor their understanding; provision, initially by a teacher, of an expert model of metacognitive processes; and a social setting that enables joint negotiation for understanding. The knowledge-acquisition strategies that students learn in working on a specific text are not acquired as abstract memorized procedures, but as skills instrumental in achieving subject-area knowledge and understanding. The instructional procedure is reciprocal in the sense that a teacher and a group of students take turns in leading the group to discuss and use strategies for comprehending and remembering text content.

A program of procedural facilitation for teaching written composition (Scardamalia, Bereiter, and Steinbach, 1984) shares many features with reciprocal teaching. The method prompts learners to adopt the metacognitive activities embedded in sophisticated writing strategies. The prompts help learners think about and reflect on the activities by getting them to identify goals, generate new ideas, improve and elaborate existing ideas, and strive for idea cohesion. Students in the procedural facilitation program take turns presenting their ideas to the group and detailing how they use prompts in planning to write. The teacher also models these procedures. Thus, the program involves modeling, scaffolding, and taking turns which are designed to help students externalize mental events in a collaborative context. Alan Schoenfeld (1983; 1985; 1991) teaches heuristic methods for mathematical problem solving to college students. The methods are derived, to some extent, from Polya's (1957) problem-solving heuristics. Schoenfeld's program adopts methods similar to reciprocal teaching and procedural facilitation. He teaches and demonstrates control or managerial strategies and makes explicit such processes as generating alternative courses of action, evaluating which course one will be able to carry out and whether it can be managed in the time available, and assessing one's progress. Again, elements of modeling, coaching, and scaffolding, as well as collective problem solving and whole-class and small group discussions, are used. Gradually, students come to ask self-regulatory questions themselves as the teacher fades out. At the end of each of the problem-solving sessions, students and teacher alternate in characterizing major themes by analyzing what they did and why. The recapitulations highlight the generalizable features of the critical decisions and actions and focus on strategic levels rather than on specific solutions.

The important role of metacognition for learning has been demonstrated in the context of a "thinker tools" program that lets students run simulations of physics experiments (White and Frederiksen, 1986), as well as in adding a metacognitive component to a computer program designed to help college students learn biology. The value of using video to model important metacognitive learning procedures has also been shown to help learners analyze and reflect on models (Bielaczyc, Pirolli, and Brown, 1995). All of these strategies engage learners as active participants in their learning by focusing their attention on critical elements, encouraging abstraction of common themes or procedures (principles), and evaluating their own progress toward understanding.

Training in the use of metacognition pertaining to the regulation of task-relevant cognitive strategies leads to dramatic improvement in performance. This has been found to be true in reading (Brown, Armbruster, and Baker, 1986), writing (Bereiter and Scardamalia, 1987) and the use of general learning strategies (Corkill and Koshida, 1993; Kluwe, 1987; Weinstein and Mayer, 1986). It should be noted, however, that metacognitive regulation always applies to particular, task-related cognitive strategies, and thus calls for the acquisition of the latter together with training in metacognition. Although theoretically, cognition and metacognition are not interchangeable, they nevertheless operate in a correlated manner (Weinert, 1987). A current emphasis in psychology and education is what Brown, Campione and Day (1982) referred to as devising instructional routines to "help students learn to learn" (p. 14), and "learning how to learn from reading" (p. 22). Brown and his colleagues (1982) discussed 'blind' training (in which students are induced to use strategies without understanding the significance of the activity), 'informed' training (in which students are induced to use a strategy and are given some information about its significance) and 'self-control' training (in which students are instructed in the use of the strategy and are also explicitly taught how to employ, monitor, check, and evaluate the strategy). Recent research indicates that self-control training results in superior benefits (efficacy, durability, generalizability). In an integrative study concerning attempts to teach metacognitive reading strategies, Haller et al. (1988) synthesized 20 studies and found an average effect size of 0.71. This means that, on the average, the treatments studied improved students' reading by 70 percent of a standard deviation. An effect size this large in instructional intervention is considered very high. Brown and Campione (1978) described the properties that cognitive activities to be taught require: (a) trans-situational applicability; (b) the sense on the part of children that these are reasonable activities that work; (c) a counterpart in real-life experiences; and (d) an understanding of component processes so that effective training techniques can be devised. These studies found that systematic training increases the quantity and quality of children's metacognitive knowledge and monitoring skills.

Paris and Winograd (1990) maintained that metacognition can promote academic learning and motivation. The idea is that students can enhance their learning by becoming aware of their own thinking as they read, write, and solve problems at school. Teachers can promote this awareness by simply informing students about effective problem-solving strategies and discussing cognitive and motivational characteristics of thinking. Paris and Winograd (1990) argued that such "consciousness-raising" has twin benefits: "(a) it transfers responsibility for monitoring learning from teachers to students themselves, and (b) it promotes positive self-perceptions, affect, and motivation among students. In this manner, metacognition provides personal insights into one's own thinking and fosters independent learning" (p. 15). They concurred with other researchers that strategic reading can be taught to students who need it through carefully devised instructional techniques (e.g., Brown et al., 1986). However, they cautioned that "metacognition should not be regarded as a final objective for learning or instruction." Instead, it should be regarded as an opportunity to "provide students with knowledge and confidence that enables them to manage their own learning and empowers them to be inquisitive and zealous in their pursuits" (Paris and Winograd, 1990, p. 22). According to Garner (1987), reading strategies, which she operationally defined as "generally deliberate, planful activities undertaken by active learners, many times to remedy perceived cognitive failure" (p. 50), facilitate reading comprehension and may be teachable. Garner (1994) concurred with Paris, Lipson, and Wixson (1983) that reading strategies can and should be learned to the point of automaticity, after which they become skills, and that learners must know not only what strategies to use but also when, where, and how to use them. The research on metacognition and reading comprehension is extensive (for recent reviews of the multidimensional nature of text comprehension, see especially Alexander and Jetton, 2000; and Pressley, 2000). This work has been very important in prompting reading researchers to examine readers' own awareness of their cognitive and motivational processes while reading and the actions they use to monitor comprehension. In addition, such research has provided teacher educators and practicing teachers with practical suggestions for helping struggling readers increase their awareness and use of reading strategies while reading.

Another major justification for promoting and fostering metacognitive skills in teaching is that they appear to have 'ecological validity'; that is, there are recognizable counterparts in real world, everyday life situations. Checking the results of an operation against certain criteria of effectiveness, economy, or common-sense reality is a metacognitive skill applicable whether the task under consideration is solving a math problem, reading for meaning, memorizing a passage of prose, following a recipe, or assembling an automobile or a piece of furniture. Self-interrogation concerning the current state of one's own knowledge during any reading or problem-solving task is an essential skill in a wide variety of situations: those of the laboratory, the school, and everyday life.

Marzano (1998) analyzed 4,000 intervention studies in education involving over 1,237,000 subjects. He found that nearly all interventions worked to some extent but that interventions that focused on the level of metacognition, (i.e., teaching thinking and learning strategies), and the level he called the 'self-system' (i.e., how students feel about themselves as learners) were most effective in improving measures of learning.

A "Psychology Tool" within Vygotsky's Zone of Proximal Development

Vygotsky (1978) argued that one cannot understand the child's level of development unless one considers two aspects: the actual development level and the potential development level. "The zone of proximal development is the distance between the actual development level as determined by independent problem solving and the level of potential development as determined through problem solving under adult guidance, or in collaboration with more capable peers" (Vygotsky 1978, p. 86). He argued that measuring the level of potential development is just as crucial, if not more so, as measuring the level of actual development.

In assessing a learner's performance and outcomes, the importance of conducting a separate analysis of the potential level of development derives from the fact that it may vary independently of the actual level. Vygotsky illustrated this point as follows:

> Imagine that we have examined two children and have determined that the mental age of both is seven years. This means that both children solve tasks accessible to seven-years-olds. However, when we attempt to push these children further in carrying out the tests, there turns out to be an essential difference between them. With the help of leading questions, examples, and demonstrations, one of them easily solves test items taken from two years above the child's level of [actual] development. The other solves test items that are only a half-year above, his or her level of [actual] development (in Wertsch, 1985, p. 68).

Given this set of circumstances, Vygotsky asked whether the mental development of these two children was the same and argued that in an important sense they were not:

> From the point of view of their independent activity they are equivalent, but from the point of view of their immediate potential development they are sharply different. That which the child turns out to be able to do with the help of an adult points us toward the zone of the child's proximal development. This means that with the help of this method, we can take stock not only of today's completed process of development, not only the cycles that are already concluded and done, not only the processes of maturation that are completed; we can also take stock of processes of maturation that are not completed; we can also take stock of processes that are now in the state of coming into being, that are only ripening, or only developing (in Wertsch 1985, p. 68).

Another notable aspect of Vygotsky's theory is that it claims "that instruction is most efficient when students engage in activities within a supportive learning environment and when they receive appropriate guidance that is mediated by tools" (Vygotsky 1978, cited by Gillani and Relan, 1997, p. 231). In Vygotsky's words, a 'psychology tool' serves "as a conductor of humans' influence on the object of their activity. It is directed towards the external world; it must stimulate some changes in the object; it is the means of humans' external activity directed towards the subjugation of nature" (in Wertsch 1985, p. 78). These instructional tools can be defined as "cognitive strategies, a mentor, peers, computers, printed materials, or any instrument that organizes and provides information for the learner." Their role is to help learners complete a task near the upper end of their zone of proximal development (ZPD) and then to systematically withdraw this support. Psychological tools enable us to bridge the gap between lower and higher mental functions. They do not serve simply to facilitate mental processes that would otherwise exist, but rather, they fundamentally shape and transform them.

Researchers have noted that performance must be assisted, and assisting performance by combining a 'psychology tool' and a 'stimulus' with an assessment task will make a difference in the learner's performance and outcomes (Brown, Campione, Reeve, Ferrara, and Palincsar, 1991; Brown and Ferrara, 1985; Brown and French, 1979). The 'stimulus' or the 'scaffolding' given the learners became, in time and with social support, part of the learner's repertoire of understanding. In Vygotsky's formal language, understanding means moving from the 'interpsychic' plan to the 'intrapsychic' plan. Implicitly, what we are first able to do with others, we are eventually able to do by ourselves.

In the framework of relating to computers as cognitive tools, Lajoie (1993) identified four types of cognitive tools:

- tools that support cognitive and metacognitive processes
- tools that share the student's cognitive load by providing support for lower level cognitive activities so that the student may concentrate more on higher level cognitive activities
- tools that allow the student to engage in cognitive activities that otherwise would be out of his reach
- tools that make it possible for the student to generate and test hypotheses in problem solving activities

Salomon (1993), in taking up the metaphor of the computer program as a cognitive tool, further distinguishes between performance-oriented tools and pedagogical tools. While the former help the learner in a given situation to improve his or her actual performance, the latter aim to help the students acquire and cultivate generalizable skills, particularly higher order thinking skills that later on may be employed in the absence of the tool. An example of the former would be a word processor, examples of the latter are the 'Writing Partner', a computer program that helps students write a creative story (Zellermayer, Salomon, Globerson, and Givon, 1991); and the 'Reading Partner', a computer program that helps students to better comprehend a text (Salomon, Globerson, and Guterman, 1989).

The 'Writing Partner' is based on the psychological analysis of written composition Bereiter and Scardamalia (1987), on the theory of procedural facilitation (Scardamalia, Bereiter, Swallow, and Woodruff, 1989), on Vygotsky's (1978) socio-historical theory of development, and on Salomon's theory of technology and mind (Salomon, 1990). It was designed to help students shift from writing composition in the free-association, less-than-thoughtful mode of 'knowledge telling' to writing better planned, self-guided, self-diagnosed and revised compositions of the 'knowledge transformation' mode (Salomon, 1993, p. 185). The program offers the student four types of assistance (procedural facilitations):

1. The student is guided through a forced process of planning of his or her story, brainstorming and outlining.
2. While writing, students can ask for assistance which will be given to them in the form of expert-like questions that depend on the key-words typed earlier in the composition.
3. If the student does not know how to continue his or her story ("I am stuck"), the program will help the student diagnose where and with what she or he is stuck (opening, lost the main idea, plots don't meet, need a word, etc.).
4. Finally, ideas that the student downloaded from his or her mind into the program (idea list and outlines) may be retrieved at any time during the writing process.

The 'Reading Partner' functions as "more capable peers". In order to achieve a transferable cognitive residue in reading comprehension, the tool was designed to aid the reader to comprehend texts better by modeling, activating and raising awareness of the relevant cognitive reading strategies. The 'Reading Partner' had two main components. The first component introduced three general self-guiding statements used by successful readers who think while reading: "Think what *message* a text is trying to convey to you," "Think what *thoughts* the text brings to your mind," and "Ask yourself whether you *understand* the text". The subject were urged to remember the three elements – Message, Thoughts and Understanding (MTU) – and to relate to them during all subsequent readings. A reminder to think of MTU was inserted into the text and was repeated at the beginning of each reading session. The second component introduced specific reading principles and prompted students to ask themselves questions while reading, such as "What image can I make of what I am reading?", "What can I predict from the title?", "Does the text make sense?", "Does it ring a bell?" and "What are the key sentences here?". Each of these specific suggestions was accompanied by examples based on the text presented on the screen.

The general hypothesis underlying the 'Writing Partner' and the 'Reading Partner' studies was that intellectual partnership with 'psychological tool' that provides metacognitive awareness guidance leads to the internalization of the guidance, which in turn, facilitates better learning. The main question that Salomon addressed in his studies was whether the interaction of a psychological tool within the learner's zone of proximal development could leave a transferable cognitive residue. Indeed, his findings confirmed that the subjects' reading comprehension improved substantially and students who worked with the 'Writing Partner' exhibited significant improvement in writing quality.

This suggests that even a simple psychological tool serves as a "more capable peer" in the learner's zone of proximal development and can facilitate and enhance the development of the learner's competency. Thus, one might ask whether similar results could be obtained with the use of a written tool, based on the same principles.

METACOGNITIVE AWARENESS GUIDANCE (MCAG) – A "PSYCHOLOGICAL TOOL"

Written metacognitive awareness guidance (MCAG) was developed to serve as a psychological tool for students being assessed on reading comprehension skills (Guterman, 2002). The uniqueness of this cognitive tool lies in the expert-like guidance that it affords. It does not teach nor does it correct errors. It is based on the assumption that students are the ones who need to do the thinking (planning, self-diagnosing, self-guiding) and that the tool ought only to provide the learner with the stimulation and guidance for doing so (activating and engaging learners' awareness of their existing prior knowledge). More specifically, it was based on the following assumptions, derived from the theoretical background above:

- Metacognitive awareness of prior knowledge accompanies the process of learning from a text and constitutes part of the reading behavior used by the expert learners/readers: metacognitive awareness relates to proficiency in reading
- Metacognitive awareness of prior knowledge will determine the level of performance and outcome of any learning or assessment task

- Students can be trained to be aware of the influence of their existing prior knowledge, and of characteristics of text, task, learning strategies, and of themselves as learners
- The written MCAG affords learners the opportunity to engage in higher order operations: to test their knowledge, discover new links, anticipate, raise questions, suggest possible answers – and these operations will facilitate their learning and improve the outcomes on reading assessment tasks
- The MCAG creates a 'zone of proximal development' and addresses the learner's potential level of development. It is based on Vygotskian theory and leads to internalization of the guidance
- Increasing learners' metacognitive awareness by means of well-planned guidance which builds on prior knowledge will increase learners' chances of internalization the guidance components and applying them in changing learning situations

Thus, written MCAG provides the assistance of 'others' in situations where learners are encouraged to perform activities more 'mindfully' and 'meaningfully', before attempting to process the assessment tasks. It affords learners the opportunity to engage in higher order operations: to test their knowledge, discover new links, anticipate, raise questions, suggest possible answers, etc. As such, the MCAG functions in the 'zone of proximal development', and addresses the learner's potential level of development. Based on Vygotsky's theory, the written MCAG and should lead to the internalization of the guidance. According to Tharp and Gallimore, Vygotsky's stages can be broken down as follows (1988, p. 35):

- Stage 1: assistance provided by more capable others (coaches, experts, teachers)
- Stage 2: assistance by self
- Stage 3: internalization automatization (fossilization)
- Stage 4: de-automatization: recursiveness through prior stages

The MCAG is based on the assumption that increasing learners' metacognitive awareness by means of well-planned guidance, built on prior knowledge, will not only facilitate their learning and improve their outcomes on a specific assessment task, but will also increase their chances of internalizing the guidance components and applying them in changing learning situations. Thus, the main objectives of the written MCAG were:

- To help learners become aware of what they already know about the topic of the assessment text before they receive the assessment task
- To help learners concentrate on and invest mental effort in 'constructing' meaning rather than identifying 'correct' answers, by focusing on what they already know and understand
- To help learners make an active effort to construct meaning by predicting what the text may be about, by leading the learners to make judgments about how new information relates to what they already know, so that they can fit new pieces into the partially-assembled puzzle which already exists in their minds

- To help learners focus on their existing knowledge by asking them to discover for themselves "what they already know about...", and direct this knowledge to their 'working memory'
- To help learners build and create an 'advanced organizer' for the task by building bridges and making connections between existing knowledge and the ideas which are communicated in the text
- To help learners activate schema by anticipating, raising questions, suggesting possible answers, and extending thinking about the task/topic/issue before "going to work on it"
- To raise the learners' awareness of:

  - their prior knowledge (schema) of the task
  - the role and function of prior knowledge in understanding and in answering the assessment task questions
  - the effect of the use of prior knowledge on their performance and outcomes
  - the active and dynamic nature of their existing knowledge and the need to re-examine this knowledge (vis-à-vis what they will read)

The metacognitive guidance was also designed to stimulate interest, arouse curiosity, and draw the learner into the assessment task. An open-ended question format (which requires a written response) as opposed to multiple choice was chosen, because of its potential to drive the learner's metacognitive awareness. The written responses required by the open-ended questions stimulate learners to think about the topics, issues and problems, and enable the learner to integrate their schema into their thinking. Open-ended questions provide learners the opportunity to think for themselves, and express their knowledge and ideas. Furthermore, open-ended questions

- call for learners to construct their own response instead of selecting a single 'correct' answer
- allow learners to demonstrate the depth of their understanding – almost impossible with multiple choice items
- encourage learners to think about the topic/issue/problem in many ways, and in their own style

The MCAG also employs direct explicit self-talk. Learners were asked to use self-talk to monitor their activities and to establish meaningful connections with their MCAG activities. The instruction to stop and reflect on what they did, why they did it, and how to use what they did, breaks down their spontaneous tendency to 'start working' – to answer the question immediately. Through the use of self-talk, their processing of the assessment tasks becomes less impulsive and more mindful.

The MCAG implements four main principles through various kinds of activities. The first principle, *Providing context information* (building readiness by putting topics, issues, and subjects of assessment tasks into context) was implemented by introducing the reading text ("The title of the passage you are about to read is ..."; "In the passage, the writer describes

..."; "You are about to read a poem by ..."; "The passage that you are about to read is from an Encyclopedia and is called ...").

The second principle, *Building, creating, or discovering (BCD) relevant schema* was implemented by asking questions such as: "What do you think ... is made of?"; "What problem could arise when manufacturing it?"; "What solution can you suggest to the problem that you raised?", or "Before reading the passage, write 5 questions that you think will be answered in the passage".

The third principle, *Activating the relevant schema* was implemented as follows: "Write a short paragraph to fit the title of the passage, using the following words: ..."; "Of the five questions you have written, select two, and answer them"; "The sentences below describe what you may read in the passage. If you think that a sentence may be from the encyclopedia, about the passage, circle the word Yes. If, in your opinion, a sentence does not describe the passage, circle the word No"; "I think that the sentences I marked Yes describe the reading passage because ...".

The fourth principle, *Creating and raising metacognitive awareness of prior knowledge* through direct instruction was implemented by asking learners to repeat the following words out loud before receiving the assessment task: "Now I know more about .... This knowledge will help me to understand the passage. Now it will be easier for me to study the passage" or "I know a lot about .... Everything I already know helps me understand. Everything I already know will help me to study the passage".

INVESTIGATING THE EFFECTS OF WRITTEN MGAC ON STUDENT ACHIEVEMENT IN READING

An experimental study was designed to test the effect of metacognitive awareness guidance on students' achievement and performance on three authentic reading assessment tasks. Each item in the reading assessment task was classified according to two parameters: cognitive level and level of difficulty, on a scale of 1 to 3. A total of 300 students (aged 9-10) studying in ten 4th grade classes, in four different schools participated in the research. The study utilized three modalities: (1) a control group, which received no intervention (N = 102). The students were asked to read the text and answer the questions that followed. (2) a placebo group that received content instruction (CI) guidance (N = 85). The CI consisted of instructions that focused on content and procedure, i.e., "Read the passage... carefully. When you finish reading it, you will be asked questions on what you read. Pay attention. Before you begin to answer the question, be sure that you understand the passage.... After you answer all the questions, go back and check your answers." When they finished reading, they were asked to raise their hands to signal that they were ready to proceed to the reading assessment tasks; and (3) the intervention group (N = 113), that was given written metacognitive awareness guidance for each of the three reading assessment tasks. The MCAG was given to students before performing the reading assessment tasks. After answering the metacognitive awareness questions, they were asked to say out loud, "Now I know a lot about.... What I know about... will help me to understand the passage. Now it will be easier for me to study the passage," and only then to signal that they were ready to process the assessment task.

A Metacognitive Strategy Index questionnaire (MSIQ) was administered 14 days after the three assessment tasks were performed and was given to all three groups. It was based on the MSI, a questionnaire designed by Schmitt (1990) to measure children's awareness of metacognitive reading strategies. The MSI is a 25-item, 4-option, multiple-choice questionnaire that asks students about strategies they could use before, during, and after reading texts and stories. The strategies assessed by the MSI are consistent with those taught in several meta-comprehension instructional studies (e.g., Braun, Rennie, and Labercane, 1986; Palincsar and Brown, 1984; Riscko and Feldman, 1986). Students were asked to read a list of four statements and decide which would help them the most to understand the story. The instructions clarify that "there are no right answers. It is just what you think would help the most, circle the number of the statement you choose". The 25 questions had four statements each, a total of 100 statements, and related to three time periods: Before reading, while reading, and after reading. The 'correct' response for each item is that which is indicative of a meta-comprehension awareness strategy. The MSI has been shown to be a reliable measure of meta-comprehension strategy awareness (Braun et al., 1986; Palincsar and Brown, 1984; Paris and Jacobs, 1984; Riscko and Feldman, 1986; Schmitt and Baumann, 1986). The study used a 17-item questionnaire, MSIQ, which also defined a more generalized category: building, creating and discovering relevant prior knowledge (BCD), represented by questions specifically related to the MCAG intervention.

The achievements of the learners in the treatment group were compared to those of learners in the control and the placebo groups, and in relation to other research variables: gender, school, and level of awareness of metacognitive reading strategies. Teachers' views about the role and effects of metacognitive awareness guidance on learner performance and outcomes were also examined. (For a full description of the results of the study, see Guterman, 2002, 2003; Guterman and Boxall, 2002. Details on the effectiveness of the MCAG intervention are presented in the Appendix).

The findings of the study indicate that engaging learners in metacognitive awareness guidance affected their performance on assessment tasks – they attained a higher level of achievement on these tasks. Learners who received metacognitive awareness guidance also demonstrated a significantly higher level of awareness of metacognitive reading strategies. However, no relation was found between the quality of students' answers on the MCAG questions and their level of awareness of metacognitive reading strategies. In general, the students' performance on the MCAG questions was very disappointing, and only a small number of students furnished satisfactory answers to the MCAG questions. If learners' did not give satisfactory responses to the questions, what is it about the MCAG questions that can explain their effect? Clearly, it is not necessarily the quality of students' responses on the MCAG that made the difference in their level of achievement on the reading tasks or on their level of awareness according to the MSI questionnaire. What seems to be significant is the role of the MCAG in creating engagement between the students and the reading process. Students were guided to construct their own responses, to use context information, to focus on what they already know and understand, to express their opinions, to anticipate, to raise questions, to suggest possible answers, to use direct explicit self-talk, and to reflect on what they know and how they can use it. Extrapolating from this, we can say that the MCAG created commitment, involvement, connection, obligation and responsibility. It weakened the detachment between the task and the students. Thus, the MCAG seems to act as a trigger to involvement and commitment to the process of reading.

CONCLUSION

"What they don't know will hurt them" – Wilson and Anderson, 1986

Driven by three learning theories – schema theory, metacognitive awareness theory, and the Vygotskian 'zone of proximal development' – written MCAG addresses four main metacognitive learning principles. *Context information* - putting topics, issues, and subjects of assessment tasks into context, and guiding learners to use context information, to read with purpose and anticipation. *Building, creating, or discovering relevant schema* - focusing on what the learners already know and encouraging them to make connections between their prior knowledge and the new knowledge in the assessment task. *Activating relevant schema* - by involving the students through anticipating, raising questions, suggesting possible answers, and extending thinking about the task or topic before "going to work on it". *Creating and raising metacognitive awareness of their prior knowledge* and its role and effect on their performance and outcomes - by employing direct explicit self-talk.

The findings of the study described here showed that integrating metacognitive principles into reading assessment tasks significantly enhanced student achievement in reading, especially when answering questions on high cognitive and difficulty levels. The findings provide initial evidence to suggest that the MCAG engaged the students in actions within the zone of proximal development (ZPD) and through this process enabled them to transcend their present level of performance and to approach their potential level. The ZPD is one of the more exciting concepts in cognitive development as it perceives the individual as an active agent in his or her own cognitive development. Individuals can achieve some of their goals by recruiting means already in their repertoire, and can be taught the skills needed to reach other goals.

Iser (1978) argued that the process of reading is a dynamic one, to which readers bring personal experience and social and cognitive schemata, in which predictions, assumptions and inferences are constantly made, developed, challenged and negated. If our goal is that students construct meaning for themselves in their reading, we have to acknowledge the concept of meaning and the role of the reader in determining meaning. We need assessment tasks that recognize the importance of the individual and that attempt to capture the authenticity of the learner's reading processes and outcomes.

Incorporating MCAG into assessment tasks affords learners the opportunity to engage in higher-order operations: to test their knowledge, discover new links, anticipate, raise questions and suggest possible answers. As such, it functions within the ZPD and leads to internalization of the guidance. Thus, it not only facilitates students' learning and improves outcomes on specific assessment tasks, but also increases the likelihood that they will apply it to higher order operations and to other learning situations. These findings were supported by a teacher who incorporated MCAG into a history test. Her observations about the link she noted between the MCAG and the students' performance on the history test are valuable and substantial:

> One of the most interesting things I discovered as a result of this experience was that the answers to the questions on the test were longer and more detailed, and more relevant to the subjects we studied. The pupils used the introductory questions that they answered in the guidance for explanations, reinforcement and as a basis for their answers on the test.

For me this was fantastic because usually their answers are short and trite (Guterman and Boxall, 2002, p. 41).

Students' engagement was enhanced because the MCAG encouraged students to take responsibility for their performance by employing what Flavell (1976, p. 282) calls "active monitoring and consequent regulation and orchestration" of cognitive processes to achieve cognitive goals. The findings underscore the role of the MCAG as a cognitive tool used in cognitive activities. Metacognitive awareness refers to one's awareness of the different kinds of cognitive tools that are available, and to one's competence in choosing those which are best suited for a given task and applying them intelligently. However, as Salomon points out, "No tool is good or bad in and of itself; its effectiveness results from and contributes to the whole configuration of events, activities, contents, and interpersonal processes taking place in the context of which it is being used" (Salomon, 1993, p. 186). The role of the teacher in this context is to provide students with a tool kit and to train them how and when to use the tools. To do this successfully, teachers need to understand the conceptual framework underlying their teaching. Such understanding will allow teachers to apply familiar learning and teaching principles in new learning, teaching and assessing situations. But more importantly, it can empower teachers by providing them with tools for intelligent criticism of these learning principles. Teachers are the key – they are the classroom practitioners.

The research described here is a fusion of

- A child-centered view of teaching and assessment that acknowledges the importance of the individual and views every pupil as unique and special.
- A constructivist view of knowing and meaning-making that acknowledges the notion of meaning in text and places a different interpretation on the privileged role of the reader in determining meaning. In learning which occurs as students give meaning to experiences in light of their existing knowledge, assessment techniques should allow students to express their personal understanding of concepts in ways that are uniquely theirs.
- The Vygoyskian 'zone of proximal development' which suggests that assessment methods must take into account that what children can do on their own is their level of actual development, and what they can do with help is their level of potential development. Assessment methods must target both.
- Metacognitive learning theory that focuses on (a) the role of awareness and management of one's thinking, (b) individual differences in self-appraisal and mastery of cognitive development and learning, (c) knowledge and monitoring abilities that develop through experience, and (d) constructive and strategic thinking (Paris and Winograd, 1990). Thus, the promise of metacognitive theory is that it focuses precisely on those characteristics of cognition that can contribute to pupils' awareness and understanding of being masters of their own thinking.
- Post-modern assessment, or what Harrison, Bailey and Dewar (1998) and Harrison, Bailey and Foster (1998) call 'responsive assessment', relates to teachers and learners as subjects rather than objects of the assessment process. They suggest using a wide range of methods and approaches to assess achievement, and actively involving pupils in negotiating and determining what serves as evidence of their learning. They acknowledge the importance of the readers' role in determining

meaning and state that assessment tasks should capture the authenticity of the reader's active response through interview and small group discussion to ensure the reader's central, powerful role as an active and purposeful user of text and creator of meaning.

Reading is the most fundamental skill needed in learning, and literacy assessment is one of the most important issues in literacy education today. The findings of the research, its results and implications, raise suggestions regarding "what ought to be" that will hopefully influence policy formation and contribute to reconsideration of assessment in the educational system. But more important, the research provides evidence relating to "how to do it". It thus has the potential value to improve teaching, learning and assessment, and to make a difference in the evaluation of students' reading performance.

REFERENCES

Alexander, P. A., and Jetton, T. L. (2000). Learning from text: A multidimensional and developmental perspective. In M. Kamil, P. Mosenthal, P. D. Pearson and R. Barr (Eds.), *Handbook of reading research* (Vol. 3, pp. 285-310). Mahwah, NJ: Erlbaum.

Anderson, R. C. (1983). Role of the reader's schema during comprehension, learning, and memory. In R. C. Anderson, J. Osborn and R. Tierney (Eds.), *Learning to read in American schools* (pp. 85-121). Hillsdale, NJ: Erlbaum.

Anderson, T. H. (1980). Study strategies and adjunct aids. In R. J. Spiro, B. C. Bruce and W. F. Brewer (Eds.), *Theoretical issues in reading comprehension* (pp. 483-503). Hillsdale, NJ: Erlbaum.

Baker, L., and Brown, A. L. (1984a). Cognitive monitoring in reading. In J. Flood (Ed.), *Understanding reading comprehension* (pp. 35-52). Newark, DE: International Reading Association.

Baker, L., and Brown, A. L. (1984b). Metacognitive skills and reading. In P. D. Pearson (Ed.), *Handbook of reading research* (pp. 353-394). New York, NY: Longman.

Bereiter, C., and Scardamalia, M. (1987). *The psychology of written composition*. Hillsdale, NJ: Erlbaum.

Bereiter, C., and Scardamalia, M. (1989). Intentional learning as a goal of instruction. In L. B. Resnick (Ed.), *Knowing, learning, and instruction: Essays in honor of Robert Glaser* (pp. 361-392). Hillsdale, NJ: Lawrence Erlbaum.

Bielaczyc, K., Pirolli, P. L., and Brown, A. L. (1995). Training in self-explanation and self-regulation strategies: Investigating the effects of knowledge acquisition activities on problem-solving. *Cognition and Instruction, 13*(2), 221-252.

Bloom, B. (1964). *Stability and change in human characteristics*. New York, NY: Wiley.

Bransford, J. D., and Johnson, M. K. (1972). Contextual prerequisites for understanding: Some investigation of comprehension and recall. *Journal of Verbal Learning and Verbal Behavior, 11*, 717-726.

Braun, C., Rennie, B. J., and Labercane, G. D. (1986). A conference approach to the development of metacognitive strategies. In *Solving problems is literacy: Learners, teachers, and researchers* (pp. 204-209). The 35th Yearbook of the National Reading Conference.

Brown, A. L. (1978). Knowing when, where and how to remember: A problem of metacognition. In R. Glaser (Ed.), *Advances in instructional psychology.* Hillsdale, NJ: Erlbaum.

Brown, A. L. (1980). Metacognitive development and reading. In R. Spiro, B. Bruce and W. F. Brewer (Eds.), *Theoretical issues in reading comprehension* (pp. 453-482). Hillsdale, NJ: Erlbaum.

Brown, A. L. (1982a). Learning and development: The problems of compatibility, access, and induction. *Human Development, 25,* 89-115.

Brown, A. L. (1982b). Learning how to learn from reading. In J. A. Langer and M. Smith-Burine (Eds.), *Reader meets author: Bridging the gap* (pp. 18-31). Newark, DE: International Reading Association.

Brown, A. L. (1994). The advancement of learning. *Educational Researcher, 23,* 442.

Brown, A. L., Armbruster, B. B., and Baker, L. (1986). The role of metacognition in reading and studying. In J. Orasanu (Ed.), *Reading comprehension: From research to practice* (pp. 49-76). Hillsdale, NJ: Erlbaum.

Brown, A. L., Bransford, J. D., Ferrara, R. A., and Campione, J. C. (1983). Learning remembering and understanding. In J. H. Flavell and E. M. Markman (Eds.), *Child development* (4th ed., Vol. 3, pp. 77-166). New York, NY: Wiley.

Brown, A. L., and Campione, J. C. (1978). Permissible references from the outcome of training studies in cognitive development research. *Quarterly Newsletter of the Institute for Comparative Human Development, 2,* 46-53.

Brown, A. L., Campione, J. C., and Day, J. D. (1982). Learning to learn: On training students to learn from text. *Educational Researcher, 10,* 12-14.

Brown, A. L., Campione, J. C., Reeve, R. A., Ferrara, R. A., and Palincsar, A. S. (1991). Interactive learning and individual understanding: The case of reading and mathematics. In L. T. Landsmann (Ed.), *Culture, schooling, and psychological development* (pp. 136-170). Norwood, NJ: Ablex.

Brown, A. L., and Ferrara, R. A. (1985). Diagnosing zones of proximal development. In J. V. Wertsch (Ed.), *Culture, communication, and cognition: Vygotskian perspectives* (pp. 273-305). Cambridge: Cambridge University Press.

Brown, A. L., and French, L. A. (1979). The zone of potential development: Implications for intelligence testing in the year 2000. *Intelligence, 3,* 255-273.

Campione, J. C., and Brown, A. L. (1990). Guided learning and transfer. In N. Frederiksen, R. Glaser, A. Lesgold and M. Shafto (Eds.), *Diagnostic monitoring of skill and knowledge acquisition* (pp. 141-172). Hillsdale, NJ: Erlbaum.

Chi, M. T. H. (1978). Knowledge structures and memory development. In R. S. Siegler (Ed.), *Children's thinking: What develops?* (pp. 73-96). Hillsdale, NJ: Erlbaum.

Chi, M. T. H., Feltovitch, P. J., and Glaser, R. (1981). Categorization and representation of physics problems by experts and novices. *Cognitive Science, 5,* 121-152.

Chi, M. T. H., Glaser, R., and Reese, E. (1982). Expertise in problem solving. In R. Steinberg (Ed.), *Advances in the psychology of human intelligence* (Vol. 1, pp. 7-75). Hillsdale, NJ: Erlbaum.

Chi, M. T. H., and Koeske, R. D. (1983). Network representation of a child's dinosaur knowledge. *Developmental Psychology, 19,* 29-39.

Cobb, P. (1994). *Theories of mathematical learning and constructivism: A personal view.* Paper presented at the Symposium on Trends and Perspectives in Mathematics Education, Institute for Mathematics, University of Klagenfurt, Austria.

Cohen, J. (1977). *Statistical power analysis for the behavioral sciences* (revised ed.). New York, NY: Academic Press.

Cohen, J. (1988). *Statistical power analysis for the behavioral sciences* (2nd ed.). Hillsdale, NJ: Lawrence Erlbaum.

Collins, A., Brown, J. S., and Larkin, K. M. (1977). *Inference in text understanding.* Urbana, IL: University of Illinois, Center for the Study of Reading.

Corkill, A. J., and Koshida, D. T. (1993). *Level of metacognition awareness and calibration of performance: Strategic knowledge makes a difference.* Paper presented at the annual meeting of AERA, Atlanta, GA.

Flavell, J. H. (1976). Metacognitive aspects of problem solving. In L. B. Resnick (Ed.), *The nature of intelligence* (pp. 281-299). Hillsdale, NJ: Erlbaum.

Flavell, J. H. (1979). Metacognition and cognitive monitoring. *American Psychologist, 23*(10), 906-911.

Flavell, J. H., and Wellman, H. M. (1977). Metamemory. In R. V. Kail and J. W. Hagen (Eds.), *Perspectives on the development of memory and cognition.* Hillsdale, NJ: Erlbaum.

Garner, R. (1987). *Metacognition and reading comprehension.* Norwood, NJ: Ablex.

Garner, R. (1994). Metacognition and executive control. In R. B. Ruddell, M. R. Ruddell and H. Singer (Eds.), *Theoretical models and processes of reading* (4th ed., pp. 715-732). Newark, DE: International Reading Association.

Garner, R., and Reis, R. (1981). Monitoring and resolving comprehension obstacles: An investigation of spontaneous text lookbacks among upper-grade good and poor comprehenders. *Reading Research Quarterly, 16,* 569-582.

Gillani, B. B., and Relan, A. (1997). Incorporating interactivity and multimedia into web-based instruction. In B. H. Khan (Ed.), *Web-based instruction* (pp. 231-237). Englewood Cliffs, NJ: Educational Technology Publications.

Guterman, E. (2002). Toward dynamic assessment of reading: Applying metacognitive guidance to reading assessment tasks. *Journal of Research in Reading, 25*(3), 304-319.

Guterman, E. (2003). Integrating written metacognitive awareness guidance as a 'psychological tool' to improve student performance. *Learning and Instruction, 13*(6), 633-651.

Guterman, E., and Boxall, W. (2002). Teachers' voices on integrating metacognitive awareness guidance into assessment tasks in reading. *Reading - A Journal about Literacy and Language in Education, 36*(1), 38-43.

Haller, E. P., Child, D. A., and Walberg, H. J. (1988). Can comprehension be taught? A quantitative synthesis of "metacognitive" studies. *Educational Researcher, 17,* 5-8.

Harrison, C., Bailey, M., and Dewar, A. (1998). Responsive reading assessment: Is post-modern assessment of reading possible? In C. Harrison and T. Salinger (Eds.), *Assessing reading 1: Theory and practice - International perspectives on reading assessment* (pp. 1-20). London: Routledge.

Harrison, C., Bailey, M., and Foster, C. (1998). Responsive assessment of reading: Seeking evidence on reading attainment from students. In M. Coles and R. Jenkins (Eds.),

Assessing reading 2: Changing practice in classrooms - International perspectives on reading assessment (pp. 1-8). London: Routledge.

Holmes, B. L. (1983). The effect of prior knowledge on the question answers of readers. *Journal of Reading Behavior, 15*(4), 1-18.

Iser, W. (1978). *The act of reading: A theory of aesthetic response.* Baltimore, MD: Johns Hopkins University Press.

Johnston, P. (1984). Prior knowledge and reading comprehension test bias. *Reading Research Quarterly, 19*, 219-239.

Kluwe, R. H. (1987). Executive decision and regulation of problem solving behavior. In F. E. Weinert and R. H. Kluwe (Eds.), *Metacognition, motivation and understanding* (pp. 31-64). Hillsdale, NJ: Erlbaum.

Lajoie, S. P. (1993). Computer environments as cognitive tools for enhancing learning. In S. P. Lajoie and S. J. Derry (Eds.), *Computers as cognitive tools* (pp. 261-288). Hillsdale, NJ: Erlbaum.

Langer, J. A., and Nicholich, M. (1981). Prior knowledge and its effect on comprehension. *Journal of Reading Behavior, 13*(4), 373-379.

Lipson, M. Y. (1982). Learning new information from text: The role of prior knowledge and reading ability. *Journal of Reading Behavior, 14*(3), 243-261.

Markman, E. M. (1979). Realizing that you don't understand: Elementary school children's awareness of inconsistencies. *Child Development, 50*, 643-655.

Marr, M. B., and Gormely, K. (1982). Children recall of familiar and unfamiliar texts. *Reading Research Quarterly, 18*, 89-104.

Marzano, R. J. (1998). *A theory-based meta-analysis of research on instruction.* Aurora, CO: Mid-continent Research for Education and Learning.

Means, M. L., and Voss, J. (1985). Star wars: A developmental study of expert novice knowledge structures. *Journal of Memory and Language, 24*, 746-757.

Miller, G. A., Golanter, E., and Pribram, K. H. (1960). *Plans and structure of behavior.* New York, NY: Holt.

Neisser, U. (1976). *Cognition and reality: Principles and implications of cognitive psychology.* San Francisco: Freeman.

Nolte, R. Y., and Singer, H. (1985). Active comprehension: Teaching a process of reading comprehension and its effect on reading achievement. *The Reading Teacher, 39*, 24-28.

Norris, S., and Phillips, L. (1987). Explanation of reading comprehension: Schema theory and critical thinking theory. *Teachers College Record, 89*(2), 282-306.

Palincsar, A. S., and Brown, A. L. (1984). Reciprocal teaching of comprehension- fostering and comprehension-monitoring activities. *Cognition and Instruction, 1*, 117-175.

Paris, S. G., and Jacobs, J. E. (1984). The benefits of informed instruction for children's reading awareness and comprehension skills. *Child Development, 55*, 2083-2093.

Paris, S. G., Lipson, M. Y., and Wixson, K. K. (1983). Becoming a strategic reader. *Contemporary Educational Psychology, 8*, 490-509.

Paris, S. G., and Winograd, P. (1990). How metacognition can promote academic learning and instruction. In B. F. Jones and M. C. Idol (Eds.), *Dimensions of thinking and cognitive instruction* (pp. 15-51). Hillsdale, NJ: Erlbaum.

Pearson, P. D. (1993). Teaching and learning reading: A research perspective. *Language Arts, 70*(6), 502-511.

Pearson, P. D., Hansen, J., and Gordon, C. (1979). The effect of background knowledge on young children's comprehension of explicit and implicit information. *Journal of Reading Behavior, 11*, 201-209.

Pearson, P. D., Roehler, L. R., Dole, J. A., and Duffy, G. G. (1992). Developing expertise in reading comprehension. In S. J. Samuels and A. E. Farstrup (Eds.), *What research has to say about reading instruction* (pp. 145-191). Newark, DE: International Reading Association.

Polya, G. (1957). *How to solve it: A new aspect of mathematical method* (2nd ed.). Princeton, NJ: Princeton University Press.

Pressley, M. (2000). What should comprehension instruction be the instruction of? In M. Kamil, P. Mosenthal, P. D. Pearson and R. Barr (Eds.), *Handbook of reading research* (Vol. 3, pp. 545-561). Mahwah, NJ: Erlbaum.

Pressley, M., and Afflerbach, P. (1995). *Verbal protocols of reading: The nature of constructively responsive reading*. Hillsdale, NJ: Erlbaum.

Riscko, V. J., and Feldman, N. (1986). Teaching young remedial readers to generate questions as they read. *Reading Psychology, 23*, 54-64.

Rumelhart, D. E. (1980). Schemata: The building blocks of cognition. In R. J. Spiro, B. C. Bruce and W. F. Brewer (Eds.), *Theoretical issues in reading comprehension* (pp. 33-58). Hillsdale, NJ: Erlbaum.

Salomon, G. (1990). Cognitive effects with and of computer technology. *Communication Research, 17*, 26-44.

Salomon, G. (1993). On the nature of pedagogic computer tools: The case of writing partner. In S. P. Lajoie and S. J. Derry (Eds.), *Computers as cognitive tools* (pp. 179-196). Hillsdale, NJ: Lawrence Erlbaum.

Salomon, G., Globerson, T., and Guterman, E. (1989). The computer as a zone of proximal development: Internalizing reading-related metacognition from a reading partner. *Journal of Educational Psychology, 81*, 620-627.

Salomon, G., and Perkins, D. N. (1989). Rocky roads to transfer: Rethinking mechanisms of a neglected phenomenon. *Educational Psychologist, 24*, 118-142.

Scardamalia, M., Bereiter, B., and Steinbach, R. (1984). Teachability of reflective processes in written composition. *Cognitive Science, 8*, 173-190.

Scardamalia, M., Bereiter, B., Swallow, M. J., and Woodruff, E. (1989). Computer-supported intentional learning environments. *Journal of Educational Computing Research, 5*(1), 51-68.

Schmitt, M. C. (1990). A questionnaire to measure children's awareness of strategic reading processes. *The Reading Teacher, 43*(3), 454-461.

Schmitt, M. C., and Baumann, J. F. (1986). How to incorporate comprehension monitoring strategies into basal reader instruction. *The Reading Teacher, 40*, 28-31.

Schoenfeld, A. H. (1983). Problem solving in the mathematics curriculum: A report, recommendation and an annotated bibliography. *Mathematical Association of America Notes, 1*.

Schoenfeld, A. H. (1985). *Mathematical problem solving*. Orlando, FL: Academic Press.

Schoenfeld, A. H. (1991). On mathematics as sense-making: An informal attack on the unfortunate divorce of formal and informal mathematics. In J. F. Voss, D. N. Perkins and J. W. Segal (Eds.), *Informal reasoning and education* (pp. 311-343). Hillsdale, NJ: Erlbaum.

Schwartz, D., and Bransford, J. D. (1998). A time for telling. *Cognition and Instruction, 16*(4), 475-522.

Snow, C. E., Burns, M. S., and Griffin, P. (Eds.). (1998). *Preventing reading difficulties in young children.* Washington, DC: National Research Council, National Academy Press.

Spilich, G. J., Vesonder, G. T., Chiesi, H. L., and Voss, J. F. (1979). Text processing of domain-related information for individuals with high and low domain knowledge. *Journal of Verbal Learning and Verbal Behavior, 18,* 275-290.

Tharp, R. G., and Gallimore, R. (1988). *Rousing minds to life: Teaching, learning and schooling in a social context.* New York, NY: Cambridge University Press.

Tierney, R. J., and Pearson, P. D. (1994). Learning to learn from text: A framework for improving classroom practice. In R. B. Ruddell, M. R. Ruddell and H. Singer (Eds.), *Theoretical models and processes of reading* (4th ed., pp. 496-513). Newark, DE: International Reading Association.

Vacca, J. A. L., Vacca, R. T., and Gove, K. M. (1995). *Reading and learning to read.* New York, NY: Harper Collins.

Vygotsky, L. S. (1962). *Thought and language.* Cambridge, MA: MIT Press.

Vygotsky, L. S. (1978). *Mind in society: The development of higher psychological processes.* Cambridge, MA: Harvard University Press.

Wagner, R. K., and Sternberg, R. J. (1987). Executive control in reading comprehension. In B. K. Britton and S. M. Glyn (Eds.), *Executive control processes in reading* (pp. 1-21). Hillsdale, NJ: Erlbaum.

Weinert, F. E. (1987). Introduction and overview: Metacognition and motivation as determination of effective learning and understanding. In F. E. Weinert and R. H. Kluwe (Eds.), *Metacognition, motivation and understanding* (pp. 1-16). Hillsdale, NJ: Erlbaum.

Weinstein, C. F., and Mayer, R. F. (1986). The teaching of learning strategies. In M. C. Wittrock (Ed.), *Handbook of research on teaching* (3rd ed., pp. 315-327). New York, NY: Macmillan.

Wertsch, J. V. (1985). *Vygotsky and the social formation of mind.* Cambridge, MA: Harvard University Press.

White, B. Y., and Frederiksen, J. R. (1986). Progressions of quantitative models as a foundation for intelligent learning environments. *Technical Report # 6277,* Bolt, Beranek, and Newman.

Wilson, P. T., and Anderson, R. C. (1986). What they don't know will hurt them: The role of prior knowledge in comprehension. In J. Orasanu (Ed.), *Reading comprehension: From research to practice* (pp. 31-49). Hillsdale, NJ: Erlbaum.

Zellermayer, M., Salomon, G., Globerson, T., and Givon, H. (1991). Enhancing writing-related metacognitions through a computerized writing partner. *American Educational Research Journal, 28*(2), 373-391.

APPENDIX: ASSESSING THE EFFECT OF THE MCAG TREATMENT

Effect size (ES) was used to quantify the effectiveness of the MCAG intervention. ES quantifies the size of the difference between two groups, and may therefore be said to be a true measure of the significance of the difference. As Coe (Cohen, 1977, 1988) notes, ES allows us to move beyond the simplistic, "Does it work or not?" to the far more sophisticated, "How well does it work in a range of contexts?". Statistical significance does not tell us the most important thing: the size of the effect.

An SAS G* power analysis was used to provide a quantitative expression of how well the treatment group and the placebo group performed, relative to the control group. The results shown calculated the value of Cohen's d using the means and standard deviations of two groups (treatment and control). The Effect Size index d, uses Cohen's level of effect size: Small: 0.20; Medium: 0.50; Large: 0.80. An ES of 0 means that, on average, a student receiving the intervention did no better or worse than a student who did not receive it. A positive ES means that the average student who received the intervention performed better than the average student who didn't; the larger the ES, the more powerful the intervention.

Tables 1 and 2 compare the effect size of the two treatments (MCAG and CI) relative to the control group and relative to each other for the following variables:

- Students' achievements (level of performance) on each of the three reading assessment tasks separately; and for all three together
- Students' performance on the reading assessment tasks questions according to cognitive and difficulty levels
- Students' awareness of metacognitive reading strategies measured using the Metacognitive Strategy Index two weeks after the intervention (MSIQ-T: overall score; MSI-D: during reading and MSI-A: after reading – reading strategies that were not incorporated in the written MCAG; MSI-BCD: building, creating and discovering relevant schemata – reading strategies specifically dealt with by the written MCAG)

Table 1: Effect sizes of intervention on students' level of performance on reading assessment tasks

	Control group N=102 Mean	SD	Content Instruction N=85 Mean	SD	Metacognitive awareness N=113 Mean	SD	$ES_1(d_1)$[a]	$ES_2(d_2)$[b]	$ES_3(d_3)$[c]
Reading assessment task 1 *	1.64	0.53	1.73	0.55	2.05	0.55	0.67	0.17	0.58
Reading assessment task 2 *	1.40	0.68	1.54	0.70	1.96	0.69	0.82	0.20	0.60
Reading assessment task 3 *	1.62	0.58	1.95	0.48	1.89	0.46	0.52	0.62	-0.13
All tasks *	1.57	0.47	1.73	0.47	1.99	0.42	0.94	0.34	0.58
Level of difficulty 1	2.39	0.62	2.53	0.52	2.56	0.40	0.50	0.24	0.06
Level of difficulty 2	1.55	0.60	1.53	0.62	1.91	0.58	0.61	-0.03	0.63
Level of difficulty 3	1.14	0.49	1.43	0.51	1.65	0.52	1.00	0.58	0.43
Cognitive level 1	2.20	0.59	2.53	0.51	2.45	0.45	0.48	0.60	0.48
Cognitive level 2	1.69	0.75	1.60	0.71	1.97	0.60	0.40	-0.12	0.57
Cognitive level 3	1.24	0.51	1.36	0.53	1.71	0.52	0.91	0.23	0.00

* Reading achievement adjusted for students' prior reading ability
[a] Control, MCAG
[b] Control, CI
[c] CI, MCAG

The findings in Table 1 suggest that integration of metacognitive learning principles within reading assessment tasks enhances students' achievements and makes a significant difference in their performance. Students in the MCAG group attained significantly higher scores on each of the three reading tasks after adjusting for their prior reading ability. Furthermore, the medium to large ES values of the MCAG treatment group suggest that, on average, students given the intervention performed better than students who did not. In contrast, the CI treatment group shows a negligible ES on two of the three assessment tasks and a medium ES on task 3, a finding explained by the low cognitive and difficulty levels of this task.

The results of the study indicate that written MCAG not only improved students' achievements on specific reading tasks, but also increased their awareness of metacognitive reading strategies. Table 2 illustrates these findings.

Table 2: Effect sizes of intervention on students' level of awareness of metacognitive reading strategies (MSI)

	Control group N=102		Content Instruction N=85		Metacognitive awareness N=113		$ES_1(d_1)$[a]	$ES_2(d_2)$[b]	$ES_3(d_3)$[c]
	Mean	SD	Mean	SD	Mean	SD			
MSI - total (17 items)	7.25	2.94	7.71	2.87	9.14	3.16	0.62	0.16	0.47
MSI-B - before reading (7 items)	2.95	1.64	3.14	1.74	4.54	1.81	0.92	0.11	0.79
MSI-D - during reading (6 items)*	2.48	1.36	2.60	1.26	2.66	1.38	0.13	0.09	0.05
MSI-A - after reading (4 items) *	2.81	1.15	1.96	1.03	1.94	1.18	-0.75	-0.79	-0.02
MSI-BCD - prior knowledge (7 items)	2.47	1.60	2.68	1.65	3.60	1.91	0.64	0.13	0.56

* Not incorporated in the written MCAG
[a] Control, MCAG
[b] Control, CI
[c] CI, MCAG

Subjects in all three research groups exhibited a low level of awareness of metacognitive reading strategies. Of a possible score of 17 (one point for each question answered correctly) the mean score of the control group is 7.25, the CI group is 7.71, and the MCAG treatment group is 9.14. However, examining the different parts of the MSI questionnaire reveals significant differences. On those sections relevant to the MCA treatment - MSI-B (before reading) and MSI-BCD (building, creating and developing relevant schemata), the results of the treatment group are significantly higher than those of the other two groups. And the ES values establish the correlation between MSI achievements and MCAG treatment.

The findings suggest a noticeable contribution of the MCAG treatment to the students' level of awareness of metacognitive reading strategies. The analysis revealed an extremely high and significant ES value of the MCA treatment for 'before reading' metacognitive strategies (ES=0.92). This indicates that the MCAG treatment had a powerful effect on subjects' level of awareness of these strategies. In contrast, for the CI treatment group meaningless ES values were found for all relevant indicators of the MSI questionnaire. This suggests that the CI treatment had no effect on subjects' level of awareness of metacognitive reading strategies. ES values for MSI-D and MSI-A reflected the fact that 'during reading' and 'after reading' metacognitive strategies were not part of the MCAG treatment, and this is validated by the lack of effect found in the analysis (0.13 and 0.11, respectively).

Chapter 6

EFFECTS OF IQ AND KNOWLEDGE COHESIVENESS ON MEMORY TASK PERFORMANCE IN EARLY ELEMENTARY SCHOOL

Joyce M. Alexander, Che-yu Kuo, Kathy E. Johnson, Victoria M. Fleming, James B. Schreiber and Katrina M. Daytner

Indiana University
Indiana University Purdue University – Indianapolis
Northwestern University
Duquesne University
Western Illinois University

ABSTRACT

This article summarizes results from two separate studies concerning the role of IQ and knowledge cohesiveness in memory task performance. Results from Study 1 suggest that some degree of domain cohesiveness is necessary to facilitate sophisticated strategy use though IQ exerted additional effects on recall that were not mediated by more sophisticated strategy use. Study 2 examines the role of IQ when children are taught a cohesive organization for a domain. Results suggest that IQ facilitates knowledge acquisition and, over time, facilitates the use of multiple strategies. Implications for theory development and educational applications are discussed.

When confronted with a demanding memory task, children often have a variety of strategies with which to respond. The choices they make will ultimately affect both the amount recalled and the quality of memory task performance. Factors that influence strategy deployment have been hypothesized to include both knowledge base cohesiveness and intelligence (Bjorklund, 2005). Previous investigations of the effects of knowledge base cohesiveness on strategy use have concluded that items from more cohesive domains generally are more facilitative of recall and strategy use than those from less cohesive domains, presumably because the information is connected together in meaningful ways (e.g.,

Kee and Davis, 1990; Rabinowitz and Kee, 1994). In addition, research from studies of expertise or knowledge base effects shows that experts use more sophisticated strategies in more effective ways within their domain of expertise (e.g., Schneider and Bjorklund, 1992). Evidence suggests, however, that intelligence also plays an independent, facilitative role in strategic tasks. Research has demonstrated that gifted children are more likely to use strategies on free-recall tasks than their non-gifted peers (Gaultney, Bjorklund, and Goldstein, 1996). In fact, many researchers have hypothesized that strategies are central to a defensible definition of intelligence (Bray, Fletcher, and Turner, 1996; Das, 1984).

Although working with information from a highly cohesive knowledge base would be ideal for the facilitation of sophisticated strategy use, children completing typical school tasks are rarely in this position. On the contrary, these "universal novices" (Brown and DeLoache, 1978) are seldom in situations where they have a pre-existing cohesive knowledge base. They spend most of their time working with information from domains that are less cohesive. DeMarie-Dreblow (1991) contends that only those learners with some critical level of initial domain knowledge are able to encode additional knowledge during a learning situation. Thus, a lack of cohesive knowledge can put a learner at a distinct disadvantage in new learning situations. Given these assumptions, it is unclear what facilitates children's strategy choices when they are operating in situations where their knowledge base is less cohesive or rapidly developing. The present studies investigate this question.

We begin with a definition and overview of strategy use in early elementary school. We review literature that examines relations among intelligence, knowledge, and strategy use, concentrating particularly on studies that have examined these factors together. Next, we discuss the challenges of strategy use when knowledge is less cohesive or still developing. We then present results from two studies that examine the respective roles of intelligence and knowledge on strategy use at different points along the continuum of knowledge acquisition. Finally, implications of the combined set of results for theory building are discussed.

STRATEGY USE IN EARLY ELEMENTARY SCHOOL

In concordance with Siegler and Jenkins (1989) we assume that for behavior to be considered strategic, it must be both goal-directed and non-obligatory. Research indicates that children rarely select and use one strategy throughout a task (Siegler, 1990, 1995). Instead, children use multiple strategies. For example, McGilly and Siegler (1989) found that 77% of kindergartners and 59% of third graders used multiple strategies on a math task. Coyle and Bjorklund (1997) reported similar results for a memory task. They found that the average number of strategies used by children in second through fourth grade increased from 1.6 to 2.4 during a 2-minute memory task. They also found that children used different combinations of strategies on different trials.

Crowley, Shrager, and Siegler (1997) maintain that children's strategy choices are seldom controlled by rational calculations, as some researchers have assumed. They argue instead that, within familiar contexts, an associative strength model best explains strategy choices. At any given point in time, and for any given problem, there is a strategy which has optimal associative strength based on past performance, regardless of metacognitive knowledge about specific strategies. Interestingly, newly-generated strategies get additional "novelty credit" to assure their continued use in this model. Siegler (1990) hypothesizes that strategy choice is then a function of "the local value of the strategy (how well it has done on that problem in the past in terms of speed and accuracy) and of its global value (how well it has done across all problems)" (p. 82-83). The strategy that fits the above criteria is then used on the specific task with little metacognitive reflection involved in the selection process.

Children in the early elementary school years typically are able to use several developing strategies when confronted with a memory task. A sorting strategy is often adopted, though levels of recall and organization usually increase with age. Preschool children's use of sorting is typically minimal, and the extent to which their recall is organized by adult groupings is frequently at chance levels (Schneider and Bjorklund, 1998). By first grade, sorting is evident (particularly with highly cohesive or highly typical items) and performance is significantly greater than chance (Alexander and Schwanenflugel, 1994). By second grade, Coyle and Bjorklund (1997) found that children tended to use a combination of sorting, clustering (recalling related items together), and rehearsal (labeling an item more than once or labeling several items together). Thus, children of the ages tested in the present studies were expected to have rudimentary versions of rehearsal, clustering, and sorting available.

THE EFFECTS OF INTELLIGENCE AND KNOWLEDGE ON STRATEGY USE

Individual differences in cognitive abilities have been studied from various theoretical perspectives. The present study adopts an information processing perspective, in which differences in how easily information is encoded, categorized, and recalled are important to explaining how people learn. Researchers adopting this perspective often contrast groups that significantly differ in cognitive ability level in order to understand some of the underlying processes responsible for developmental and group differences (Bjorklund, 2005). Although multiple definitions of cognitive ability have been proposed (Sternberg, 1985; Gardner, 1999), we view cognitive ability as a domain-general resource that facilitates processing speed, vocabulary development, and problem solving. Individual differences in cognitive ability (or IQ) often are discussed as existing along a continuum from those with mental retardation and learning difficulties to gifted individuals. The following section reviews research on the effects of cognitive ability on strategy use as well as the interplay of cognitive ability and the cohesiveness of to-be-learned materials.

Hettinger Steiner and Carr (2003), in a recent review of cognitive development in gifted children, noted that gifted children seem better able to acquire, produce, and use strategies than nongifted children (e.g., Cho and Ahn, 2003; Davidson and Sternberg, 1984; Montague, 1991; Scruggs and Mastropieri, 1985, 1988). They note, however, that research has not always shown advantages for gifted children in the early primary grades (Alexander, Carr, and Schwanenflugel, 1995; Muir, Masterson, Weiner, Lyon, and White, 1989; Perleth, 1994), nor have tests of strategy generation and near transfer always proven easier for gifted children (Borkowski and Peck, 1986; Ferretti and Butterfield, 1992; Harnishfeger and Bjorklund, 1990). On the other hand, Gaultney, Bjorklund, and Goldstein (1996) found that gifted middle school children were consistently more strategic than their nongifted peers on a task involving free recall. At least some of the gifted children's advantage in their study came from nonstrategic factors such as a more elaborated knowledge base or faster speed of processing allowing for easier identification of individual items. Similar arguments have been made by Geary and Brown (1991) for early mathematics addition strategies.

Several studies have attempted to manipulate the cohesiveness of the to-be-remembered materials in order to investigate the effects of cohesiveness and cognitive abilities on strategy use. Bjorklund and Bernholtz (1986) gave 13-year-olds two lists of items to remember that differed on typicality. On the first list, typicality was based on adult norms. On the second list, typicality was based on the individual's own self-generated norms. Significant differences in memory performance for good and poor readers were observed, but only for the adult-generated lists. Recall of items derived from the child-generated norms did not differ as a function of reading level, suggesting that better readers (typically those with higher cognitive abilities) were not more strategic. The superior performance of the good readers when presented with items derived from the adult-generated norms was assumed to be based on increased world knowledge. Alexander and Schwanenflugel (1994) also gave first and second grade children lists of items that varied in typicality (high versus low). Again, cohesiveness of the list, and not intelligence or metacognitive knowledge about a strategy's usefulness, was the best predictor of recall and strategy use.

Similarly, Schneider, Korkel and Weinert (1989) gave German children in grades 3, 5, and 7, classified as soccer "novices" or "experts," a well-organized soccer narrative to recall. Measures of cognitive ability also were available, enabling a factorial design in which ability and knowledge were crossed, yielding four groups. High knowledge children recalled the narrative well, regardless of whether they were assigned to the high or low ability group. Low ability experts outperformed high-ability novices. Possessing detailed subject-matter knowledge was sufficient to yield high levels of performance. Importantly, high levels of domain knowledge compensated for low levels of cognitive ability. Similar results have been presented by Recht and Leslie (1988) and Walker (1987) for adult experts on baseball, and by Ceci and Liker (1986, 1988; Ceci, 1993) for adult experts on horse racing.

However, knowledge does not always eliminate the effects of cognitive ability on memory task performance. Schneider and Bjorklund (1992) and Schneider, Bjorklund, and Maier-Bruckner (1996) used a similar factorial design in which IQ groups (high versus low) were crossed with soccer knowledge groups (4th grade experts versus novices). Text recall and sort-recall memory tasks were administered that either were soccer-related or not. In both studies, experts remembered more than novices from the soccer related materials but not from the non-soccer related materials. The effect of IQ, however, was not eliminated in these studies. High IQ children remembered more than low IQ children on both soccer and nonsoccer materials, at each level of expertise. Schneider and Bjorklund (1992) argued that intelligence played a greater role in these tasks because of the requirement for more deliberate encoding strategies. Therefore, when strategic behavior is required for task completion, as in the present studies, high levels of knowledge may not totally eclipse the impact of intelligence on task performance.

THE CONTINUUM OF KNOWLEDGE ACQUISITION

As reviewed above, numerous studies illustrate that students' ability to understand texts, solve mathematical problems, and learn new concepts in the social or natural sciences, depends on what students already know (see Glaser, 1987). Young children, by definition, are in a position of low knowledge when they are exposed to new topics in school, and yet, investigations on the effects of heightened knowledge levels have failed to address what happens during knowledge construction in a new domain (e.g., Chi, 1978; Schneider, Korkel, and Weinert, 1989). Likewise, we know very little about how children's strategy use changes as knowledge in a domain is acquired and becomes more cohesive.

At least two potential hypotheses about the interaction between knowledge acquisition and strategy use have been proposed in the literature. First, one could predict that a minimum amount of domain knowledge is necessary to facilitate strategy use (e.g., Alexander and Judy, 1988). Thus, domain knowledge growth would have to occur first, followed by strategy use. Second, one could argue that memory strategies could be learned in the absence of specific domain knowledge. Once those strategies have been mastered they should, theoretically, facilitate acquisition of knowledge within any new domain (e.g., Hasselhorn and Korkel, 1986). The literature supporting each of these hypotheses is reviewed below.

Domain Knowledge is Necessary to Facilitate Strategy Use

Previous studies have shown that children both learn and use strategies more effectively within a more familiar domain (Bjorklund and Buchanan, 1989). Age-related changes in domain knowledge have been found to be related to, (1) children's tendency to use strategies, (2) the likelihood that children will benefit from strategies, (3) the degree to which strategy training is successful, and (4) the likelihood that such strategy use will transfer outside of the domain in which it has been learned (Bjorklund, Muir-Broaddus, and Schneider, 1990; Corsale and Ornstein, 1980; Rabinowitz, 1984, 1988).

Within this framework, Alexander and Judy (1988) have advanced the argument that "a foundation of domain-specific knowledge seems requisite to the efficient and effective utilization of strategic knowledge" (p. 384). They hypothesize that domain-specific knowledge, as it is proceduralized, gives rise to domain-related strategies (Anderson, Greeno, Kline, and Neves, 1981; Chi, 1981). Any given task should require knowledge about a domain, general strategy use, and typically some higher-level planning or metacognitive-type strategies for monitoring task completion (i.e., McCutchen, 1986). Indeed, research has shown that children who possess low levels of knowledge seem to lack prerequisite skills that allow them to benefit from strategy use (Alexander, Pate, Kulikwoich, Farrell, and Wright, 1989). In sum, a child's ability to be an effective strategy user depends on requisite amounts of domain-relevant knowledge.

THE POSSESSION OF KNOWLEDGE-INDEPENDENT STRATEGIES CAN FACILITATE KNOWLEDGE ACQUISITION

Although increases in strategy use typically covary with increases in knowledge, there clearly are aspects of strategic performance that develop throughout the preschool and elementary school years, independently of the influences of knowledge. First, the speed with which information is processed increases in a linear fashion as a function of age (Hale, 1990; Kail, 1986, 1988, 2004). Increased processing efficiency subsequently enables the discovery and execution of strategies to promote learning. Second, strategy use might be mediated by individual differences that are not developmentally based (e.g., intelligence), even when knowledge is equated (see discussion above). Strategy use might also be mediated by peer-assisted discussions involving metacognitive insights and not just discussions about content (Fleming and Alexander, 2001; Manion and Alexander, 1997). Finally, the context of school, where most children engage in deliberate memory tasks for the first time, may promote the acquisition of multipurpose strategies such as rehearsal and naming, regardless of the status of the knowledge base (Best and Ornstein, 1986; Morrison, 1987).

These two hypotheses may not be mutually exclusive and perhaps oversimplify relations between strategy learning and knowledge acquisition. There may be instances in which less well-integrated knowledge conditions could promote strategy execution (Alexander and Schwanenflugel, 1994). Schauble (1996) introduces further complexity by noting that while available strategies affect the way knowledge develops, knowledge can simultaneously affect the way that strategies are applied. Indeed, strategic and conceptual knowledge acquisition may occur in parallel (Schauble, 1996). Alternatively, DeMarie-Dreblow (1991) argued that increases in knowledge may not automatically lead to increases in strategy use. Rather, knowledge may need to be transformed or restructured before it is capable of facilitating strategy execution. We believe that aspects of both theories must be integrated to provide a more satisfactory explanation of interactions between knowledge cohesiveness, IQ, and strategy use. We begin with an investigation in which the degree of knowledge cohesiveness was explicitly manipulated to examine the impact of intelligence and knowledge cohesiveness on strategy use and recall. We then present a mini-longitudinal investigation of domain-specific knowledge acquisition in which we examine the impact of intelligence and developing knowledge on strategic memory task performance.

STUDY 1: THE RELATION OF INTELLIGENCE TO STRATEGIC MEMORY PERFORMANCE WITH MORE AND LESS COHESIVE MATERIALS

In the first study, we investigated the effects of more and less cohesive knowledge on strategy use and recall. Our specific goals were: 1) to explore the types of strategies children use in response to task demands with more and less cohesive materials; 2) to determine whether IQ predicts recall and strategy use differently for materials varying in cohesiveness.

Method

Participants

Ninety second-grade children from a rural elementary school in southern Indiana participated (age range 92-112 months, M = 8 years 4 months). Ten children were subsequently dropped from the study due to technical difficulties (n = 1), inability to complete both sessions (n = 2), or a lack of an appropriate IQ match (n = 7). The remaining 80 children were matched on IQ (range 80-130) and assigned to either a low or high cohesive condition. There were equal numbers of girls and boys in each condition. Two pairs of children were eliminated from data analyses after all data were collected in order create groups that did not overlap in terms of IQ scores (range 80-100 for low IQ group and 103-130 for high IQ group).

Materials

Children were presented with two decks of 20 4-color pictures (8.5 cm X 8.5 cm), each including 4 pictures from 5 categories: vehicles, furniture, fruit, weapons, and clothing. All items were highly identifiable by picture and had a greater than 60% inclusion rate from Lin, Schwanenflugel, and Wisenbaker's (1991) second grade norms. One deck consisted of items rated as "low" in typicality relative to other items in the category. The other deck consisted of the 4 highest-rated typicality items in the category (see Appendix A).

Procedure

The researcher arranged 20 pictures on a table in a random grid so that no category exemplars were contiguous and covered the cards so as to hide them as the child entered the room. To ensure that identification would not be a problem, the researcher lifted the cover and the child named each of the pictured objects before he or she was introduced to the task. If the child could not name the object, the researcher named the object and asked the child whether she knew the object. All children reported being familiar with all 20 stimuli.

The researcher told the child she would have three minutes to study the pictures and instructed her to do anything she thought would help her remember them. The researcher said, "You don't have to leave the pictures where they are. You can pick them up or leave them alone, whatever you think will help you remember them." During this explanation, the researcher picked up two random pictures momentarily placing each in the other's location on the grid before returning them to their original positions. During the three-minute study phase, a video camera recorded the child's behavior. After the study phase, the researcher covered the stimuli and prompted the child to recall the items, terminating the recall period after the child had either exhausted his memory, sitting silent for 15 seconds following a prompt for additional words, or after the child recalled all 20 items. After approximately 2 minutes of a filler task, the researcher re-set the cards in their original random grid and administered Trial 2, a repeat trial in which the researcher presented the same stimuli with the same instructions and repeated the recall measure. The Kaufman Brief Intelligence Test (K-BIT; Kaufman and Kaufman, 1990) was administered during a separate session two weeks earlier by a different researcher. The K-BIT was used as a general measure of intelligence to match children assigned to the high and low cohesive conditions.

Coding

Strategy Use. We measured sorting and clustering with Adjusted Ratio of Clustering (ARC) scores (Roenker, Thompson, and Brown, 1971). The ARC score ranges from a chance level (0.0) to perfect sorting or clustering (1.0), and represents how closely a child's sorting (movement of the cards into physical categories during study) and clustering (use of categories to facilitate ordered or clustered recall) approximate adult categories.

A video camera recorded other study behaviors during each three-minute study period. Researchers (blind to participants' knowledge cohesiveness condition assignment and to the hypotheses of the present study) viewed tapes and rated each child's strategy use during 1-minute intervals. They coded external indications of both rehearsal (pointing to cards and saying names or simply saying the names of the cards) and self-testing (involving covering pictures or closing eyes and reviewing item names) as either 1 for present or 0 for absent during each 1-minute interval, for a potential sum total range from 0-3 for each strategy. Children could receive credit for more than one strategy in a 1-minute interval. The initial agreement rate on the entire set of tapes was 96.08%. The research team discussed and resolved all disagreements. This agreement percentage is similar to Coyle and Bjorklund (1997) and Lange, MacKinnon, and Nida (1989).

Results

Effects of Knowledge Cohesiveness on Strategy Use

Table 1 presents means and standard deviations for all strategy and recall variables for children assigned to both knowledge cohesiveness conditions. Paired sample *t*-tests revealed higher recall on both trials for children in the high cohesive condition than for those in the low cohesive condition, trial 1 $t(39) = 5.29$, trial 2 $t(39) = 5.58$, both p's $< .01$. The high cohesive condition also facilitated greater use of sorting on trial 1, $t(39) = 3.29$, $p < .01$, and clustering on both trials, trial 1 $t(39) = 3.21$, trial 2 $t(39) = 3.23$, both p's $< .01$. Finally self-testing, although not common, was significantly more likely to occur in the low cohesive condition, trial 1 $t(39) = 2.48$, $p < .05$; trial 2 $t(39) = 1.99$, $p = .05$. Given the similarities in strategy use between the two trials, recall and strategy variables were averaged for further analyses.

IQ as a Predictor of Recall and Strategy Use

A 2 (IQ: high, low) x 2 (knowledge cohesiveness condition) ANOVA on number of items recalled revealed significant main effects for both knowledge cohesiveness [$F(1,72) = 36.60$, $p < .001$, partial $\eta^2 = .34$] and IQ [$F(1,72) = 4.94$, $p < .05$; partial $\eta^2 = .06$] with no significant interaction [$F(1,72) = .32$]. Children assigned to the high cohesiveness condition remembered more items than those assigned to the low cohesiveness condition ($M = 14.37$ and 10.71, respectively). Children with higher IQs recalled more items than those with lower IQs ($M = 13.21$ and 11.87, respectively).

We conducted similar analyses on recall ARC, sorting ARC, and rehearsal scores. Recall ARC scores were significantly higher for those assigned to the high knowledge cohesiveness condition than those assigned to the low knowledge cohesiveness condition, $M = .57$ and .25 respectively; $F(1,72) = 17.88$, $p < .001$, partial $\eta^2 = .20$. There was neither a main effect nor interaction with IQ [$F(1,27) = 1.2$ and $F(1,72) = .37$ respectively]. We found similar results for sorting ARC scores, with scores significantly higher for children assigned to the high knowledge cohesiveness condition than for those assigned to the low knowledge cohesiveness condition, $M = .38$ and .16 respectively; $F(1,72) = 7.46$, $p < .01$; partial $\eta^2 = .09$. Again, we found neither interactions nor main effects involving IQ [$F(1,72) = .59$ and .17 respectively]. In addition, neither IQ nor knowledge cohesiveness significantly predicted the use of rehearsal [$F(1,72) = .02$ and 1.97 respectively] nor was there a significant interaction [$F(1,72) = .26$]. Though the absolute level of self-testing was low, our results indicate a main effect of knowledge cohesiveness [$F(1,72) = 5.66$, $p < .05$, partial $\eta^2 = .07$], with children in the *low* knowledge cohesive condition more likely to demonstrate self-testing than those in the high knowledge cohesiveness condition ($M = .37$ and .05, respectively). We found no main effect or interaction with IQ on self-testing [both F's < 1].

Table 1. Means and standard deviations for all variables in Study 1

Variable	High Knowledge Cohesiveness M	SD	Low Knowledge Cohesiveness M	SD
Intelligence	101.75	11.19	101.80	11.51
Recall				
Trial 1	13.75	2.93	10.17	2.94**
Trial 2	14.98	3.18	11.58	3.18**
Sorting ARC (0-1 scale)				
Trial 1	46	52	18	28**
Trial 2	28	.52	15	28
Clustering ARC (0-1 scale)				
Trial 1	54	42	25	42**
Trial 2	59	39.	26	41**
Rehearsal (0-3 scale)				
Trial 1	1.20	99	.95	1.06
Trial 2	1.38	1.00	1.08	1.97
Self-testing (0-3 scale)				
Trial 1	00	00	18	45*
Trial 2	05	22	18	38*

*$p < .05$; ** $p < .01$.

Discussion

The results from Study 1 illustrate that children experience recall benefits from both high levels of knowledge cohesiveness and high IQ. Interestingly, higher IQ children did not demonstrate more sophisticated strategy use. Differences in strategy use were predicted solely by knowledge cohesiveness. These results suggest that some degree of domain cohesiveness is necessary to facilitate more sophisticated strategy use. IQ exerts an additional effect on recall performance through mostly non-strategic factors. We speculate speed of processing or item familiarity may be responsible for the higher recall levels of the children with higher

IQs. These results, however, do not help us understand the role of cognitive ability in the process of learning about a new domain. Thus, we turn to Study 2.

STUDY 2: THE EFFECT OF IQ AND INCREASING DOMAIN KNOWLEDGE ON MEMORY TASK PERFORMANCE

The objective of Study 2 was to address the complex interplay between IQ and increasing knowledge for kindergarten children who completed a specially-designed 3-week curricular unit on dinosaurs. We were specifically interested in the relative effects of cognitive ability and increasing domain-specific knowledge on young children's recall performance and strategy use on a memory task. There has been only one other curricular study aimed at examining the effect of growing domain knowledge on memory task performance. DeMarie-Dreblow (1991) presented a curricular unit on birds to college students and children in the second through fifth grades. Although the students' domain knowledge increased, there was no improvement in recall performance or execution of strategies on a memory task. Importantly, DeMarie-Dreblow did not teach the organizing features of the domain. In the present study, we designed a curriculum that was intended to explicitly teach children information pertaining to distinctive features correlated with taxonomic group membership as well as interrelations among taxonomic groups of dinosaurs. We expected that the curriculum would help young children to construct a cohesive and organized knowledge base pertaining to dinosaurs that could serve as a foundation for knowledge-dependent memory strategies (e.g., grouping by taxonomic families to facilitate recall). This study also allowed us to examine the interaction of knowledge and verbal intelligence on memory performance at early points along the continuum of knowledge acquisition.

Method

Participants

Twenty-six kindergarteners (mean age 74.27 months; range 68 to 83 months) participated in this study. There were 12 girls and 14 boys.

Curriculum

An experienced kindergarten teacher, blind to the hypotheses of the present study, introduced a 3-week curriculum about the dinosaur domain to children. The curriculum was designed to explicitly teach children the taxonomic organization of the domain. Five taxonomic families were introduced in the first week (large flesh eaters, small flesh eaters, sauropods, four-legged ornithiscians, two-legged ornithischians). General information pertaining to all dinosaurs including diet, habitat, defense, and ambulation was also provided in week 1. During weeks 2 and 3, the curriculum focused on information concerning the names and distinguishing features for each of 3 "basic level" species within the 5 target families. More details about the curriculum can be found in Alexander, Johnson, Leibham, and DeBauge (2005).

Measures

Production of species name and attributes. Production tests designed to assess name and attribute knowledge for the 15 target dinosaur exemplars were administered throughout the curriculum. A picture of each species introduced in the curriculum was presented to the child and the child was asked to first name, and then tell all that they knew about that dinosaur. Pictures in the testing phase were always different from those presented in the curriculum.

Comprehension of Dinosaur Name

Comprehension of species names was assessed through structured comprehension trials. Each trial consisted of four realistic color pictures of dinosaurs arranged in two consecutive pages within a loose-leaf binder. The four dinosaur pictures included one species "target," one closely related and perceptually similar distractor, and two perceptually different dinosaurs from unrelated species. The positions of the four pictures were determined randomly. At baseline, there were 36 trials designed to test knowledge across 10 subfamilies within the 5 target families in order to estimate how much children knew about dinosaurs before the curriculum began. During the curriculum, 2 comprehension tests involving 15 trials were used to test knowledge of the 5 families taught in the curriculum. Each species introduced in the curriculum was included in one of the 15 trials in order to monitor developing knowledge of names.

Pile Sort Task

The pile sort task was used to assess children's developing knowledge of the taxonomic structure of the dinosaur domain. It included pictures of 4 dinosaur species from each of five target families. It included an example of each of the 15 target species introduced in the curriculum as well as one novel exemplar drawn from each of the 5 target families, yielding a total set of 20 pictures.

Memory Task

One set of nine farm animal pictures with one background picture of a barnyard scene (14 x 21.5 inches) was used for a practice trial. The sizes of the animal pictures were proportional to the background picture provided. A set of 12 dinosaur exemplars that could be positioned against a background "prehistoric scene" was used for the test trials. Again, the exemplars were proportional to each other and to the background scene (38 x 28 inches). The barnyard scene included a barn, a pasture, a pond, and a fence. The prehistoric scene included cues for specific diets or habitats (brush, a carcass, water, and tall trees)

Procedures

Children were tested individually by one of five trained researchers in a quiet area of the school. All verbal responses were audiotaped and behaviors during the memory task were videotaped for later coding and analysis. Baseline measures were administered two school days before the curriculum began. The baseline session involved the verbal section of the Kaufman Brief Intelligence Test (K-BIT; Kaufman and Kaufman, 1990) and a test of dinosaur name comprehension, which provided information about cognitive ability and background dinosaur knowledge levels. Session 1 and Session 2 data were collected toward the end of week 1 and week 3 of the curriculum, respectively (with name comprehension assessed at the beginning of weeks 2 and 4; see Table 2 for the complete testing schedule for Study 2). At Session 1 and Session 2, children completed tests of species name and attribute production and dinosaur name comprehension. In addition, the pile sort task was administrated before the memory task was completed.

Table 2 Assessment Schedule for Study 2 including all knowledge tasks, the memory task, and K-BIT across the curriculum.

Session	Comprehension	Production	Pile Sort	Memory Task	K-BIT
Pretest	X				X
Session 1	X	X	X	X	
Session 2	X	X	X	X	

Production of Species Name and Attributes

During the name production task, a researcher presented dinosaur pictures to each child and asked the child to provide the dinosaur's name. During the attribute knowledge production task, the researcher provided children with the name of the 15 dinosaurs and the child was asked to provide attribute information. "What do you know about X? (1st prompt) Can you think about what it might have that's special, or what it might do that's special?" (2nd prompt). If the child presented no additional information for 10 seconds after the 2nd prompt, the researcher presented the next dinosaur. Children's responses were audiotaped for subsequent transcription and later analysis.

Comprehension of Names

Children were randomly assigned to complete the comprehension task in either a forward or reverse order. On each trial, the researcher presented the child with a set of four dinosaur pictures and asked, "Is there a(n) X?" (Where X was the species name of the target dinosaur). The researchers assured the child that it was fine to select more than one picture, to say there was not an X, or to say they did not know the answer. As there were no differences in comprehension scores by order of presentation, order of presentation was subsequently collapsed for all analyses.

Pile Sorting Task

The researcher laid out 20 dinosaur pictures on the table in front of the child and asked her to create her own groups saying, "I'd like you to put these dinosaurs into piles so that the ones that are like the same kind of things are together in the same pile." After the child created her piles, the researcher asked for verbal justifications as to why the dinosaurs belonged together in each pile.

Memory Task

During the memory task practice trial, nine farm animals were randomly positioned on the table in front of the child and next to the scene picture of the farmyard. The researcher introduced this task by saying, "In this game, I'm going to give you some farm animal pictures that I want you to remember. But first, I need to make sure that you know what all the farm animals are." The researcher asked each child to provide a name or nickname for each animal.

Following the naming phase, the researcher invited the child to "Do whatever you think will help you remember. You can put them on the picture (as the researcher demonstrated placing an animal exemplar on the scene), or leave them where they are (as the researcher took the example back from the scene). I'm going to give you a couple of minutes to study the pictures and then I'm going to take them away and ask you to remember them." The researcher gave the child 2 minutes to study the exemplars and then removed them from sight, leaving the scene background in front of the child. The researcher terminated the recall period after the child had either exhausted his memory, sitting silent for 15 seconds following a prompt for additional words, or after the child recalled all 9 items. The test trials involved using the same procedure with 12 dinosaur exemplars. In the test trials, the researcher gave the child 2.5 minutes for study, as there were more exemplars to remember than during the training trial.

Coding

We were interested in the effects of IQ and knowledge on three strategies children used while engaging in the memory task: rehearsal (a strategy not necessarily dependent on domain knowledge), sorting (a measure of strategic use of grouping-related knowledge during encoding) and clustering (a measure of strategic use of grouping-related knowledge during retrieval). Other strategies (e.g., self-testing) did not occur frequently enough in children this young to be considered. Children of this age are typically very obvious with their strategy use (Alexander and Schwanenflugel, 1994). Mouthing of words is easily seen and rehearsal can be heard both out loud and in whispers. Given the age of the children and questions about their ability to accurately report strategy use, we chose to rely on the obvious behaviors we could code from the videotapes. Thus, the occurrence of overt rehearsal behaviors was credited when the child either verbalized out loud or silently mouthed dinosaur names (or nicknames) during each of five consecutive 30-s intervals during the study phase of the memory task.

The extent to which children arranged the dinosaur exemplars in cohesive ways was evaluated in two ways: adherence to either taxonomic or cue-related organization. The taxonomic organization score was derived from counting the number of dinosaurs from the same family group that clustered together spatially on the background scene at the end of the study time. Groups were defined by taxonomic membership (based on either 4 basic categories or the 5 family groups taught in the curriculum). Children were given the higher count as their score. Two dinosaurs were counted as spatially clustered when the distance between the pair of related dinosaurs was smaller than the distance between each member of the pair and unrelated dinosaurs on the habitat.

The cue-related organization score was also derived from counting the number of dinosaurs which were placed on the habitat picture by the appropriate diet cue (brush, carcass, tall trees). Proximity to the appropriate cue was defined as within 1.5 cm distance of the diet-related cue on the habitat background picture. The taxonomic membership and the cue-related organization scores were intended to capture whether children used a knowledge-based organization to aid study in the memory task. Each child then received the higher of these two standardized scores as an index of cohesive organization during study.

The degree to which children clustered their recall lists was evaluated using an Adjusted Ratio of Clustering (ARC) score (Roenker, Thompson, and Brown, 1971). This score was based on taxonomic membership (either 4 basic categories or 5 family groups taught in the curriculum), and was intended to capture whether children used the cohesive knowledge structure they learned in the curriculum to organize their recall. Scores for both taxonomic membership groupings were calculated and the child received the higher of the two scores. A perfect ARC score was equal to 1 and the chance level was 0; thus children who did not demonstrate clustering during recall by taxonomic groups were given an ARC of 0.

Two authors independently coded from videotapes 30% of children's study behaviors. The agreement between the coders for the presence of rehearsal during each 30-second interval was 97.5 % and for the cue-related and taxonomic organization scores agreement was 95.8 %. Given that the 30% established the reliability of the coding schemes, the first coder then coded the remaining 70% of the trial data.

Results

The Effect of the Curriculum on Knowledge Acquisition

In order to provide information about what children learned from our curriculum, scores were derived from each knowledge task. Detailed analyses of knowledge acquisition from our curriculum have been presented elsewhere (Alexander, Johnson, Leibham, and DeBauge, 2005) and thus will be described only briefly here.[1] Name production scores for Sessions 1 and 2 were transformed into the proportion of correct species names (or nicknames presented in the curriculum e.g. "t-rex" for tyrannosaurus rex; "long neck" for diplodocus) provided by each child in reference to the 15 target dinosaurs. Attribute production scores were also calculated for Session 1 and Session 2 by averaging the total number of meaningful propositions generated in reference to each of 15 target dinosaurs. Those propositions involving perceptual features that were superficial (e.g. " it's green") or subjective evaluations (e.g. "it's pretty") were not counted. Name comprehension scores were derived for Baseline, Session 1, and Session 2 by calculating the proportion of correct targets and/or closed related distractors picked by the child. Finally, children's understanding of domain organization was inferred through scores on the pile sort task. The proportion of exemplars (out of 20) included in piles that were based on features or similarity dimensions explicitly taught through the curriculum (e.g., meat-eaters; having crests) was calculated at each Session.

All children learned from the curriculum (see Table 3). Comprehension of dinosaur names increased significantly from Baseline to Session 1. Name comprehension, production of names, attribute production and pile sort scores increased significantly across all three weeks of the curriculum, suggesting that domain knowledge continued to develop throughout the period through which memory performance was assessed. Increases in pile sorting scores, in particular, suggest that the organization and cohesiveness of the domain continued to increase.

---

[1] The knowledge acquisition data presented here were based on the total number of children who performed the memory task (n=26) and not the total number of children who participated in the curriculum as reported in Alexander, Johnson, et al. (2005).

The relation between IQ and knowledge was also examined (see Table 4). IQ scores were significantly correlated with Baseline name comprehension scores ($r = .56$, $p<.01$), but not with comprehension scores from either Sessions 1 or 2. Children with higher IQ scores tended to comprehend more dinosaurs than children with lower IQ scores at the beginning of this study, but this advantage disappeared when children learned information from our curriculum. IQ scores were not related to scores on either the attribute listing or the pile sort task. Given that children placed 44% of dinosaurs in piles corresponding to taxonomic groups at Session 1, they (regardless of IQ) seemed to have already begun constructing an organized knowledge base pertaining to dinosaurs by the time the first assessment occurred at the end of week 1 (remember that children had been taught the organizing features of the domain during that week). Children also produced about one curriculum-related attribute for each dinosaur (.84 for Session 1 and 1.22 for Session 2), suggesting that all children started connecting featural information to each of the dinosaur exemplars.

It is interesting that name production scores from Sessions 1 and 2 were the strongest knowledge measures correlated with IQ scores ($r = .60$, $p<.01$ for Session 1; $r = .61$, $p<.01$ for Session 2).

Table 3. Study 2 Knowledge Measures over Time

Variable	Baseline M	Baseline SD	Session 1 M	Session 1 SD	Session 2 M	Session 2 SD	Paired *t*-test Result
Production (proportion correct)			.16	.11	.22	.14	$t(25)=3.38*$ (Session 1 vs. Session 2)
Comprehension (proportion correct)	.38	.14	.56	.15	.68	.19	$t(25)=5.50*$ (baseline vs. Session1) $t(25)=3.08*$ (Session 1 vs. Session 2
Attribute (avg. attributes produced per exemplar)			.84	.38	1.22	.43	$t(25)=4.13*$ (Session 1 vs. Session 2)
Pile Sort (proportion of species sorted based on taxonomic membership)			.44	.27	.52	.26	$t(25)=2.03*$ (Session 1 vs. Session 2

*$p<.05$; **$p<.01$

Since IQ was correlated with the Baseline comprehension score, we examined partial correlations between IQ and the name production score (with the Baseline comprehension score controlled) for both sessions (partial $r = .42$, $p<.05$ for Session 1; partial $r = .45$, $p<.05$ for Session 2). These partial correlations suggest that IQ was related to production scores over and above initial knowledge scores. Since name production scores have been argued to be the best proxy for depth of domain-related knowledge (Johnson, Scott and Mervis, 2004), these significant correlations suggest that individual differences in intelligence influenced the rate at which children acquired information from the curriculum (cf. Johnson and Mervis, 1994).

In order to explore the effects of both knowledge acquisition and intelligence on recall performance at each session, a knowledge index score was derived by summing the standardized scores from each knowledge task. There were significant correlations between IQ and the summed knowledge scores at both sessions ($r = .54$, $p<.01$ for Session 1 and $r = .52$, $p<.01$ for Session 2). This lends additional support to our conclusion from the name production data. Although all children learned from the curriculum, high-IQ children did seem to learn domain exemplar names more quickly from our curriculum and have higher overall knowledge scores than their low-IQ peers.

Table 4. Correlations between knowledge measures and IQ across time for Study 2

	Measure	Baseline Comp.	Pile Sort	Name Prod.	Name Comp.	Attribute Prod.
Session 1	K-BIT	.56**	.22	.60**	.33	.17
	Baseline Comprehension		.10	.54**	.28	.14
	Pile Sort Score			.36	.11	.47**
	Production				.52**	.13
	Comprehension					-.20
Session 2	K-BIT		-.02	.61**	.38	.32
	Pile Sort Score			.07	-.13	.08
	Production				.56**	.30
	Comprehension					.25

The Effects of Knowledge and IQ on Recall

Children recalled a mean of 5.80 dinosaur names (or nicknames) during the first session and 6.77 during the second session. We were interested in whether high IQ would facilitate recall over and above the effects of knowledge. Separate ANOVAs were completed for each session, as knowledge levels increased over time, and some children moved across knowledge groups between Sessions 1 and 2. For Session 1, a 2 (IQ: high and low based on median split) × 2 (knowledge: median split) ANOVA was conducted on the numbers of dinosaur names recalled.[2] The main effect of IQ was significant, $F(1, 22) = 6.7$, $p=.01$, partial $\eta^2 = .23$. There was no main effect of knowledge, $F(1,22) = 1.50$, nor was there a significant interaction, $F(1,22) = .02$. This suggests that children's recall performance early in the curriculum was influenced by IQ. At Session 2, results indicated a significant main effect of knowledge on items recalled, $F(1,22) = 4.46$, $p < .05$, partial $\eta^2 = .17$. There was no main effect of IQ, $F(1,22) = 2.01$, nor was there a significant interaction. Later in the curriculum, performance seemed to be related only to children's relative levels of domain-specific knowledge.

Given that there was a correlation between IQ and baseline comprehension, baseline knowledge could have been mediating the main effect of IQ on recall at Session 1. A partial correlation between IQ and recall with baseline comprehension scores partial was calculated, $r_{23} = .38$, $p = .07$. This suggests that IQ may directly impact recall during the early stages of knowledge acquisition.

The Effects of IQ and Knowledge on Strategy Use

We were curious about the relative roles of IQ and knowledge on the use or non-use of strategies. Children were classified as rehearsal users if they demonstrated rehearsal behaviors during any interval of the study phase or as rehearsal non-users if they did not. One way to use rehearsal more strategically is to rehearse items late in the study period, increasing the number of items held actively in working memory at the beginning of the recall period. Thus, children were additionally categorized either as late rehearsal users if they demonstrated rehearsal behaviors in either of the last two intervals or late non-rehearsers if they had not. For clustering, a 0 ARC score represents recall inconsistent with the organization of the selected categories (or chance). Thus, children were categorized either as clustering users (ARC>0) or non-users (ARC=0). In order to compare the influence of the relative cohesiveness of children's study placement behaviors on recall, children were divided into high and low cohesive placement groups based on a median split of the cohesive placement scores.

Previous research has indicated that strategy diversity (or using multiple strategies on a trial) is positively related to recall in children (Coyle, 2001; Coyle and Bjorklund, 1997). Thus, children were given one point for each strategy for which they were classified as users (scores ranged from 0-3; late rehearsal was not included in this analysis). Figure 1 shows the mean number of strategies used by each group.

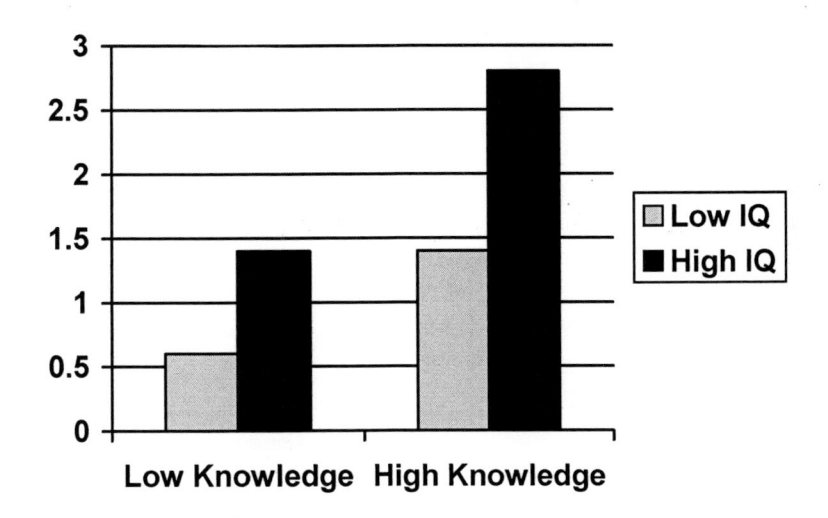

Figure 1. Mean number of strategies used at Session 2

Separate 2 (IQ) x 2 (Knowledge) ANOVAs were run for each session. For Session 1, relatively few strategies were evident and neither IQ nor knowledge predicted the number of strategies children used, $F(1,21) = .14$ and 2.26, respectively. By Session 2, strategy scores had increased substantially (paired $t(21) = 1.9$, $p = .07$), and there were main effects for IQ, $F(1,19) = 13.31$, $p < .01$ and for knowledge, $F(1,19) = 13.31$, $p < .01$. There was not a significant interaction[3]. Interestingly, strategy scores were correlated with recall performance both at Session 1 ($r_{25} = .42$, $p = .03$) and Session 2 ($r_{25} = .55$, $p < .01$).

---

[2] Data from one child were not included for analysis because the videotape was of poor quality.

[3] We realize this analysis combines both domain-neutral and domain-specific strategies. A similar analysis using only the domain-specific strategies of sorting and clustering returned identical results.

The Relation Between Strategy Use and Recall

Given the results from Session 2, we were interested in whether IQ and knowledge had direct effects on recall independent of strategy use, or whether the role of IQ or knowledge was only to facilitate sophisticated strategy use. As noted above, Session 1 results indicated only a direct effect of IQ on recall, with no mediation by strategy use. For Session 2, a partial correlation was used to examine the relationship between IQ and recall after controlling for strategy use, $r_{20} = -.11$, ns. Thus, after controlling for strategy use, IQ had no direct effect on number of items recalled at Session 2. A similar analysis was conducted examining the relationship between knowledge and recall after controlling for strategy use at Session 2. Results indicated that knowledge did continue to have an independent relationship with recall, over and above the influence on strategy use, $r_{20} = .58, p < .01$.

To examine each strategy individually, the mean number of dinosaur names recalled by users and non-users for each strategy at each session was examined (see Table 5). Independent group t-tests revealed no significant differences in children's recall performance comparing rehearsal users and late rehearsal users with non-users at either session [$t(23)=1.14$ for rehearsal at Session 1 and $t(23)=.60$ at Session 2 as well as $t(23)=.64$ for late rehearsal at Session 1 and $t(23)=.86$ at Session 2]. In contrast, children who demonstrated clustering based on taxonomic categories recalled significantly more items than those who did not during both sessions [$t(23)=2.77, p=.01$ at Session 1 and $t(23)=3.54, p<.01$ at Session 2]. Although there were no significant differences in children's recall performance between children with higher and lower placement cohesiveness scores at Session 1 [$t(24)=.11$], children who had higher placement cohesiveness scores recalled significantly more items than their peers with lower placement cohesiveness scores at Session 2 [$t(22)=2.82, p=.01$][4]. In sum, the results suggest that children's cohesiveness of placement during studying facilitated recall later in the curriculum, but their use of clustering benefited recall at both sessions.

Surprisingly, children did not benefit from the use of every type of strategy. Patterns of results consistent with utilization deficiencies were seen for cohesive placement at Session 1 and rehearsal at Session 2. Utilization deficiencies are typically defined as a stage in strategy development in which children use a strategy but gain no benefit from that use (Miller, 1990). Children actually generated comparably cohesive placements across both sessions, but recalled fewer dinosaurs in Session 1. The teaching of the dinosaurs in the curriculum seemed to promote cohesive placement at Session 1 but the children were unable to capitalize on this developing knowledge to aid recall. Once a more cohesive knowledge organization was constructed (week 3 of the curriculum), however, recall performance increased. By contrast, no such improvement over the course of the curriculum was found for the rehearsal strategy. Thirty-six (36%) percent of children who attempted to implement the rehearsal strategy at Session 1 and 48% of those who attempted rehearsal at Session 2 did so without concomitant improvement on recall performance. Thus, improvement in the effectiveness of strategy use was seen only for strategies dependent on curricular knowledge and not for those strategies typically viewed as more domain-neutral.

---

[4] Data from two children's final placements were not included for analysis because the photograph was of poor quality.

Table 5 Mean items recalled by strategy users and non-strategy users across sessions for Study 2

	Measure	Strategy user M SD	Non-strategy user M SD	T-test Result
Session 1	Rehearsal	6.67 1.66	5.50 2.78	t(23)=1.14
	Late Rehearsal	6.43 1.81	5.72 2.70	t(23)=.64
	Recall ARC	7.40 1.84	4.93 2.37	t(23)=2.77**
	Study Cohesive Placement	5.72 2.14	5.86 2.82	t(24)=.11
Session 2	Rehearsal	7.08 2.27	6.46 2.85	t(23)=.6
	Late Rehearsal	7.30 2.41	6.40 2.67	t(23)=.86
	Recall ARC	7.88 1.75	3.78 2.64	t(23)=3.54**
	Study Cohesive Placement	8.00 1.81	5.42 2.61	t(22)=2.82**

* $p < .05$; ** $p < .01$

Discussion

The purpose of this study was to examine the interplay of knowledge and cognitive aptitude on kindergarteners' memory performance during the early acquisition of knowledge from a curriculum about dinosaurs.

Our curriculum was designed to facilitate cohesive family-based understanding of the dinosaur domain and performance on all knowledge measures increased over time, demonstrating that children clearly learned from the curriculum. The correlations between IQ scores and knowledge measures further suggest that children with higher aptitude learned domain-specific knowledge faster than those with lower aptitude throughout the curriculum. The question remained, however, whether or not children would be able to use this knowledge on a strategic task.

The present study suggests that children can use developing knowledge to facilitate strategy use and recall, particularly at intermediate stages of knowledge acquisition. In contrast to earlier research that specified that IQ effects on recall performance are mediated by strategy use, we found that IQ also exerted direct effects on recall, particularly early on in the curriculum. We also found that children with higher IQ scores tended to acquire domain-specific knowledge more efficiently. Higher levels of cognitive aptitude and higher levels of knowledge worked together additively to facilitate strategy use, particularly strategy use that was dependent on domain knowledge.

GENERAL DISCUSSION

Together, these two studies help to increase our understanding of the roles of strategies and cognitive aptitude along the continuum of young children's knowledge acquisition, although our findings must be interpreted with some caution given the small samples recruited. As noted earlier, two potential hypotheses have been introduced in the literature. Alexander and Judy (1988; Alexander, 2003) have argued that at least some domain-specific knowledge is necessary for the efficient use of strategies. Others, however, have argued that strategies can be executed independently of domain-specific knowledge (e.g., Hasselhorn and

Korkel, 1986). We suggest that a hybrid model is worthy of further study. In particular, higher levels of domain-specific knowledge may support the deployment of those strategies that depend heavily on organization (e.g., sorting, clustering). The same effects may result when the cohesiveness of the material to be learned is particularly high, as seen in Study 1. On the other hand, possessing cohesive, domain-specific knowledge should have little or no impact on the execution of strategies that are domain-neutral (e.g., rehearsal). These relations between knowledge and particular types of strategy use may be unique to early childhood, when metacognitive awareness of strategy utility is particularly low. They also may have been amplified in Study 2 by the highly structured curriculum used to support knowledge acquisition, which will be considered further below.

A second contribution of these studies is the delineation of alternative means through which cognitive aptitude may impact children's learning and memory. Not surprisingly, children with higher IQ scores generated better recall scores in Study 1, and in Session 1 of Study 2. Since IQ effects were not mediated by more sophisticated strategy use at these points in time, we propose that IQ exerted non-strategic or item-specific influences on recall performance, perhaps by enabling more efficient information processing during encoding. In Study 2, the relation between IQ and recall at Session 1 remained strong even when baseline levels of knowledge were statistically controlled. This suggests that IQ may impact recall directly at very early points along the continuum of knowledge acquisition, particularly when children are very young. Cognitive aptitude also impacted the rate at which knowledge was acquired, replicating past findings from a mini-longitudinal analysis of the construction of shorebird knowledge (Johnson and Mervis, 1994). Because higher IQ facilitated the process of knowledge acquisition, and because acquired knowledge subsequently impacted strategy use, very young children with high cognitive aptitude potentially benefit from multiple advantages to information processing. Future research should investigate whether this still holds true for older children, for whom metacognitive awareness of strategy use is considerably higher and potentially more important in strategic tasks (DeMarie and Ferron, 2003).

Third, our results suggest that particular kinds of strategy use are best predicted by the density and cohesiveness of the knowledge base. Although knowledge acquisition was not tracked in the first study, we found that the cohesiveness of the knowledge base, and not IQ, facilitated domain-related strategy use such as sorting and clustering during recall. This is similar to the proposal by Alexander and Judy (1988) suggesting that at least some critical foundation of knowledge is necessary for the early application of domain-specific strategies. In Study 2, once sufficient amounts of knowledge had been acquired through the curriculum (in the second testing session), both IQ and domain knowledge exerted effects on strategy use, and strategy use remained significantly correlated with recall. Partial correlations indicated that the influence of IQ on recall, however, was mediated solely through its influence on strategy use; no direct influence of IQ on recall was detectable. On the other hand, the present studies suggest that the effective use of domain-neutral strategies (e.g., rehearsal) is not related to knowledge cohesiveness or IQ. This fits with the hypothesis that memory strategies may develop without the support of domain knowledge.

Two caveats potentially limit the generalizability of these conclusions and suggest directions for future research. First, the children participating in Study 2 were kindergartners, and were deliberately recruited because of their fledgling status as "strategic rememberers" and because we were highly confident that they would possess little, if any, declarative metacognitive knowledge related to memory task performance. It is possible that the beneficial effects of knowledge and cognitive aptitude are most evident when children are very young and metacognitive awareness is minimal (Hasselhorn, 1995). Indeed, DeMarie-Dreblow's (1991) findings that older children do not derive immediate benefits of domain-specific knowledge for strategy use suggests that knowledge may affect strategy execution in different ways throughout developmental time.

Second, the curriculum introduced to facilitate knowledge acquisition pertaining to dinosaurs was highly structured and was intended to emphasize groups of dinosaurs and relations among those groups. Thus, sorting and grouping strategies were heavily scaffolded by the very medium through which knowledge was acquired. Young children may first happen upon such strategies rather spuriously, but upon reflecting upon the consequences of those "accidental executions" may gradually develop understanding that can lead to deliberate strategy use. In this sense, deliberate strategy execution may be bootstrapped through contexts that enhance the likelihood that grouping and sorting will occur. Teachers who want to help children use strategies may wish to provide opportunities for children to practice strategic behaviors with carefully designed materials that enhance the organizational structure of the domain. A well-designed curriculum and more cohesive materials may facilitate strategy use, regardless of the individual differences children bring to the classroom.

AUTHOR NOTE

This research was supported by grants BCS-9907865 and BCS0217466 from the National Science Foundation and a Proffitt Research Endowment from the School of Education at Indiana University. The authors wish to thank the principals, teachers, and students of Spencer Elementary and Templeton Elementary for their patience and help. We also wish to thank W. Perry, L. James, and the K-Club program for access to the kindergarten classrooms. We are very thankful to Fabiola Reis-Henrie, Steven Spencer, Christiane DeBauge, and Mary E. Leibham for their assistance in conducting the research. Correspondence concerning this article should be addressed to Joyce M. Alexander, Department of Counseling and Educational Psychology, 201 N. Rose Avenue, Room 4018, Indiana University, Bloomington, IN 47405.

REFERENCES

Alexander, J. M., Carr, M., and Schwanenflugel, P. J. (1995). Development of metacognition in gifted children: Directions for future research. *Developmental Review, 15,* 1-37.

Alexander, J. M., Johnson, K. E., Leibham, M. E., and DeBauge, C. (2005). Constructing Domain-Specific Knowledge in Kindergarten: Relations among Knowledge, Intelligence, and Strategic Performance. *Learning and Individual Differences, 15,* 35-52.

Alexander, J. M., and Schwanenflugel, P. J. (1994). Strategy regulation: The role of intelligence, metacognitive attributions, and knowledge base. *Developmental Psychology, 30,* 709-723.

Alexander, P. A. (2003). The development of expertise: The journey from acclimation to proficiency. *Educational Researcher, 32*(8), 10-14.

Alexander, P. A., and Judy. J. E. (1988). The interaction of domain-specific and strategic knowledge in academic performance. *Review of Educational Research, 58*, 375-404.

Alexander, P. A., Pate, P. E., Kulikowich, J. M., Farrell, D. M., and Wright, N. L. (1989). Domain-specific and strategic knowledge: The effects of training on students of differing ages and levels of competence. *Learning and Individual Differences, 1*, 283-325.

Anderson, J. R., Greeno, J. G., Kline, P. J., and Neves, D. M. (1981). Acquisition of problem-solving skill. In J. R. Anderson (Ed.), *Cognitive skills and their acquisition* (pp. 191-230). Hillsdale, NJ: Erlbaum.

Best, D. L., and Ornstein, P. A. (1986). Children's generation and communication of mnemonic organizational strategies. *Developmental Psychology, 22*, 845-853.

Bjorklund, D. F. (2005). *Children's thinking: Developmental function and individual differences (4th. Edition)*. Pacific Grove, CA: Brooks/Cole.

Bjorklund, D. F., and Bernholtz, J. F. (1986). The role of knowledge base in the memory performance of good and poor readers. *Journal of Experimental Child Psychology, 41*, 367-373.

Bjorklund, D. F., and Buchanan, J. J. (1989). Developmental and knowledge base differences in the acquisition and extension of a memory strategy. *Journal of Experimental Child Psychology, 47*, 451-471.

Bjorklund, D. F., Muir-Broaddus, J. E., and Schneider, W. (1990). The role of knowledge in the development of strategies. In D. F. Bjorklund (Ed.), *Children's strategies: Contemporary views of cognitive development*. Hillsdale, NJ: Erlbaum.

Borkowski, J. G., and Peck, V. A. (1986). Causes of consequences of metamemory in gifted children. In R. J. Sternberg, and J. C. Davidson (Eds.), *Conceptions of giftedness*. Cambridge, England: Cambridge University Press.

Bray, N. W., Fletcher, K. L., and Turner, L. A. (1996). Cognitive competencies and strategy use in individuals with mild retardation. In W. E. MacLean, Dr. (Ed.), *Handbook of mental deficiency, psychological theory and research* (3rd ed.). Hillsdale, NJL Erlbaum.

Brown, A. L., and DeLoache, J. S. (1978). Skills, plans and self-regulation. In S. R. Siegler (Ed.), *Children's thinking: What develops?* Hillsdale, NJ: Erlbaum.

Ceci, S. J. (1993). Contextual trends in intellectual development. *Developmental Review, 13*, 403-435.

Ceci, S. J., and Liker, J. (1986). A day at the races: A study of IQ, expertise, and cognitive complexity. *Journal of Experimental Psychology: General, 115*, 255-266.

Ceci, S. J., and Liker, J. (1988). Stalking the IQ-expertise relation: When the critics go fishing. *Journal of Experimental Psychology: General, 117*, 96-100.

Chi, M. T. H. (1978). Knowledge structure and memory development. In R. Siegler (Ed.), *Children's thinking: What develops?* (pp. 73-96). Hillsdale, NJ: Erlbaum.

Chi, M. H. T. (1981). Knowledge development and memory performance. In M. P. Friedman, J. P. Das, and N. O'Connor (Eds.), *Intelligence and learning* (pp. 221-229). New York: Plenum.

Cho, S., and Ahn, D. (2003). Strategy acquisition and maintenance of gifted and nongifted young children. *Exceptional Children, 69*, 497-505.

Corsale, K., and Ornstein, P. A. (1980). Developmental changes in children's use of semantic information in recall. *Journal of Experimental Child Psychology, 30*, 231-245.

Coyle, T. R. (2001). Factor analysis of variability measures in eight independent samples of children and adults. *Journal of Experimental Child Psychology, 78,* 330-358.

Coyle, T. R. and Bjorklund, D. F. (1997). Age differences in, and consequences of, multiple- and variable-strategy use on a multitrial sort-recall task. *Developmental Psychology, 33,* 372-380.

Crowley, K., Shrager, J., and Siegler, R. S. (1997). Strategy discovery as a competitive negotiation between metacognitive and associative mechanisms. *Developmental Review, 17,* 462-489.

Das, J. P. (1984). Cognitive deficits in mental retardation. A process approach. In P. H. Brooks, R. Sperber, and C. McCauley (Eds.), *Learning and cognition in the mentally retarded.* Hillsdale, NJ: Erlbaum.

Davidson, J. E., and Sternberg, R. J. (1984). The role of insight in intellectual giftedness. *Gifted Child Quarterly, 28* (2), 58-64.

DeMarie, D., and Ferron, J. (2003). Capacity, strategies, and metamemory: Tests of a three-factor model of memory development. *Journal of Experimental Child Psychology, 84,* 167-193.

DeMarie-Dreblow, D. (1991). Relation between knowledge and memory: A reminder that correlation does not imply causality. *Child Development, 62,* 484-498.

Fleming, V. M., and Alexander, J. M. (2001). The benefits of peer collaboration: A replication with a delayed post-test. *Contemporary Educational Psychology, 26,* 588-601.

Ferretti, R. P., and Butterfield, E. C. (1992). Intelligence-related differences in the learning, maintenance, and transfer of problem-solving strategies. *Intelligence, 16*(2), 207-223.

Gardner, H. (1999). *The disciplined mind: What all students should understand.* New York: Simon and Schuster.

Gaultney, J. F., Bjorklund, D. F., and Goldstein, D. (1996). To be young, gifted, and strategic: Advantages for memory performance. *Journal of Experimental Child Psychology, 61,* 43-66.

Geary, D. C., and Brown, S. C. (1991). Cognitive addition: Strategy choice and speed-of-processing differences in gifted, normal, and mathematically disabled children. *Developmental Psychology, 27,* 398-406.

Glaser, R. (1987). Thoughts on expertise. In C. Schooler and K. W. Schaie (Eds.), *Cognitive functioning and social structure over the life course* (pp. 81-94). Norwood, NJ: Ablex.

Hale, S. (1990). A global developmental trend in cognitive processing speed. *Child Development, 61,* 653-663.

Harnishfeger, K. K. and Bjorklund, D. F. (1990). Memory functioning of gifted and nongifted middle school children. *Contemporary Educational Psychology, 15,* 346-363.

Hasselhorn, M. (1995). Beyond production deficiency and utilization inefficiency: Mechanisms of the emergence of strategic categorization in episodic memory tasks. In R. W. Weinert and W. Schneider (Eds.), *Memory performance and competencies: Issues in growth and development* (pp. 141-159). Mahwah, NJ: Erlbaum.

Hasselhorn, M., and Korkel, J. (1986). Metacognitive versus traditional reading instructions: The mediating role of domain-specific knowledge on children's text processing. *Human Learning, 5,* 75-90.

Hettinger Steiner, H., and Carr, M. (2003). Cognitive development in gifted children: Toward a more precise understanding of emerging differences in intelligence. *Educational Psychology Review, 15,* 215-246.

Johnson, K. E., and Mervis, C. B., (1994). Microgenetic analysis of first steps in children's acquisition of expertise on shorebirds. *Developmental Psychology, 30,* 418-435.

Johnson, K. E., Scott, P., and Mervis, C. B. (2004). What are theories for? Concept use throughout the continuum of expertise. *Journal of Experimental Child Psychology, 87,* 171-200.

Kail, R. V., Jr. (1986). Sources of age differences in speed of processing. *Child Development, 57,* 969-987.

Kail, R. (1988). Developmental functions for speeds of cognitive processes. *Journal of Experimental Child Psychology, 45,* 339-364.

Kail, R. V. (2004). Cognitive development includes global and domain-specific processes. *Merrill-Palmer Quarterly, 50,* 445-455.

Kaufman, A. S., and Kaufman, N. L. (1990). *Kaufman Brief Intelligence test.* Circle Pines, MN: American Guidance Service.

Kee, D., and Davies, L. (1990). Mental effort and elaboration: Effects of accessibility and instruction. *Journal of Experimental Child Psychology, 49,* 264-274.

Lange, G., MacKinnon, C. E., and Nida, R. E. (1989). Knowledge, strategy, and motivational contributions to preschool children's object recall. *Developmental Psychology, 25*(5), 772-779.

Lin, P., Schwanenflugel, P.J., and Wisenbaker, J. M. (1991). Category typicality, cultural familiarity, and the development of category knowledge. *Developmental Psychology, 26,* 805-813.

Manion, V., and Alexander, J. M. (1997). Benefits of peer collaboration on strategy use, metacognitive causal attributions, and recall. *Journal of Experimental Child Psychology, 67,* 268-289.

McCutchen, D. (1986). Domain knowledge and linguistic knowledge in the development of writing ability. *Journal of Memory and Language, 25,* 431-444.

McGilly, K., and Siegler, R. S. (1989). The influence of encoding strategic knowledge on children's choices among serial recall strategies. *Developmental Psychology, 26,* 931-941.

Miller, P. H. (1990). The development of strategies of selective attention. In D. F. Bjorklund (Ed.), *Children's strategies: Contemporary views of cognitive development.* Hillsdale, NJ: Erlbaum.

Montague, M. (1991). Gifted and learning-disabled gifted students' knowledge and use of mathematical problem-solving strategies. *Journal of Education of the Gifted, 14,* 393-411.

Morrison, F. (1987). *Making the cut: Contrasting developmental and learning influences on cognitive growth.* Paper presented at the annual meeting of the Psychonomics Society, Seattle.

Muir, J., Masterson, D., Weiner, R., Lyon, K., and White, J. (April, 1989). *Training and transfer of an organizational strategy in gifted and high-average children.* Presentation at the Society for Research in Child Development. Kansas City, MO.

Perleth, C. (1994). Strategy use and metamemory in gifted and average primary school children. In K. A. Heller and E. A. Hany (Eds.). *Competence and responsibility, Vol. 2* (pp. 46-52). Ashland, OH: Hogrefe and Huber Publishers.

Rabinowitz, M. (1984). The use of categorical organization: Not an all-or-none situation. *Journal of Experimental Child Psychology, 38,* 338-351.

Rabinowitz, M. (1988). On teaching cognitive strategies: The influence of accessibility of conceptual knowledge. *Contemporary Educational Psychology, 13,* 229-235.

Rabinowitz, M., and Kee, D. (1994). A framework for understanding individual differences in memory: Strategy-knowledge interactions. In P. A. Vernon (Ed.), *Handbook of the neuropsychology of individual differences.* New York: Academic.

Recht, D. R., and Leslie, L. (1988). Effect of prior knowledge on good and poor readers' memory of text. *Journal of Educational Psychology, 80,* 16-20.

Roenker, D. L., Thompson, C. P., and Brown, S. C. (1971). Comparison of measures for the estimation of clustering in free recall. *Psychological Bulletin, 76,* 45-48.

Schauble, L. (1996). The development of scientific reasoning in knowledge-rich contexts. *Developmental Psychology, 32,* 102-119.

Schneider, W., and Bjorklund, D. F. (1992). Expertise, aptitude, and strategic remembering. *Child Development, 63,* 461-473.

Schneider, W., and Bjorklund, D. F. (1998). Memory. In D. Kuhn and R. S. Siegler (Vol. Eds.), Cognitive , language, and perceptual development, Vol. 2. In W. Damon (Gen. Ed.), *Handbook of child psychology.* New York: Wiley.

Schneider, W., Bjorklund, D. F., and Maier-Brücker, W. (1996). The effects of expertise and IQ on children's memory: When knowledge is, and when it is not enough. *International Journal of Behavioral Development, 19,* 773-796.

Schneider, W., Korkel, J., and Weinert, F. E. (1989). Domain-specific knowledge and memory performance: A comparison of high-and low-aptitude children. *Journal of Educational Psychology, 81,* 306-312.

Scruggs, T. E,. and Mastropieri, M. A. (1985). Spontaneous verbal elaboration in gifted and nongifted youths. *Journal of Education of the Gifted, 9*(1), 1-10.

Scruggs, T. E., and Mastropieri, M. A. (1988). Acquisition and transfer of learning strategies by gifted and nongifted students. *Journal of Special Education, 22*(2), 153-166.

Siegler, R. S. (1990). How content knowledge, strategies, and individual differences interact to produce strategy choice. In W. Schneider and F. E. Weinert (Eds.), *Interactions among aptitudes, strategies, and knowledge in cognitive performance.* New York: Springer-Verlag.

Siegler, R. S. (1995). Children's thinking: How does change occur? In W. Schneider and F. E. Weinert (Eds.), *Memory performance and competencies: Issues in growth and development.* Hillsdale, NJ: Erlbaum.

Siegler, R. S., and Jenkins, E. (1989). *How children discover new strategies.* Hillsdale, NJ: Erlbaum.

Sternberg, R. J. (1985). *Beyond IQ: A triarchic theory of human intelligence.* Cambridge: Cambridge University Press.

Walker, C. H. (1987). Relative importance of domain knowledge and overall aptitude on acquisition of domain-related information. *Cognition and Instruction, 4,* 25-42.

APPENDIX A. STIMULI LIST STUDY 1

	High Cohesive Stimuli		Low Cohesive Stimuli	
Category	Item	Typicality Rating	Item	Typicality Rating
Vehicles	Bus	2.70	Bicycle	1.73
	Car	2.63	Tricycle	1.53
	Airplane	2.47	Skates	1.33
	Motorcycle	2.37	Canoe	1.30
Fruit	Grapes	2.83	Cantaloupe	2.43
	Apple	2.80	Lemon	2.17
	Pineapple	2.80	Tomato	1.80
	Strawberry	2.73	Coconut	1.40
Weapons	Arrow	2.23	Grenade	1.47
	Gun	2.13	Scissors	1.30
	Knife	1.97	Poison	1.23
	Axe	1.63	Hammer	1.00
Furniture	Chair	2.63	Piano	1.83
	Sofa	2.47	Mirror	1.73
	Bed	2.43	Lamp	1.70
	Desk	2.17	Stereo	1.70
Clothing	Shirt	2.70	Glove	2.17
	Pants	2.67	Swimsuit	2.13
	Shorts	2.67	Belt	2.10
	Coat	2.61	Shoes	2.03

Highest rating possible = 3.0; lowest rating possible = 0.0. Each category differed as to range of ratings.

In: New Developments in Learning Research
Editor: Samuel N. Hogan, pp. 145-163

ISBN 1-59454-669-X
© 2006 Nova Science Publishers, Inc.

Chapter 7

FOREIGN LANGUAGE LEARNING: THE ROLE OF PHONOLOGICAL MEMORY

Marcella Ferrari and Paola Palladino
University of Pavia

ABSTRACT

The present chapter reviews recent research on the role of phonological memory skills in typical and disordered foreign language learning. We will briefly illustrate a working memory model and its phonological component, focusing on its relationship with foreign language learning. In the last part of the chapter two recent experiments that add significant data in favour of a crucial role of phonological memory in foreign language learning are presented. In the two experiments, the authors examined working memory problems in groups of 7th and 8th grade Italian students who studied English as a second language. Participants were tested on a visuo-spatial working memory task, on passive verbal working memory tasks and more active ones, in order to clarify which component of working memory may be involved in the foreign language learning ability. Phonological awareness was tested comparing experimental and control groups on phonological memory tasks. Results are discussed within the working memory framework (Baddeley, 1986).

INTRODUCTION

Foreign language learning has become an important topic within language learning research. In particular a number of studies have been interested in the locus of individual differences in foreign language acquisition. In other words, research on second language acquisition has been asking the question "why do some foreign language learners do better than others?". Different areas in psychology have addressed the issue during past decades. In the '50s-'60s, systematic analysis of Second Language Acquisition (SLA) focused both on natural and classroom learning. Some authors suggested lack of motivation (Gardner, 1985) or language attitude (Carrol, 1998) as factors accounting for individual differences. Between

1960 and- 1980 research focused on investigating whether there were other abilities which could better predict foreign language learning. Studies with university students found in the Modern Language Aptitude Test (MLAT) a good predictor of foreign language learning success. Students who exhibited a low performance in syntax sensitivity, phonological coding and in the associative and inductive language learning areas (these were the areas examined by the MLAT) were also the students that later tended to show more foreign language learning problems. Furthermore, a factor that seemed to influence the acquisition of a foreign language was the linguistic transfer process. In recent years, the interest in language learning in general has produced interesting findings also in the foreign language acquisition field, resulting in a definition of a cognitive profile of students with a specific foreign language learning problem.

Foreign language learning doesn't involve conceptual reorganisation because the conceptual organisation has already been formed within the native language vocabulary (Bernahrdt, 2000). In other words, foreign language learning may be more a phonological than a semantic process as sensitivity to new sounds and correspondences and memory for new words, sequences and structures, are skills influenced by the efficiency of phonological processing within memory.

The present chapter reviews recent research on the role of phonological memory skills in typical and disordered foreign language learning. We will briefly illustrate a working memory model and its phonological component, focusing on its relationship with foreign language learning. In the last part of the chapter two recent experiments that add significant data in favour of a crucial role of phonological memory in foreign language learning are presented. In the two experiments, the authors examined working memory problems in groups of 7th and 8th grade Italian students who studied English as a second language. Participants were tested on a visuo-spatial working memory task, on passive verbal working memory tasks and more active ones, in order to clarify which component of working memory may be involved in the foreign language learning ability. Phonological awareness was tested comparing experimental and control groups on phonological memory tasks. Results are discussed within the working memory framework (Baddeley, 1986).

1. THE PHONOLOGICAL COMPONENT OF WORKING MEMORY AND LANGUAGE LEARNING

Research that investigates the relationship between memory and language learning suggests that phonological memory abilities can be considered as specific prerequisites which contribute to language learning, in reading, writing and oral skills. According to the memory model proposed by Baddeley and Hitch in 1974, short term memory was conceptualised as a sort of workspace mainly responsible for the cognitive functioning of every day life e.g. language processes, learning and reasoning. The tripartite working memory model, as proposed by Baddeley (1986) can be considered as a reliable theoretical tool to clarify memory involvement in language learning (Andrade, 2001; Gathercole and Baddeley, 1990). It is composed of the central executive, conceptualised as a general processing system that supervises two slave systems: the phonological loop (a verbal short term memory) which is the most studied and best known component and the visuo-spatial sketch-pad.

The phonological loop can be fractionated into the articulatory loop, which can refresh the decaying verbal trace through rehearsal, and the phonological store which functions as a temporary store system. The phonological component of working memory seems to be a device for language learning and specifically for the acquisition of novel unfamiliar phonological forms, as such it facilitates the creation of accurate representations and thus new language learning (for a review see Baddeley, Gathercole, and Papagno, 1998).

Furthermore, findings from a number of longitudinal research and several studies conducted with young children tested in native vocabulary knowledge, digit span task and word and non-word repetition tasks, reveal that children who performed better in phonological memory tasks at the age of four years old, also tended to exhibit a better vocabulary knowledge (e.g., Gathercole and Baddeley, 1989; Gathercole, Willis, and Baddeley, 1991 b; Gathercole, Hitch, Service, and Martin, 1997), thus supporting the hypothesis of a close relationship between phonological memory, measured by the digit span and the non-word repetition task, and language learning. Although these data cannot support a causal relation, they however provide further elements in favour of the involvement of the phonological loop in learning new words. As suggested by the authors in the studies reviewed above, the verbal memory trace is likely to be recalled when accurate representations are made in the phonological loop.

A central issue within the working memory conceptualisation is the phenomenon that people tend to recall short words more than long words (i.e., the word length effect) in an immediate serial recall task . This phenomenon has been thought to depend on the spoken duration of the words and it has been explained in terms of the time-limited capacity of the phonological loop component of working memory: the faster an item can be rehearsed within 2 seconds, the greater the probability that it will be stored in the phonological store and then recalled (Baddeley, Thomson, Buchanan, 1975). Thus, the first explanation of the word length effect focused on the rehearsal process so that a slower articulatory coding of longer items leads to a decreased rehearsal rate. Many other explanations have been suggested as regards the word length effect. It could depend on the items phonological complexity (Caplan, Rochon, and Waters 1992). In recent years, experiments carried out by Service (1998) have noticeably contributed to discussion on this issue. In some experiments, Service examined the immediate serial recall of consonant-vowel-consonant-vowel pseudowords stimuli based on Finnish phonotactic in Finnish participants. The pseudowords were matched for length of articulatory duration but differed in number of phonemes. If the word length effect is based on a rehearsal process, pseudowords with shorter articulatory duration should have been remembered better than long-duration pseudowords. Results showed that there was no difference between the short and the long duration items with four syllables. This data suggests that phonological complexity not the articulatory duration could be more responsible for the item-length-effect in the pseudowords' immediate serial recall (Service, 1998).

Immediate serial recall of verbal stimuli was explored further by Service and Maury (2003) in a set of experiments in which the authors examined the phenomenon of redintegration, which operates to support immediate recall of verbal stimuli using all available long-term information. In these experiments the redintegration effect was based on episodic learning during the experiment. Participants were in fact required to study lists of redundant pseudowords composed by CVCVCV (consonant-vowel) stimuli that in turn shared the same first, middle (e.g., /kunela/, /janelu/) or end redundant syllable and non redundant pseudowords (no syllable was shared between pseudowords lists). They were then presented with lists of different lengths and asked to recall them. The redundancy effect was particularly strong when the first syllable was shared, whilst there was no effect when the middle syllable was shared, and recall actually improved when the last syllable was shared. Considering that the items used in the experiments had no previous existing lexical representation in the memory system, it is plausible to conclude that episodic learning during the experiment influenced recall performance. This finding was explained by the authors as being a redintegration process operating during either recall or storage. In particular the study showed how difficulties were greater in redintegrating or reconstructing CVCVCV stimuli that shared the same syllable in the first position than in the middle or end position. Moreover, not only the first syllable appeared to have a stronger weight than the middle and last ones, but also vowels and consonants seemed to behave in different ways in pseudoword recall. Results from a similar set of experiments conducted by Service, Maury and Luotoniemi (submitted), showed that vowels seemed to have more weight in form access than consonants.

Significant empirical evidence for the involvement of phonological memory in language learning derives from research on a specific learning disability classified as a Specific Language Impairment (SLI), a developmental disability defined by the observed discrepancy between poor language learning and adequate non verbal intelligence (for a review see Baddeley, Gathercole, and Papagno, 1998; Bishop and Snowling, 2004). Children with SLI showed phonological memory deficits when compared both to age matched controls and to language matched controls.

Research was also carried out with the aim of better specifing what mechanisms might underpin the association between phonological memory and language learning (Gathercole and Baddeley, 1990). Studies on sensitivity to the word length effect (i.e., shorter words should be recalled better than longer words) and phonological similarity (i.e., memory traces for similar-sounding items are assumed to be harder to recall, Baddeley, 1990, p. 72) have been conducted, for example, by Gathercole and Baddeley (1990) with six children with a specific language impairment (SLI). The authors assessed the phonological memory of the six participants comparing them to two control groups, one matched on verbal abilities and the other matched on non verbal intelligence. The groups were compared in tasks like nonwords repetition, recall of phonologically dissimilar and phonologically similar words, and in recall of one-syllable words and three–syllables words in order to investigate the phonological encoding skills and rehearsal abilities of the language disordered children and explore their sensitivity to similarity and the word length effect. Given their lower performance on the serial recall of words and non-words the main result of this study shows that children with SLI have a worse immediate phonological memory than control groups. However all groups were sensitive to the word similarity and word length effect, suggesting that children with SLI were also using subvocal rehearsal to maintain items. Thus, findings from this study indicate that neither the initial encoding phonological processes nor subvocal rehearsal are impaired in children with SLI. A number of hypotheses have been made as regards the SLI children's poorer immediate phonological memory performance; for example suggesting it is linked to a faster decay of the phonological trace in their phonological loop, or to some noisy factor that could affect the adequate phonological representation of the stimuli or to a poorer capacity of the phonological store. Gathercole and Baddeley (1990) are in favour of an impairment of phonological storage in working memory as the most likely source of SLI.

A further step towards the investigation of phonological memory in foreign language learning has been made by more recent studies, showing a phonological loop involvement in the older children's learning of new words. Studies assessing phonological memory skills, measured by both digit span and non-word repetition revealed that they were significantly linked to new word learning in children of both 5 and 13 years of age (Gathercole, Hitch, Service, and Martin, 1997; Gathercole, Service, Hitch, Adams, and Martin, 1999).

2. THE PHONOLOGICAL COMPONENT OF WORKING MEMORY AND *FOREIGN* LANGUAGE LEARNING

Only a few studies have specifically approached the critical role of phonological memory on individual and developmental differences in foreign language learning. Service (1992) showed that the 9 years old Finnish children's phonological memory for non-words that sound like English predicted their acquisition of English as a foreign language two and a half years later. Three tasks were presented to participants. The first, was a pseudoword repetition task with non words sounding like English, the second was a pseudoword copying task, in which strings of letters looking like English or Finnish were presented to the pupils who had to write them down as accurately as possible after the strings had disappeared from view. The third task was intended to measure high level language skills and consisted of a comparison of the syntactic-semantic structure. In this task pupils were presented with two lists of sentences with a similar structure (subject-verb-object vs. subject-verb-adverb) distributed in two columns and were asked to join the sentences they thought went together. The three tasks were examined in a longitudinal study and were correlated with scholastic achievement in English learning after two and a half years from the first measurement. Results showed that repetition accuracy was a better predictor of learning English since repetition scores accounted for 44% of the variance in the English grades obtained.

Similar results emerged with older Finnish children, where a strong correlation was observed between non-word repetition and learning English as a foreign language (measured by the performance in listening comprehension and vocabulary tests) even after controlling for general school achievement (Service and Kohonen, 1995).

Further contributions come from studies carried out in order to investigate which abilities were the best predictors of foreign language. Starting from Service's findings, Cheung (1996) tested the hypothesis of a relationship between phonological memory and foreign language word learning. In Cheung' s experiments, English vocabulary and English word learning processes were directly examined with an English vocabulary score and an English reading comprehension score, differently from Service's study (1992) in which the overall English performance at school was taken as an outcome measure. The other variables considered were chronological age, non verbal intelligence score, nonword span (as a measure of phonological memory) simple word span and a vocabulary learning ability. Participants were a group of bilingual seventh-grade high school students who spoke Cantonese-Chinese as their native tongue and started learning English as a second language at the age of 3 or 4 years in a classroom situation. The main finding was that in the group of participants with low vocabulary scores nonword span was the only predictor of the students' ability to acquire new English words $F(1,28) = 5.34$, $MSE = 24.52$, $p<.03$. It is important to note that in this study the relationship between nonword span and English word acquisition was preserved only in participants with an English vocabulary score below the median value.

One plausible conclusion suggested by Cheung is that foreign language word learning relies on phonological memory in the first stages of language acquisition but relies more on the amount of long-term vocabulary knowledge obtained, when there is greater proficiency (see Cheung, 1996).

In order to substantiate previous findings, Masoura and Gathercole (1999) developed a study in which phonological memory skills and vocabulary knowledge were assessed in both the native and second language. Forty-five Greek children (age range from 8 years and 8 months to 11 years and 8 months) learning English as a second language were tested on: phonological short-term memory measures in both languages, using English and Greek sounding-like nonword repetition tasks; nonverbal ability, measured by the Coloured Progressive Matrices (Raven, 1986); native vocabulary, using measures for assessing both productive and receptive vocabulary, and foreign vocabulary measures, involving word translation tasks from the foreign–to-native and native-to-foreign language. Results showed that both the foreign and native language vocabulary measures were significantly correlated with nonword repetition for both the foreign and native language, implying a close relationship between vocabulary knowledge and phonological memory. Knowledge of foreign but not native vocabulary was associated with nonword repetition. Foreign vocabulary acquisition seemed to rely mostly on phonological memory rather than native vocabulary knowledge, perhaps because of the unfamiliarity of foreign words.

Also Dufva and Voeten (1999), in a longitudinal study with Finnish children from first to third grade, conclude that a crucial prerequisite for learning English as a foreign language is phonological memory. Their study measured phonological memory with a non-word repetition task whilst native language literacy, was assessed based on word recognition skills. Both these skills had positive effects on foreign language learning.

As conceptualised by Baddeley et al. (1998) the phonological loop functions as a device supporting the long-term acquisition of the sound pattern of the unfamiliar words both in native and second language learning. It is plausible to hypothesise some lexical influence on the storage of memory stimuli in the phonological loop, in light of the relation between vocabulary knowledge and phonological memory skills. The prediction would thus be that the availability of familiar sound patterns would be better than for unfamiliar ones, thanks to the availability in the long term memory of this well established pattern.

In order to test the hypothesis that short term memory accuracy could be higher for native language stimuli than for stimuli belonging to an unfamiliar language, Thorne and Gathercole (1999) investigated children with different degrees of familiarity with English and French. Three groups of children participated in the experiment: a group of monolingual children with English as their native language, a group of bilingual English-French speaking children and a group of bilingual children with English as their first language and French as a second language from the age of three years old. They were administered a vocabulary measure i.e. a digit span task and a phonological memory measure, i.e. a nonword repetition task. The main findings revealed that children's short term memory performance in each language mirrored their familiarity with English and French. Greater vocabulary knowledge was associated with a higher level of phonological memory, in terms of recall of both words and nonwords in that language. In conclusion, phonological short term memory appears to be a language dependent system which is also specifically linked to a given language (see Thorn and Gathercole, 1999).

A significant contribution to the foreign language research field comes from the investigation of students with specific difficulty in foreign language learning (FLLD).

Individuals with a foreign language learning difficulty (FLLD) have been described as having average or above average intelligence (usually non-verbal) and adequate scholastic achievement but a specific problem in the acquisition of a foreign language, either Spanish (for a review see Ganschow and Sparks, 1995; Ganschow, Sparks, and Javorsky, 1998) or English (Palladino and Cornoldi, 2004).

Although students with FLLD exhibit different disability profiles (Sparks and Ganschow, 1993), they typically seem to show problems in language learning, mostly related to a foreign language, although less severe difficulties are also present in learning their native language. Although several studies have consistently found that phonological but not semantic coding and processing difficulties in a native language are closely related to foreign language learning difficulties (Linguistic Coding Deficit Hypothesis, Sparks and Ganschow,;1993; Ganschow and Sparks, 1989;1993; Sparks, Ganschow, Javorsky, Pohlman and Patton, 1992) little attention has been paid to systematically investigate phonological memory in FLLD students. The study of foreign language learning disorders may thus be used to develop and extend research on the relationship between memory and language learning.

3. WHICH OTHER COMPONENTS OF WORKING MEMORY ARE INVOLVED IN FOREIGN LANGUAGE LEARNING?

Till now, in the present chapter the focus has been on the relationship between foreign language and phonological memory. The assumption that phonological working memory plays a more important role than other working memory components in foreign language learning needs to be substantiated by taking into consideration also those studies that investigated the involvement of the central executive and the visuospatial component of working memory.

Working memory measures of simultaneous maintenance and processing of verbal information such as the listening span procedure (Daneman and Carpenter, 1980), which requires understanding the meaning of a sentence and recalling its final words, have also been related to foreign language learning. Results from studies looking at working memory tasks in a foreign language showed a strong relationship between working memory performance and foreign language proficiency both in adults (Harrington and Sawyer, 1992) and children (Geva and Ryan, 1993). However the conclusions that can be drawn from this line of study are somewhat limited due to the fact that the authors did not clearly separate second language learning measures, assessed in terms of grammar and vocabulary knowledge, and reading comprehension.

Similar weaknesses may be found in Miyake and Friedman (1998) although they tested the relationship between working memory and foreign language learning with a path model. Partcipants were 59 Japanese native speakers studying English as a second language, who were presented listening span tests in both their native and foreign language, as well as a syntactic comprehension task. An overall best-fitting path model was described (CFI = .96).

In the model native language working memory influences second language working memory, which in turn influences syntactic comprehension. In other words, Miyake and Friedman's model supports the hypothesis that second language proficiency can be affected by working memory demand, using a methodology which goes beyond the limitations of the typical correlational study. However the use of the typical listening span procedure (which requires sentence comprehension and recall of the final words) (Daneman and Carpenter, 1980) as a measure of working memory in both languages partly overlaps with the syntactic comprehension task (also requiring sentence comprehension, albeit of greater syntactical complexity). This aspect could make the results rather circular and their interpretation somewhat problematic.

A first step towards clarifying which of the multiple components of working memory (Baddeley, 1986), e.g. the phonological loop, visuo-spatial sketchpad and central executive, may be related to a foreign language learning ability were taken by Palladino and Cornoldi (2004) with participants with Foreign Language Learning Difficulties (FLLD). They compared groups of 7th and 8th grade Italian students with different proficiency levels in the acquisition of English as a second language. The students were matched for non-verbal intelligence, age and gender according to the classical group comparison design used in learning disabled studies (for a methodological discussion see for example Cornoldi and Oakhill, 1996; Palladino, Cornoldi, De Beni and Pazzaglia, 2001). They were tested on a visuo-spatial working memory task, different phonological memory tasks (e.g. a forward and backward digit span task and a non-word repetition test) and verbal working memory tasks (such as the Italian version of Daneman and Carpenter's Listening Span Task) (1980; De Beni , Palladino, Pazzaglia, and Cornoldi 1998). Results showed significant differences between the two groups only on phonological memory tasks, i.e. the forward digit span and non-word repetition test. Differences in the Listening span test disappeared when non-word repetition performance was partialled out. The groups' performance was similar in the visuo-spatial working memory task. Results thus suggest that the main component involved in foreign language learning difficulties is the phonological loop, similarly to what was observed with native language learning and specific language disorders. Whereas the visuo-spatial sketchpad and central executive appeared to play a less critical role in foreign language acquisition (Palladino and Cornoldi, 2004).

The fact that only a few studies have occasionally pursued the goal of disentangling the relevance of the different phonological memory components may be due to the difficulty of referring to a clear theoretical framework in which the relevant variables are accurately represented, detailing their specific functions, boundaries and interconnectedness.

Considering the afore mentioned Palladino and Cornoldi's experiment (2004), similar but not identical predictions could be made following the different working memory models. For example, the model proposed by Cornoldi and Vecchi (2000, 2003) is based on two continua according to an active vs. passive process dichotomy and a verbal vs. visuo-spatial modality dichotomy. Findings from Palladino and Cornoldi (2004) could be more consistent with this recent model, since the differences between the group with FLLD and the control group could be accordingly explained in light of the active vs. passive and verbal vs. visuo-spatial continua. In fact the groups differed significantly in the forward digit span and the non-word repetition test, both considered as being the more passive tasks. In the Listening span test, considered as a more active and controlled task measuring the Central Executive component and when non-word repetition performance was partialled out, differences between groups disappeared.

Palladino and Cornoldi (2004) concluded that the FLLD participants' working memory problem should be located along the continuum of the control-activity dimension within the verbal areas of working memory.

Starting from the findings showing that both foreign language and native language vocabulary learning (or nonword learning) depend on a phonological STM resource, Morra, Camba and Calvini (2004) tested the hypothesis that new word learning depends on the interaction between central attentional resources and phonological variables. Measures of phonological sensitivity (i.e. syllable discrimination including Russian phonemes, syllable repetition and non-word repetition of 2 - 4 syllables, with and without Russian phonemes) and measures of articulation rate (i.e. speed articulation of high frequency Italian nouns) were presented to 8-11 years old children. Central attentional resources (M capacity) were tested with tasks involving more executive processes, like the backward digit span task. A linear structural relations model was fitted, with three latent predictors (phonological sensitivity, M capacity, rehearsal speed) and four latent dependent variables (learning of short legal, long legal, short non-legal, and long non-legal nonwords). Phonological sensitivity appeared, for all kinds of material the best predictor of vocabulary learning, while M capacity and articulation rate appeared to be important only with short non-words and with phonologically legal non-words, respectively.

In summary Morra et al. concluded that phonological representation more strongly influences the contextual binding of phoneme sequences and that rehearsal appears to be a strategy which works better for familiar sounds (i.e. the Italian non-words). The attentional resources are likely to be thought of as useful when phoneme sequences are familiar enough and the demand is not excessive.

4. PHONOLOGICAL AWARENESS

As regards phonological awareness, it is defined as the awareness of the sound units which make up a spoken word (e.g. phonemes and syllables). It also refers to different abilities, such as analysing a word's sub-components and manipulating (blending, deleting, synthesising) the spoken word units.

Phonolgical awareness should be involved in foreign language learning since it contributes to a correct analysis, representation and manipulation of the phonological trace.

However phonological awareness is not clearly defined within the phonological memory model and a large debate has arisen as regards which variable must be indicated as the main source of individual and developmental differences in language learning, specifically questioning whether the relationship between the phonological memory measures and vocabulary learning could be mediated by metaphonological skills (see Bishop and Snowling, 2004; Gathercole, Willis, Emslie and Baddeley, 1992).

Bishop and Snowling (2004) discussed the role of the general term "phonological processing" in one of their works on Specific Language Impairment (SLI) and developmental dyslexia. Starting from some other authors' speculations considering SLI and dyslexia as different points on a continuum of language learning impairments, they took into consideration the relationship between these in an attempt to find out whether they are different manifestation of the same deficit. A child's ability to learn literacy (i.e. the ability to learn reading and writing) is affected by an impaired phonological processing system. In particular a number of studies on dyslexia and SLI, reviewed by Bishop and Snowling, emphasised the role of poor phonological awareness in literacy acquisition. adequate phonological representation in the memory system, leading to reading impairment. Nevertheless, the authors outlined the importance of considering the role of phonological memory, measured by nonword repetition tasks, when the phonological origins of dyslexia and SLI are being studied. Phonological memory is in fact thought to play a crucial role in maintaining an adequate representation of the phoneme-grapheme correspondence. It seems however difficult to establish a causal direction between literacy skills or vocabulary acquisition and phonological memory.

For example, among the researchers that tried to clarify this issue, Gathercole and Baddely (1990) compared two groups of 5-6 years old children, one with low and one with high nonword repetition performance. Both groups were asked to learn labels for unfamiliar toy animals. Results showed significant differences between groups as participants with a low repetition performance were slower at learning phonologically unfamiliar names, while no differences emerged in speed for familiar names. The authors suggested a direct and causal involvement of memory processes in learning new vocabulary items, at least in young children.

Bowey (1996; 1997) carried out a number of studies in order to examine the nature of the contribution of phonological memory to vocabulary learning. His conclusion included a criticism of Gatercole, Willis and Baddeley's (1991a) findings which suggested a direct contribution of phonological memory in the acquisition of new vocabulary. In their study, Gathercole et al. (1991a) investigated phonological memory and rhyme awareness in order to find out whether they reflected a common phonological processing skill or differentiable phonological abilities. Participants were 4 and 5 years old children, who were administered a phonological memory test, a rhyme oddity detection task as well as reading, vocabulary, and nonverbal intelligence measures. Results showed that the association between receptive vocabulary and phonological memory, measured with the nonword repetition task and digit span test, was stronger than the association between vocabualry and phonological awareness. Bowey highlighted that the direct link between phonological memory, measured by non word repetition and vocabulary learning should be interpreted with greater caution given the evidence for the causal contribution of phonological memory on vocabulary development (Bowey, 1997).

She carried out a study with 5 years old children who were administered tests of vocabulary and grammatical comprehension, phonological sensitivity (i.e. phonological awareness), assessed with a rhyme oddity task and phoneme identity task, and phonological memory measures such as the forward digit span and non word repetition task, as well as a general intelligence test.

The specific link between phonological memory and receptive vocabulary was not supported by Bowey's data, but an association between receptive vocabulary and phoneme identity and rhyme oddity was found.

First of all she argued that the non word repetition task is a complex psycholinguistic task that reflects different processing components, among which speech perception and the construction of phonological representation that cannot be neglected when considering vocabulary learning. In addition it includes a memory component although this aspect was expressed only implicitly. In particular, she criticised Gathercole et al.'s (1991a; 1991b) thesis that only phonological memory can explain subsequent vocabulary learning, after controlling for the phonological sensitivity effect. On the contrary, she hypothesised that phonological memory and phonological sensitivity are both manifestation of a latent phonological processing ability. Results of her study supported this claim (see Bowey, 1996). In turn, Gathercole and Baddeley (1997) highlighted a number of methodological constrains in Bowey's study. For example the weak correlational relationship between the nonwords repetition task and vocabulary acquisition could be due to the fact that not all children received a common prerecorded sequence of non words as is recommended for the standard administration of this test. This live presentation would lead to potential noise in phonological memory measurements resulting, in ultimate analysis, in a lack of empirical power. Furthermore Gaterhole and Baddeley (1997) indicated other bodies of evidence coming from correlational studies with neuropsychological patients which added support for a concrete involvement of phonological memory in non words repetiton, showing that ".. phonological memory is not in any simple sense the same as other aspects of phonological function" (Gathercole and Baddeley, 1997, p. 293).

Actually, efficient maintenance of phonological traces could be masked by a disturbed phonological analysis and fuzzy or absent phonological representation.

5. THE ROLE OF THE PHONOLOGICAL COMPONENTS IN FOREIGN LANGUAGE LEARNING

In light of the findings reviewed above and in order to replicate the findings from Palladino and Cornoldi (2004), two experiments carried out by Palladino and Ferrari (submitted) further investigated the central and peripheral working memory components in children with Foreign Language Learning Difficulty (FLLD). An added objective of the study was to investigate the efficiency of phonological processing and awareness in children with FLLD and to better clarify its role in phonological memory.

The research design, common to both the experiments, compared two groups differing in foreign language learning abilities but matched on other potentially confounding variables. It also excluded participants with more general and severe learning problems following the research tradition on individual differences and learning disabilities (see for example Cornoldi and Oakhill, 1996; Gillam, Cowan, and Day, 1995).

Following this research design, a group with a specific foreign (English) learning difficulty, but adequate non-verbal intelligence was accurately selected within a wide sample of 7th and 8th grade students and compared to a control group matched for non-verbal intelligence, age and gender but with an average foreign language learning capacity.

In the first experiment participants with FLLD were administered a verbal working memory task (i.e. a forward and backward digit span task, Orsini, 1993) and a visuo-spatial working memory task (i.e. Corsi Blocks Test, Corsi, 1972; Milner, 1971) in order to examine the peripheral working memory components separately (i.e. the phonological loop and visuo-spatial sketchpad). A first goal was to replicate the dissociation between the two peripheral components observed by Palladino and Cornoldi (2004) in order to support a specific phonological memory impairment in children with FLLD.

A further goal was to assess the performance on phonological awareness comparing groups in a phoneme deletion task, considered one of the more difficult phonological awareness tasks and thus more apt to discriminate performance in older children. The task was composed of matched trials differing for language (native vs. foreign language) and unit (letter vs. syllable). The two languages and units were introduced in order to investigate the role of familiarity with the language and sensitivity to linguistic units, respectively, following results obtained by Service (1992).

Results revealed that children with FLLD have a poorer verbal working memory, when assessed with both the forward and backward digit span, but a preserved visuo-spatial working memory, measured with a visuo-spatial working memory task that requires both processing and maintenance of information. Thus, such findings replicate what emerged from the previous study by Palladino and Cornoldi (2004).

The performance of FLLD participants in phonological awareness, as measured by the syllable and letter deletion task, shows how this group has a specific difficulty in representing and manipulating linguistic sounds. However, a significant interaction was found between Language and Group, in that the FLLD group was less efficient in manipulating the sounds of English non-words than Italian non-words whilst no difference was observed in the control group.

These problems could have influenced phonological memory performance since word representation and processing are sub-components of the digit span task. However, when phonological awareness was partialled out, phonological memory differences between groups were still significant.

Therefore preliminary conclusions seem to indicate that children with FLLD have two main independent problems: poor phonological representation and processing and a less efficient phonological memory.

The latter deficit could be due to poor rehearsal abilities that would reduce the phonological memory capacity inducing faster trace decay.

The efficiency of the rehearsal mechanism could be tested looking at the FLLD children's specific sensitivity to the word length effect, which provided the initial support for the existence of an articulatory loop within the working memory model.

In a second experiment a group of individuals with FLLD and a control group were compared in a series of tasks. First, the phonological processing and storage components were examined by manipulating the word length and output modality of a word span task. An immediate serial recall task similar to that used by Gathercole and Baddeley (1990) was devised. List length and word length were increased in order to adapt the task to older children. It was composed of disyllabic and four-syllable word lists. List length ranged between 4 and 6 words according to the digit span observed in the groups tested in the previous experiment.

In half the trials, participants' output consisted of pointing to picture stimuli that matched list words instead of giving the spoken output pronouncing the words aloud.

A specific phonological memory problem due to an output difficulty would be demonstrated by a better performance in the pointing output modality.

A second task, used to explore the groups' central executive working memory efficiency, was the listening span test. The listening span test is a working memory task requiring a contemporary maintenance and processing of verbal information and is considered a measure of the central executive component of working memory (Daneman and Carpenter, 1980; De Beni, Palladino, Pazzaglia and Cornoldi, 1998; Just and Carpenter, 1992).

The last tasks administered in this experiment replicated the letter-syllable deletion task, similar to the one presented in the first experiments except for some improvements according to a "sounding like English" evaluation of English items.

As regards the word length and output modality measures, three separate mixed design analysis of variance performed for each list showed a main effect for the lists of 4 5 and 6 words, where participants with FLLD were poorer in the serial recall than the control group. Thus, results showed that the group with FLLD did not exhibit sensitivity to the word length effect and showed no advantage in the picture pointing recall condition.

However the significant interaction between Length and Group indicated that the Length effect was observed exclusively in the Control group. Furthermore the interaction between Output and Length was significant.

Results clearly show that the word length manipulation was effective with a list length of 6 words, immediately higher than the children's span. Lists with shorter words (e.g. composed of two syllables) produced larger spans than lists with longer words (e.g. of four syllables). However this effect is clearly evident only in the control group's performance. Children with FLLD did not decrease their recall when word length increased thus showing no sensitivity to word length. The absence of a word length effect implies a dysfunctional subvocal rehearsal. Children with FLLD thus appear to have a deficient subvocal rehearsal mechanism which could, at least partially, account for their phonological memory problem. The FLLD group showed a different pattern of results as compared to children with SLI. In a similar task the latter group did show a phonological memory deficit, but was as sensitive as the control group to the word length effect (Gathercole and Baddeley, 1990).

Furthermore in the spoken output condition the recall task consisted of pointing to the correct sequence of pictures corresponding to the words just listened to. Comparison of the two conditions showed no advantage for the picture pointing recall in either group. Children with FLLD did not show a specific decrease in performance as a consequence of producing a spoken output. Therefore it is possible to exclude that their phonological memory deficit is due to a difficulty in pronouncing aloud lists of words, caused either by a slower pace, which would increase trace decay (Cowan, day, Saults, Keller, Johnson and Flores, 1992; Cowan, Keller, Hulme, Roodenrys, McDougall and Rack, 1994) or by difficulties in setting or executing the motor program required.

Group differences were still significant for disyllabic words, but no longer significant for four-syllable words, even when the total score of the Letter/Syllable deletion task was covariated.

Memory differences between groups in recalling disyllabic words was not accounted for by group differences in manipulating language sounds. However with four-syllable words memory differences between groups are explained by the phonological processing skill. One possible interpretation of these results is that FLLD children show major problems when they have to process longer words such as four-syllable words because of deficient phonological processing and awareness. An impaired phonological processing system affects the FLLD children's memory performance with longer words but does not affect, to such an extent, their memory performance for disyllabic words.

Analysis of the Listening span test as a measure of the central executive component of working memory showed no significant difference in neither memory performance (number of final words recalled: Control group, M=27.5 SD=8.68; FLLD group, M=24.27 SD=4.7) nor sequence errors (number of words recalled in the wrong sequential position: Control group, M=3.07 SD=3.01 ; FLLD group, M=3.08 SD=2.73). The absence of a deficit in the central executive component in children with FLLD is consistent with previous results (Palladino and Cornoldi, 2004). This result indirectly restricts the nature of the deficit to a more peripheral processing in memory such as the phonological component.

As regards phonological awareness assessed with the syllable/letter deletion task, the FLLD group showed to be less capable of manipulating language sounds than the control group. A main effect of Language was found, the deletion task with Italian phonemes was easier than with English phonemes.

This difficulty was not only observed with relatively new sounds (sounding like English non-words) but also occurred with familiar sounds from their native language. This result seems to indicate that although the memory problem falls into the verbal domain it cannot be specified further.

The deficit in phonological awareness is not limited to less familiar linguistic sounds but concerns all the verbal domain even though in this case the native and foreign languages are quite different in several respects (Leonard, 1998).

Children with FLLD are poorer than controls in phonological awareness confirming results obtained in the previous reported experiment. However the more stringent methodology, i.e. choosing English sounding non-words, resulted in a sensitivity to language familiarity in children with FLLD. They showed a greater impairment when English sounding non-words were presented and their sound composition had to be manipulated, than when Italian non-words were presented for manipulation. Their gap between languages was about twenty times bigger (1.33) than the control group's (0.06). The phonological processing difficulty of children with FLLD appeared more severe with the foreign language phonology in accordance with what was previously observed by Service (1992) in Finnish children learning English. However both Finnish and Italian, differently to English, have a transparent correspondence between phonemes and graphemes. Therefore it is possible that in both studies the easier orthographic representation could have helped children in doing the deletion task in their native language. Nevertheless in the present research children with FLLD showed a more marked sensitivity to language than children in the control group.

Although the deletion task used in this second experiment highlighted a language sensitivity in the FLLD group, the control group's mean performance on this task showed that it was too easy for those children not impaired in foreign language learning. Therefore it is possible that the control group's ceiling effect had an influence on group differences.

Overall, the pattern of results demonstrates a dissociation between phonological and visuo-spatial memory in children with FLLD (Palladino and Cornoldi, 2004). Their memory problem appears to be confined to verbal material given that the sequence maintenance of both forward and backward positions is as good as that of controls. Furthermore the FLLD group appears to have a specific difficulty in representing and manipulating linguistic sounds, independently of the language i.e. it is manifest both with native and foreign sounding non-words. These problems could have influenced phonological memory performance since word representation and processing are sub-components of the digit span task. However, when phonological awareness was partialled out phonological memory differences between groups were still significant in both short term memory measures, forward and backward.

Therefore preliminary conclusions seem to indicate that children with FLLD have two main independent problems: poor phonological representation and processing and a less efficient phonological memory.

Results consistently showed, in both experiments, that participants with FLLD have a phonological processing and memory deficit. A significant difference between groups was observed in both digit and word span tasks. Results from the First experiment lead us to exclude a visuo-spatial memory deficit whilst results from the Second experiment eliminate the possibility of a difference between groups due to a central executive deficiency. Both these exclusions are consistent with evidence obtained by Palladino and Cornoldi (2004). These authors had found a specific impairment in digit span and non-word repetition resulting in a memory deficit profile of FLLD children limited to phonological working memory. In this respect the FLLD children's deficit overlapped with that of children with SLI examined by Gathercole and Baddeley (1990).

Children with FLLD seem therefore to have a poor phonological working memory also because their articulatory loop does not function properly, and no rehearsal effect emerged from their memory performance.

Nonetheless phonological memory performance could also be disturbed by an inaccurate phonological processing such as phoneme representation and manipulation. Indeed participants with FLLD consistently demonstrated, throughout both experiments, a phonological processing deficit in linguistic unit manipulation in both languages but more marked in the foreign language. The attempt to define the influence of phonological processing on phonological working memory differences between groups was repeated in both experiments with consistent results. The FLLD children's less accurate phonological processing did not contribute to determine their poor phonological memory performance. However an opposite result was obtained in the memory performance of four-syllable words, since in this case phonological processing explained the memory differences between groups. A tentative explanation would be that phonological processing is required to a larger extent when dealing with longer words, and thus memory for such stimuli depends more heavily on phonological processing. A direct manipulation and control of these variables could contribute to highlight a possible effect due to length similarity between verbal items in phonological processing and memory tasks.

Results of the two experiments show that children with FLLD have a memory deficit specifically limited to phonological working memory. On the one hand their poor performance seems to depend, at least in part, on an inadequate rehearsal process that in a regular memory system works as an articulatory loop to refresh memory traces avoiding faster decay (Baddeley, 1986). On the other their poorer memory seems to depend on an inaccurate phonological processing and manipulation particularly when longer words are presented. This result is less immediately accounted for by Baddeley's working memory model (although it is not incompatible with it) because it asks for a clearer definition and a precise relative location of phonological processing within the model.

By contrast the output modality should not have affected the word length effect according to Baddeley's model. Results of the second experiment showing that the word length effect is sensitive to the output modality fit better with Cowan et al.'s model (1998). In fact the study shows consistent evidence that output duration affects the word length effect leading the authors to suggest updating Baddeley's model taking into consideration a memory-retrieval process that plays a significant but distinct role from the well known articulatory loop. According to this updated model the absence of the word length effect in the picture pointing modality observed in the Second experiment is due to the fact that picture pointing eliminates word duration in response to which it is possible to attribute the effect.

CONCLUSION

Overall results strengthen the idea that the phonological working memory is a language learning device (Baddeley et al., 1998). Results are consistent with Baddeley's memory model and its articulation into different components, although, according to several authors, a better specification of the phonological loop's components could significantly increase, not only the present data comprehension, but also the possibility of further developing research in this field (see for a review Andrade, 2001 and for a model updating proposal, Cowan et al., 1998).

Research from different perspectives and with different designs consistently demonstrates that language learning and also foreign language learning is strongly related to phonological memory and processes.

Future research should further clarify the memory component involved in language learning in order to add a significant contribution to knowledge in this field. Not only, a better understanding of language processing could improve the opportunity of offering adequate diagnostic instruments and appropriate intervention strategies to children suffering from FLLD.

REFERENCES

Andrade, J. (2001). *Working memory in perspective*. Hove, UK: Psychology Press.

Baddeley, A. D. (1990). *Human memory: Theory and practice*. Needham Heights, MA, US: Allyn and Bacon.

Baddeley, A.D. (1986). *Working memory*. New York: Oxford University Press.

Baddeley, A.D., Gathercole, S., and Papagno, C. (1998). The phonological loop as a language learning device. *Psychological Review,* 105, 158-173.

Baddeley, A.D., and Hitch, G. (1974). Working memory. In G.A. Bower (Ed.), *Recent advances in learning and motivation*, 8. New York: Academic Press.

Baddeley, A.D., Thomson, N., and Buchanan, M. (1975). Word length and the structure of short term memory. *Journal of Verbal Learning and Verbal Behaviour*, 14, 575-589.

Bernhardt, E. B. (2000). Second-language reading as a case study of reading scholarship in 20th century. In M.L. Kamil, P.B Mosenthal, P.D. Pearson, and R. Barr (Eds.), *Handbook of reading research*, Vol. III (pp 791-811). Mahwah, NJ: Lawrence Erlbaum Associates.

Bishop, D. V. M., and Snowling, M. J. (2004). Developmental dyslexia and specific language impairment: same or different? *Psychological Bulletin*, 6, 858-886.

Bowey, J. A. (1996). On the association between memory and receptive vocabulary in five years olds. *Journal of Experimental Child Psychology*, 63, 44-78.

Bowey, J: A. (1997) What does nonword repetition measure? A replay to Gathercole and Baddeley. *Journal of Experimental Child Psychology*, 67, 295-301.

Caplan, D., Rochon, E., and Waters, G. (1992). Articulatory and phonological determinants of word length effect in span tasks. *Quarterly Journal of Experimental Psychology*, 45A, 177-192.

Carrol, J.B. (1998). Second language abilities. In R. Sternberg (Eds.), *Human abilities: An information processing approach.* New York: Freeman, pp.83-101.

Cheung, H. (1996). Nonword span as a unique predictor of second language vocabulary learning. *Developmental Psychology*, 5, 867-873.

Cornoldi, C., and Oakhill, J. (Eds.) (1996). *Reading comprehension difficulties: processes and intervention*. Mahwah, NJ: Erlbaum

Cornoldi, C., and Vecchi, T. E. (2000). Mental imagery in blind people: The role of passive and active visuospatial processess. In M.A. Heller (Ed.) *Touch, representation and blindness* (pp. 143-181). Oxford, UK: Offord University Press.

Cornoldi, C., and Vecchi, T. E. (2003). *Visuo-spatial working memory and individual differences.* Hove, UK: Psychology Press.

Corsi, P.M. (1972). Human memory and the medial temporal region of the brain. (Doctoral dissertation, McGill University, Montreal, 1972). *Dissertation Abstract International*, 34(2-B).

Cowan, N., Day, L., Saults, J. S., Keller, T. A., Johnson, T., and Flores, L. (1992). The role of output time in the effect of word length on immediate memory. *Journal of Memory and Language,* 31, 1-17.

Cowan, N., Keller, T. A., Hulme , C., Roodenrys, S., McDougall S., and Rack, J. (1994). Verbal memory span in children: Speech timing clues to the mechanisms underlying age and word length effects. *Journal of Memory and Language*, 33, 234-250.

Cowan, N., Wood, N., Wood, P., Keller, T. A., Nugent, L., Keller, C. V. (1998).Two separate verbal processing rates contributing to short-term memory span. *Journal of Experimental Psychology: General*, 127(2), 141-160.

Daneman, M., and Carpenter, P.A. (1980). Individual differences in working memory and reading. *Journal of Verbal Learning and verbal Behaviour*, 19, 450-466.

De Beni, R., Palladino, P., Pazzaglia, F., and Cornoldi, C. (1998). Increases in intrusion errors and working memory deficit of poor comprehenders. *The Quarterly Journal of experimental Psychology*, 51 A, 305-320.

Dufva, M., and Voeten, M.J.M. (1999). Native language literacy and phonological memory as prerequisites for leraning English as a foreign language. *Applied Psycholinguistic*, 20, 329-348.

Ganschow, L., and Sparks, R.L. (1989). Linguistic Coding Deficit in Foreign Language Learners. *Annals of Dyslexia*, 39, 179-195.

Ganschow, L., and Sparks, R.L. (1993). Foreign language learning disabilities: Issues, research, and teaching implications. In S. A. Vogel and P. B. Adelman (Eds.), *Success for college student with learning disabilites* (pp. 283-322). New York: Springer- Verlag.

Ganschow, L., Sparks, R.L., and Javorsky, J. (1998). Foreign language learning difficulties: An historical perspective. *Journal of Learning Disbilities*, 31, 248-258.

Gathercole, S.E., and Baddeley, A.D. (1989). Evaluation of the role of phonological STM in the development of vocabulary in children: A longitudinal study. *Journal of Memory and Language*, 28, 200-213.

Gathercole, S.E., and Baddeley, A.D. (1990). The role of phonological memory in vocabulary acquisition: A study of young children learning new names. *British Journal of Psychology*, 81(4), 439-454.

Gathercole, S.E., and Baddeley, A.D. (1990). Phonological memory deficits in language disordered children: Is there a causal connection? *Journal of Memory and Language*, 29, 336-360.

Gathercole, S.E., and Baddeley, A.D. (1993). *Working memory and language.* Lancaster, England UK: Lawrence Erlbaum Associates.

Gathercole, S.E, and Baddeley, A.D. (1997). Sense and sensitivity in phonological memory and vocabulary development: A reply to Bowey (1996). *Journal of Experimental Child Psychology,* 67(2), 290-294.

Gathercole, S.E., Hitch, G.J., Service, E., and Martin, A.J. (1997). Phonological short term-memory and new word learning in children. *Developmental Psychology*, 33(6), 966-979.

Gathercole, S.E., Service E., Hitch, G.J., Adams and Martin, A.J. (1999). Phonological short-term memory and vocabulary development: Further evidence on the nature of the relationship. *Applied Cognitive Psycholog,.* 13(1), 65-77.

Gathercole, S.E, Willis, C., and Baddeley, A.D. (1991a). Differentiating phonological memory and awareness of rhyme: Reading and vocabulary development in children. *British Journal of Psychology.* 82(3), 387-406.

Gathercole, S. E., Willis, C., Baddeley, A. D. (1991b). Nonword repetition, phonological memory, and vocabulary: A reply to Snowling, Chiat, and Hulme. *Applied Psycholinguistics.* 12(3), 375-379.

Gathercole, S.E., Willis, C.S., Emslie, H., and Baddeley, A.D. (1992). Phonological memory and vocabulary development during the early school years: evidence from a longitudinal study. *Developmental Psychology*, 28, 887-898.

Gardner, R. C. (1985). *Social Psychology and Second Language Learning: The role of Attitudes and Motivation.* London: Arnold.

Geva, E., and Ryan, E. B. (1993). Linguistic and cognitive correlates of academic skills in first and second languages. *Language Learning*, 43, 5-42.

Gillam, R. B., Cowan, N., and Day, L. S. (1995). Sequential memory in children with and without language impairment. *Journal of Speech an Hearing Research*, 38, 393-402.

Harrington, M., and Sawyer, M. (1992). L2 working memory capacity and L2 reading skill. *Studies in Second Language Acquisition*, 14, 25-38.

Just, M.A., and Carpenter P.A. (1992). A capacity theory of comprehension: Individual differences in working memory. *Psychological Review*, 99, 1, 122-149.

Leonard, L. B. (1998). *Children with specific language impairment.* Cambridge, MA: MIT Press.

Masoura, E. V., and Gathercole, S.E. (1999). Phonological short-term memory and foreign language learning. *International Journal of Psychology*, 34 (5/6), 383-388.

Milner, B. (1971). Interhemispheric differences in the localization of psychological processes in man. *British Medical Bulletin*, 27, 272-277.

Miyake, A., and Friedman, N. (1998). Individual differences in second language proficiency: Working memory as language aptitude. In A. Healy, and L. Bourne (Eds.), *Foreign language learning* (pp. 339-364.) London: Lawrence Erlbaum Associates.

Foreign language learning: Psycholinguistic studies on training and retention (pp. 139-164). Mahwah, NJ: Lawrence Erlbaum Associates.

Morra, S. (2000). A new model for verbal short term memory. *Journal of Experimental Child Psychology* 75, 191-227.

Morra S., Camba R., Calvini G. (2004). Learning non-words as a function of attentional capacity and phonological variables. *18th Biennal Meeting of the I.S.S.B.D.* Ghent, July 11-15.

Orsini, A (1993). *WISC-R. Contributo alla taratura italiana (Contribution to italian norms).* Firenze: O.S.

Palladino, P., and Cornoldi, C. (2003). Working memory performance of Italian students with Foreign Language Difficulties, *Learning and Individual Differences*, 14, 137-151.

Palladino, P., Cornoldi, C., De Beni, R., and Pazzaglia, F. (2001). Working memory and updating processes in reading comprehension. *Memory and Cognition*, 29, 344-354.

Raven, J.C. (1986). *Raven's Progressive Coloured Matrices.* London: H.K. Lewis

Service, E. (1992). Phonology, working memory, and foreign language learning. *Quarterly Journal of Experimental Psychology*, 45(1), 21-50.

Service, E. (1998). The effect of word length on immediate serial recall depends on phonological complexity, not articulatory duration. *Quarterly Journal of Experimental Psychology*, 51A, 283-304.

Service, E., and Maury, S. (2003). All parts of an item are not equal: Effects of phonological redundancy on immediate recall. *Memory and Cognition*, 31 (2), 273-284.

Service, E., and Kohonen, V. (1995). Is the relation between phonological memory and foreign language learning accounted for by vocabulary acquisition? *Applied Psycholinguistics*, 16, 155-172.

Service, E., and Maury, S. and Luotoniemi, E. (in preparation). *Forgetting and redintegration of consonants and vowels in pseudowords lists.*

Sparks, R. L., and Ganschow, L. (1993). The impact of native language learning problems on foreign language learning: Case study illustrations of linguistic coding deficit hypothesis. *Modern Language Journal*, 76, 149-159.

Sparks, R., Ganschow, L., Javorsky, J., Pohlman, J., and Patton, J. (1992). Test comparison among students identified as high-risk, low-risk and learning disabled in high school foreign language courses. *Modern Language Journal*, 76, 142-159.

Thorn, A.S.C., and Gathercole, S.E. (1999). Language-specific knowledge and short-term memory in bilingual and non-bilingual children. *Quarterly Journal of Experimental Psychology*, 52A, 303-324.

In: New Developments in Learning Research
Editor: Samuel N. Hogan, pp. 165-190

ISBN 1-59454-669-X
© 2006 Nova Science Publishers, Inc.

Chapter 8

SITUATED KNOWING AND LEARNING DURING SCIENCE LABORATORY ACTIVITIES: MODELS, METHODS, AND EXAMPLES

Wolff-Michael Roth
University of Victoria

ABSTRACT

We teach according to our understanding of how students know and learn. Conducted from a perspective of phenomenological sociology, my research has shown that many science teaching practices are inconsistent with the state of the art on knowing and learning. An important instructional method lies in hands-on activities; these are said to help students learn science concepts. However, there is no theory that would help us understand the microlevel details of how doing something with the hands is helping to learn and understand general concepts. Correlatively, most science teachers consider laboratory activities as add-ons and fun, but with little benefit for doing better on tests. In recent years, researchers have come to understand cognition as a situated and distributed process (Roth, 2001b). Here, I present a model of and a methodology for studying situated knowing and learning as they arise from laboratory activities in school science. This allows us to make a direct connection between manual activity and general concepts. I use case studies from an extensive database established during a four-month study of learning during school science laboratory activities to illustrate both model and method. In addition, the case studies presented here illustrate cognitive development of different types at shorter and longer time scales. As students engage science activities, the entities that they are attuned to change in character and kind, which affords changes in their cognitive development. Collective activities, including discussions with a teacher or peer, coordinate and scaffold the complexity of individual cognition.

INTRODUCTION

Hands-on laboratory activities have been a stable feature of science and mathematics education for many decades. Yet, there exists virtually no research to show what type of cognition arises from such activities and how this process unfolds (Nersessian, 1995). There is evidence that existing models of concepts and conceptual change are inappropriate to describe and theorize learning as it occurs in real time as students engage with materials, talk to one another and their teacher, and build new understandings of physical systems (Roth and Duit, 2003). There is little evidence that shows a tight link between the material activities students engage in and the general concepts they develop; and it remains unclear how situations influence knowledge construction in the way situated learning theories presuppose (Billett, 1996). It is therefore not surprising that we know little about the development of scientific competence from childhood to professional science (Pickering, 1995). Understanding such a development is the central concern of my research agenda and that of the present article. I focus on what students actually do in school physics laboratories to understand the relationship between sensorimotor and verbal actions, knowing, and learning and thereby find more definitive answers about the pedagogic value of laboratory work.

Take the following situation recorded during an innovative curriculum on simple machines in a mixed sixth- and seventh-grade classroom that I taught a few years ago. Two students (J, D) gather around a second-class lever (weight is suspended from a beam between fulcrum and point of effort) held up by a rubber band and supporting a one-kilogram weight and I ask them some questions.[1] (The episode is also represented as S_2 in Figure 1.)

In the course of this lesson, Jon and Dave developed from (a) never having seen a second-class lever to (b) understanding the relationship between weight, effort, and their respective positions along the beam to hold the lever in equilibrium. Such cognitive changes can be described, among others, in terms of the complexity of students' verbal and sensorimotor actions. Here, this increase in complexity involved (a) focusing on an aspect of the lever, (b) operating on the elastic, (c) establishing the property of extension, and (d) coordinating two properties, "stretchability" of the elastic and heaviness of the weight. In essence, Dave (and Jon) constructed a relation between the stretching of an elastic band and different weights. In the course of the episode, the actions increased in complexity from operating on entities to describing properties (lines 03, 04) and ended with the link between two properties (stretch and weight). In the course of the entire lesson, the two students extended this relation to a variation between properties, as expressed in the statement "the closer the weight is moved to the fulcrum, the less the elastic is stretched." A plot of the complexity of individual verbal and sensorimotor actions (levels of complexity are defined below) shows an increase in the course of the episode (Figure 1, S_2). Here, cognition increases in complexity as students learn to operate on and combine less complex entities.

While such episodes may appear at first trivial, I show in this chapter that they constitute the foundation of the scientific knowledge that students develop as they engage in laboratory activities. This learning is remarkable given the number of inherent uncertainties in this as in any learning situation (e.g., Roth, McRobbie, Lucas, and Boutonné, 1997a). First, students' and teachers' ways of perceiving physical events, their *domain ontologies*, are more likely to

---

[1] The following transcription conventions have been observed: [,] – square brackets show where two consecutive speakers overlap in their talk; (GESTURES) – parentheses enclose actions denoted by capital letters.

differ than to be the same.[2] Second, learning occurs despite the use of highly indexical language with utterances such as "this" (line 01) and "it" (lines 04, 05). Third, although sensorimotor and verbal actions are intertwined during the activity, that is, simultaneously occur at the neural level, students' conceptual understandings eventually become independent of the actual situation at hand—which literally constitutes abstraction, a kind of trans-situational knowledge.

```
01   J:    See like this. (J POINTS TO ELASTIC)
02         (J PULLS UP ON RUBBER BAND)
03   T:    Now, what happens to your elastic?
04   D:    (OBSERVES BAND) It stretches.
05   T:    Why would it stretch?
06   J:    [Because the]
07   D:    [Cause the ] weight is heavy. (D GESTURES DOWNWARD PULL)
```

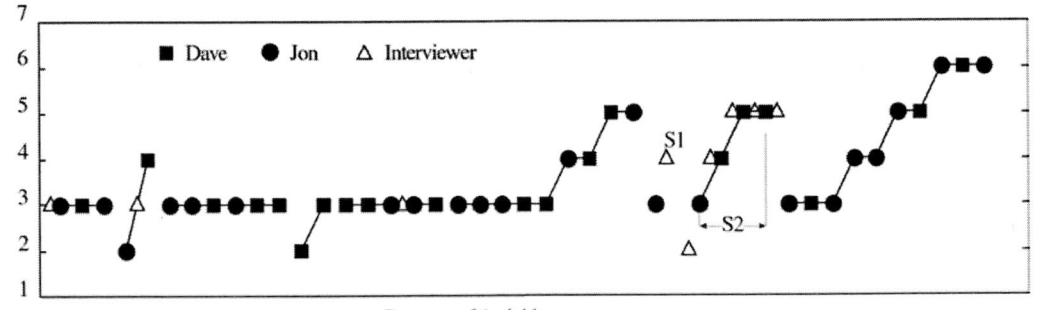

Figure 1. Complexity of situated cognition for two students in the course of one activity during which they construct a relationship between the distance of a weight hanging from a second-class lever and the amount of effort it takes to hold the lever.

Any endeavor designed to show a linkage between physical activity and conceptual understanding has to include detailed, continuous studies of students in activity and tease out what the current domain ontologies are, what it is that students attend to and act upon (Roth, 1998b, 2001a). It is hereby important to account for the learning environment as it is viewed by the students, for it is in response to opportunities for and constraints to sensorimotor and verbal actions that are salient to them that students change rather than to the things as they appear to science teachers and science education researchers. This leads me to conduct research on knowing and learning in science from a situated cognition perspective. The purpose of this chapter thus is threefold. First, I present a way of thinking about cognition that allows me to track science learning in real time as students enact laboratory activities. Second, I provide details of my analytical approach. Finally, I exemplify the approach in providing a detailed case study of learning about levers from a split sixth- and seventh-grade

---

[2] The ontology of a domain consists of all salient entities and operations as registered by the acting individual in the current situation (Roth, 2001a); that is, the ontology describes a particular individual's way of perceiving the world. We may also say that the domain ontology describes all the entities and processes in the *lifeworld* of a person. The lifeworld is the world as experienced, known, and felt by the individual subject rather than the world as described by scientists.

classroom. To be explicit, I present a model of knowing and learning as it has arisen from more than a decade of research in physics classrooms in many of which I was the teacher.

SITUATED COGNITION

Following one line of recent work in cognitive science and sociology, I take a ecological perspective on cognition. In this perspective, cognition is not considered a property of the individual student, but the result of acting-in-setting (Snow, 1992); this makes "student-in-setting" an appropriate unit of analysis of cognition (Lave, 1988). I view cognition as a structural coupling of the ideal types "student" and "setting" in terms of which earlier research has been conducted. This implies that aspects of cognition traditionally considered to be *in*dependent are now *inter*dependent. First, what an individual student senses (sees, feels, smells) and what he or she acts (manipulates, talks) towards is never some true, objective environment, but always a *lifeworld* in which entities are salient as a function of the species and individual history. Second, patterns of actions arise from intentions (mental) and the salient, situated aspects that already have collective motives built in (e.g., Leont'ev, 1978). Third, sensations are both a function of the physical stimuli received at the periphery (e.g., ear, and retina, skin) and the interpretative horizon that the student has built through prior experience. Finally, consciousness has evolved both as a function of genetic *and* environmental pressures; its structure is therefore the result of prior experience as well as its historical development.

Changes in students or their lifeworlds change the patterns of actions observed, and therefore the characteristics of cognition inferred by analysts. At the heart of my perspective lies the recognition that in lived cognition, perception and action are fundamentally inseparable and not merely contingently linked; they are two sides of the same coin (Weizsäcker, 1973). An inward direction (perception, interpretation) and an outward direction (verbal, physical action) simultaneously characterize cognitive activity. That is, perception and action are treated at the same level because in many cases, they cannot be meaningfully separated: perception is guided action (Varela, Thompson, and Rosch, 1993). Inward and outward cognitive activities are related to previous experiences that shape inward and outward action: actions and perceptions are guided by anticipations. This enactive approach conceptualizes cognition in terms of three, circularly dependent processes: perception, anticipation, and action. New perceptions change students' anticipations that then allow the projection of new possibilities for action and different engagement in activity.

This model provides an answer to the oft-asked question, "Where and how is cognition situated?" (Roth, 2001b). Thus, stable and recurrent structures in knowing and learning arise from regularities associated with any of the four elements mind, acting, lifeworld, or sensing. For example, students do not need to construct internal representations of the world because they can rely on structures *in* the world. When a short-order cook takes a knife's present position as an indication of what has to happen next, he does not have to memorize and remember a plan; rather, the next step, cleaning the knife or chopping garlic, is determined by a structure of his or lifeworld (Agre and Horswill, 1997). Each situation is therefore characterized by constraints (in both positive and negative senses) as perceived by students; they are a function of students' familiarity with the details of the physical and social setting.

Modifications of the settings will change the nature of cognition that can be observed and active exploitation of the setting to simplify and improve problem solving is typical of situated cognition. From this perspective, learning is constituted by the changes in one's lifeworld, that is, the extension of the possibilities for acting in the world (Lave, 1993). It is observable in the form of changing patterns of patterned actions, ever-increasing resources of experienced situations, and evolving notions of what the world is like.

This way of looking at knowing and learning distinguishes itself from other ways current in science education in its assumption about how the world looks to different students. I use the term *domain ontology* to denote the ensemble of elements that make a student's lifeworld, that is, the objects and events that populate the world as experienced by some student. Most research in education takes the teacher or researcher's domain ontology as a starting point against which students' cognitive performances are evaluated. However, human interpretation is flexible and therefore not ontologically bound. Evidence from a variety of disciplines suggest that concepts and categories are not in the world but are enacted by individual students who must constantly change in response to new experiences and new realities in their environment (Smith, 1987). These domains include the neurosciences and biology, linguistics, psychology, cognitive anthropology, science education, sociology, and philosophy. Because of the irreducible triad of perception, anticipation, and action, students always live and act in *their* worlds, only parts of which are shared because students interact with others. The checks for the validity and viability of categories constructed by individuals occur through structural coupling to the world. In this sense, there are considerable constraints on the categories that are viable (fruitful) for students.

Science teachers and science education researchers should not take their own domain ontology as a starting point for understanding cognition but they should construct students' lifeworld based on the data. To build appropriate models of knowing and learning in science, we need appropriate understandings of the students' domain ontology (or we may end up ascribing unexpected cognitive behaviors to defects in the cognitive system rather than contingencies of the system's historical development). Once the students' perspective on the world is taken into account, failures to learn physics can often be attributed to different domain ontologies rather than to malfunctioning cognitive processes (Roth *et al.*, 1997a, 1997b).

LEVERS AND THE DEVELOPMENT OF REASONING

To make a case in point, I provide an example from studies of how students know and learn about levers. I have studied levers since my dissertation work (e.g., Roth, 1991) and, most recently, designed and taught a unit on simple machines as part of which we investigated what students know and learn about levers (e.g., Roth, McGinn, Woszczyna, and Boutonné, 1999).

Levers have been used as a context for developing and testing theories of cognitive development for over four decades (e.g., Inhelder and Piaget, 1958; Metz, 1993). But the resulting theories of reasoning and its development on lever problems are far from commensurable. Inhelder and Piaget suggested three stages of cognitive development in the context of first-class levers. According to this theory, reasoning at the first two stages is largely of qualitative nature, whereas proportional reasoning in the form

$$\frac{\text{weight}_1}{\text{weight}_2} = \frac{\text{distance}_2}{\text{distance}_1}$$

is developed in the third stage (distance$_i$ is the distance of weight$_i$ from the fulcrum). Most individuals, however, do not appear to use ratio rules for solving lever problems (Siegler, 1976). Accordingly, most individuals use one of four rule systems in the form of decision trees of increasing depth (or number of decision nodes). The simplest rule system consists of a binary decision tree that compares the two weights on a lever. The most advanced rule system includes four levels of decisions the last of which contains the product moment rule that relates weights and distances through the equation:

$$\text{weight}_1 \times \text{distance}_1 = \text{distance}_2 \times \text{weight}_2.$$

There also exists a linear-logistic model (Spada and Kluwe, 1980) in which development occurs in terms of quantitative changes for dealing with problem difficulty rather than in terms of the quality of cognitive operations. I modeled cognitive development related to balance beams using an artificial neural network (Roth, 2000a). The results showed that for each level of complexity of items, the network's performance follows the linear logistic curve observed by Spada and Kluwe. Furthermore, performance on easier problems precede those that are cognitively more complex both in Siegler's and Piaget's terms.

In all of these and similar studies, it was assumed that individuals attend to *weight* and *distance of weight from fulcrum* as basic properties that they use to reason about balance beam problems. However, in these studies, children and students generally did not manipulate levers. Furthermore, these studies were primarily concerned with the development of numerical rules using the elements of researchers' ontologies of the domain rather than the ontologies of the experimental subjects. Thus, none of the studies investigated whether children and students actually focused on the conceptual relations between weights and distances and rather than on the relations between numbers that they can see.

My theoretical framework does not make the assumption that students experience the experimental situation on the basis of the researchers' ontology. Rather, I expect that individual students develop their own ways of perceiving the situation as they engage with the materials and resources provided. If students have no prior experience, they will be concerned predominantly with the construction of conceptual primitives and a set of relationships that can be made between these primitives (see Table 1). Subsequent experiences will allow the students to evolve a domain ontology that includes increasingly complex elements.

When I observe physics students as they engage in laboratory activities, I see changes in their actions over time and at different time scales. Table 1 shows different levels of cognitive processes related to first-class level (balance beam) activities. To reconstruct cognition independently from our situation-theoretic formulation, I first rewrite the detailed transcripts in the form of actions and motivations from the perspective of the student. That is, I reconstruct how students and their settings are related during the actions in the science classrooms. Great care is taken to reconstruct students' cognitive activity to reflect what they see and how they see these objects and events. I then assign a complexity to each action or utterance according to the heuristic in Table 1.

Table 1. Categories of cognitive complexity with examples from the domain of levers

Level, Complexity	Sample Salient Entities	Sample Student Actions
1		SEPARATES[lever, ground].
2		DISCRIMINATES[parts].
3		OPERATES[lever] ∩ CHANGES[aspect]
4		DISCRIMINATES[weight, distance].
5		OBSERVES[Δw ⇒ Δd]
6		CHANGES[w] ∩ OBSERVES[d].
7		COVARIES[w, d]
8		COVARIES[w, d, left] and COVARIES[w, d, right]

Table 1. Continued

Level, Complexity	Sample Salient Entities	Sample Student Actions
9	(diagram: lever with height h on left, distance d across fulcrum, weight w on right)	VARIES([height] and COVARIES[force, distance]
10	(diagram: lever with height h, distance d, weight w, var[ρ])	COVARIES[distance, weight] and VARIES[density] and VARIES[height]

UNIT ON SIMPLE MACHINES

The present case studies of cognition derive from an extended empirical *in situ* study of learning science in a sixth- and seventh-grade class where students studied simple machines as part of their regular curriculum. I designed and taught the unit (e.g., Roth *et al.*, 1999). During data collection and initial analysis phases, it became quite clear that our assessments showed considerable within-student variations in performance across format such as paper-and-pencil test, group interviews, and practical problems (McGinn and Roth, 1998; Roth, 1998a; Welzel and Roth, 1998). The framework presented above was developed to account for these variations and understand cognitive activity as it arises in real time when students engage in activity.

Students were tested, using a variety of formats, at the beginning and end of this unit. During the four-month long curriculum, students enacted four types of activities. First, there were whole-class discussions over simple machines and teacher-produced visual representations. Second, students conducted small-group investigations using simple machines and teacher instructions. Third, I had planned small-group open-ended activities in which students designed their own machines. Fourth, students presented their designs in whole-class sessions that provided opportunities for peers to voice comments and critique.

The entire curriculum unit was videotaped using two cameras. During small-group activities, each camera followed one student group; at the same time, I carried around a cassette tap to record all my interactions with the different student groups in class. Interviews with individual and pairs of students were also videotaped. Two graduate student research assistants completed ethnographic observations that entered the database in the form of field notes. All videotapes were transcribed. For this study, I analyzed all data related to levers, including whole-class sessions on first-, second-, and third-class levers, a whole-class review lessons concerning all levers, small-group activities with first and second class levers, and pretest and posttest interviews. The following case studies were developed with data from the activities of two sixth-grade boys, Dave and Jon.

SITUATED COGNITION IN SCIENCE CLASSROOMS

In this section I exemplify my analyses in several detailed case studies. My analyses show that situated cognition develops from lower to higher complexity on two time scales. On a short time scale (from seconds to a few minutes), one observes series of bottom-up developments of cognitive activity from lower to higher complexity. Over longer time scales (across several lessons in the same context), the average complexity reached over short time scales drifts to higher values. A change in the complexity to higher levels requires considerable experience at lower levels. Close observations of students during their activities suggest that their domain ontologies changed and developed as they became more familiar with the materials and as they built up cognitive processes from lower to higher complexity. With each change of situation, new processes of situated cognition begin. Utterances are intimately tied to and rely on the setting. Interactions with peers show a remarkable coordination of the complexity of the respective situated cognition. These findings are elaborated in the following subsections.

SITUATED ACTIONS OF INCREASING COMPLEXITY

In the course of the unit on simple machines, I observed increases in the complexity of students' cognitive activity. This increase is evident from the plot of the complexity of sensorimotor actions and verbal utterances for the pretest and posttest interviews with one of the sixth-grade students (Jon) who did not have prior experiences with a balanced lever (Figure 2). Correspondingly, the average complexity lay between Level 3 and 4. That is, during the interview he began by identifying aspects of the lever device (Level 2) such as the metal nuts (serving as weights) and positions along the lever arms (i.e., his domain ontology included at a minimum the set {weight, position}). Later, and concurrently with moving weights along the lever arm, he developed operational notions (what to do) to balance the lever. Subsequently (right half of Figure 2.a), he used the rudimentary distance notion of "from here to there."

The posttest interview provided evidence that Jon's cognitive activity was of a higher complexity. He consistently coordinated changes in one property (distance) with those of another (weight) without, however, providing evidence that he coordinated a continuous covariation of two properties (Figure 2.b). Thus, we can ascertain that the actions and utterances were at Level 6, without having enough evidence that the enacted cognition was at Level 7. (Students may use the product-moment rule as an algorithm to do pencil and paper lever problems without understanding the inverse relationship between weight and distance, or without having a phenomenological understanding of lever devices.)

For students, the interviews about levers already constituted the beginning of their learning process about levers. For example, Jon began to build up distance as a relevant property of levers. Initially, Jon provided answers in terms of locations where the weights need to be placed using the indexical labels "here" and "there" accompanied by pointing that anchored the utterance in the situation. That is, in the initial phases, specific locations along the lever arm were aspects that Jon isolated from others and the ontology consisted of the items in the set {here, there}. In the course of the first interview and throughout the activities, Jon, like many of his peers, built up an understanding of distance through Level 2 (operations). While Jon moved weights along the lever arms, his answer to the question where the weight should go changed. These answers included "from here to there," "between here and there," to "between here and there" and were associated with moving weights along the beam (or simply drawing the fingertip along the beam), to a notion of distance. That is, the entities salient to him (i.e., his domain ontology) changed.

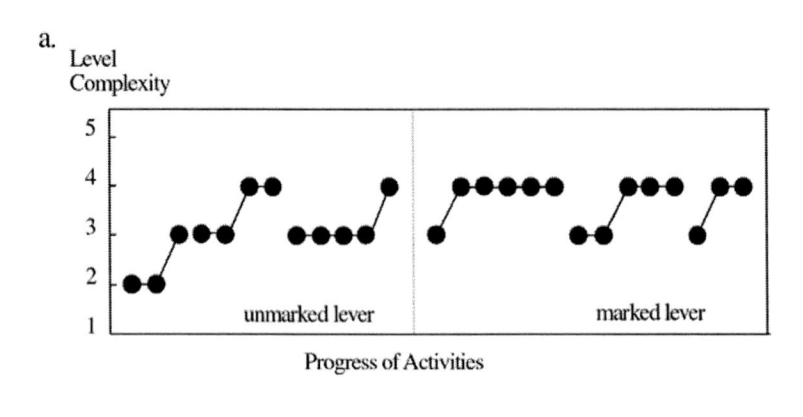

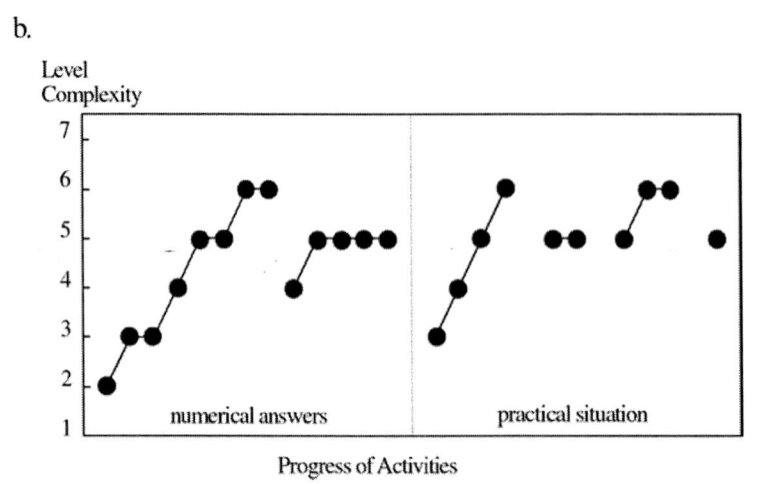

Figure 2. Complexity of situated cognition inferred from Jon's pretest (a) and posttest (b) interviews. One observes repeated bottom-up developments within interviews and a drift of the average level of complexity from the pretest to posttest.

Table 2 shows that after having separated the lever as an object, Jon discriminated at first positions ("here") which he later differentiated such as to have two elements ({"here," "there"}). These elements were then combined by an operation that occurred, by means of a process of differentiation, both at the level of practical action and discourse (Level 3). Finally, he derived the property of "distance" as a relevant property of the object lever by integrating across (by means of type abstraction) across repeated changes of position (Level 4). Here, the operation of moving weights along the beam has been integrated into the student's description that evolved into that of differences in location to that of distances (between locations). Developing a notion of distance in the context of first-class levers does not mean here that the salient property is the distance between fulcrum and weight. Jon's first mention/use of distance concerned that from the end of the lever to the weight on one side, but from the fulcrum to the weight on the other side. That is, although he attended to distance, this distance could not lead him to a generalization of rules for balanced levers.

During the posttest interview, Jon explained how he calculated the weight on paper-and-pencil problems with first- and second-class levers. During this explanation, traces of the learning history were observable in the association of utterances with the corresponding movements of his index finger along the property described. He enacted distances and weight: he moved the finger along the lever while talking about the magnitude of the distance, and gestured pulling downward (in the direction the force of gravity would be expected) when talking about the weights. Both properties (Level 4) were based on phenomenological experiences of weight and distance. In his case, across different paper-and-pencil problems, he identified load, effort, and the associated distances. Jon's explanation also provides evidence that during his development, at least two type abstractions had occurred. First, he treated balanced levers and drawings of them as members of the same type, a first-class lever, which could exist as device or drawing. Second, he formed a general class of levers in the context of which the product moment rule could be used to find the measures of properties not given by the teacher-researcher. The domain ontology now contained a set that includes both first- and second-class levers (i.e., {Class I levers, Class II levers}). This constitutes a structural change in which Jon has made an object-type abstraction as he has generalized across different objects to form a new classification of objects into a family.

Table 2 Development of Situated Cognition on the Lever

Confirmed Set of Elements in Domain Ontology	Level
{l| here}	2
{l| here, there}	2
{l| here, there, from-to[here, there]}	3
{l| here, there, from-to[here, there], between[here, there]} ∩ {R |Δl|}	3
{l| here, there, from-to[here, there], between[here, there], distance} ∩ {R |Δl|}	4

NOTE: R|Δl| = MOVES finger/weight along lever arm.

We see here, how the notion of "distance" as a relevant property of levers was grounded in a student's interactions with the phenomena at hand. (For detailed demonstrations how abstract discourse is embodied in physical activity see Roth, 1999; 2000b; Roth and Welzel, 2001.) Traditional science education assumes that students learn a more inclusive concept before knowing specific cases (e.g., students are told about chemical reactions before seeing one). In contrast, my research shows that Jon's notion of distance was grounded bottom up through the coordination of less complex cognitive activity by means of deliberate and consistent operations. It should be emphasized that the development of "distance" as it relates to levers is a situated one, for Jon was certainly familiar with distances as a relevant property in other situations (e.g., walking to school). That is, notions such as distance that students build up through experience are situated notions relevant properties (or principles, systems) for the phenomena at hand.

LEARNING FROM ENGAGING IN ACTIVITIES

Situated cognitive activity at higher levels of complexity arises when students coordinate cognitive activity from lower levels. Through experience, students differentiate existing entities and collect existing entities into families. With increasing experience, students begin to link sensorimotor and verbal actions to yield cognitive activity of higher complexity. Thus, we expect considerable exploratory phases before higher order abstractions can be made. The data from this study are consistent with these hypotheses as the following example illustrates. I had asked students to explore second-class levers by moving a load along the lever arm and observing the changes in an elastic band that they used to hold up the arm (indication of the effort).

In Figure 1, we saw that much of the initial activity was at Level 3, that is, students largely operated with existing entities (objects, aspects). The graph represents actions that included setting up, getting the lever to work, discovering new aspects (e.g., through breakdowns), and discovering the meaning of the teachers' instructions (e.g., through their own embodied action). Here, literal breakdowns provided occasions during which Dave and Jon began to attend to new aspects of the lever. They saw the specific nature of the fulcrum only after the pivoting mechanism had slipped from its seat in the lever beam. In terms of my theoretical perspective, breakdowns occur when the student perceives a significant difference between anticipations and actions. These periods of operating with materials were necessary because they allowed students to integrate repeated cognitive activity at Level 3 to form new entities at Levels 4, 5, and 6. The following excerpt (involving Dave, Jon, and an interviewer) exemplifies the role physical activity played in learning about second-class levers.

```
01      (DAVE PULLS UP LEVER WITH ELASTIC)
02      (WEIGHT SLIPS TOWARDS FULCRUM)
03  J:  But the this one (POINTS TO WEIGHT) will slip.
04  I:  Maybe you should make it tighter.
05  D:  Maybe it is supposed to go like that.
```

This excerpt illustrates several important issues. First, students have to discover in their own actions the sense of the instructions; that is, what an instruction instructs can be known only *after* one has already followed the instruction successfully.[3] Whether they have actually enacted the instructions as intended or done something else inherently had to be unclear to them. The slipping weight was not expected (line 03) and therefore constituted another breakdown that made students investigate the suspension of the weight—the interviewer's "it" can be read as "clip." On the other hand, Dave proposed (line 05) that this might just be the phenomenon they were to look at. This may be so for many instructions that students attempt to enact. Confirmation for a sequence of action may be derived from a plausible observation. Students are therefore in a fundamental double bind where they need confirmation for their actions when they know that their observation is the desired one; but this confirmation depends on the evaluation of the courses of action (Roth *et al.*, 1997a).

Breakdown also led to students' investigation and discovery of the fulcrum mechanism ("It's broken right here. (PULLS LEVER OUT OF POSITION. WORKS ON FULCRUM)"). In students' ontologies, the lever became an object with an increasing number of aspects and properties through actions and breakdown resulting from actions. The aspect (part of the lever) was not named, but made salient through the utterance "right here" and the accompanying movement which took the lever out of its position and the immediate attention (gaze, manipulation) to and manipulation of the fulcrum piece. The meaning of "right here" arose from the grounding of the utterance in the sensorimotor interactions with the setting ("right here" becomes connected to the fulcrum by means of his gesture and orientation that is noticed by other students). Once the fulcrum was fixed, Jon confirmed that "it is working." If a thing "works," it literally does the required work, fulfilling the function it was designed for. It is a shift in the perspective from a student who works to a thing that does the work. The thing (tool) does no longer interfere with the student's actions and returns to the nature of a transparent tool.

The instructions allowed students to reach Level 6. At first, students were asked to observe what happened to the elastic when they suspended a weight from the lever. Then, they moved the load closer to the pivot. "What happens to the elastic as you move closer to the pivot?" Here, students found their observation (that is, the situation) to support the claim that moving (operation) the load closer to the fulcrum is associated with a decrease (inverse variation) in effort (i.e., variation in (DISTANCE) implies inverse variation in (EFFORT)). As Figure 1 shows, this upward development occurred only after longer periods of operating with the materials at hand. The process of development of higher complexity was identical to that described in the previous section.

CONTINGENCY OF COGNITION

During this study, the contingent nature of cognition became quite clear, especially during those moments of the study when students had little experience with levers. The nature of students' answers to balance beam problems changed when the context of the question was changed. For example, during the pretest, we first asked students to respond to lever problems without providing for equidistant markers and numbers on the lever arm in front of them. Of thirteen interviewees, only three made explicit references to distance by conducting approximate measurements with their fingers (McGinn and Roth, 1998). The others "eyeballed" the distance (three students), used trial and error (five students) or haphazard guessing (two students) procedures to answer the interviewers' questions. These answers changed to using numbers explicitly to reference locations (five students) or do calculations (five students); however, using numbers to do calculations does not mean that students reasoned with distances as earlier developmental research had falsely assumed. Rather, the

---

[3] This may sound strange to some readers, but in fact corresponds to the familiar phenomenon of following a new recipe in the kitchen. Whether one has done what the recipe says can be known only after the finished dish (which we can compare to the photograph in the cookbook) looks like what we were supposed to get.

students are likely to use numbers as objects on which they do some common operation, some arithmetic operation addition and subtraction being the ones normally employed at that stage. These aspects are featured in the following example.

Figure 1 shows the complexity of Jon's cognitive activity across two contexts: lever arm with marks and numbers and unmarked lever. A drift of level to the next higher complexity from operation to properties can be observed. (Note that there also was a change of situation.) More interesting, Jon's answers changed qualitatively when the situation was changed. First, he treated position as something approximate and in terms of "farther in" (on the lever arm) and "farther out." In the course of the interview with the unmarked lever arm, Jon proceeded moving his finger along the beam (or push weights):

```
06          (JON MOVES WEIGHT FURTHER OUT)
07 I:       Is there anything to help tell you where you got to put it?
08 J:       Oh, judging between here (POINTS POSITION LEFT WEIGHT) and
09   here (POSITION FULCRUM) and then between here (POSITION
10          FULCRUM) and here (POSITION RIGHT WEIGHT)
```

In this situation, Jon isolated the beam as an important aspect (Level 2), noticed positions on the beam (i.e., a differentiation of the aspect), and operated on the aspects such that differences in positions were noted (Level 3). The domain ontology in this example consisted of elements {lever arm, position, "here," "there," fulcrum} and operations {MOVES}. The reasoning therefore was in terms of parts of the lever as a physical device. When the interviewer turned the balance beam around so that the equidistant lines and numbers became visible, the elements that were salient to Jon changed and therefore the entities on which his reasoning was based.

With the marks and numbers along the beam visible, they became salient in Jon's actions. However, marks and numbers were aspects (Level 2) rather than a quantification of property (distance, Level 4), and there was little to suggest that Jon actually used distance. Rather, he treated the marks and numbers as resources (at the level of aspects) to reference the position and *not* to specify distance. In one episode, the numbers related to distance were salient in his explanation.

```
11 J:       Because (ADJUSTS WEIGHT), because that's 2 here (ON RIGHT, 2
12   UNITS) and that's two (ON LEFT, 2 UNITS FROM OUTSIDE IN) so it
13   could be even . . . about two in there (STRIKES ALONG BEAM) and
14   that's two there (DISTANCE OF WEIGHT FROM END OF BEAM)
```

In another situation, the salient aspects in the explanation were the one-unit weights Jon had seen the interviewer add to each side.

```
15 J:       Because, since you add one more there (LEFT WEIGHT) and
16   one more there (RIGHT WEIGHT), it would be the same.
```

Thus, although a student reasoned in terms of two unit distances in the first episode, one-unit weights were salient in the present situation. In both situations, however, what was salient to the students were numbers rather than positions or distances along the beam (i.e., his domain ontology consisted of the elements {1, 2, 3, 4, 5, 6} and operations {+, -}).

Comparing this domain ontology and available operations with the former, we see that the operations completed where those on numbers (arithmetic ones) rather than on aspects and properties of the lever as a physical device. It is important to note the change of the domain ontology with change in situation and corresponding changes in students' activities. All students enacted qualitatively different cognitive operations when the situation was changed such that there was no overlap in the practices between the two contexts. Much of the prior research attributed such responses to random behavior or "knowledge in pieces" (diSessa, 1988). I do not perceive the situation in terms of deficits. Rather, in the absence of previous experiences, students produce explanations on the spot drawing on the most salient resources currently available in the setting (including the linguistic resources they bring with them). Questions of coherence between the two settings become relevant only once students are intimately familiar with both.

ANCHORING OF UTTERANCES IN MATERIAL SETTINGS

Students, as all speakers, typically rely on the efficiency of language. If entities are part of the surroundings which students can take as accessible to all, they do not express these verbally. A simple deictic reference (uttering "it," "that," etc. or POINTING) suffices to enter the entities into the communicative process. (A famous adage suggests that conversation participants do not talk about entities "that go without saying.") The meaning of indexical utterances becomes fixed by the particulars of the situation. In situation-theoretic terms, there exists some function that anchors a specific utterance (i.e., "it") to some specific item (i.e., "elastic") in this specific context ("it" = elastic); or, equivalently, in terms of my framework, the communicative representation has been partially shifted into an aspect of the lifeworld. "It" and an entity in the lifeworld are therefore structurally coupled and should be considered as part of one cognitive system. In other words, the world is taken by speakers as its own representation and is used as part of their verbal actions without that any further explanation is necessary. This is evident from the following episode.

```
17  J:(DAVE PICKS UP RULER. PLACES FULCRUM, PLACES RULER NEXT TO
18  BOX) I'd put it right there, and, well it goes like
19  that. (OPERATES LEVER) Then I'd put it close (PUTS
20  FULCRUM CLOSE) so you'd have more leverage (OPERATES
21  HIS LEVER). Instead of right here (PUTS FULCRUM AT 4 TIMES DISTANCE)
    then it's harder.
```

Dave used the word "it" four times. But each time he used the indexical "it," he referred to a different element: lever, fulcrum, operation of lever pushing, and effort. That is, the nature of the reference changed. However, the situation made it possible for listeners to track the meanings of "it." Associated with the current activities of Dave's hands, the referential function allowed listeners to track what was talked about without that miscommunication arose. Grounding words directly in the world helps conversation participants to follow the shifting use of the same syllable "it" and to reconstruct the intended sense. Viewing the situation from the outside, the position of listener or analyst, I take Jon and his lifeworld as *one* communicative cognitive system. In this system, what is communicated is then represented in different locations of the model. In contrast to analyzing only words emanating from a talking head we obtain a meaningful communication by considering the individual student-in-setting as one system.

We see here that meaning lies not just in the utterances as many discourse analysts treat it, but arises from the very structural coupling of the words in the material aspects of the setting; the materiality of sensorimotor action provides the link between individual and world. Tracking information in the world therefore also means that any salient aspects of the situation are invoked as necessary (Roth and Lawless, 2002). I begin with the reconstruction of things salient to students and then describes situated actions in terms of complexity that arises by combining and coordinating these elements whatever the level of complexity. I am therefore able to explain how learning arises despite continuously shifting reference and ontologies without having to build internal world models.

A different kind of grounding was responsible for the earlier emergence of the notion of "distance" as a relevant property (Level 4). Notions such as "distance" are built up from basic level categories such as "location" and operations on objects and properties. We described above how Jon built up distance from the fulcrum as a property. In the process, his domain ontology changed from {here} to {here, there, from-to[here, there], distance} $\cap$ {R | Δl} (where $\cap$ corresponds to the logical "and"). In a similar way, students in this class constructed the concepts of leverage from pushing levers or mechanical advantage from operating their machines and measuring loads and efforts.

INTERACTIONS WITH OTHERS

Research on interaction—particularly that done from an interactionist and ethnomethodological perspective—provided insights to the interindividual coordination of multiple actors. Thus, what is communicated even in highly structured interviews is the outcome of a collective endeavor rather than a transmission of data from interviewee to interviewer. Even if a "psychiatrist" answered questions with randomly distributed "yes-no" responses, subjects nevertheless reconstructed a coherent motivation underlying this "advice" (Garfinkel, 1967). In the light of such studies, one may ask how the actions and utterances from different actors relate in terms of their complexity. Two general observations can be made in the context of my study. First, there is a considerable coherence in the cognitive complexity of interacting individuals. Second, if the level of complexity by one participant (in our case teacher, interviewer) is too high, the complexity of the response begins at a considerably lower level. Both cases are observable in the interactional sequence from the posttest interview with Dave and Jon (Figure 3). It should be noted that in the middle section of Figure 3, actions and utterances are mostly at Level 5 although interpretations of these episodes may have allowed an assignment at Level 6. There was not enough evidence to support the claim that the near/far distinction that provided "lots of leverage" or made it "harder to lift" (a) was an instance of extreme case reasoning (with an underlying understanding of continuous variation) or (b) was merely the distinction of two locations. I read the situation as in (b) and therefore assigned Level 5 rather than Level 6 as it would be possible under reading (a).

First, the complexity-time graph of Dave and Jon shows similar patterns as graphs representing individual activity. Exchanges were at the same level of complexity or built on each other so that consecutive utterances and actions by different increase in complexity. In other words, there existed a high degree of coordinated cognitive activity and intersubjectivity. This high level of agreement was confirmed by the ethnographic data collected throughout the study. Furthermore, even during discussions in which different perspectives were argued (and different arguments supported), the level of complexity was coordinated. This is evident in the following sample episode in which the interviewer asked Dave and Jon to explain a situation in which the fulcrum was far away from the load in a first class lever (S_1 in Figure 3). It is evident that in the first part of this discussion, Dave ($\sigma_0 \Rightarrow \sigma_1$) and Jon ($\sigma_0 \Rightarrow \sigma_2$) proposed two types of constraints in the form of the implicative IF . . . THEN . . . structure (each sigma [σ] stands for a statement and the arrow [$\Rightarrow$] stands for a logical implication). By beginning his turn with the connective "but" ("but it will be easier to push"), Jon asserted both the conjunct of the two assertions and their contrast leading to the claim that their situation suppers both claims, that is, that

$$(\sigma_0 \Rightarrow \sigma_1) \cap (\sigma_0 \Rightarrow \sigma_2).$$

Here, the students achieve a higher order of complexity by linking the implicative statements previously uttered by Jon and Dave. The entire exchange to this point was maintained at the same level of complexity; it moved up one level when Dave formulated a more general constraint which linked a continuous variation (moving the fulcrum) of fulcrum position to a corresponding change in the height of the load. That is, we understand more complex cognition to arise as it is distributed across the two participants whose mutual contributions get linked and thereby constrain each other. I depict this increase in complexity supported by the situation available to the students, from

$$\{(\sigma_0 \Rightarrow \sigma_1), (\sigma_0 \Rightarrow \sigma_2)\}$$

To

$$\{(\sigma_0 \Rightarrow \sigma_1), (\sigma_0 \Rightarrow \sigma_2), (\sigma_0 \Rightarrow \sigma_1) \Rightarrow (\sigma_0 \Rightarrow \sigma_2)\}.$$

That is, two elements do not simply coexist but constrain one another increasing both the total number of elements and the complexity. In three contributions, the interviewer simply repeated the previous contentions—which is normally read by conversation participants as agreement and confirmation of intersubjectivity.

Second, when the complexity of the questions asked by interviewer or teacher were too high, the complexity of the response generally began considerably below the complexity of the question. In everyday situations, one can often hear expressions such as "You lost me there" or "I don't get it." These comments on the part of the listener are indications that the complexity of the previous utterance was too high or that it lacked grounding as described earlier. Both situations lead to a communication breakdown signaled by expressions such as the ones cited.

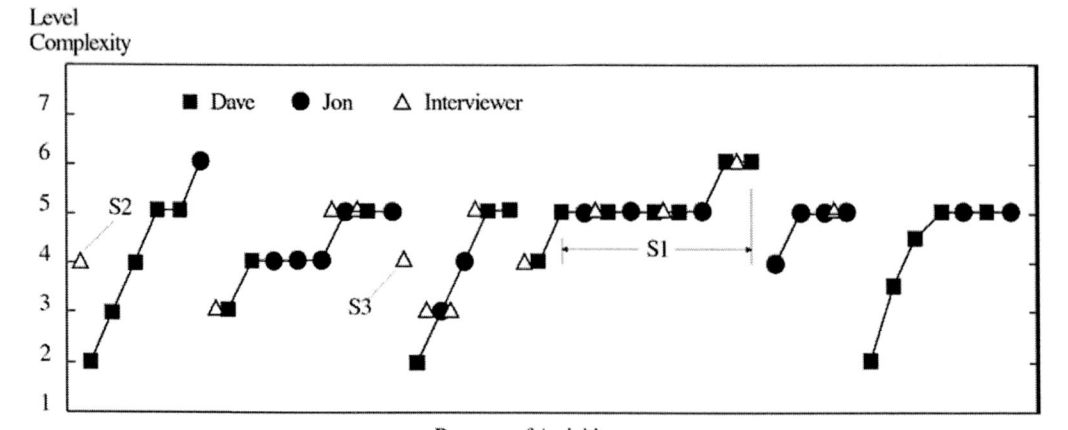

Figure 3. Complexity of situated cognition during the conversation with a teacher. One observes considerable coordination among students and between students and teacher. When the level of complexity of the question is too high (S_2, S_3), student cognition begins a new sequence of bottom-up development.

Two such instances are marked in Figure 3 as S_2 and S_3. Sometimes, students did not even respond or the interviewer followed with a second question (double-barreled question) at a much lower level. In situation S_3, the interviewer followed Dave's attempt to understand the questions (focusing, identifying aspects) with another question that asked in which action (operation) students would engage. Such a situation in which the interviewer followed with another question at a much lower level appears in Figure 1. Dan had used "leverage" to explain why he would place a fulcrum close to a heavy load that he had to lift.

22	I:	What does leverage mean?
23	D:	Well?
24	I:	Where is leverage measured or what does it?
25	J:	Like when you lift something.

The videotape revealed that Dave was at a loss with the first question to explain "leverage" (property). The interviewer then followed up asking for an operational definition of the same notion (operation). At this point, Jon responded in terms of an operation that exemplified his notion of "leverage" (operation).

DISCUSSION

A theoretical framework is presented that allows science educators, researchers and teachers, to track situated knowing and learning in real time. In this model, students are not bounded by their skin, but cognition is considered as a system in which mind, actions, lifeworld (world as available to individual), and perceptions irremediably (that is, structurally) coupled. Thus, rather than arguing that external physical actions were increasingly internalized—as the authors of a similar case study in the domain of early number use have done (Davydov and Andronov, 1981)—I suggest that any activity always occurs inside and outside the person simultaneously. A methodology was presented that allows documenting how aspects of the individual and setting are coupled via grounding functions. These ideas are exemplified by means of descriptive accounts of knowing and learning in a mixed sixth- and seventh-grade classroom for which I had designed and taught a special curriculum on simple machines.

The case studies illustrate that cognitive development is observable at different time scales. First, on short time scales, I observed sequences of situated cognitions with increasing complexity, bottom-up developments. Over longer time scales, I observed that the average complexity of situated cognitive activity drifted to higher complexity. At the same time, the number of elements at each level of complexity increased through processes of differentiation, resulting in an increase of the elements in a student's domain ontology (expressed as a set). This methodology allows teachers and researchers to track this development in real time and therefore to show how and when new levels of complexity emerge from laboratory activities and how and when the ontology of individual students change. This methodology and framework also allows teachers and researchers to track cognition during interactions and show how cognitive complexity of individual students is scaffolded during the activities of collectives. The work presented here raises new questions about knowing and learning and provides new challenges to the modeling of learning as it occurs in real time. I discuss these in the context of knowing in a reasonably studied domain (i.e., levers).

My theoretical approach provides a plausible account of knowing and learning by individual mind, actions, lifeworld, and perception as one system. The examples show how communication, because it also considers aspects of the setting, is meaningful although utterances alone are not. This model does not contest that there are neuronal configurations that constitute a brain where imagery and declarative statements can be evoked; rather, the model suggests that to understand what students do, and therefore, science educators need to account for the entire system of "student-in-laboratory-setting." The methodology takes account for the elements that constitute the setting as perceived by the individual student, her actions, and the linkage between structures that in the past have been dualistically associated with the setting *or* the individual mind. The gains arising from this approach to science education research on knowing and learning are discussed in the context of research levers.

KNOWING AND LEARNING ABOUT LEVERS

There exists a long tradition of studies of reasoning involving equal arm levers. However, this study provides important new insights about students' activities in the context of lever problems. Specifically, the present work suggests that the students' experiences of handling the lever during the interview may lead to rapid adaptation of cognitive activity in terms of the construction of complex actions. For example, the interactions of Jon led to the progressive construction of distance as a relevant property. On the other hand, previous research prevented this form of adaptation because of the contingencies of the interview contexts. Specifically, Siegler (1976) used an equal arm balance with pegs at unit distances onto which weights were mounted. In his situation, the interviewed children were not in a position to build up an understanding of distance through their embodied experiences (moving weights, moving finger along beam) as we observed it in the present study. In the Hardiman *et al.* (1986) study, respondents answered paper and pencil questions during the pretest; during the training sessions, they were allowed to observe in which way the lever tipped, but could not manipulate weights and distances themselves. I am not surprised that most participants in the Hardiman et al study "did not use the scale until after Trial 20" (p. 75), that 23 percent "did not appear to be counting the number of distance units" (p. 73), and that the participants had to be prompted after forty trials to attend to distance. That is, even if the marks on the lever appear to be salient from a researcher perspective, they may not sufficiently constrain cognitive processes to make distance a salient property (Level 4). The present study suggests that pointing to the scale and using numbers are not necessarily evidence of using distance as a property (as Hardiman et al. assumed). Instructional cycles such as that used in the Hardiman *et al.* study embody dangers: they focus students on developing algorithms for dealing with sets of numbers devoid of meaning rather than building embodied understanding of relations between phenomenological properties. The present work suggest that students are more likely to construct covariation of two properties when they actually experience continuous variation of forces as the result of the corresponding continuous variation of distance.

The example of Jon and Dave's cognitive activity during the second-class lever activity showed how conceptual understandings arose from physical activity. The value of hands-on activities in school science is apparent from our research. In situations such as levers, hands-on allows students to construct conceptual understandings of properties relevant to the physical system at hand. This construction begins with cognitive activity that is directed towards objects and increase in complexity as the student learns to differentiate and coordinate them. In contrast to Zietsman and Clement (1997), I do not think that descriptions such as "naive physical intuition," "primitive mechanism," or "primitive case" are suitable descriptions for the development of cognition about levers. Rather, students' sound conceptual understandings require the transformation of embodied experiences of levers in many situations. Furthermore, the present work suggests that rather than encoding "conceptions" and schemata (notions which suggest structural changes), students adapt so that they can provide complex situated actions more rapidly than they did before training (see e.g., differences between pretest and posttest). In this light, Zietsman and Clement's results seem to confirm my own studies as they needed to introduce "temporary conceptual change" and "reversion to preconceptions" to account for their data. (Alleta Zietsman [March 3, 1997, private email communication] confirmed that the students in their study did not develop a phenomenological understanding of distance as a relevant property of second-class levers.) These notions are counterintuitive in a framework that models learning as permanent structural change (as modeled in conceptual change approaches).

What is not clear from most existing studies is the exact role that the weights shown in lever problems play the students' responses. In many studies, there is little evidence that individuals treated the weights as physical forces that are experienced in different ways or whether they simply treated them as numerical codes. However, one study with preschool children showed that children did not encode weights as "weight" (Metz, 1993). Rather, the concept of weight emerged from children's manipulative activities, "primitive yank and align repairs, in the proprioceptive sense of weight felt or exerted in interaction with the apparatus"

(p. 83). In line with the present work, Metz suggested that children's pre-weight responses are not so much misconceptions than building blocks for the construction of conceptual knowledge. Learning from actual examples (rather than drawings as Zietsman and Clement suggested) promotes embodied forms of scientific "conceptual knowledge" that is robust in many situations. This is particularly the case when these examples include extreme cases. One example of such a case was observed when Jon and Dave could not lift a videocassette when the effort arm of their lever system was too short.

SCAFFOLDING COMPLEX COGNITION

My approach suggests different instructional approaches than those that were used in past training studies. Instructional modules provide opportunities for the successive construction of increasingly complex situated action on levers. This includes structuring the instructional setting such that students make distance a salient property before scales and numbers are made salient. I showed how interactions with actual levers allowed Jon to build up a notion of distance beginning with a localization of loads ("here," "there") to differences in localization ("from here to there") and the explicit registration of distance. This change illustrated was illustrated in Jon's utterances concurrent with his physical activity that changed from pointing, to moving (or gesturing movement of) weights, to explicit encoding of distance as distance between thumb and index and numerical value. These changes can be read as physically instantiating changes of "deictic representations" (which encode relations between student and things) from point-like locations over pairs of distant points and extended spaces that need to be covered (movement of finger, hand) to notions of distance. My study therefore suggests that an understanding of distance arises, as other aspects of cognition, from "the kind of experiences that come from our having a body with various sensorimotor capacities" (Varela, Thompson, and Rosch, 1993, p. 173). Complexity of activity was not determined primarily by complexity of the student (Jon likely individuated distance in other situations) or complexity of the setting (levers are rather simple devices). Rather, complexity was an emergent property of situated students-in-laboratory-settings. This complexity changed rapidly and repeatedly. Changes occurred first on one side of the lever before the concurrent changes were observable on both sides. As Table 1 shows, the association and consistent coordination of two covariations are expected to occur only after sufficient experiences of the students with simple covariations (e.g., qualitative, numerical, on either side of lever, possibly different kinds of levers).

SITUATED COGNITION AND EXPERTISE

My work has important implication for the construction of expertise in a science domain. "Experts" usually have great familiarity with their domains. Much as familiarity and experience allowed our students to engage in bringing forth complex activities, experts can be expected to bring forth rather complex activities scaled up many times. This expertise involves a different domain ontology than that which can be expected from newcomers to a domain. Thus, "expert" and "novice" performance cannot be compared on a par because different domain ontologies are involved. Furthermore, it is not so much that novices could simply be trained in the cognitive processes derived from descriptions of expert performance, because novices first need to have the opportunities to develop the conceptual ontologies of and familiarity with the domains of the expert. For example, it would not help to teach students the ratio or product-moment rules to do balance beam problems if they had not yet developed distance and weight as a relevant physical properties of lever systems, unless we want students to plug salient numbers into algorithms they recall. (This is the predominant result of current science education.)

If "novices" are asked to respond to paper and pencil questions or interviewed in domains where they have no experience, we expect their responses to be a bricolage from available resources. This includes only those resources that are salient to students within that particular situation and in everyday common sense (i.e., their current lifeworld and its domain ontology). The responses therefore reflect the salient structured resources as much as structures of the mental apparatus. My own paper and pencil tests and interviews with marked and unmarked levers suggest a strong relationship of responses with those aspects that novices may construct as salient. Even if students were to view distance as a salient property of levers, it could be distances other than those from load/effort to fulcrum (Hardiman *et al.*, 1986).

Some studies showed that students do learn about mechanical systems without having manipulated and worked with such systems (White, 1993). At least one of these studies showed, however, that the learners involved generally understood little about the forces operating in the system and did very poorly on practical application tasks (Ferguson and Hegarty, 1995). Furthermore, particular aspects of a mechanical system only become apparent and salient when learners interact with real systems rather than representations of them. Ferguson and Hegarty also contended that "it seems unlikely that the kinesthetic information would affect the ability to encode details of [a system's] configuration" (p. 156). My research does not support this contention and, to the contrary, suggests that individuals construct important properties of mechanical systems only through interacting with physical instantiations of them.

UNDERSTANDING LEARNING FROM ACTIVITIES

The results of this study have considerable implications for teachers and researchers wanting to understand and explain cognition and learning in realistic settings. Modeling learning of children using neural networks, Elman (1993) notes that learning is suboptimal when training occurs with a constant set of input data. Learning increases dramatically in two conditions: (a) when the training started with input data of low complexity that was increased over time and (b) when the cognitive capacities allowed data to be processed only partially. Elman argues that in human learners processes of the second type are more likely occur.

Similar processes occur with older children. Here, the initial domain ontology available to a student in a new domain is fairly small—children initially act towards levers (e.g., talk, actions, and gestures) as indiscriminate wholes. With experience of acting in the setting (domain), the number of elements in their ontology increases and so does the complexity of situated activity. In new situations, cognitive activity deals with reduced ontologies: there are few salient elements and relations (actions). With familiarity in a particular situation, the number of salient elements increases; elements are also linked ("chunked") into more complex elements. Because entities can be interpreted in different ways, the associated uncertainty affords a great deal of flexibility to cognitive activity and therefore learning from activity. Although the retinal stimulus generated by some focal situation may stay constant, the perception of this situation changes because perception is also a function of the learning dynamic and the anticipations of the individual. Thus, although the environment may be held constant in some absolute sense (in terms of an agreed upon ontology), it is not for the individual student, especially during the learning phases and before it is enculturated in a particular ways of seeing and classifying a domain. The present research suggests that essential elements of understanding in a domain (as levers) come from having a body and acting in the world. I explain this observation by making perceptions and anticipations functions of the experience of acting in the world.

But does such a process of changing ontology and increasing complexity hold for adults or even scientists? Although case studies using my framework have not been conducted in any detail, there exists a detailed historical case study of Faraday's work on the electromagnetic motor (Gooding, 1990). My research would suggest that there was a process of interdependent development in which Faraday's actions in the world, his observation language (an expression of his perceptions), and his formal representations converged and mutually constituted one another. Gooding concluded that "practical manipulation is necessary to propositional representation" (p. 93) during discovery work when new phenomena are constructed; the development of skill affords a differentiation of material things, events, and representations and therefore a fixation of their ontological status. Thus, Faraday did not observe some abstract phenomena that he learned to interpret in some new way. Rather, his domain ontology of the situation changed and with it the actions that the materials afforded and the conceptual framework that provided a consistent explanations. The importance of modeling anticipations to cognition became evident from an independent analysis of Faraday's work on the electromagnetic motor. A neural network—as a pure empiricist—presented with the same evidence as Faraday did not learn to predict successful from unsuccessful experiments if it was exposed to the entire set of experiments he conducted (Tweney and Chitwood, 1995). After ruling out alternative hypotheses, it was concluded that Faraday's theoretical anticipations mediated his perceptions and assessments of any experiment. Faraday simply ignored unsuccessful experiments and disconfirmatory evidence.

EPILOGUE

In order to advance their field, learning researchers in general and science educators in particular need to closely inspect whether the theories and methodologies to study knowing and learning are consistent with the state of the art. I began this article suggesting that science educators generally hold ideas about knowing and learning that are no longer consistent with the theories that cognitive scientists, anthropologists, and sociologists have constructed over the past decade. Because theories of knowing and learning have tremendous impact on curriculum development and teaching strategies, the science education community needs to do update the conceptual framework from which it conducts its work. This chapter is a contribution on how to understand knowing and learning and how to study these phenomena given the different theoretical commitments that I developed. This framework pays close attention to the way in which the world appears to learners, and therefore to the grounds these have for acting in the way they do.

ACKNOWLEDGMENTS

This work was made possible in part by Grants 410-93-1127 and 410-96-0681 from the Social Sciences and Humanities Research Council of Canada. I thank Sylvie Boutonné, Michelle K. McGinn, Carolyn Woszczyna, and Manuela Welzel for their help and feedback during different stages of the study.

REFERENCES

Agre, P., and Horswill, I. (1997). Lifeworld analysis. *Journal of Artificial Intelligence Research, 6*, 111–145.

Billett, S. (1996). Situated learning: Bridging sociocultural and cognitive theorizing. *Learning and Instruction, 6*, 263–280.

Davydov, V. V., and Andronov, V.P. (1981). The psychological conditions for the origination of ideal actions. *Soviet Psychology, 19* (3), 3–28.

diSessa, A. A. (1988). Knowledge in pieces. In G. Forman and P. B. Pufall (Eds.), *Constructivism in the computer age* (pp. 49–70). Hillsdale, NJ: Lawrence Erlbaum Associates.

Elman, J. L. (1993). Learning and development in neural networks: the importance of starting small. *Cognition, 48*, 71–99.

Ferguson, E. L., and Hegarty, M. (1995). Learning with real machines or diagrams: Applications of knowledge to real-world problems. *Cognition and Instruction, 13*, 129–160.

Garfinkel, H. (1967). *Studies in ethnomethodology*. Englewood Cliffs, NJ: Prentice-Hall.

Gooding, D. (1990). *Experiment and the making of meaning: Human agency in scientific observation and experiment*. Dordrecht: Kluwer Academic Publishers.

Hardiman, P. T, Pollatsek, A., Well, A. D. (1986). Learning to understand the balance beam. *Cognition and Instruction, 3*, 63–86.

Inhelder, B., and Piaget, J. (1958). *The growth of logical thinking from childhood to adolescence*. New York: Basic.

Lave, J. (1988). *Cognition in practice: Mind, mathematics and culture in everyday life*. Cambridge: Cambridge University Press.

Lave, J. (1993). The practice of learning. In S. Chaiklin and J. Lave (Eds.), *Understanding practice: Perspectives on activity and context* (pp. 3–32). Cambridge: Cambridge University Press.

Leont'ev, A. N. (1978). *Activity, consciousness and personality*. Englewood Cliffs, NJ: Prentice Hall.

McGinn, M. K., and Roth, W.-M. (1998). Assessing students' understandings about levers: better test instruments are not enough. *International Journal of Science Education, 20,* 813–832.

Metz, K. E. (1993). Preschoolers' developing knowledge of the pan balance: From new representation to transformed problem solving. *Cognition and Instruction, 11,* 31–93.

Nersessian, N. J. (1995). Should physicists preach what they practice? Constructive modeling in doing and learning physics. *Science and Education, 4,* 203–226.

Pickering, A. (1995). *The mangle of practice: Time, agency, and science.* Chicago: The University of Chicago Press.

Roth, W.-M. (1991). The development of reasoning on the balance beam. *Journal of Research in Science Teaching, 28,* 631–645.

Roth, W.-M. (1998a). Situated cognition and assessment of competence in science. *Evaluation and Program Planning, 21,* 155–169.

Roth, W.-M. (1998b). Starting small and with uncertainty: Toward a neurocomputational account of knowing and learning in science. *International Journal of Science Education, 20,* 1089–1105.

Roth, W.-M. (1999). Discourse and agency in school science laboratories. *Discourse Processes, 28,* 27–60.

Roth, W.-M. (2000a). Artificial neural networks for modeling knowing and learning in science. *Journal of Research in Science Teaching, 37,* 63–80.

Roth, W.-M. (2000b). From gesture to scientific language. *Journal of Pragmatics, 32,* 1683–1714.

Roth, W.-M. (2001a). Designing as distributed process. *Learning and Instruction, 11,* 211–239.

Roth, W.-M. (2001b). Situating cognition. *Journal of the Learning Sciences, 10,* 27–61.

Roth, W.-M., and Duit, R. (2003). Emergence, flexibility, and stabilization of language in a physics classroom. *Journal for Research in Science Teaching, 40,* 869–897.

Roth, W.-M., and Lawless, D. (2002). Signs, deixis, and the emergence of scientific explanations. *Semiotica, 138,* 95–130.

Roth, W.-M., McGinn, M. K., Woszczyna, C., and Boutonné, S. (1999). Differential participation during science conversations: The interaction of focal artifacts, social configuration, and physical arrangements. *Journal of the Learning Sciences, 8,* 293–347.

Roth, W.-M., McRobbie, C., Lucas, K. B., and Boutonné, S. (1997a). The construction of knowledge in traditional high school physics laboratories: A phenomenological analysis. *Learning and Instruction, 7,* 107–136.

Roth, W.-M., McRobbie, C., Lucas, K. B., and Boutonné, S. (1997b). Why do students fail to learn from demonstrations? A social practice perspective on learning in physics. *Journal of Research in Science Teaching, 34,* 509–533.

Roth, W.-M., and Welzel, M. (2001). From activity to gestures and scientific language. *Journal of Research in Science Teaching, 38,* 103–136.

Siegler, R. S. (1976). Three aspects of cognitive psychology. *Cognitive Psychology, 8,* 481–520.

Smith, D. E. (1987). *The everyday world as problematic: A feminist sociology.* Toronto: University of Toronto Press.

Snow, R. E. (1992). Aptitude theory: Yesterday, today, and tomorrow. *Educational Psychologist, 27,* 5–32.

Spada, H., and Kluwe, R. (1980). Two models of intellectual development and their reference to the theory of Piaget. In R. Kluwe and H. Spada (Eds.), *Developmental models of thinking* (pp. 1–28). New York: Academic Press.

Tweney, R. D., and Chitwood, S. T. (1995). Scientific reasoning. In S. Newstead and J. S. B. T. Evans (Eds.), *Perspectives on thinking and reasoning: Essays in Honour of Pater Wason* (pp. 241–260). Hillsdale, NJ: Lawrence Erlbaum Associates.

Varela, F. J., Thompson, E., and Rosch, E. (1993). *The embodied mind: Cognitive science and human experience*. Cambridge, MA: MIT Press.

Weizsäcker, V. von (1973). *Der Gestaltkreis: Theorie der Einheit von Wahrnehmen und Bewegen*. Frankfurt a/M.: Suhrkamp.

Welzel, M., and Roth, W.-M. (1998). Do interviews really assess students' knowledge? *International Journal of Science Education, 20*, 25-44.

White, B. Y. (1993). ThinkerTools: Causal models, conceptual change, and science education. *Cognition and Instruction, 10*, 1–100.

Zietsman, A., and Clement, J. (1997). The role of extreme case reasoning in instruction for conceptual change. *Journal of the Learning Sciences, 6*, 61–89.

Chapter 9

TEACHER COMMUNICATION BEHAVIOUR AND ENJOYMENT OF SCIENCE LESSONS

Harkirat S. Dhindsa[1]
Universiti Brunei Darussalam

ABSTRACT

Teacher communication behavior in a classroom is an important dimension of classroom learning environment that significantly contributes towards a unique learning environment. The aim of this research was to study secondary students' perceptions of science teacher communication behaviour and its association with enjoyment of science lessons. Data were collected (a) by administering a teacher communication behaviour questionnaire and students' enjoyment of science lesson questionnaire to 1098 students in 53 classes and (b) by direct observation of 20 science classes. Factor analysis, alpha reliability and discriminant validity coefficients for the five scales in the instruments using a student or a class or a school as a unit of analysis supported internal consistency and the distinct nature of the scales, thus the high quality of the data collected. The results of the study revealed that Bruneian science students perceived their teachers to some extent friendly and understanding who exercise dominance in the classrooms controlling the overall classroom interaction without so often challenging their students with higher order questions. The students seldom received praise, non-verbal support, and encouragement from their science teachers despite a large number of the teachers are expatriates with qualifications from and experience in developed countries. The female students perceived their teachers to be statistically significantly more challenging as well as understanding and friendly than the male students. A low level statistically significant difference in favour of Form 5 (Grade 10) students was observed on encouragement when compared to Form 4 students. Low to moderate level statistically significant differences between class means as well as school means revealed that teacher communication behavior varied marginally between the classes and schools. Statistically significant positive simple correlation values between students' perceptions of enjoyment of and factors of teacher communication behaviour in science lessons suggest that teacher communication behaviour directly influence enjoyment of science lesson. The

---
[1] hdhindsa@shbie.ubd.edu.bn

implication of this research is (a) for classroom teachers to optimse their classroom communication behaviour and (b) for teacher educators to redesign their training programs to optimize pre-service teachers' communication behaviour to make science lessons more enjoyable.

INTRODUCTION

Teacher and student communication plays a central role in establishing a quality classroom learning environment (Wubbels and Levey, 1993). Teacher communication behavior in a classroom, therefore, is an important dimension of the classroom learning environment that significantly contributes towards a unique classroom learning environment which is a result of interactions of students with peers, curriculum and teachers. These interactions last for approximately 15,000 hours per year (Fraser, 1989) the time secondary students spend in their classes to pursue their social and academic goals (Ryan and Patrick, 2001). According to Good and Brophy (1991) on an average teachers in secondary school have interactions with 150 students per day. The teachers are not aware of these interactions. Based on the interview results Good and Brophy (1991) concluded that the teachers were not aware of the number and types of questions they asked in their classes and the feed back they provided to their students. The influences of teacher-student interactions on classroom discipline (Rosenholtz, Bassler, and Hoover-Dempsey, 1986), constructivist learning (Watts and Bentley, 1987), and, attitudes and achievement (Wubbels and Levey, 1993) have been demonstrated.

There is a large number of dimensions of teacher communication behaviour. Some of these dimensions include questioning (Carlsen, 1991), wait time (Jegede and Olajide, 1995; Rowe, 1974), communication rate (Dhindsa and Anderson, 1992), helping, friendly and understanding teacher behaviour (Fisher, Henderson and Fraser, 1996; Wubbels and Levey, 1993), controlling behaviour (Fisher and Rickards, 1997; Wubbels and Levey, 1993), verbal reinforcement (She, 2000), non-verbal reinforcement (She, and Fisher 2000, van Tartwijk, 1993). These dimensions of teacher communication behaviour directly influence students' attitudes and learning outcomes (Fisher and Rickards, 1997; Wubbels and Levey, 1993). Wait time and communication rate dimensions have been extensively studied, whereas other dimensions listed above need attention. This study will concentrate on five dimensions of teacher communication behaviour namely challenging, encouragement and praise, non-verbal support, understanding and friendly, and, controlling. The importance of studying these dimensions has been highlighted in the literature. For example van Tartwijk (1993) reported that 63% of the measured variance of perceived influence of teachers on what happens in the class was explained by non-verbal behaviour of the teacher. She and Fisher (2002) reported statistically significant correlation (association) between teachers' encouraging and praise behaviour to students' affective and academic outcomes. In 1997, Fisher and Rickards reported an association between friendly and understanding behaviour of teachers, and, students' learning outcome and positive attitude to learning the subject. They also reported that controlling or strict behaviour is associated with students' cognitive gains not with attitudes. Challenging scales in this instrument covered questioning. Effective classroom questions promote relevance, encourage ownership, help students to interpret their observations and link new learning to extant knowledge (Deal and Sterling, 1997). Most of the research in the area has been conducted in developed countries, and very little attention has been paid in developing countries especially in Asia.

Communication is also a dimension of culture, hence it is not context free. The communication behaviours of teachers and students in a classroom are therefore, influenced by their cultural backgrounds. Chan (2004) observed that Asian students generally tend to be quieter than North American students, because they have been taught not to speak unless they are asked to as a respect to their teachers. According to Delpit (1988), white teachers used indirect statements or veiled commands instead of direct commands when speaking to black children. Moreover, the managerial strategies developed by lower secondary white American teachers did not meet the needs of children from other cultures. The communication behaviours of teachers and students are further influenced by subcultures identifiable by nation, tribe, language, location, religion, gender, occupation, race, ethnicity, and social class (Aikenhead, 1997). Communication occurring in physical and social contexts especially verbal communication reflects the thought patterns of a culture or sub-culture. Many cultures or subcultures express emotional overtone of messages with different nonverbal behaviour (Atwater, 1996). For example in Brunei, pointing at something with the thumb is acceptable, but not with the first finger. According to Rasool and Curtis (2000) cultures develop a variety of acceptable modes of verbal and nonverbal communication that can confuse and misinform outsiders. It can happen very often in classroom situations, because in many such situations teachers from a culture or subculture are involved teaching students from other cultures or subcultures.

Often there are cultural overlaps between neighboring societies and even between neighboring countries. Bruneians share cultural values to some extent with neighboring countries. Therefore the research done in these countries could be useful in reflecting the situation in Brunei without doing actual research in local context. There are studies on the classroom learning environment reported from Singapore, Malaysia and Indonesia (Wahyudi and Treagust, 2003; Goh and Fraser, 1998 ; Liau and Arellano, 2003). But no research has been reported using the instrument (TCBQ) used in this study. Moreover, minor variations in cultural context may be highly important in a classroom context. She and Fisher (2002) conducted a study in Taiwan and Australia using this instrument. Both Taiwan and Australian cultures are significantly different from Bruneian culture indicating a need for this study. In Brunei itself, a reasonable amount of work on the classroom learning environment has been conducted. For example, Dhindsa (2005) and Dhindsa and Fraser (2004) studied the cultural learning environment in secondary and tertiary institutions respectively, Riah (2001) studied learning environment in secondary chemistry classes and Poh (1995) investigated the learning environment in upper secondary biology laboratory classes. Riah (2001) has used QTI to study teacher interactions in chemistry classrooms in Brunei, but the dimensions of QTI are different to than of TCBQ. The author has not come across any research conducted on teacher communication behaviour in secondary science classes in Brunei. Under these conditions, it is important to study teacher classroom communication behaviour in a specific cultural context that is Bruneian, rather than importing research done in another non-compatible culture to solve local problems. This study was therefore planned and conducted to evaluate teacher communication behaviour in science classes and the association between teacher communication behaviour and the students' enjoyment of science lessons.

The dimensions of teacher communication behaviour in a classroom setting can be studied by using systematic observations of classroom interactions as well as of video recorded files, descriptive base studies and using students' and teachers' perceptions (She, 2000). The major limitation of using observation and descriptive approaches is their ability to deal with small samples of data. Since generalization requires large volumes of data and a computer can process large quantities of data, a trend over the years has been to use the students' and teachers' perceptions approach. The advantage of using students' perceptions as indicators of the quality of the classroom environment has been highlighted in many studies (Walberg and Haertel, 1980; Fraser 1998). These studies suggest that students are directly involved in classroom activities and observe more of their teacher's behaviour than does an external observer.

A number of instruments have been developed to study teacher interactions in a classroom: questionnaire on teacher interactions (QTI) by Wubbels and Levey (1993) and teacher communication behaviour questionnaire (TCBQ) by She and Fisher (2000). In this study the instrument developed by She and Fisher (2000) is considered for studying secondary students' perceptions of teacher communication behaviour, because it is based on the theory of communication behaviours (Waltzlawick, Beavin and Jackson, 1967), also it has accounted for research based on the use of QTI. However, these dimensions are not directly covered in QTI. The TCBQ instrument consists of 40 items covering five dimensions namely challenging, encouragement and praise, non-verbal support, understanding and friendly, and, controlling. The instrument has been reported as valid and reliable for data collection (She and Fisher, 2000). They reported that the Chonbach's alpha reliability coefficients for the scales in the instrument ranged from 0.86 to 0.93 for Taiwan as well as for the Australian data. The discriminant validity (mean partial correlation of a scale with other scales) data for the scales varied from 0.16 to 0.50 for the Taiwan data and from 0.06 to 0.45 for the Australian data. These data suggest internal consistency and independence of the scales used in the instrument. Moreover, eta^2 values ranged from 0.17 to 0.22 for Taiwan and from 0.05 to 0.15 for the Australian data. Eta^2 values indicate the variance in teacher communication behaviour (dependent variable) that is accounted for by class memberships (independent variable).

The research data have been analysed in numerous ways to study the effects of different variables. For example, researchers have evaluated the relationship between affective domain and academic outcomes and have reported a significant relationship between these variables (Fraser, 1994; Gardner and Gauld, 1990; Weinburgh, 1995). She and Fisher (2000) using 7-item "Attitude to This Class" scale has reported significant correlation between affective domain and the students' perceptions of teacher communication behaviour in classes. In the present study a 5-item enjoyment scale was used to investigate if the teacher communication behaviour scales significantly correlate with enjoyment of science in the classes of the respondents involved in this study. The enjoyment scale used in this study was previously used by Riah (2000) to study students' enjoyment. He reported the reliability coefficients for the scale as 0.84 for chemistry theory classes data and 0.89 for practical classes data.

The researchers have also analysed the data using individual students and a class as units of analysis (Fisher and Waldrip, 1997; She and Fisher, 2002). The trend in this direction is growing. Using the class as a unit of analysis, researchers have computed eta^2 values to validate their instruments (Fisher and Waldrip, 1999; Riah, 2000). On similar grounds, one can argue that schools have their own culture that influences the communication behaviour of teachers. It is therefore important to analyse the data using the school as the unit of analysis. However, the limitation of analyzing data using a school as a unit of analysis is the number of data points (degrees of freedom) becomes small. Furthermore, the social roles of males and females in a culture are usually different (Thomas, 2000). The communication styles or behaviours of males and females in a culture are therefore expected to be different. The students from different cultures or sub-cultures observe these practices at home and they exercise these practices in classroom situations. Therefore, it is also important to compare the perceptions of male and female students on teacher communication behaviour. Researchers also believe that students are directly involved in observing their teachers in a classroom setting (Walberg and Haertel, 1980; Fraser 1998). It implies from these studies that the students' observation experience should make a difference. In other words the observations of students in lower grades should be different from that of students in higher grade. It is therefore worth comparing Form 4 and Form 5 students' perceptions of teacher communication behaviour. The overall analysis of the above literature suggests that it is worth studying students' perceptions of teacher communication behaviour in Bruneian schools by analyzing the data in the various modes of grouping discussed above, firstly because of the cultural distinctiveness of the local population and secondly because of the lack of research in the area not only in the country but also in the neighbouring countries.

AIMS

The aims of the research reported here were (a) to determine reliability and validity of the Teacher Communication Behaviour Questionnaire (TCBQ) for collecting data on upper secondary students' perceptions of science teachers' communication behaviour (TCB), and (b) to evaluate the magnitude of dimensions of teacher communication behaviour in science classes of the upper secondary science at government schools. More specifically, the following research questions were answered in this study.

1. Was the TCBQ suitable for collecting data on upper secondary students' perceptions of science teachers' communication behaviour in their classes?
2. What were the students' mean perceptions on the five dimensions of TCB?
3. Were there gender differences in students' perceptions on the five dimensions of TCB?
4. Were there differences in Form 4 and 5 students' perceptions on the five dimensions of TCB?
5. Were there any associations between students' perceptions on dimensions of teacher communication behaviour and their enjoyment of science lessons?

METHODOLOGY

This section reports the descriptions of respondents, instrument, procedure, and contexts: cultural and classroom.

Respondents

The population for this study comparised Form 4 and 5 secondary science students at Government schools in Brunei Darussalam. The subjects of the study were 1098 upper secondary science students from 15 schools. These students were attending 53 classes in these schools. The sample consisted of 33 % males and 67% females with an overall mean age of 16.6 $\pm$ 0.9 years. The data on national enrolment in schools, including science subjects, show that the number of female students is higher than that of male students (BDSY, 1996-97). Moreover, the mean achievement score in science for female students is higher than that of male students (unpublished data). The male and female students occupy separate rows and seats.

Table 1. Description of Dimensions of Teacher Communication Behaviour and Example Items

Scale	Description	Sample item
Challenging	Extent to which the teacher uses higher-order questions to challenge students in their learning.	This teacher asks me questions that require me to apply what I have learned in class in order to answer
Encouragement and Praise	Extent to which the teacher praises and encourages students.	This teacher praises me for asking a good question.
Non-verbal Support	The extent to The teacher uses non-verbal communication to interact positively with students.	This teacher smiles at me to show support while I am trying to solve a problem.
Understanding and Friendly	Extent to which the teacher is understanding and friendly towards students.	This teacher understands when I doubt something.
Controlling	Extent to which the teacher controls and manages student behaviour in the class.	This teacher requires us to be quiet in his/her class.
Enjoyment	Extent to which respondents enjoy their science lesson.	Science is fun.

This table containing 5 scales of TCB and an enjoyment scale is partly adapted from She and Fisher (2000).

Instruments and Procedure

The instrument (TCBQ) developed empirically by She and Fisher (2000) was used in this study. It contained 40 items representing five scales. The test items in each scale are written in English language. The instrument was given to three university lecturers of science education who evaluated its language, content and constructs. They reported that the content and constructs were valid for the use of the instrument in Brunei. However, the items are wordy and are somewhat difficult to understand especially for those students who lack English language proficiency, especially student at lower secondary schools. They believed that the use of instrument should be satisfactory for upper secondary students. During a pilot study, the students in lower secondary science classes found the items wordy and difficult. A group of 20 upper secondary students who were not part of this study found the questions in the instrument easy to understand. The 40-item instrument consisted of five scales: Challenging, Encouragement and Praise, Non-verbal Support, Understanding and Friendly, and, Controlling. The enjoyment scale consisted of five items. The enjoyment scale has been previously used by Riah (2000)

The descriptions of the TCB scales and enjoyment scale are reported in Table 1. Each TCB scale contained eight items and the enjoyment 5 items. Each TCB item was responded to on a five-point scale response format with the extreme alternatives from "Almost never" to "Almost always" (Strongly agree to Strongly disagree for enjoyment scale). The instrument covering TCB scales and enjoyment scale was administered to the students in their classes and the students were asked to indicate to what extent they agreed to that each item described their classroom. The higher the score for a given scale the more prominent is the behaviour. The scores for negative items were reversed before the analysis. The data were analysed using ANOVA and the significance of the results was further evaluated using effect size data. The effect size classification reported by Cohen (1969) was used to evaluate the effects of treatment.

The observation of teacher communication behaviour in 20 classes followed non-participant field note taking. Every effort was made to thoroughly record the five dimensions of teacher communication behaviour and enjoyment activities in the classes. The field notes were then summarised for the observations to make overall comments.

Contexts

There are two types of contexts discussed under this heading: Cultural and Classroom. The cultural context explains the actual cultural diversity in local population that affects the classroom composition. The classroom context describes the classroom situation and public perception of classroom.

Cultural Context. The Brunei although small in size, is rich in cultural diversity. The major sources of cultural diversity in the Brunei are the cultural variations within the population as well as in temporary (migrant) population. In 2001, there were about 80,000 (about 23% of the total population) temporary workers from many countries working in Brunei Darussalam. A considerable fraction of temporary workers is involved in teaching at primary, secondary and tertiary institutions. Children of the temporary workers attend primary, secondary and tertiary educational institutions. The Bruneian population mainly consists of Malay, Kedayan, Tutong, Belait, Bisaya, Dusan, Murut, Iban, Kelabit and Chinese communities. The population (344500; estimated for 2001) of Brunei Darussalam consists of 53% male and 47% female. On the basis of race, there are 73.8% Malays, 6% indigenous people, 14.8% Chinese and 11.4 % Others (see Borneo Bulletin Brunei Year Book, 2002 for details). The literacy rate, that is ability to sign one's name in a local language, is 90%. There are also sub-cultures co-existing within a culture such as rural, urban, water-village culture, rich, well to do and poor. The language as well as style of communication in these cultures and sub-cultures are so diverse. For example, the students from rural and water village sub-cultures often speak louder than other students The data reported in this paragraph show cultural diversity in Brunei Darussalam that students from various cultures and sub-cultures bring to their classes that influence the teaching and learning processes in the schools. .

Classroom context. In general, classrooms are coeducational. The government however, has also provided the facility of single sex schools for parents to make a choice of educational institution type for their children. The classrooms have single students desks arranged in rows. Almost all classrooms have electricity and fans fitted. The climate is hot and humid. The boys and girls usually occupy different rows. However, gender equity is quite high in the classes. Local culture is highly hierarchical, that provides teachers a higher level on the *priori* scale of hierarchy. Therefore teachers are usually authoritarian. Their teaching style is more traditional that further adds to the teacher authority in the classroom. The students often are quiet in their classes and do not argue with the teacher. This may be the cultural effect as stated by Chan (2004). According to her, Asian students are much quieter than their American counterparts. However, in the absence of teacher or in after hour social context, they may be very expressive. A compression of two situations is very aptly captured in the following *cartoo*n (Cuboi, 2001).

Figure1. Brunei classrooms: A cartoonists' view point

RESULTS

The results of this study are described under three major heading: (a) Validation of instruments, (b) Teacher communication behvaiour and (c) Associations between teacher communication behaviour scales and enjoyment of science lessons.

Validation of Instruments

This section deals with validations of TCBQ and the enjoyment scale.
Validation of TCBQ. Under this heading, Chi-square, factors analysis, reliability, discriminant validity and the eta^2 coefficients for the scales in the TCBQ are discussed.

Chi-square analysis values for all the items in the instrument using the data collected from all the subjects were calculated to examine if the distribution of the responses was different from the randomly distributed (equal for all possible choice). The Chi-square values obtained were over 157 for all items and were highly significant at P<.001. These results demonstrated that the respondents' responses to the test items were not randomly selected.

Table 2. Factor Loading for Items in the 30-item Version of the Personal Form of the CLEQ for the Individual Students as the Unit of Analysis

Item	CHA	EAP	NVS	UAF	CON	h^2
1	0.60					0.41
2	0.56					0.39
3	0.66					0.48
4	0.41	0.33				0.34
5	0.65					0.47
6	0.57					0.40
7	0.62					0.48
8	0.43					0.30
9		0.64				0.48
10	0.36	0.51				0.44
11		0.45				0.33
12		0.67				0.53
13		0.66				0.48
14		0.62				0.45
15		0.75				0.63
16		0.70				0.55
17			0.56			0.39
18			0.62			0.46
19			0.74			0.63
20			0.74			0.62
21			0.73			0.62
22			0.74			0.63
23			0.74			0.62
24			0.67			0.51
25				0.61		0.43
26				0.68		0.54
27				0.67		0.49
28				0.58		0.43
29				0.70		0.53
30				0.76		0.62
31				0.70		0.56
32				0.64		0.52
33					0.42	0.32
34					0.63	0.51
35					0.75	0.58
36					0.76	0.60
37					0.75	0.57
38					0.67	0.47
39					0.53	0.34
40					0.62	0.44
% variance	4.47	6.44	22.76	9.86	5.44	
Eigenvalue	1.79	2.58	9.10	3.95	2.18	

CHA = Challenging; EAP = Encouragement and Praise; NVS = Non-verbal Support; UAF = Understanding and Friendly; CON = Controlling; Cut-off point for factor loadings = 0.3. h^2 is the commonality.

Factor analysis was performed to refine and validate TCBQ. It involved a series of factor analyses whose purpose was to examine the internal structure of the set of 40 items. Using SPSS, principal components analysis with varimax rotation was used to generate orthogonal factors. Because the instrument was designed with five scales, a five-factor solution was first tried. All the 40 items grouped into the five factors reported in Table 2 in the same fashion as reported by She and Fisher (2000). The table also shows the factor loadings for the five factors obtained from this analysis using the individual student as the unit of analysis. All factor loadings less than 0.3 have been omitted.

Table 2 shows that, for each of the 40 items, the factor loading is larger than 0.4 on the *a priori* scale. The percentage variance extracted and eigenvalue (rotation sum of squared loading) associated with each factor are also recorded at the bottom of each scale. The five factors reported in this study accounted for a total of 49% of the variance. Similar values for the total variance explained have been reported (see Dhindsa, 2005; Salta and Tzougraki, 2004). The amount of variance for each factor explained varied from 4.5% to 22.8 %. The communality values (h^2) reported in Table 2 represent the fraction of variance explained by an item when grouped into a factor. The communality data were within an acceptable range and vary from 0.32 to 0.63.

Reliability is a measure of the internal consistency of each scale and it was evaluated using Cronbach's alpha coefficient. Table 3 shows that, for this sample of students, the alpha reliability coefficient ranged from 0.77 to 0.86 and from 0.87 to 0.94 when individual student and class as units of analysis respectively were considered. The overall reliability coefficients for the 40 items instrument were 0.91 and 0.93 when individual student and class as a units of analysis respectively were used. These data suggest that each scale as well as the instrument have acceptable reliability.

Table 3. Cronbach Alpha Reliability Coefficients and Discriminant Validity for each Scale Using a Student, a Class and a School means as unist of analyses

Scale	N	Alpha Reliability		Discriminant Validity		
		Ind.	Class	Ind.	Class	School
Challenging	8	0.77	0.87	0.21	0.31	0.41
Encouragement and Praise	8	0.83	0.92	0.21	0.31	0.42
Non-verbal Support	8	0.88	0.94	0.19	0.24	0.21
Understanding and Friendly	8	0.86	0.90	0.19	0.14	0.29
Controlling	8	0.82	0.87	0.17	0.29	0.17
Instrument	40	0.91	0.93	-	-	-

N = Number of items in a scale. Ind. = individual

Discriminant validity is a measure of overlap between the scales. The mean partial correlation of a scale with the other scales was used as a convenient measure of the discriminant validity or independence of the instrument scales. The mean correlations of each scale with the other scales, reported in Table 3, ranged from 0.17 to 0.21, 0.14 to 0.31 and 0.17 to 0.42 when data were analysed using an individual student, a class and a school as units of analysis respectively. These values suggest that the instrument scales measure relatively distinct aspects of the learning environment. Moreover, the factor analysis results (individual student data) attest to the independence of factor scores on CLEQ scales.

The eta² values reported in Table 4 were computed to evaluate the variance explained when a class or a school as a unit of analysis was used. This measure was adopted because of some limitations of SPSS-ANOVA analysis of large data (also details discussed later in this paragraph). Table 4 shows that eta² values ranged from 0.16 to 0.25 and from 0.05 to 0.16 for class and school memberships respectively. These data suggest that 16% – 25% of the variance in teacher communication behaviour data on the five scales was explained by class membership and 5% - 16% by school membership. These eta² values lend further support to the validity of TCBQ in the local context.

Table 4. Eta² Data for Each Scale Using Class and School as a Unit of Analysis

Scale	N	Eta² Class	Eta² School
Challenging	8	0.22	0.10
Encouragement and Praise	8	0.25	0.16
Non-verbal Support	8	0.19	0.11
Understanding and Friendly	8	0.16	0.07
Controlling	8	0.17	0.05

N = Number of items in a scale.

The ANOVA analysis of data using a class or a school as units of analysis produced F-values highly significant at $p< .001$ for all the five scales. These results indicated that at least one of the compared pairs was statistically significantly different. The post-hoc analysis was difficult to summarise due to (a) large numbers of pairs of schools and (b) inability of the SPSS program to handle large number of class pairs for comparison. Therefore, the scale item mean values averaged over classes or schools are reported in Table 5 for reference and are not discussed further in this manuscript.

Validation of Enjoyment scale. The enjoyment scale contained five items. The scale is described in Table 1 along with TCBQ scales. This is a uni-dimensional scale with a Chrobach alpha value of 0.82 and mean inter item correlation of 0.47. The factor analysis revealed that the five items converge into a factor with factor loading values ranging between 0.68 and 0.80 on a priori scale. The communality data were within an acceptable range and vary from 0.46 to 0.65. The communality values (h^2) reported represent the fraction of variance explained by an item when grouped into a factor. This scale explained 57.8% of the total variance. When the data on these items was grouped with TCBQ data, these items got grouped together as a factor without any interference to or from the TCBQ scales. For this scale, the values of eta² for class and school as units of analysis were 0.14 and 0.05 respectively. Eta² represents the proportion of variation accounted for class or school membership. These results indicate that 14% and 5% of the variation in enjoyment data is accounted for by class and school variables.

Teacher Communication Behaviour

The results of this study dealing with scales of teacher communication behaviour are described quantitatively and qualitatively. The quantitative results deal with students' perception of teacher communication behaviour data collected using survey instruments and the qualitative with classroom observation data.

Quantitative data. The results in this section are discussed under three sub-headings representing: (a) The students' perception of TCB in general, (b) the gender differences in students' perceptions, and (c) the difference in perception of Form 4 and Form 5 students. The students' perceptions of TCB in general are reported as the scale item mean values averaged over individual student, a class and a school on the five teacher communication behaviour factors assessed by the instrument. These data hereafter are referred to as average scale item mean value(s), average scale item mean-C value(s), average scale item mean-S value(s) respectively.

The students' perceptions of TCB in general are reported in Table 5. The data in the table show average scale item mean, average scale item mean-C, average scale item mean-S, standard deviation and 95% confidence interval data for five factors of teacher communication behaviour. The mean data for individual student, class and school reported in the table ranged 2.60 - 3.70, 2.62 - 3.70 and 2.59 - 3.71 respectively for TCB scales. The average scale item mean values for these three types of data are almost the same with differences in standard deviation data therefore the scale item mean values averaged over a student will be further discussed in detail.

Table 5. Average Scale Item Mean, Standard Deviation, N and 95% Confidence Interval for Mean Data Average Item Mean, Standard Deviation, N and 95% Confidence Interval for Mean Data

Scales	Analysis unit	N	Mean	SD	95% Confidence interval (Mean)
Challenging	Indiv.	1098	3.49	0.61	3.45 – 3.52
	Class	53	3.50	0.30	3.42 – 3.58
	School	15	3.44	0.21	3.32 – 3.55
Encouragement and Praise	Indiv.	1108	2.60	0.71	2.55 – 2.63
	Class	53	2.62	0.38	2.52 – 2.73
	School	15	2.59	0.32	2.53 – 2.77
Non-verbal Support	Indiv.	1104	2.74	0.80	2.70 – 2.79
	Class	53	2.73	0.36	2.64 – 2.83
	School	15	2.71	0.31	2.53 – 2.88
Understanding and Friendly	Indiv.	1109	3.70	0.72	3.66 – 3.74
	Class	53	3.70	0.31	3.61 – 3.78
	School	15	3.71	0.18	3.61 – 3.81
Controlling	Indiv.	1108	3.68	0.69	3.64 – 3.72
	Class	53	3.67	0.29	3.58 – 3.75
	School	15	3.62	0.20	3.51 – 3.73

Indivi. = Individual, N = Number of data points

The average scale item mean values reported in the Table 5 can be divided into two categories: (i) greater than 3 and (ii) less than 3. A value of 3.00 represented sometimes on the five point scales indicating that teachers exhibited the behaviour sometimes only. The average scale item mean values for Understanding and Friendly, controlling and challenging were greater than three indicating that students perceived their teachers exhibiting these behaviours in their classes to some extent, that is between "sometimes" and "often" may be more close to often. However, the average scale item mean values for the non-verbal support, and, the encouragement and praise scales were less than three. These data indicated that teachers exhibited these behaviours "seldom" to "sometimes". The highest average scale item mean value was 3.70 for understanding and friendly and the lowest 2.60 for encouragement and praise. These data suggest that teachers teaching upper secondary science classes are often understanding and friendly, but they seldom encourage and praise their students. The data in the table also suggest that the teachers were in control of their classes and challenged their students with questions. However, they seldom provided non-verbal support. In the table, standard deviation values for the data ranged from 0.61 to 0.80. The highest value of 0.80 was obtained for non-verbal support scale, with the average scale item value just above the minimum mean value (4th out of five). The standard deviation values indicate that the teachers varied in providing non-verbal support more than exhibiting challenging behaviour where the standard deviation value was 0.61. The variations in the students' perceptions of TCB for other three scales were in between the above stated two extremes as reflected by the standard deviation values for non-verbal ands challenging scales.

Table 6. Average Scale Item Mean, Average Item Standard Deviation, and ANOVA Results for Difference in TCBQ Mean Scale Data for Male and Female Respondents

Scales	Male N	Mean	SD	Female N	Mean	SD	Significance of Difference F /(p)	Effect size
Challenging	351	3.36	0.59	747	3.55	0.61	23.31 (.000)	0.31
Encouragement and Praise	357	2.65	0.70	740	2.57	0.71	2.05 (.086)	0.11
Non-verbal Support	352	2.67	0.78	745	2.78	0.81	4.77 (.029)	0.14
Understanding and Friendly	355	3.52	0.72	743	3.78	0.70	34.04 (.000)	0.37
Controlling	354	2.58	0.68	744	3.72	0.69	10.65 (.001)	0.20

N = number of respondents.

The gender differences in students' perceptions of teacher communication behaviour are reported in Table 6. The data in the table show no statistically significant differences in average scale item mean values on encouragement and praise scale for male and female subjects. These results suggest that both male and female students perceived encouragement and praise in their classes to the same extent. For the remaining four TCB factors, statistically significant gender differences (p< .03) were observed. However, the effect size values for non-verbal support, and, controlling scales were 0.14 and 0.20 respectively. Therefore, these low (see Cohen 1969 for classification) level significant differences are of little educational importance and might have been contributed by some other factors such as the large sample size. It was therefore concluded that there were no gender differences in non-verbal support, and, controlling dimensions of teacher communication behaviour. The table also shows statistically significant low to medium level gender differences on Challenging, and, Understanding and Friendly scales with effect size values of 0.31 and 0.37 respectively. These results show that the female as compared to male students perceived their teachers to be more challenging as well as understanding and friendly.

The overall results show that the gender differences on three out of five factors were statistically significantly different with effect size >= 0.20. Based on the quantitative data, it was therefore concluded that there were gender differences in students' perceptions of teacher communication behaviour in science classes. However, readers should consider these results with caution because in a complex situation like this where TCB dimensions interact with a large number of variables associated with the school, content, teacher and students during teaching and learning, the low effect size and small differences such as for non-verbal support and controlling may be of some importance especially if they are observed in repeat studies (see Rennie, 1998).

Table 7. Average Scale Item Mean, Average Item Standard Deviation, ANOVA and Effect Size Results for Difference in TCBQ Mean Scale Data for Form 4 and Form 5

Scales	Form 4			Form 5			Significance of Diff.	
	N	Mean	SD	N	Mean	SD	F/ (p)	ES
Challenging	658	3.46	0.62	440	3.52	0.63	1.92 (.166)	0.10
Encouragement and Praise	651	2.50	0.72	446	2.73	0.70	27.11 (.000)	0.32
Non-verbal Support	650	2.68	0.81	445	2.84	0.81	10.74 (.001)	0.20
Understanding and Friendly	651	3.66	0.72	446	3.76	0.74	5.11 (.024)	0.14
Controlling	655	3.67	0.70	442	3.67	0.70	0.00 (.956)	0.00

N = number of respondents; ES = effect size; Diff. = Difference

The difference in perceptions of Form 4 and Form 5 students on the TCB scales are reported in Table 7. The ANOVA analysis of Form 4 and 5 students' data revealed that the average scale item mean score representing Form 4 and 5 students' perceptions of TCB in their classrooms were comparable (not statistically significantly different) for the factors except for Non-verbal Support, and, Encouragement and Praise scales (see table 7). These results suggest that Form 5 students perceived statistically significantly higher level (p = 0.001; ES = 0.20) of non-verbal support as compared to Form 4 students. The low effect size suggests that the perceptions of both the groups were only marginally different on this scale.

The results in the table also suggest that Form 5 students perceived that they received statistically significantly more encouragement and praise (p = 0.000; ES = 0.32) from their teachers when compared to Form 4 students. The effect size values suggest that the difference between the two groups' perceptions was low to moderate. Form 5 students were to sit for the GCE – O level examination at the end of the year, therefore teachers and students appeared to have become more serious about optimizing learning in their classes. The overall results demonstrate that Form 4 and Form 5 students' perceptions' were statistically significantly different for two out of five factors. Out of these two factors, the difference on one factor was of low level (Effect size = 0.20), which is of little educational importance and on the second factor low to medium level. Therefore based on the survey data, it was concluded that the perceptions of both groups of students on TCB were comparable.

The qualitative classroom observation data. The observation data is summarised under five sub-heading representing five dimensions of TCB and an enjoyment of science lessons scale.

The challenging nature of TCB is summarised as follows. In general the teachers asked chorus questions to whole class where any student who knew the answer initiated the response and others mumbled with him or her. It was therefore difficult to know if the teachers asked more question to male or female students. Most of the questions were recall type and very few questions were of the thinking type or higher order. Often the higher order questions were linked to what is expected from them in final examination. The response from the students was minimal. When the teachers were faced with stunned silence after they ask a question, they will answer the questions themselves. Many times teachers did not give enough wait-time. However, there were only a few teachers who asked higher level questions. The following field note indicates a summary of classroom observation of a teacher.

> "The nature of questions often posed in the class were more geared towards finding out students' recall of certain facts. These questions did little to determine the depth of students' understanding of particular concepts. Very few of the questions challenged the students to think creatively or to analyse and organise information. It was observed that some times there was a certain tendency for the teacher to answer his/her own question, particularly if the questions required a certain amount of application."

Encouragement and Praise classroom observation data revealed that the teachers often praised the students when their responses to the questions were correct. However, the praise was very much limited because teachers did not ask many questions to individual students. Teachers tended to overlook the value of praising students for their efforts when they did not give correct responses. There are teachers who even did not praise the students after they responded the questions correctly and simply used the word OK. The praise was mostly linked to the responses to the questions only, however, the classroom has much more where teachers should praise their students. The home-work and class-work marked by teachers had practically no praise or encouraging comments. Both male and female students are often not praised for their good behaviour in the class. The students were not encouraged to discuss answers among themselves. In the majority of times, students' ideas were not used in the development of the concepts. The following field note indicates a summary of classroom observation of a teacher:

> "This teacher does tend to praise students for giving correct responses. Apart from that, teachers tend to overlook the part where they should praise students for their efforts as well. Also while observing the classes of the teacher, it seems to be a general lack of teacher encouraging his/her students to ask questions and express their opinions."

Nonverbal support provided to the students by their teachers during the lessons was limited. The teachers displayed hand movements while explaining the concepts to the students. More common non-verbal support observed was nodding straight-faced head. Facial expressions were more used to show anger rather than happiness. Eye and shoulder movements were rarely used during the lesson. The overall impression of the classroom observations was that there is a need for improvement of non-verbal support for both males and female students in science lessons. The following field note indicates a summary of non-verbal support in a typical classroom:

> "The teacher nodded her head to approve students' actions but did not display lot of facial expression. Very little eye contact occurred in this class and the teacher did not use the shoulder movements at all to express non-verbal support."

Friendly and Understanding nature of a teacher as observed in the classes showed that in general teachers are fairly friendly to students but they still keep some distance. They may think that this distance is required to maintain discipline in their classes. Teachers often were willing to repeat the points over and again for all students without any preference for a gender. They trusted their students and were patient with their students. In general, the students were not afraid of their teachers, but some authoritarian teachers were also observed. Most of the times students trusted their teachers, but the degree of trust showed a wide range from low to high. The students seemed to accept everything their teacher say in the class. A specific example is described in the following field note.

> "Despite the teacher being friendly and willing to respond to students question over and again, does not seem to trust her students. This is obvious because the teacher thinks that the students know nothing and don't even wait for students' response to the questions before giving response to the question. Some intelligent students got angry and argued with her about the explanations."

Controlling scale data collected during observation revealed that the teachers were often in control of classes. They expected their students to obey set rules, did not allow them to do things differently, demanded students to listen to them and do things as told. For example, don't talk to anyone irrespective of the nature of subject to be discussed, don't leave the desk and walk to student in the next row etc. Teachers often exhibited authoritarian attitude in the class and exercise teacher centred teaching to keep class in control. However, there is concern in the country about the increased problems with student discipline. The following field note highlights an incidence.

> "The most disappointing situation was when male students started talking while the teacher was explaining and the class began to make noise. They threw crumbled papers on the floor."

Enjoyment of science lessons was often difficult to assess. One of the problems was the authoritarian nature of the teachers. Classes were silent and doing what they were told to do. In most of the classes students appeared to be comfortable. They did not show any expression of enjoyment during experimental activities. Was it enjoyment of real teaching or playing with the apparatus? Both male and female students were doing the class work in the class, but not very enthusiastically. Were they looking forward to their next science class? Following field note gives some hint.

> "Students didn't show that they were looking forward to next science class, may be the relief that the class for the day finally ends."

Observation notes in Form 4 and Form 5 revealed that the perceptions of these two groups of students were not different. They were behaving very similarly on all the aspects evaluated in this study, may be because most of the teachers involved in this study were teaching classes of both the Forms.

Table 8. Association between TCBQ Scales and Students Enjoyment of Science Lesson in Terms of Simple (R) and Multiple (β) Correlations

Scale	Enjoyment					
	Individual student		Class		School	
	r	β	r	β	r	β
Challenging	0.30**	0.13**	0.50**	0.40*	0.65**	0.40
Encouragement and Praise	0.24**	0.08*	0.19	0.04	0.13	0.14
Non-verbal Support	0.20**	-0.05	0.21	-0.07	0.33	-0.12
Understanding and Friendly	0.42**	0.37**	0.54**	0.38*	0.63**	0.63
Controlling	0.20**	0.05	0.13	-0.17	0.01	-0.31
Multiple correlation, R	0.47**		0.61**		0.80	
R^2	0.22		0.37		0.64	

**p = .000; *p = .01

Associations Between Teacher Communication Behaviour Scales And Enjoyment Of Science Lessons

The association between the teacher communication behaviour scales and the enjoyment of science lessons was computed using individual student, class and the school as units of analysis. The results are reported in Table 8. The multiple correlation data in the table show that students' perception of their teacher communication behaviour contributed 22% of the measured variance in the students' enjoyment of science lessons. The simple correlation values ranged from 0.20 to 0.42 and all these values were significant at p = .000. These values for the association between TCB scales and enjoyment scale suggest that there were significant relationships between students' perceptions of their teachers' communication behaviour for all the five scales of the TCB with their enjoyment of science lessons. That is, students' enjoyment of their science lesson was higher when they perceived that their teachers provided them encouragement, praise and non-verbal support. The enjoyment of science lessons was also higher when they perceived their teachers' nature is understanding, friendly, controlling and challenging. The highest correlation value of 0.42 for understanding and friendly scale and enjoyment scale suggests that Bruneian students enjoy learning science from teachers who trust, are willing to explain things over and again to, listen to, care, friendly with and are patient with, their students. The simple correlation values of 0.20 for non-verbal support (or controlling) and enjoyment scales indicated the close associations of these scales with students' enjoyment of science lessons. β is a more conservative standardised regression coefficient that measured the association between enjoyment and a scale of TCBQ while keeping the effect of other TCBQ scales constant. The data in Table 8 show that values of the β coefficient for associations between enjoyment and understanding and friendly (p = .000) or challenging (p = .000) or encouragement scales (p = .01) were statistically significant. This data further support that students enjoy more the science lessons of those teachers who are understanding and friendly. The β values for controlling and non-verbal support scales were 0.05 and -0.05 respectively.

The analysis of associations between teacher communication behaviour and the enjoyment of science lessons using class and school as units of analysis revealed a strong association between enjoyment of the science lesson and the challenging as well as friendly and understanding behaviours of teacher (see r values in Table 7). As expected with a decrease in degrees of freedom from individual students through classes to schools, the number of significant associations between TCB scales and enjoyment decreased. However for the understanding and friendly behaviour scale the beta coefficient for class-data was statistically significant.

ANSWERS TO RESEARCH QUESTIONS

The research questions in this section are answered by triangulating conclusions drawn based on quantitative data, qualitative data and research data in the literature.

1. *Were the TCBQ and Enjoyment questionnaires suitable for collecting data of upper secondary science students' perceptions of (i) teachers' communication behaviour and (ii) enjoyment of their lessons?*

Teachers' Communication Behaviour Questionnaire. The results on instrumental variables obtained by analysing the data using individual student, class and school as units of analysis revealed that 40 items in the instrument factorised into five factors clearly as reported by She and Fisher (2000). The percentage variance extracted associated with the factors varied from 4.5 % to 22.8%. The five factors reported in this study accounted for 49.0% of the variance. These data are comparable to the values reported in Bruneian studies in the field of learning environment (see Dhindsa, in press; Dhindsa and Fraser, 2004). These studies reported the variance explained by a cultural learning environment questionnaire (CLEQ) as 51.1% (Dhindsa, 2005) and 52.7% (Dhindsa and Fraser, 2004). She and Fisher (2002) used this instrument to study teacher communication behavior, however they did not report these data.

The Cronbach alpha reliability coefficient for five factors ranged from 0.77 to 0.88 (0.87 – 0.93 for Taiwan; 0.86 – 0.93 for Australia) and from 0.87 to 0.94 when data were analysed using individual and class as units of analyses respectively. The reliabilities of the 40-item instrument were 0.91 and 0.93 when data were analysed using individual and class as units of analyses. These data suggest that the instrument was reliable.

The discriminant validity values for the scales ranged 0.17 - 0.21, 0.14 - 0.31 and 0.17 to 0.42 when data were analysed using individual student, class and school as units of analysis respectively. The upper limits for individual and class data were lower than the values from 0.14 to 0.50 and from 0.05 to 0.44 reported for Taiwan and Australia respectively (She and Fisher, 2002). These data suggest that the TCBQ scales measure distinct, although somewhat overlapping aspects of the teacher communication behaviour. The conceptual distinctions among the scales are therefore justified by both the factor analysis and the discriminant validity.

Eta^2 is a measure of the amount of variance explained by class and school memberships. In this study the Eta^2 values ranged from 0.16 to 0.25. These values are comparable to the data (0.17 – 0.22) reported from Taiwan, but higher than the data (0.05 – 0.15) reported from Australia.

Based on the Chi-square analysis, factor analysis, discriminant validity, alpha reliability coefficient and eta^2 values in this study and their comparison to published data, it was concluded that the TCB instrument was valid and reliable for the data collection in this study.

Enjoyment Scale. The enjoyment scale is a uni-dimensional scale with a Chrobach alpha value of 0.82 and mean inter item correlation of 0.47. The factor analysis revealed that the five items converge into a factor and explained 57.8% of the total variance. The mean values of eta^2 for a class and a school as units of analysis were 0.14 and 0.05 respectively. Eta^2 represents the proportion of variance accounted for by class or school membership. These values are comparable to data reported using this scale in Brunei (see Riah, 2000). Based on these instrumental variable data it was concluded that the enjoyment scale was also valid and reliable to collect data for this study.

2. *What were the students' mean perceptions on the five dimensions of TCBQ?*

The scale item mean values of 2.60 and 2.74 for encouragement and praise, and non-verbal support respectively, fall below the sometimes level of 3.0. These results suggest that students perceived that their teachers only sometimes praised, and encouraged them. The teachers also sometimes use body language to express their praise, encouragement and concerns. She and Fisher (2002) reported 2.96 and 2.85 as the average scale item mean values for encouragement and praise, and non-verbal support scales respectively, as perceived by lower secondary students from Taiwan. Their data though are higher than that for the Bruneian sample, but still fall just below sometimes level. These results are further supported by the observation data. During classroom observation, it was found that the teachers often did not use body language to express their feeling and concerns. They also provided low-level encouragement and praise to their students. Based on the qualitative and quantitative data it is concluded that science students in their classes in Bruneian schools do not receive enough encouragement, praise and non-verbal support. These aspects therefore need special attention.

The average scale-item mean values for understanding and friendly, challenging, and controlling scales were 3.7, 3.5, and 3.7 (Taiwan data 3.6, 3.3, 3.4) respectively. These values fall between "seldom" and "often". Since these values are close to often, therefore, the students perceived a reasonable amount of activities associated with these factors occurring in their classes. The values are comparable to what students from Taiwan perceived. However, when we look at qualitative data, it was observed that teachers often ask recall type of questions. Very few questions of higher-level thinking are asked in this class. It looks that the students perceived low-level questions as challenging. Moreover, a reasonable understanding and friendly behaviour was observed in these classes. Teachers like to be in control of their class, may be due to traditional teaching style they use in the classes. Most of these teachers were taught using traditional teaching style that could have influenced their teaching practices. The overall impression is although teachers exhibit these factors in their classes to a reasonable extent, but there is huge scope for improvement in teacher communication behaviours. In conclusion, teacher communication behaviour in science classes in local educational system need attention and actions towards improvement are desirable.

3. *Were there gender differences in students' perceptions on the five dimensions of TCBQ?*

A comparison of male and female respondents data revealed statistically significant differences ($p<.03$) in favour of girls in the students' perceptions of TCB scales except for encouragement and praise scale. These results are different from what She and Fisher (2002) reported. In their study they found statistically significant sex differences in favour of girls on two scales (Understanding and friendly, and, controlling) only. However when the significance levels for differences in this study were evaluated using effect size analysis scale by Cohen, (1969) the gender differences on understanding and friendly scales only were of low to moderate level. She and Fisher (2002) did not report the effect size data, but the magnitude of the difference in mean data and the standard deviation data reported suggest that statistically significant sex differences in their study for two understanding and friendly, and, controlling scales were also of very low level. In Brunei, during the class room observations, no serious gender bias in classroom communication was observed. Other studies also have reflected a higher level of gender equity in Bruneian classes (Dhindsa, 2005; Dhindsa and Fraser, 2004). Based on the quantitative (one out of five comparisons being significant at effect size of 0.3) and qualitative results it was concluded that there were no sex differences in the male and female students' perceptions of teacher communication behavior.

4. *Were there differences in Form 4 and 5 students' perceptions on the five dimensions of TCBQ?*

The results of this study suggested that Forms 4 and 5 students' perceptions were statistically significantly different on non-verbal support ($p = 0.001$; ES = 0.20), and encouragement and praise ($p = 0.000$; ES = 0.32) scales, whereas non-significantly different on the challenging and controlling scales. The effect size values suggest that the statistically significant differences in perceptions of two groups, in favour of Form 5 students, were at low to moderate level. The qualitative results based on the observations also supported these results. Based on the qualitative and quantitative data, it was concluded that the perceptions of Forms 4 and 5 students on TCB in their classes were comparable.

5. *Were there any associations between students' perceptions of teacher communication behaviour scales and their enjoyment of science lessons?*

The results of this study revealed that students' perception of their teacher communication behaviour contributed 22% (Multiple correlation, R = 0.47; p < .0001) of measured variance in students' enjoyment of science lessons. This value is higher than the one (17%; R = 0.41; p < .0001) reported by She and Fisher (2002). The statistically significant (p < .000) values of the simple correlation coefficient in the range from 0.20 to 0.42 suggest that there were significant relationships between students' perceptions of their teachers' communication behaviour for all the five scales of the TCBQ and their enjoyment of science lessons. These results are different from those of She and Fisher (2002). They reported a statistically non-significant relationship between controlling and enjoyment scales data. The results of this study are also supported by qualitative data. During the classroom observations it was observed that students seemed to be enjoying the lessons of those teachers who received more positive comments about their classroom communication behaviour. Based on quantitative data on simple correlation and standardised regression coefficients, and qualitative data it was concluded that teacher communication behaviour and enjoyment of science lessons in Bruneian schools correlated significantly.

DISCUSSION

The instrument used in this study has been shown to be valid and reliable. Despite experts' initial thinking that items are very wordy, the instrument seems suitable for upper secondary and tertiary students and it may be suitable to assess TCB in upper secondary classes in other subjects. Although, the instrument has been reported to be reliable and valid for data collection in Taiwanese and Australian lower secondary students (She and Fisher, 2002), it may not be suitable for lower secondary and primary students in Bruenian schools as stated by the experts. The author has observed a decrease in reliability coefficients from upper to lower secondary even when a simple instrument was used. The instrument, therefore, should either be translated into Malay (as it is translated in Taiwan to Chinese) or the items should be made simple. The author believes it is possible to translate as well as to simplify the items without losing the context.

Teacher communication behaviour is a very complex concept with numerous dimensions. Defining this concept in terms of five scales and each scale in terms of 8 items is rather like putting an elephant in a teapot. Therefore, the study is limited to the definitions of the scales used in the TCBQ. Addition or deletion of items might add variability to the results. Moreover, as only science students were involved in this study, the results are limited to science students' perceptions. In Brunei, so far there is no other research work done using this instrument.

In general, there was a good agreement between the qualitative and quantitative data. This agreement supports the reliability and validity of research conducted using this instrument. However, some differences have been observed. For example, students' data reflected that teachers often asked challenging questions to students, but in classroom observation this was seldom observed. It appears that even simple questions are perceived to be challenging by the students. More research is required to see the causes of this gap and possibilities of minimizing it.

The analysis of data using class (or school) as a unit of analysis has been reported in this paper which is in line with that previously reported in the literature (see Fisher and Waldrip, 1997, 1999). But a class is a non-randomized small sub-set of students from the sample, e.g. 20 out of 3785 in an Australian study (Fisher and Waldrip, 1999). Therefore, these classes are not equivalent for comparison. Even random assignment does not ensure the groups are equivalent (Rennie, 1998). Therefore, data on the comparison of classes may be misleading. For example, in a situation where two classes with the same mean values will be treated as comparable on statistical grounds, the differences in their standard deviation values will reflect the differences in the students' perception of the targeted factor. Fisher and Waldrip (1997) also felt (without giving reasons) that a detailed examination of the class as a unit of analysis was generally not meaningful. Therefore, readers are urged to consider these results with caution.

The data in this study indicate that students perceived that teachers often asked challenging questions in their classes. However, the classroom observations revealed that teachers often asked simple questions. Most of the time teachers addressed their questions to the whole class. The teachers rarely asked challenging questions in the class. This finding was also supported by data collected for another study (unpublished data). It appears that simple questions asked by the teachers appeared to be challenging to the students. These differences may be associated with traditional teaching and learning styles used in the classes. Teachers often give notes and students cram these notes without understanding. Therefore, the students are unable to integrate the rote learned knowledge to answer any questions that require something more than free recall of crammed knowledge.

There are studies that report a decline in students' interest in science learning (DeBoer, 1984; Erb, 1983; Utmost, 1998) and it has been linked to teacher related factors (She, 1995). Brunei is not different from the rest of the world. There was a decline of about 7% in the number of secondary science students from 1990 to 1996, thereafter it gradually improved due to intervention by the ministry of education (Monaliza, 2001). The ministry of education (MOE) asked schools to encourage more students in science subjects. Despite that, the concern about students not opting for science subjects is still serious in the country. The deputy minister of education, Brunei, while reporting a forecast for a demand of science related personals in Brunei, stated at the present rate, it would rather be impossible to meet the national demand of professionals in the science related fields. One way to achieve this goal is by increasing the number of science students at school level. The government tried introducing an N-level program to increase the number of science students (N-level students are of lower standard than normal students). This system was not successful and it was abolished in 2005. However, the author feels that improvements in teacher communication behaviour could help to make science lessons more enjoyable and attract more students to science. In this study, statistically significant positive correlation coefficients values between enjoyment of science lesson and the scales of TCB suggest that enjoyment of lessons can be improved by improving TCB. Enjoyment of science lessons is more strongly associated with understanding and friendly, and, challenging behaviours of teachers. Teachers are perceived to be fairly understanding and friendly (3.7 out of 5) by `students. However, the mean value of 3.7 suggests that there is scope for improving upon this factor. Similarly, there is a need for teachers to add more challenging questions in their lessons. Research suggests that questions asked by teachers are indicators of the quality of teaching (Carlsen, 1991; Smith, Blakeslee, and Anderson, 1993) and they promote relevance, encourage ownership, help students interpret their observations, link new learning to prior knowledge and promote students' thinking (Deal and Sterling, 1997: King 1994). Moreover, this research supports a strong association between enjoyment of science lessons and teachers' understanding, friendly, and challenging behaviours. Since attitudes have been associated with academic achievement, it is therefore assumed that there is a grater chance of improving upon students' achievement by improving teacher communication behavior. These scales have also been reported to strongly correlate with students' academic outcomes. For example, She and Fisher (2002) reported that teachers' improved understanding and friendly, and challenging behaviours will improve students academic achievement, and hence an increase in the number of students with a science qualification, that is required for the achievement of national goal, could be expected.

Teacher training institutions can help to improve the teacher communication behaviour of pre-service teachers. Universiti Brunei Darussalam is the major teacher training institution in the country. The Sultan Hassanal Bolkiah Institute of Education, Universiti Brunei Darussalam (equivalent to Faculty of Education) should concentrate more upon improving teacher communication behaviour especially in the area of non-verbal support, and, encouragement and praise. The author believes that these factors are improving as a whole in the country as the government is replacing the foreign teachers with local teachers. This will bring more cultural understanding between students and teachers. There has been an undefined border between expatriate teachers and local students. Most of the expatriate teachers have been unaware of the extent to which the local culture will accept them and their own cultural expressions. They received no orientation in this regard. However, despite possible improvement on this front in the country, the institute of education still needs to review its curriculum to put more emphasis on improving teacher communication behavior. The ministry of education being the sole caretaker of school education in the country should concentrate on the staff development in this area. The seminars and workshops for the extant teachers in the area of teacher communication behaviour will be useful.

CONCLUSION

The students' perception of teacher communication behaviour and observation data revealed that although teachers are to some extent understanding and friendly, challenging their students with questions and controlling their classes, they lacked not only in praising and encouraging students but also in providing adequate non-verbal support. The perceptions of male and female students and of both Form 4 and Form 5 students were comparable. The enjoyment of science lessons significantly correlated with the teacher communication behaviour scales. To improve the enjoyment of science lessons, there seems to be strong need to improve the teacher communication behaviour. It is recommended that the teacher training institution focus on improving the teacher communication behaviour of pre-service teachers. Further research in developing the techniques to improve upon the teacher communication behaviour in the local cultural context is recommended. In order to verify the results reported here in this study it is highly desirable to replicate the study at lower secondary and tertiary level institutions. The research finding of such a study will hopefully provide insightful makers for making definitive recommendations to the ministry of education for to enhance improvements in science teaching and learning at schools.

REFERENCES

Aikenhead, G. (1997). Student views on the influences of culture on science. *International Journal of Science Education, 19*, 419-428.

Atwater, M. M. (1996). Social constructivism: Infusion into multicultural science education research agenda. *Journal of Research in Science Teaching*, 33, 821-837.

Borneo Bulletin (2002). *Brunei Yearbook*. Gadong: Brunei Press SDN BHD, Brunei.

BDSY(1996-97). *Brunei Darussalam Statistical Yearbook*. Brunei Darussalam: Statistical division, Department of Economic Planning and Development, Ministry of Finance.

Carlsen, W. S. (1991). Questioning in classrooms: A sociolinguistic perspective. *Review of Educational Research, 61*, 157-178.

Chan, E. (2004) Embracing cultural diversity and enhancing students' learning environment. Triannual Newsletter 8(3). Singapore: NIE, *Center for Development of Teaching and Learning.*

Cohen, J. (1969). *Statistical power analysis for behavioural sciences.* New York: Academic press.

Cuboi. (2001, 10 September). *Borneo Bulletin.*

Deal, D., and Sterling, D. (1997). Kids ask the best questions. *Educational Leadership, 54*, 61-63.

DeBoer, G. E. (1984). A study of gender effects in the science and mathematics course-taking behaviour of a group of students who graduated from college in late 1970s. *Journal of Research in Science Teaching, 21*(1), 95-105.

Delpit, L. D. (1988). The silenced dialogue: power and pedagogy in educating other people' children. *Harvard Educational Review*, 58(3), 280-298.

Dhindsa, H. S. (2005). Cultural Learning environment of upper secondary science students. *International Journal of Science Education, 27*(5), 575-592.

Dhindsa, H. S. and Anderson, O. R. (2004). Using a conceptual change approach to help pre-service science teachers reorganize their knowledge structures for constructivist teaching. *Journal of Science Teacher Education*, 15(1), 63-85.

Erb, T. O. (1983). Career preferences of early adolescents: Age and sex differences. *Journal of Early Adolescence, 3,* 349-359.

Fisher, D., and Rickards, T. (1997, April). *A way of assessing teacher-studnets interpersonal relationshipd in science classes.* Paper presented at the national Sceince Teachers Association Annual National Convention, New Orleans, USA.

Fisher, D. L. and Waldrip, B.G. (1997). Assessing culturally sensitive factors in leaning environments of science classrooms. *Research in Science Education*, 27(1), 41- 48.

Fisher, D.L. and Waldrip, B.G. (1999). Cultural factors of science classroom learning environments, teacher – student interactions and student outcomes. *Research in Science and Technological Education*, 17(1), 83-96.

Fraser, B. J. (1989). Assessing and improving classroom environment. *What research says to the science and mathematics teacher*, (Number 2), Perth, Australian: National Key Centre for School Science and Mathematics, Curtin University of Technology.

Fraser, B. J. (1994). Research on classroom and school climate. In D. Gabel (Ed.), *Handbook of research on science teaching and learning* (pp. 493-541). New York: Macmillan.

Fraser, B. J. (1998). Science learning environments: Assessment, effects and determinants. In B. J. Fraser and K. G. Tobin (Eds.), *The Inrternational Hansbook of Science Education* (pp. 527-564). Dordrecht, The Neatherlands: Kluwer.

Fraser, B. J. (2001). Twenty thousand hours: Editor's introduction. *Learning Environment Research, 4*, 1-5.

Gardner, P., and Gauld, C. (1990). Labwork and students' attitudes. In E. Hegarty-Hazel (Ed.), *The student laboratory and science curriculum* (pp. 132-156). London, England: Routledge.

Goh, S. C., and Fraser, B. J. (1998). Teacher interpersonal behaviour, classroom environment and student outcomes in primary mathematics in Singapore. *Learning Environment Research, 1*, 199-229.

Good, T., and Brophy, J. (1991). *Teacher-student relationships: Causes and consequences.* New York: Holt.

Jegede, O. J., and Olajide, J. O. (1995) Wait-time, classroom discourse, and the influences of sociocultural factors in science teaching. *Science Education, 79*(3), 233-249.

Khadijah Mohd. Salleh and Dhindsa, H. S. (2004). Teachers' predictions of students' perceptions of sociocultural dimensions in science classes. *Journal of Science Teacher Education, 8*(1), 135-147.

King, A. (1994). Guiding knowledge construction in the classroom: Effects of teaching children how to question and how to explain. *American Educational Research Journal, 31*, 338-368.

Liau, M. T. L. and Arellano, E. L. (2003, April). *Learning environment in science classes in Penang secondary schools: Implications to secondary science education reform.* Paper presented at the ICASE 2003 world conference on science and technology education, Penang, Malaysia.

Monaliza, A-H (2001). *The teaching and learning of heat energy in lower secondary science: A case study.* Unpublished Master of Education, dissertation, Universiti Brunei Darussalam, Brunei.

Poh, S. H. (1995). *An evaluation of O-level biology laboratory teaching across government secondary schools in Brunei Darussalam: process skills and learning environment.* Unpublished M. Sc. project, Curtin University of Technology, Perth, SA, Australia.

Rasool, J. A. and Curtis, A. C. (2000). *Multicultural education in middle and secondary classrooms: Meeting the challenge the diversity and change.* USA: Wadsworth.

Rayn, A. M. and Patrick, H. (2001). The classroom social environment and changes in adolescents' motivation and engagement during middle school. *American Educational Research Journal, 38*(2), 437-460.

Rennie, L.J. (1998). Improving the interpretation and reporting of quantitative research. *Journal of Research in Science Teaching, 35*, 237-248.

Riah, H. (2000). Bruneian secondary students' environment of Chemistry. In H. S. Dhindsa (Ed.). *Teaching and learning of Chemistry* (pp. 42-48). Brunei: ETC-Universiti Brunei Darussalam.

Rosenholtz, S. J., Bassler, O., and Hoover-Dempsey, K. (1986). Organisational conditions of teacher learning. *Teaching and Teacher Education, 2*, 91 – 104

Rowe, M. B. (1974). Wait-time and rewards as instructional variables, their influence on language, logic and fate control: Part one-wait time. *Journal of Research in Science Teaching, 11*(2), 81 – 94.

Salta, K., and Tzougraki, C. (2004). Attitudes toward Chemistry among 11th grade students in high schools in Greece. *Science Education, 88*(4), 535-547.

She, H-C. (1995). Elementary and middle school students' perception of science, scientists, and their work. *Proceedings of the National Science Council, Part D: Mathematics, Science , and Technology Education, 5*(1), 19-28.

She, H-C. (2000). The interplay of a biology teacher's beliefs, teaching practices and gender-based students-teacher classroom interaction. *Educational Research, 42*(1), 100-111.

She, H-C and Fisher, D. (2000). The development of a questionnaire to describe teacher communication behaviour in Taiwan and Australia. *Science Education, 84*, 706-726.

She, H-C and Fisher, D. (2002). Teacher communication behaviour and its association with students' cognitive and attitudinal outcomes in science in Taiwan. *Journal of Research in Science Teaching, 39(1)*, 63-78.

Smith, E. L., Blakeslee, T. D., and Anderson, C. W. (1993). Teaching strategies associated with conceptual change learning in science. *Journal of Research in Science Teaching, 20*, 111-126.

Thomas, E. (2000). *Culture and Schooling: Building Bridges Between Research, Praxis and Professionalism.* New York: John Wiley and Sons, Ltd.

Utmost, M. E. (1980). Occupational sex-role liberality of third-, fifth- and seventh-grade females. *Sex Roles,* 6(4), 611-617.

van Tartwijk, J. (1993). Sketches of teacher behaviour (in Dutch). Docentgedrag in beeld. Utrecht, The Neatherlands:W.C.C.

Wahyudi and Treaguest, D. F. (2003, April). *Science classroom learning environments and their association with students' cognitive and attitude outcomes in Indonesian lower secondary schools.* Paper presented at the ICASE 2003 world conference on science and technology education, Penang, Malaysia.

Walberg, H. J. and Haertel, G. D. (1980). Validity and use of educational environment assessments. *Studies in Educational Evaluation, 6*, 225-238.

Waltzlawick, P., Beavin, J., and Jackson, D. (1967). *The pragmatics of human communication.* New York: Norton.

Watts, M., and Bentley, D. (1987). Constructivism in the classroom: Enabling conceptual change by words and deeds. *British Educational Journal, 13*, 121-135.

Weinburgh, M. (1995). Sex differences in students' attitudes towards science: A meta analysis of the literature from 1970 to 1991. *Journal of Research in Science Teaching, 32,* 387-398.

Wubbel, T., and Levey, J. (Eds.), (1993). *Do you know what you look like? Interpersonal relationships in education.* London, England: Falmer Press.

In: New Developments in Learning Research
Editor: Samuel N. Hogan, pp. 217-233
ISBN 1-59454-669-X
© 2006 Nova Science Publishers, Inc.

Chapter 10

WHAT MAKES DESIRABLE LEARNING ACTIVITIES? EXPLORING THE RHETORIC AND PRACTICE IN HONG KONG KINDERGARTENS

Yuen Ling Li
The Hong Kong Institute of Education

ABSTRACT

There is a good deal of evidence within the psychological literature that desirable learning activity is an interactive event, where the child actively constructs his/her own understandings within a social and physical environment. This kind of learning is sometimes referred to as 'active learning'. Active learning refers to the interactive process between teacher and learner, and it is also applied to include the provision of some aspects of the learning environment. These ideas were introduced to kindergarten teachers when they received their in-service teacher education started in 1981. In a two-year school-based project, sixty teachers in five schools were to develop some videos on models of good practices collaboratively after sharing each others' 'effective' teaching episodes with peer teachers who were experimenting with 'desirable learning activities' in their classrooms. This study is to report the planning, implementation, assessment, classroom ethos and adult support displayed in the project deliverables (videos) so as to portray the context in which children are expected to learn in Hong Kong kindergartens. Records of dialogues during sharing sessions/case discussion sessions and post-project evaluation meetings, and project deliverables (four to five vignettes from each of the five schools) were collected and analysed. Teaching records (lesson plans), and commentary of videos were sources of data collected for triangulation. The aim was to capture the belief of teachers and a variety of 'desirable learning activities'/learning and teaching episodes so they could be analysed for learning environment and pedagogy. During sharing/case discussion sessions, the principles of 'high child participation' and a joyful and harmonious learning environment were upheld and teachers in general consented their initiation to engage children in learning activities. The project deliverables showed that teachers tended to introduce activities that targeted a 'collaborative and permissive learning environment' but freely chosen play activities or child initiated learning were absent in the vignettes. Items that were found to be 'worked' in peers' classrooms were internalized and absorbed into the teachers' repertoire. The findings of the study suggest that there was some evidence of significance in the use of case discussions/worked examples to shape instruction, though strategies concerning the scrutiny of the pool of knowledge for the development of 'cases' are of concern.

INTRODUCTION

Direct instruction has found to hinder children's learning, generating higher anxiety and lower self esteem (Burts, Hart, Charlesworth and Kirk, 1990). There is a good deal of evidence within the psychological literature that learning is an interactive event, where the child actively constructs his/her own understandings within a physical and social environment. Some researchers termed it "active learning" and define this as "learning in which the child, by acting on objects and interacting with people, ideas and events, constructs new understandings" (Hohmann and Weihart 1995). This means that young children require direct and immediate experiences that will enable them to derive meaning from these experiences based on their previous ones (Siraj-Blatchford, Sylva, Muttock, Gilden and Bell, 2002). The learning environment must, therefore, provide children with opportunities to be active and take the initiative to learn. The role of the adult is to provide these opportunities and experiences through setting the physical and intellectual environment and through consistent planning and rigorous assessment so that appropriate opportunities may be given. Adult support is also important to encourage children to learn in active and participatory way by enabling the child to discover contradictions or 'disequalibria' with her/his prior knowledge and understanding (Sylva, Siraj-Blatchford, and Taggart, 2003). According to Piaget, learning took place when the learner was involved in active elaboration of his/her mental structures as they assimilated and accommodated new experiences and the active elaboration was triggered by the 'disequilibria' between the learner's new experience and the prior knowledge (Sylva et al., 2003). The child's interest in the new phenomenon or experience might be the spontaneous result of their natural curiosity but it could also be influenced by the adults and peers around them, as suggested by Vygotsky (Forman, 1995). Social constructivism further emphasizes creating discourse communities whereas the holistic constructivist perspective emphasizes developing student ownership of the learning process (Green and Gredler, 2002). The role of an adult and learner in the learning and teaching process has been defined as interactive.

The provision of in-service initial teacher education programmes for early childhood teachers in Hong Kong began in 1981. As there were a number of early childhood teacher education programmes offered for in-service teachers' initial training and professional advancement from then onwards (pre-service teachers' training was provided not until 1999), the vision of early childhood education and "child initiated" learning or "active learning" learning (the two terms had the same translation in Chinese) were introduced to early childhood teachers (Li, 2004a). However, kindergarten teachers in Hong Kong are blamed for not putting child-initiated learning theory into practice (Education Commission, 1999). Their competence is challenged. The earlier study (Li, 2004b) suggested that all the teachers tended to be rather directive and give a lot of verbal instructions involved assigning activities and monitoring children on task. In the initial report of this study, data of pre-project teaching revealed that most teachers used direct instruction to deliver teaching and required the children to be seated in an orderly manner and to be quiet before commencing teaching (Li, 2004 c).

Researches (Tharp and Gallimore, 1988; Anning and Edwards, 1999; Lieberman, 2000; Little, 2003; Abor, Holm and Horn 2003) suggested that collaboration in the form of peer-coaching would trigger practitioners to question particular aspect of their practice, to articulate the underlying values and assumptions which informed and influenced that practice, and to consider the effectiveness of their professional actions and judgements especially in the light of the impact these had on the children with whom they worked. The theoretical basis for this study draws on the philosophy of teacher development, which emphasises joint collaborative activity (Hargarves, 1992) and the presence of models (Kagan, 1992) as the keys to confront and modify the teachers' knowledge and practice.

This study is to report participants' view and implementation of desirable learning activities after going through collaborations and action research in a school-based project which was an activity on video production of good practice. There were four phases in the project. In Phase I, briefing sessions on the objectives of the project for participants were organized for each participant school. Teachers then understood the need for scriptwriting and video production. The video on teaching was based on classroom reality. Classroom teaching of team members in each school was to be videoed for one month. Each then chose the best day and presented the vignette to all team members in sharing sessions. The 'best' episodes on various aspects, such as small group activity, music and movement, storytelling, questioning or pupil-teacher interactions were discussed and selected for later scriptwriting use. In Phase II, workshops on topics like effective teaching, quality learning, responsive teaching and pupil-teacher interactions were facilitated by lecturers from the School of Early Childhood Education of the Hong Kong Institute of Education. Team members were then given two to three months to discuss and try out new ideas in their classrooms. In Phase III, classroom teaching was videoed. Each team member selected the best day for presentation in sharing sessions. Team members picked out all the episodes of 'effective teaching' in sharing sessions and developed a script of effective teaching. The teaching script was tried out before being filmed. The video filming took place in Phase IV.

The primary aim of the study was to explore the views of desirable learning activities among early childhood teachers in Hong Kong, and to examine the extent of emergent vision/innovations being adopted in reality. Of particular interest were studying the context in which children were expected to learn, and the impact of case discussion on teachers' work.

METHOD

This was a study of the lesson planning, implementation of learning activities and classroom culture of around 60 teachers in a collaborative project. Teachers were introduced to ideas of effective teaching and quality learning such as child-initiated learning or active learning while receiving their in-service teacher education. The vision of early childhood education was re-visited in a series of workshops in this study. Teachers were encouraged to participate in sharing sessions where they could observe each others' teaching (video-recorded) and to provide one another with feedback on their instruction before developing a script on 'good practice' to be video-filmed.

Four research questions framed the study:

1. What are the design and planning, implementation and classroom ethos disseminated in the 'model' lessons?
2. Whether there is a general context in which children are expected to learn?
3. What is the relationship between teacher knowledge and classroom practice?
4. What's the impact of case discussions on teachers' knowledge and practice?

Records of dialogues during sharing sessions (case discussions) /script-writing meetings and post-project evaluation meetings and vignettes and videos were collected and analyzed. Analysis of vignettes of teaching (before filming), and project deliverables (4-5 teaching episodes x 5 teams, professionally filmed) was to capture a variety of learning and teaching episodes developed so they could be analyzed for learning environment and pedagogy, the context in which children are expected to learn. Dialogues and videos were to tap the teachers' views, understanding and practice of desirable learning activities. Dialogues were to tap the teachers' views and understanding of desirable learning activities. Records of lesson plans and commentary of project deliverables were used as triangulation.

FINDINGS

It seems that teachers were keen in preparing for teaching plans and teaching materials. A number of devices such as body language, voice and pace of speech, attractive pictures and praises were introduced to buffer children's attention. 'High child participation' and a joyful and harmonious learning environment were given high priority. Teachers in general took the initiation to engage children in learning activities, though there were one or two instances of teachers allowing responsibility for the activity to be gradually transferred to the learner. Freely chosen play activities and sustained shared thinking between children and adults were absent in the videos (project deliverables). Teachers tended to assess children's learning through children's responses to questions or in a few occasions through observing children in an activity. Teachers were not mindful of children's reflection in the learning activity as well as formative assessment. The analysis has shown that the collaborative reflection has displayed the connection between the knowing and reflection-in-action of practitioners.

Lesson Design and Planning

During script writing meetings, teachers viewed the worked samples of peer teachers' teaching and tried to work out a draft lesson plan (script for the final project deliverable) consolidating all the worked strategies of quality learning and teaching episodes. Teachers' concerns informed the general principles guiding lesson design and planning.

Quite a number of general suggestions/comments made on the learning environments were recorded in the field notes. For instances,

Teacher 13: "The learning environment is important."
Teacher 37: "Teachers had to provide learning opportunities conducive to children's learning."

Teacher 51: "Children's interest in learning, new phenomenon or experience could be influenced by adults and peers."

Teacher 2: "Besides talking, the teacher could use body language such as smiling and nodding heads to encourage children's participation or to provide feedback for answers."

Teacher 45: "When a teacher uses soft voice skillfully, children are more attentive and willing to participate."

Teacher 11: "Provision of more art materials such as drawing paper, colour pencils and craft paper, bamboo sticks, wooden sticks, rubber bands and scissors would allow choices for children."

Teacher 15: "Real objects should be used as far as possible."

Teacher 40: "A lengthy session should be avoided or else children would lose their attention."

Teacher 58: "Big books and pictures should be used. Lovely pictures with beautiful colours would attract children."

Teachers also tended to pull out all the worked strategies from the vignettes/video recorded teaching episodes. For example,

Teacher10: "Providing praise, encouragement, and discussion for children helps to facilitate a harmonious learning atmosphere. Children feel safe to respond to the teacher."

Teacher 13: "The teacher is skillful in using her eye-contact. Children are very attentive."

Teacher 32: "The pace of teaching is appropriate. Children are very attentive."

Teacher 35: "Small group teaching is very effective. Teachers could take good care of the participation of children."

Teacher 44: "The lesson is well prepared. There is a lot of teaching aids which help the delivery of content. Children enjoy the learning activities."

Teacher 50: "Teaching is well prepared. The teacher uses a lot of teaching aids."

Teacher 55: "Teaching is well prepared. However, the session is rather lengthy.

Teacher 54: "The pace of teaching is good. Children are attentive and ready to give responses."

At here, teachers tended to resort to a lot of devices, speaking softly, using praises, eye contact, group size and a variety of teaching aids, and creating a well paced lesson and harmonious environment to buffer children's attention. All these were put down as remarks on the script (lesson plans) for the filming of project deliverables. Holding children's attention was very 'carefully' monitored. The following extract of transcription illustrates this:

Team A: In the morning, the class teacher greeted children with a rhyme. When children were called out as a group, the teacher sang out the names of each group. During tea time, children could listen to some pieces of music. Children were encouraged to sing along as they queued up in the corridor to go for toilets and back to their homeroom. The teacher used a few music instrument to produce the sound effect needed while reading a story to children. The teacher sang with children on the way to the special rooms such as music room and playground, and children could choose and sing the "good bye song" at their choices during the pack away time.

It seems that whether children are active attending to the learning experience or are provided with experiences to create cognitive dissonance to move on to higher levels of development are not a high priority of the teachers.

Children Participation

From the data analysis, children's attention was mentioned as parallel to children's participation which was a frequent mentioned concern. Concerning children participation, it seems the practice of introducing the children to more informal organizational structures such as experiential or hands-on activities, role-play, and small group activities preceded formal presentation/formal organizational structures such as whole class teaching or carpet time. The following extracts of transcriptions from the videos (project deliverables) illustrate this:

> In Team B: Children brought back some stems of flowers for observation ... The teacher had a brief chat with all children on the kind of flowers and its colour. Children sat in circles and were encouraged to talk about the flowers though each child was watching her or his own flowers and not many interactions were initiated. Then children could have the free choice to display the flowers in vases or pots. Some children asked to trim the flowers a bit or cut them short. Eventually, flowers of different length were displayed ... The teacher then asked children to draw stems of flowers onto the drawing paper.

> In Team C: Children in a group of eight are involved in an instructive activity through which they role-played the story "The Old Couple and the Big Carrot". Children were allowed to choose which character to act. The most popular characters were the Big Carrot and the Good Grandson. Four children become the actors and the other four become audience. The teacher scaffolded the children by providing clues or asking help from the audience so that children could pick up what was the next to act in the play. The audience then sometimes took the role of providing clues for the actors.

> In Team E, children pretended to be a group of scouts who met some problems in the event of hiking... One boy got wet and felt very cold. Team members had to think of some ways to help him out. Children were formed into 4 groups to discuss for solutions... The teacher asked for responses from children ... Some suggested him to change the wet clothes. Some suggested drying up the clothes by hanging them on trees... Some suggested using all kinds of materials at hand to make some 'clothes' for him to protect him from cold... Children presented their suggestions and then voted for the best solution... From the readings of the bar chart, children reached the consent to make some clothes for the boy. Then, they started to role play "An Accident at Hiking" and make clothes out of their creation...

In the post-project evaluation meetings, teachers expressed their satisfaction over the videos (project deliverables) as most teachers found children participation was well taken care of. The following field notes illustrate this:

> Teacher 2: "Children's participation had been well monitored."
> Teacher 15: "All children could participate as the teacher also asked passive children questions."
> Teacher 22: "Children smiled and enjoyed the flower-display activity."
> Teacher 33: "Children used different colours and material in their craft and art work."
> Teacher 40: "Children were happy and highly motivated in the physical movement session. It's a good idea to learn counting in twos through activities."
> Teacher 52: "Children were encouraged to join in with repetitive words and phrases in the text while the teacher was reading the story."

Teachers in general were sensitive with the participation of children. However the balance of who initiated the activities, teacher or child, were very different, revealing that the effective pedagogy did not encourage children to initiate activities as often as the teacher. The children in the videos experienced a different balance of initiated activities, with a much greater emphasis upon teacher initiated activities.

Learning Ethos

Teachers were less conscious of classroom management, unlike what has been described in earlier researches (Li, 2003), which was evident by some kind of relax in the learning atmosphere. The following extract of transcription illustrates this:

In Team D: When children counted to eight, the teacher showed them the number 8 on the board. The teacher asked what the shape of 8 looked like... A child spoke out and associated the shape of 8 to his pair of glasses and showed his glasses to the teacher. The teacher agreed that a laid down 8 looked very much like a pair of glasses. Children laughed. The boy smiled...The teacher smiled and then praised children' work and would like to send a sticker to every one. She asked how many children were there and how many stickers she had to give out. Children [standing up] started to count the number of children in the group and told the teacher that there were eight of them. The teacher asked how many stickers would be needed and children said it should be eight. The teacher began to distribute the stickers, with some helping hands form the children...

In general, the teachers were also apt to quote that the learning atmosphere in the videos was harmonious and teachers were very warm to children in the post-project evaluation meetings. For instances,

Teacher 7: "Pupil-teacher relations were very good. Children were ready to help the teacher when the teacher dropped some paper or word cards on the ground... Children were happy."
Teacher 25: "The teacher's voice is very soft. A very quiet and harmonious atmosphere is created in the classroom...Children wore a smiling face."
Teacher 30: "Children were willing to answer questions from the teacher... They enjoyed the learning."
Teacher 53: "The teacher smiled or nodded her head whenever children responded to her... Children smiled to the teacher."

The teachers frequently described the learning atmosphere as children were happy, children enjoyed the activity, children smiled, indicating a joyful learning environment was their high priority.

Activity-Based Learning Tasks

In some instances, a relatively weak framing of instruction as compared to earlier study (Li, 2004d) was recorded in the videos (project deliverables). There were one or two teachers allowing responsibility for the activity to be gradually transferred to the learner, contingent on his/her ability to succeed. The following extract of transcription illustrates this:

> In Team E, eight children in a group took part in a role-play "In the Country Park." The teacher told children that eight children were going for a picnic and took out eight cloth puppets. Children were allowed to choose from them. The teacher was taking one of the roles, like all the other seven children. The teacher asked children to bring along the needed items for a picnic and then initiated to have picnic in a 'country park'... The teacher pretended to be a naughty child and started to do a few mischievous deeds such as throwing banana skins on the ground. Children took a look on the teacher but didn't stop her until the teacher pretended to complain that there were flies around her. Children began to tell the teacher that banana skins attracted flies. The teacher apologized for her deeds. Children began to remind the teacher whenever she did something mischievous and then each other to clean up the place before leaving the park.... The teacher then responded by saying, "well, you are very good of reminding your friends" "if every one is like you, we'll have a lovely country park", "I am learning from you" or "you are very conscious of environmental protection". When one child was too harsh to another child, the teacher said, "Wow, the park superintendent was very strict." Children, including those two, laughed. ...

At here, the teacher tended to foster conversations which were seen as less impoverished exchanges than only posing a series of questions (Siraj-Blatchford, Sylva, Muttock, Gilden and Bell, 2002). Children were also encouraged to make alternative suggestions to keep the environment clean as well as the choices of the manner of giving advice. The lesson was designed to engage children as members of a learning community though no one teacher was aware of it in the post-project discussion sessions (Li and Li, 2004)

In the post-project evaluation meeting, some teachers found the learning activities as interactive and the classroom ethos as collaborative and permissive. In fact, all the videoed learning tasks were activity oriented which was different from the conventional practice (Li, 2004d). For instances,

> In Team A, children were exposed to music as part of the daily routine... In the music movement activity, children could move according to their imagination as animals in a Zoo.
> In Team B, children were allowed to discuss the stems of flowers and do flower displays to enrich their knowledge of flowers.
> In Team D, children took part in castle building and transporting paper bricks. In order to get 40 bricks in a time-saving manner, children modeled on the teacher to count the bricks in twos.
> In Team E, children pretended to be a group of scouts who met some problems in the event of hiking. One boy got wet and felt very cold. Team members used the materials at hand to design some 'clothes' for him to protect him from cold.
> In one or two instances, the routines which the teacher established were such that children could learn on their own pace. For example,
> In Team B, children (3-4 years old) could have great varieties of materials to choose from while making their fake ice-cream cones. There were different colour papers to represent the favour of the ice-creams like chocolate, orange or vanilla. The paper crisp became the topping. Children smiled when they chose and added the toppings once and again... Some children were busy with making the ice-cream balls...

All the learning activities were activity-based in the videos (Li, 2004c). It seems that participants in general equated activity-based learning to play. In the post-project evaluation meetings, they were confident of putting activities as central to learning for children. Many also felt that children learn best when the learning tasks, in form of activities, interested them. For instances,

> Teacher 11: "Children enjoy the learning when it is conducted through activities and play."
> Teacher 42: "Children are free from risk taking and would not be held up by jargons like beats, characteristics of flowers, and counting in two... when they are learning through activities..."
> Teacher 45: "All children wear a smiling face in the flower display activity. They can choose the stems of flowers, the length of flowers at their will and interest. They show enthusiasm when they are asked to draw flowers or the flowers displayed in the pots."

Precisely, those common concerns mentioned in the script writing and video sharing meetings were quite well monitored in the videos. In general, a high concern for children's attention and children's participation was recorded. Teachers tended to include a lot of details in the lesson plans (teaching records). Eye contact, facial expression and body language, voice and pace of speech, wording of questions and responses to children's different answers were put under remarks as reminders in the lesson plans. All the teachers in the videos prepared substantially for the sessions which were evident by the length of the activity and varieties of teaching aids.

During this school-based collaborations, practitioners' learning seemed to be scaffolded by the modeling of strategies with children by their peers, discussions for planning and reviewing, joint data collection and analysis, shared frameworks for teaching, and a shared focus on children's learning in numeracy, story-telling, social studies, music and art. It seems teachers found some ways of solving problems and grew in their ability to recognize problems, as opinions accumulated. Teachers then inclined to organize classroom settings conducive to high pupil involvement. Practitioners' learning through those scaffolding processes became evident in how the familiar strategies took on new educational meanings as teachers had a high sense of efficacy and designed lessons so that they included a lot of activity-based tasks, putting children's learning in the first priority. Teachers were rethinking what they could do to change the way they were engaging children. Informal, activity-based learning in promoting young children learning was widely adopted.

The final video product suggested that teachers were not resistant to developing new ways of interpreting classroom events and responding to them. It could be because they could experience a destabilization of prior understandings before new ones are recognized as necessary in the process of knowledge enactment or action research. The destabilizing can be professionally threatening when teachers are working in isolation. This may imply that the development of teacher will depend upon the continuous development, in action, of a common store of practical knowledge which is itself constantly open to scrutiny in a professional climate that encourages the confidence to value openness and collaboration so that the best interests of children are served.

Adult Support

Teachers were apt to talk about the questioning style in the commentary of videos. Most teachers tended to highlight that there were close questions as well as open-ended questioning to assist children's learning. For examples,

> Teacher 3: "The teacher uses good questioning skills. There are also open-ended questions during the class teaching. Open-ended questions were to facilitate children's cognitive development."
> Teacher 49: "There's quite a well balance of close questions and open-ended questions. Children were encouraged to critical thinking."

In general, teachers were conscious of the presence of open-ended questioning However, open-ended questions made up only 30% of the questioning used in even these 'effective' teaching episodes (Li, 2004e).

Students might be presumed to be actively engaged in thought-provoking activities but most of the activities did not really 'push' the child intellectually or provide cognitive challenge. On the one hand, in terms of propositional knowledge, the learning activities involved fundamental concepts of the subject rather than promoted strongly coherent conceptual understanding. On the other hand, learning assistance was mostly in form of praise and encouragement, contributing to mainly the kind of emotional support. The following extracts of transcriptions illustrate this:

> "Children, you sing very well. Well done!"
> "This is a beautiful [paper] fan! There are a lot of colours on it!"
> "Very good. You could remember the story very well and give us very good clues…"
> "Yes. You are right. Can you show me your pair of glasses?"
> "Well, a very beautiful thank you card!"

Furthermore, over 95% of teaching was conducted in the mode of small group learning. The commentary of teachers suggested that small group teaching could enhance quality interactions among children and the teacher was able to diagnose children's learning difficulties and repair wrong concepts as teacher could take better care of seven to eight children than a class over twenty-five. However, there were little signs of mutuality between learner and teacher where collaboration and negotiation is possible for turning errors or curiosity into learning opportunities. In all the videos, we found that children spent most of their time in small groups despite that the art activities and math activities were conducted in larger groups. Though 'sustained shared thinking' was most likely to occur when children were interacting with an adult or with a single peer partner, sustained shared thinking rarely happened in the videos.

Moreover there was the absence of provision of freely chosen yet potentially instructive play activities. Freely chosen play activities, which were absent in the videos, are often found to provide the best opportunities for adults to extend children's thinking (Siraj-Blatchford, et al. 2002). It may be that extending child-initiated play, coupled with the provision of teacher initiated group work, should be introduced as the main vehicles for a balance of responsibility or sustained shared thinking in the learning and teaching relationship.

Nevertheless, extended support was observed in the videos. A teacher was present whenever children were doing their group work such as matching, art, mathematics, etc. The teacher was questioning, instructing, or guiding. Regarding procedural knowledge, students were provided opportunities to use craft, drawings and graphs to represent real world objects or phenonomena. Of surprise, no one teacher mentioned these in the post-project evaluation meetings.

In general, teachers' questions and comments often determined the focus and direction of classroom discourse. In this study, teachers tended to act as classroom directors or leaders, ready to provide directives, support and guidance to children. It is true that there was a relatively higher proportion of student talk if compared with the earlier study (Li, 2004b). However, the amount of talk occurred mainly between the teacher and the child and rarely among children.

Moreover, we may need to be cautious that teachers in the study could talk about the rationale underlying the strategy but could apply it with much effort and thought and in a specific context. If we examine the final video product and the commentary closely, we might find teachers could talk about learning assistance or instructional strategy but performed it at a superficial level. For instances,

> In Team B,
> [In the video] The teacher asked children to make a paper fan according to the three steps instructed though children were showed a variety of craft work of paper fans... More assistance was provided to children working on the teacher's choice.
> [In the commentary] The teacher said, "Children are provided different stimuli before doing their art work. ... Children have free choices."
> In Team C,
> [In the video] The teacher nodded her head whenever children make suggestions and voice out opinions but tended to pick "good responses" which are directly leading to the development of the story. One or two quiet children were neglected and became the audience in most of the time.
> [In the commentary] The teacher said, "Teaching begins with stories, children can share their experiences and voice out their interests at any points of time."

It seems theories play the role as supplier of theoretical resources for practitioners to draw on when analysing and developing practice. When the new activities such as activity-based tasks engage the students, do not violate the teacher's particular need for children's participation they deemed to work and absorbed into the teachers' repertoire. However, teachers' practice was constrained by their prior knowledge which has to be deepened before innovative doctrines could be implemented in practice.

Assessing Learning

Teachers were alert and ever mindful of how rigorous the learning process was. There were insights into how learning occurred and empathy for children who struggled with the process. The following extracts of video commentaries illustrate this:

One teacher explained that announcing to children the meaning of a word, concept, idea, or theme did not mean children could then use it to comprehend what they were to learn. (Team C)

Another teacher suggested that children could not learn what was taught if the teacher just mentioned it once. Some voiced out that children had to learn from repeated rounds of activities. (Team D)

Some teachers explained the warm and encouraging interactions in the video that children were able to learn when they were confident, happy and attentive. (Team E)

Teachers tended to assess children's learning through children's responses to questions. The following field notes illustrate this:

Teacher 4: " When children could answer questions correctly, children have learnt what's taught."

Teacher 8: "By reading their eye gaze and their responses, we could see [know] children understand the lesson or not."

Teacher 23: " Children were asked questions on the previous session to check whether they could understand [follow] the content or not."

There was one stance recorded that a child was reflective in his learning. The following extract of transcription illustrates this:

Team D: The teacher taught counting to eight by asking children (of the age three) to count objects displayed on the board and clap their hands as they counted. In one instance, a child was supposed to count only one object on the board, the child was aware of his mistake when he clapped his hands two times. The child stopped clapping at once and the teacher encouraged him to clap and count again. The child did so and was happy to have his mistake corrected [clap his hand once].

However, no one teacher mentioned this in the post-project evaluation meeting. Moreover, very little on formative assessment was mentioned in the planning and evaluation meetings though there were signs of formative assessment embedded in the learning activities. Participants' failure to mention this certain point did not mean disagreement with that view. It was, however, considered to be indicative that reflective thinking and formative assessment to support children's cognitive progress or to inform children's particular needs was not a high priority in their thinking.

Teaching a model lesson displayed the knowledge and expertise that teachers had gained from teaching in the context of their classrooms. Colleagues giving feedback in ways that are "constructively critical" of the lesson (including how the lesson might be used in their own classrooms) will inform the growing cultural norms that define the group (Anning, 2000). It seems there was a general consensus or norm of effective pedagogy within a school as well as across schools.

In this study, participants gained new knowledge as information was transformed into knowledge through enactment of the information and sustained interactions to work out resolutions. The sharing of each other's teaching experience tended to build up a pool of information and thus the enacted knowledge. Concepts are changed or replaced only if 1. One becomes dissatisfied with an existing concept. This arises when it is incompatible with other existing evidence or which proves unsatisfactory when tested. 2. One finds the new concept plausible, in that it seems to present an opportunity to propose more acceptable predictions and to explain events when they are tested (Bell and Gilbert, 1996). In effect, teachers select or create practices for specific situations and learn further refinements from critical reflection on their own practice in the exercise of one's knowledge and skills. This explains why the participants in this study give up strict classroom management (Li, 2004d) and high teacher talk (Li, 2004b) and adopt the activity-based teaching or the child-doing approach. However, personal interpretation is determined largely by existing beliefs, which are prior constructions. This explains why the pool of information and knowledge mobilized was still limited to children on task, teacher-initiated activities, emotional support instead of active participation, child-initiated activities and diagnosis of learning.

Teachers' knowledge development and testing of hypotheses/action research reminds us that the ideas of theorists don't threaten practitioners if these ideas could be translated into concrete curriculum proposals that could be scrutinized in action by practitioners who then decided what should be ultimately absorbed into practice. However, the practitioner is the ultimate judge of what is useful knowledge. It seems that a balance of outside knowledge (knowledge created by research and conceptualization) and inside knowledge (the experiential knowledge of teachers) is needed before substantial teacher change could occur.

DISCUSSION AND CONCLUSION

The analysis has revealed that teachers did not have a clear conception regarding what counts as active learning in the curriculum areas. Participants in the study did not tend to diagnose the nature of children's understanding and misunderstanding and provide alternative learning experiences; might not aware of those common experiences of childhood that can be utilized to lead children towards the understandings represented by this knowledge; and thus failed to organize classroom settings conducing to high cognitive involvement of children. Teachers in general were not aware of accommodating the different ways children learn by planning for the same learning objective in a range of different ways. Evidence also suggests that the uses of verbal, nonverbal and communication techniques to foster active inquiry, collaboration and supportive interaction in the classrooms were not in the mind of the participants.

The participants in this study tended to use the same language, such as the provision of rich learning environments through setting up a stimulating environment and interacting with people, as prevailingly used by early childhood educators in other parts of the world. However, they might have different connotations. For example, the preparation for a stimulating learning environment could be more on the adults' contribution in terms of lesson planning, resources and materials which supported learning activities. Also, the provision of adult support was limited to emotional rather than learning assistance to enable children to discover contradictions or disequilibria with prior knowledge or the presence of cognitive challenge i.e. activities that really 'push' the child intellectually. The participants' desire for stimulating high child participation and buffering children's attention from distractions was evident from the data of this study. Out of their 'creation', hands-on activities were most popular across all five teams' project deliverables. This may have resulted from confusion among teachers about the difference between physical and active participation, and play and activity-based tasks. Perhaps, teachers in an attempt to practice less teacher-doing approach, choose the extreme, child-doing approach.

Participants had a high concern for children's attention and high child participation. However, we have found that most learning environments combine the provision of more focused group work/activity involving some direct instruction but not a balance between teacher-initiated group work and the provision of instructive play activities. Children's participation was monitored by small grouping, carefully chosen tasks, sequence of activities, praises and relatively permissive classroom routines, indicating provision of free choices or learning environments for free play and exploration were not a high priority of the teachers. It might be difficult to define whether when teachers are to select, sequence and pace the learning, the curriculum focus will leave less time for creative activities and knowledge and understanding of the world or when the curriculum focus leaves less time for creative activities and knowledge and understanding of the world, teachers' selection of learning activities will be constrained to more directive tasks. The findings have illustrated that the demands of teaching appeared to have influenced the nature of the planning process in these settings.

On the one hand, teachers were adhering to the daily timetables and rules (e.g. the role of teacher in the classroom) that might not facilitate children to learn on their own as teachers were the one to initiate and choose each activity, and pace the learning activities. On the other hand, some teachers tended to create a collaborative and permissive classroom which illustrated a tendency towards weak framing, as compared to a traditional didactic classroom recorded in earlier studies (Li, 2004d).

The evidence also suggests that some teachers gave sensitive conversational guidelines/guidance and helped children to see /achieve the purpose of activities despite that teachers' verbal intervention or interaction took a rather guiding role in organizing the activity/story for the child. Children were not held accountable for high-level products or processes as teachers shifted the emphasis from meaning and correctness to the participation of children. The tendency towards designing achievable learning tasks for all may, however unintentional, limit learning opportunities for children. Nevertheless when teachers used praise and encouragement as emotional support, it would contribute to a learning environment favourable for active learning.

It seems that beliefs of effective teaching principles guided kindergarten teachers' teaching and teachers' belief could be changed through workshops and sharing sessions. However, a slight change in belief might only contribute to a slight change in practice and teacher could not be changed by one project. Moreover, teachers' teaching strategies or pedagogy might not be changed without the presence of models in the same context and reinforcement of success from peers. This explains why the absence of initiating learning processes contingent on the learner's ability to succeed in the vignettes (teaching recorded in the script preparation stage) resulted in a rare occurrence of it in the videos (project deliverables).

Teachers might not, at first, be changed internally by these strategies (even through observing good models). They might need to learn through sharing and discussion to trigger their internalization. This explains why strategies that were not mentioned or reinforced during the script-writing meetings were not incorporated into the final project deliverables. If the knowledge base of teaching is to be defined as all profession-related insights that are potentially relevant to the teacher's activities (Driel et al, 2001), teachers need to talk about what they are doing and why they are doing it and so take responsibility for the generation of their own knowledge base (Anning, 1999).

There is some evidence of significance in the use of 'case method'/case-based professional development in this study. This study has facilitated discussions of what teachers know and do in their classroom practice (Darling-Hammond, 2001). These discussions are elaborated through vignettes and videos that provide vivid descriptions of teachers enacting the standards. The videos (project deliverables) illustrate how teachers draw upon many kinds of knowledge -- knowledge of teaching strategies, of curriculum, and of their students. Such videos, along with actual samples of teachers' reflections, analyses, and performances on what is believed to be desirable learning activities, closely resemble richly described cases that incorporate context and illuminate the teacher's capacity to transform knowledge into decisions in distinctive situations. If teaching is a form of transformation in which teachers create representations of complex ideas that connect with the constructions of their students. Case methods are a particular strategy of pedagogical transformation-a strategy for transforming propositional forms of information into narratives or knowledge.

The findings suggested that the teachers benefited from sharing their experiences with others. The production of videos was an opportunity for staff to engage in real analysis about what constitutes quality teaching and learning. It seems that teachers are complex thinkers, well able to examine their practices and apply new ideas to improve results in ways that complement rather than replace what they do well or are doing.

The analysis has revealed that teachers are open to change; of particular importance are acknowledging teachers' existing beliefs and practices/a common store of practical knowledge. Teacher knowledge hence becomes a critical foundation in the practice of learning to teach as instruction is shaped by what teachers know and do not know. Moreover, knowledge is constructed through the interplay between an individual's knowledge and judgement in a particular context. In considering the mechanisms by which teachers change their practice, perspectives other than that of the reflective practitioner, developed within the context of our educational systems will be needed for modeling teachers' development and change in the local context.

Some researchers suggest to research into the processes through which individuals gain or fail to gain practical knowledge and expertise of teaching (Meijier, Santing, and Verloop, 2002). It is hoped that this could contribute to a more informed understanding of the learning-to-teach process and thus teachers' knowledge-in-action. Some researchers, searched for key features of effective professional development and, based on their research, has reported that professional development should focus on deepening teacher knowledge in order to foster teacher learning and changes in practice (Driel, Beijaard and Verloop 2001). According to empirical data (Stones, 1979), teachers may change their practice if and when they are provided with feedback on the nature of their behaviour that has already been reinforced through success. Feedback can offer teachers a re-conceptualisation of their practice and a suitable vocabulary to discuss present and future improvements. To this purpose, reflective practice must cultivate activities that connect the knowing and reflection-in-action of competent practitioners to the theories and techniques taught as professional knowledge in developing teachers (Schon, 1987).

Case-based professional development may support this kind of knowledge building because they allow teachers to construct and discuss their understandings while they continually reflect on, critique, and defend their practice. There is some evidence that this kind of case-based reasoning can be deliberately developed in teaching. For example, Bliss and Mazur (1997) found that analyzing cases allowed teachers to gradually integrate standards, theory, and actual classroom practice. With repeated opportunities to reflect on cases in this way, they moved from simple awareness of teaching actions to an appreciation of principled decision-making and an ability to plan approaches to or changes in their own teaching. This initial study develops a model that provides "on-site" classroom and "joint collaboration" to equip teachers with theoretical grounding and practical application of instruction. The research will hopefully offer insights for school-based teacher development projects by illuminating on-site methods of modeling, coaching and feedback.

REFERENCES

Abor, a., Holm, L. and Horn, C. (2003) Priming schools of education for today's teachers. *The Education Digest*, 68 (7), p.25-31.

Anning, A and Edwards, A. (1999). *Promoting children's learning from birth to five: developing new early years professionals*. Buckingham, Open University Press.

Burts, D., Hart, C., Charleswoth, R. and Kird, L. (1990). A comparison of frequency of stress behaviours observed in kindergarten children in classrooms with developmentally appropriate versus developmentally inappropriate instructional practices', *Early Childhood Research Quarterly*, Vol. 5, 407-423.

Darling-Hammond, L. (2001). Teacher Testing and the Improvement of Practice. *Teaching Education*, 12 (1), 11-34.

Driel, J.H., Beijaard, D. and Verloop, N. (2001). Professional Development and Reform in Science Education: The Role of Teachers' Practical Knowledge. *Journal of Research in Science Teaching*, 38 (2), 137-158.

Education Commission (1999). Review of academic system, aims of education (Consultation Document) In *Education blueprint for the 21st century* (Hong Kong, Government Printing Department), 16-17.

Forman, G. (1995). Constructivism and the project approach. In C. Fosnot. *Constructivism: Theory, perspectives, and practice*. New York: Teachers College Press. Pp. 172-181.

Green, S. K., and Gredler, M. E. (2002). A review and analysis of constructivism for school-based practice. *School Psychology Review*. Bethesda:. Vol. 31(1) pp. 53-63

Hargarves, A. (1992). Cultures for teaching: a focus for change. In A. Hargreaves and M. Fullan (Eds). *Understanding teacher development*. New York: Teachers' College Press.

Hohmann, M. and Weihart, D.P. (1995). *Educating Young Children*. Michigan: High/Scope Educational Research Foundation.

Kagan, D.M. (1992). Professional growth among preservice and beginning teachers, *Review of Educational Research*, 62(2), 129-169.

Li, Y.L. (2003). Roadblocks to Educational Reform: Investigating Knowledge and Practice of Kindergarten Teachers in Hong Kong. *International Journal of Educational Reform*, 12 (3), 217-229.

Li, Y.L. (2004a). The Culture of Teaching in the Midst of Western Influence: the case of Hong Kong kindergartens. *Contemporary Issues in Early Childhood*, 5 (3), 330-348.

Li, Y.L. (2004b). Pupil-Teacher Interactions in Hong Kong Kindergarten Classrooms – Its Implications for Teachers' Professional Development. *Learning Environments Research: An International Journal,* 7 (1), 36-45.

Li, Y.L. (2004c). A school-based project in five kindergartens: The case of teacher development and school development. *International Journal of Early Years Education,* 12(2), 143-155.

Li, Y.L. (2004d, July). *Culture Matters: Making a Difference in Classroom Strategies in Hong Kong Kindergartens,* presented at IRA, Manila, the Philippines.

Li, Y.L. and Li, H. (2004, July). *Perceptions of effective pedagogy among teachers in Hong Kong kindergartens,* presented at PECERA, Melbourne, Australia.

Lieberman, A. and Miller, L. (2000). *The social realitites of teaching.* Teachers College Press, 80 (1), 54-68.

Little, M.E. and Houston, D. (2003). Research into practice through professional development. *Remedial and Special Education.* 24 (2), 75-89.

Schon, D.A. (1987). *Educating the reflective practitioner: toward a new design for teaching and learning in the professions.* San Francisco: Jossey-Bass.

Siraj-Blatchford, I., Sylvia, K., Muttock, S., Gilden, R. and Bell, D. (2002). *Researching effective pedagogy in the early years department for education and skills.*Research Report no. 356 (London, DfES).

Stones, E. (1979). *Psychopedagogy: Psychological theory and the practice of teaching.* London: Methuen.

Sylva, K., Siraj-Blatchford, I., and Taggart, B. (2003). *Assessing quality in the early years : early childhood environment rating scale : extension (ECERS-E), four curricular subscales.* Kathy Stoke on Trent : Trentham, 2003.

Tharp, R. and Gallimore, R. (1988). *Rousing minds to life: teaching, learning, and schooling in social context.* Cambridge: Cambridge University Press

In: New Developments in Learning Research
Editor: Samuel N. Hogan, pp. 235-261

ISBN 1-59454-669-X
© 2006 Nova Science Publishers, Inc.

Chapter 11

SITUATIONAL INTEREST: A CURRICULUM COMPONENT ENHANCING LEARNING IN PHYSICAL EDUCATION[1]

Ang Chen[2], *Catherine D. Ennis*
Department of Kinesiology of the University of Maryland - College Park

Robert Martin
Department of Health, Physical Education & Human Performance, Salisbury University

Haichun Sun
Department of Kinesiology of the University of Maryland - College Park

ABSTRACT

Learning in physical education has become more important than ever in helping young generations of Americans develop and sustain a healthy body and lifestyle. To accomplish this overarching goal, learning in physical education is operationalized in two general types. One is learner acquisition of knowledge and skills necessary for a physically active lifestyle, the other is learner participation in in-class physical activities to receive health benefits. Guided by the Model of Domain Learning and interest-based motivation theory, we examined the predictability of situational interest for both in-class physical activity and knowledge acquisition in physical education. The data for this investigation were collected from 83 lessons taught by 30 physical education teachers who and their students (n = 83 classes representing approximately 7,000 pupils) were participating in a physical education curriculum intervention study involving 30 schools. A health-science-based curriculum and a comparison curriculum were randomly assigned to 15 experimental and 15 comparison schools. Both experimental and comparison schools were represented in the current investigation. Situational interest and its sources (Novelty, Challenge, Attention Demand, Exploration, and Instant Enjoyment) were measured using the Situational Interest Scale. In-class physical activity was measured in Vector Magnitude (VM) counts using accelerometers. Knowledge acquisition was assessed using pre- and post-tests on concepts of heart, healthy

---

[1] The study was supported by a grant from the National Institutes of Health (R25 RR15674-01A1).
[2] Corresponding Author:Ang Chen, Ph.D., Department of Kinesiology, College of Health and Human Performance, University of Maryland, College Park, MD 20742, (301) 405-0344, angchen@umd.edu

exercise zone, and exercise benefits. Results show that pupils in the experimental group demonstrated higher achievement than those in the comparison group (in regression residual gain scores, $p = .001$). No differences were found in activity levels ($p > .05$) or most situational interest dimensions ($p > .05$) except Novelty ($p = .025$) and Exploration Intention ($p = .001$); both were rated higher by the experimental group. Regression analysis revealed that Instant Enjoyment was the sole predictor for in-class physical activity ($R^2 = .37$, $\beta = .37$), indicating that "fun" experiences motivated children *to become physically active*. Valid predictors ($R^2 = .55$) for knowledge acquisition included the curriculum ($\beta = -.24$, experimental = 1, comparison = 2), Total Interest ($\beta = .40$), Challenge ($\beta = -.16$), Attention Demand ($\beta = .19$), and Instant Enjoyment ($\beta = .23$). The findings suggest that motivating children *to learn* demands more than "fun". Situational Interest is an integral component of the curriculum that motivates children to be attentive and active and provides manageable challenges and instant enjoyment. The findings imply that the functions of situational interest should be emphasized in developing a coherent curriculum. Situational Interest: A Curriculum Component Enhancing Learning in Physical Education

INTRODUCTION

Since the mid 1990s, a new physical education, which emphasizes developing a healthy body and a physically active lifestyle rather than studying traditional team sports (Weir, 2000), has emerged as a curriculum model in many American schools. The curriculum reform is necessary and timely to address the child obesity epidemic in the United States. According to Freedman, Khan, Serdula, Galuska, and Dietz (2002), severe obesity among Americans has increased approximately three folds from 1990 to 2000. The obesity epidemic has been found to be associated with a sedentary life style. Due to the fact that life styles develop over time, the decrease of physical activity during childhood and adolescence will contribute to physical inactivity in adulthood (Trudearu, Laurencelle, Tremblay, Rajic, and Shephard, 1999). Although all forms of physical activity participation in childhood contribute to an active adulthood (Beunen et al., 2004), participation in school physical education, however, has been found to be the only *significant* contributor to a physically active lifestyle in adulthood (Trudeau, Laurencelle, and Shephard, 2004).

The new physical education emphasizes educating K-12 students with a body of disciplinary knowledge that integrates biological-medical sciences, socio-psycho sciences, and cultural-humanities. Enhancing learning in this integrated knowledge domain requires an approach that can maintain learners' high motivation to learn. Learning in a specific knowledge domain is conceptualized as a process for learners to encompass domain-specific cognitive and motivational factors that facilitate new knowledge and skill acquisition. Alexander (in press) proposed the Model of Domain Learning to explain the interaction of these factors during the learning process that may result in optimal learning outcome. Specifically, the model postulates that learning in a domain can be characterized as a progression from an acclimation or naïve stage, to a more competent stage, and potentially, to one of proficiency or expertise. The progression from a lower stage to a higher stage is primarily dependent on the involvement and interaction of subject-matter knowledge and a primary motivator, interest (Alexander, Jetton, and Kulikowich, 1995).

Interest has been conceptualized as individual and situational (Krapp, Hidi, and Renninger, 1992). Individual interest refers to a person's psychological disposition in preference of an activity or an action. Situational interest is defined as the appealing effect of characteristics of an activity on individuals (Krapp et al., 1992). Although both interests have been found to be motivating (Hidi and Berndorff, 1998; Schiefele, 1998), their roles in enhancing learner motivation vary in terms of the learning stages a learner is at in the learning process (Alexander, in press). For learners who are at the acclimation or naïve stage, situational interest is the sole motivator that attracts and catches the learner to focus on the learning process (Mitchell, 1993). For proficient learners, their individual interests drive them engaging in intensive exploration of and search for new knowledge. The inter-play of knowledge acquisition and interests propel the learner moving from a lower learning stage to a higher one. The progression is characterized by learner internalizing situational interest into individual interest and transforming their learning motivation from situationally elicited to personally initiated.

In the current study we examined the predictability of situational interest for learning in a newly designed health-science-based physical education curriculum (*Be Active Kids!*©) in comparison with a traditional physical education curriculum. The purpose of the study was to investigate the extent to which (a) knowledge acquisition and situational interest differed in the two different curriculum conditions and (b) situational interest contributed to the learning of scientific knowledge.

LEARNING IN THE DOMAIN OF PHYSICAL EDUCATION

Learning Defined

As a school subject, physical education provides a unique opportunity for children to learn knowledge and skills necessary for developing and sustaining a healthy, physically active lifestyle. As in other subject matter taught in schools, learning in physical education can be defined on behavioral and cognitive terms. Based on the behavioral framework, learning may be considered as manifested in an association between a stimulus and a response (Thorndike, 1913) in which the responses can be mediated or modified by reinforcement (Skinner, 1953). The reinforcement is usually imposed by people who are considered, in the behavioral framework, in control of the learning process: teachers, coaches, or parents. From this perspective, the role of reinforcement is important in learning because it helps or forces the learner to become adaptive to the desired behavior (and become conditioned, so to speak). Therefore, to enhance learning it is important that teachers should be able to use various strategies to reinforce desired behavior when it appears and to punish undesired behavior so that the desired behavior can be sustained. Learning, from this perspective, is an externally controlled process in which the learner is conditioned to acquire desired behavior. In general, the behavioral perspective provides little explanation about the nature of learning from a within-the-learner perspective (Farnham-Diggory, 1977).

From the cognitive perspective, learning is thought a behavior change resulting from the interaction between the learner's internal cognitive process and the environment. For example, Brunner's work (1957) on the influence or mental processes on behavior has profound influence on how learning should be defined. Learning, therefore, is a process governed by the learner's internal thought processes, namely cognition. It is an active, accumulative, and constructive process. Learning is associated with learners' interpretation of meaning of the content and is manifested through cognitive understanding, rather than merely performing a task as directed. In other word, learning is behavior change governed by acquired knowledge and skills and directed by a thought process consistent with the knowledge and skills. This behavior has a goal which is based on the individual's internal process (Stevenson, 1983).

It is important to distinguish the difference between the two perspectives on learning. Although there is a general agreement between behavioral and cognitive perspectives that learning is change in an individual's behavior, the two perspectives differ in explaining the nature of learning in important ways. From the behavioral perspective, learning is viewed as a passive, externally controlled process in which the learner merely responds to a series of stimuli. With positive reinforcements given to correct responses, desired behavior begins to emerge and, thereby, learning occurs. Learner motivation, defined as an internal regulatory process in an achievement setting such as schooling (Pintrich and Schunk, 2002), is rarely considered a relevant factor during this passive, externally controlled process. The cognitive perspective, on the other hand, stresses that learning is an active, constructive, and goal-oriented internal process (Shuell, 1986). During this process the learner's mental actions, including the motivational processes, determine the behavioral response.

Learning in Physical Education

Learning in physical education involves physical movement that provides unique educational experiences. In general, learning in physical education can be defined as a relatively permanent change in behavior resulting from experience of physical movement coupled with cognitive understanding of the movement (Rink, 2001). This movement-based learning is the primary goal of physical education in K-12 schools (National Association for Sport and Physical Education [NASPE], 2004).

Learning in physical education is multi-dimensional. For a student to become "physically educated," she/he should be able to "demonstrate competency in motor skills and movement patterns needed to perform a variety of physical activities (standard 1); demonstrate understanding of movement concepts, principles, strategies, and tactics as they apply to the learning and performance of physical activities (standard 2); participate regularly in physical activity (standard 3); achieve and maintain a health-enhancing level of physical fitness (stander 4); exhibit responsible personal and social behavior that respects self and others in physical activity settings (standard 5); value physical activity for health, enjoyment, challenge, self-expression, and/or social interaction (standard 6) " (NASPE, 2004; p. 11).

These goals signify that learning in physical education, a content area characterized by learning through physical movement, involves both physical and cognitive dimensions (Schmidt and Lee, 1998). As Jewett, Bain, and Ennis (1995) articulated, physical learning manifested in behavior change is inseparable from cognitive learning that can be documented in knowledge growth. Without cognitive understanding, behavior change alone should not be considered as learning in physical education (Griffin and Placek, 2001). In other words, learning in physical education can be thought to be an active and goal-oriented process of cognitive knowledge and physical skill construction that involves deep cognitive understanding of the knowledge and skills being constructed. This process is believed to lead to the desired behavior change in the learner (Rink 2001).

Because learning in physical education involves cognitive dimension, factors that influence cognitive involvement in the classroom-based learning process can also influence learning in physical education. Based on their series of studies, Lee and Solmon (1992) proposed a mediating processes paradigm specifying the function of learner thinking process in motor skill acquisition in physical education settings. They argued that learners' thinking in physical education is typically influenced by multiple motivational constructs (e.g., self perception of competence, self efficacy, interests). These motivational constructs help learners form a particular thinking pattern about the physical skills/movement to be learned, which leads to different ways to interpret the purpose of learning and thus mediates, and sometimes determines, their learning behavior and outcome.

INTEREST AS MOTIVATOR

Achieving the goal of learning necessary knowledge and skills in physical education for a healthful, physically active life relies on the extent to which learner motivation is enhanced during the learning process. Motivating learners is a challenge. For example, most adolescents choose not to take physical education during their high school years after they have met the minimal physical education credit requirement for graduation, usually a half or one credit in most high schools. It has been reported that enrollment in physical education in secondary schools decreased an average of 30% annually from 1988 to 1996 (National Center for Education Statistics [NCES], 1996) and only 19% of adolescents took physical education regularly beyond the graduation requirement to receive health benefits (CDC, 1996). If choice is considered an indicator of motivation, it is apparent that there is a motivation problem in student learning in physical education.

Although learners can be motivated by a number of motivators, interest has been considered a powerful motivator that drives the learner to pursue the outcome of knowing (Dewey, 1913; Hidi and Harackiewicz, 2000). Interest, often yielding pleasant emotional outcomes, is often considered to be associated with non-competence purposes in the learning process (Sansone and Smith, 2000). Development in educational research, however, has demonstrated that interests can directly enhance learning competence through enhancing learner cognitive functioning (e.g., increased attention, memory) during the learning process (see Hidi and Berndorff, 1998; Schiefele, 1998).

As a construct for research, interest has been re-conceptualized in a framework that consists of individual interest and situational interest. Individual interest refers to a person's psychological disposition in preference of an activity or an action. Situational interest is defined as the appealing effect of characteristics of an activity on individuals (Krapp et al., 1992). Both interests have been described as a person-environment (e.g., activity, events, ideas, objects) interactive construct (Hidi and Harackiewicz, 2000). Both are content specific and have both cognitive and affective components. In addition, it has been argued that interests are a key that underlies student motivation in all learning stages (Alexander et al., 1995).

Individual interest is evolved along with a person's knowledge repertoire and value system (Krapp et al., 1992). Therefore, individual interest is rooted in personal knowledge and values. The strong association between knowledge/value and individual interest tends to be very stable and difficult to change. Yet, because individuals vary in their knowledge and values, there are tremendous differences in individual interests. It is difficult for teachers to decide how much effort they should invest in using student individual interests to facilitate learning in a particular subject. To a certain extent, making such a decision itself is impossible when the teacher has little knowledge of how well students' individual interests match the content (Hidi and Anderson, 1992).

In contrast, situational interest is elicited by unique characteristics of an activity (e.g., puzzle problems in mathematics, Mitchell, 1993). The "catching" function of a situationally interesting task presents an appealing environment where the learner-activity interaction enables the learner to actively engage, expend effort, and persist in the activity. In a situationally interesting learning task, the learner is likely to achieve at a higher level (Mitchell, 1993). Educational researchers (Hidi and Berndorff, 1998; Renninger, Hidi, and Krapp, 1992) consider that situational interest possesses stronger motivation potential than individual interest in daily teaching-learning settings because teachers are able to enhance situational interest in learning tasks by manipulating components in learning tasks (Chen and Darst, 2001; Mitchell, 1993).

SITUATIONAL INTEREST AND LEARNING IN PHYSICAL EDUCATION

The individual-situational interest framework has been used in achievement motivation research in physical education (Chen, 2001), especially in examining motivation effects of situational interest in learning. Chen, Darst, and Pangrazi (1999) used a multi-sample and multi-stage design ($n = 674$, sampled independently in each of the four stages) to examine the multi-dimensionality of situational interest in physical education. In the study, middle school learners were asked to view jogging and gymnastic stunts on video (in Stage 1, 2, and 3) and participate in basketball chest-pass and pass-shoot activities (in Stage 4). Immediately following each activity, situational interest of the activity was assessed by having the students respond to an instrument. Exploratory and confirmatory factor analyses revealed five dimensions of situational interest: novelty, challenge, exploration opportunity, instant enjoyment, and attention demand. The researchers postulated that these dimensions represent features of physical activity tasks that may bring about situational interest.

In a later study (Chen and Darst, 2001) examine the role of cognitive and physical demands in physical activity tasks in situational interest. In the study, several physical activity tasks were designed with cognitive and physical demands manipulated for middle school students ($n = 242$) to experience and evaluate situational interest. Cognitive and physical demands in these tasks were validated by seven experienced physical education teachers. Results from a repeated-measure MANOVA, with individual interest and skill ability controlled, showed that the students rated the two tasks with high cognitive demand significantly higher ($p < .01$) in situational interest than those with low cognitive demand. In addition, ratings for all five task features (dimensions) were significantly higher ($p < .01$) for the two high cognitive demand tasks than for those with a low cognitive demand. The results show that situational interest is a function of learning task design in physical education. A pattern seems to be clear that cognitive demand of a learning task plays a critical role in generating situational interest.

Although these and other studies (Chen, 1996; Chen and Darst, 2002; Chen, Darst, and Pangrazi, 2001) have revealed promising motivational function of situational interest, the direct effect of situational interest on learning has remained unknown. Little empirical evidence is available to document the connection between situational interest and physical education learners' behavior and learning outcome. Logically, pedagogical significance of research on motivation constructs lies in observable evidence that demonstrates the effects of the motivators on the improvement of learning behavior and outcome.

Based on the aforementioned definition of learning in physical education, learning outcomes in physical education can be operationalized in two basic forms. One is the acquisition of knowledge and skill. This tangible product outcome is usually measured using achievement tests of motor skills and knowledge. The other is learner in-class movement during the learning process, which can be documented using frequency of movement or physiological intensity. This observable behavioral process outcome also indicates the extent to which the learner receives health benefits from the physical movement he/she is engaging in. The process outcome (in-class behavior) is equally important as the product outcome given the fact that physical education classes might be the only place and time for many learners, especially young children, to receive health benefits of physical activity (Corbin, 2002). The process outcome is usually measured in heart rate, number of steps, and/or consumed calories using various recording devices.

Chen and his colleagues have conducted several studies investigating the relationship between interests and the learning outcomes. Chen, Shen, Scrabis, and Tolley (2002) examined the relationship between situational interest and learning outcomes in a random sample of middle school students ($n = 104$) studying six physical activity units during 17 weeks. Situational interest was measured as the source of motivation. Individual interest was measured as a control variable for situational interest and acquired knowledge/skill. Physiological intensity was measured as the process outcome using Yamax Digiwalker® Step-recording devices and validated using a concurrent validation procedure with heart rate. Learning was measured using performance scores on summative skill and knowledge tests after each unit. Correlation analysis revealed that individual interest had a low, positive, and significant relationship with physiological intensity ($r = .35, p < .01$) and achievement ($r = .24, p < .01$), while situational interest had a highly positive correlation with physiological intensity ($r = .67, p < .01$). Follow-up regression and path analyses confirmed the relationship, suggesting a low predictability of individual interest for the two outcome measures and a relatively high predictability of situational interest for physiological intensity.

To replicate the above findings, Shen, Chen, Tolley, and Scrabis (2003) examined the relationship of individual interest, physical intensity, situational interest, and achievement outcome in a dance unit with a random sample of 60 middle school students. The results showed that girls had a higher individual interest in dance than the boys. The correlation between individual interest and achievement outcome were stronger for girls ($r = .62, p < .01$) than for boys ($r = .26, p > .05$). However, both boys and girls considered the lessons highly situationally interesting. The correlation between situational interest and physical intensity was similar between boys ($r = .69, p < .01$) and girls ($r = .73, p < .01$). The researchers did not find meaningful correlation between situational interest and achievement outcomes. The findings seem to imply that situational interest may overcome the effect of low individual interest in boys, indicating a universal effect of situational interest on motivation for all students.

The strong association between situational interest and process outcome implies that the motivation effect of situational interest is immediate and engaging, supporting Hidi and Harackiewicz (2000) argument that although short-lived, situational interest can attract the learner to the learning process effectively. In addition, the results may suggest motivation specificity of interests. While situational interest may effectively attract learners to the learning process, individual interest may assist in knowledge and skill acquisition.

The findings may have significant curricular implication. We now know that to enhance learner motivation to engage in the learning process, physical activity tasks should be situationally interesting. We also know that to design situationally interesting learning tasks, we need to emphasize cognitive demand when maintaining a high physical demand in physical activity tasks. Although situational interest can motivate students to actively engage in the learning process, resulting in high level physiological responses (health benefits), we do not know, however, that the engagement in the tasks will lead to a higher level of knowledge acquisition. In the current study, we used a controlled experimental design to examine the role of situational interest in learning health-related scientific knowledge in physical education. We hypothesized that situational interest should be an integral component of a physical education curriculum whose goal is to facilitate the learner to master health-related scientific knowledge as well as to engage them in a physically active learning process. We assumed for this study that the learners in elementary schools are at the acclimation / naïve learning stage and situational interest is their primary motivator to learn.

METHODOLOGY

The investigation reported here is part of a large, on-going physical education curriculum intervention study to field test a science-enriched elementary physical education curriculum, *Be Active Kids!*©, to increase students' knowledge and interest in health-related science. The study is being conducted in one of the largest multi-cultural metropolitan school districts in the United States and involves more than 6,000 third, fourth, and fifth grade students and their physical education teachers. A general pretest – intervention - post-test design is used to assess the effects of the curriculum in 15 experimental schools with matched 15 comparison schools. The current investigation examined the outcome of one of the three curriculum modules, "Dr. Love's Health Heart," a content unit focusing on scientific concepts and knowledge related to improving cardiovascular function through physical activity. In the space below we report research methods relevant for the current study.

A Brief Overview of the Curricula

The Experimental Curriculum

The *Be Active Kids!*© Curriculum consists of nine science-based physical education curriculum modules, three each for third, fourth, and fifth grade students. The modules for each grade include "Dr. Love's Healthy Heart," "Mickey's Mighty Muscles," and "Flex Cool Body" that teach students about cardiovascular system health, skeletal muscular system capacity, and exercise principles and programming, respectively. Each module consists of 10

30-minute lessons that emphasize processes of scientific inquiry. Throughout the lessons, emphasis is placed on unifying concepts and processes appropriate for an integrated or cross disciplinary application of science content in physical education. Instruction of the curriculum is centered on a constructivist approach that utilizes a 5-E scientific inquiry mechanism: engagement, exploration, explanation, elaboration and evaluation. In each lesson, students are actively engaged in moderate to vigorous physical activity tasks designed and sequenced in terms of the 5-Es to learn health-related scientific knowledge. The curriculum also provides opportunities in each lesson to engage students in highly cognitive learning process. Students experiment different activities, predict possible physiological or other outcomes, come to a conclusion about the activity, and document the outcome and conclusion in a workbook. The curriculum provides a high cognitive demand and physical demand context to enhance student learning.

The Comparison / Traditional Curriculum

The comparison curriculum is the one that the school board has approved for elementary school physical education. The curriculum is based on the national and state current learning standards for elementary school physical education. the content includes a variety of physical activities including sports, games, basic locomotor movement patterns, health-related fitness, and educational dance. The goal of the curriculum is to provide opportunities for elementary school students to experience many different forms of physical activities and movement and expose them to various sports and games as part of their social-cultural experiences. Instruction of the curriculum is determined by individual teachers. Some use direct teaching style, others use guided inquiry or problem-solving approaches. Student learning assessment is based on a variety of indicators including daily participation, skill tests, and written tests.

Research Design

Sampling and Participating Schools

Because knowledge about general science and social-economic background are likely to be associated with learning of health-related science content in physical education, participating schools were matched on the two variables to control for possible bias on the dependent measures due to unequal student scientific knowledge and social-economic background. All 140 elementary schools in the district were analyzed on their students' scores of Maryland state standardized science test and poverty levels. The schools were placed in 15 brackets differentiated using average science test scores for grades 3 and 5 (testing grades in the state standardized science test) and the percentage of students receiving free and reduced meals (FARM). Two schools matched on the two indicators were randomly selected from each bracket, with one school randomly assigned to the *Be Active Kids!*© curriculum and the other to the Comparison curriculum condition. The sampling procedure resulted in 15 schools in each curriculum condition. Thus, the school sample represented a range of performance and poverty levels in this large urban/suburban district (total elementary school enrollment = 72,492 students).

An initial analysis of school, teacher, and student demographics from school district data (2003-2004) indicated that the school enrollment ranged from 294 to 765 students. Seventeen of the 30 project schools (8 in *Be Active Kids!*© and 9 in Comparison) qualify for Title 1 status with from 57.2% to 82.29% of students receiving free and reduced lunches. Five additional schools had over 50% of their students receiving free and reduced lunches. Five schools in the *Be Active Kids!*© and four in the Comparison had gymnasiums; in the other schools physical education was taught in the multipurpose room, classrooms and outside on the blacktop, weather permitting. Instructional time allocated to physical education was 150 minutes every two weeks in 12 *Be Active Kids!*© and 14 Comparison schools, 120 min/ bi-weekly in one experiment school, and 90 min./bi-weekly in one *Be Active Kids!*© and one Comparison school. The participating schools provided a highly representative sample of the elementary schools in the district and the metropolitan area.

Participating Tteachers and Classes

Physical education teachers ($n = 30$) of the participating schools participated in the study. All the teachers were certified to teach physical education in K-12 schools. Their demographics indicated a diverse group with 8 white and 7 African-American teachers in both the *Be Active Kids!*© and Comparison curriculum. Twelve of the teachers in the *Be Active Kids!*© group were males and three were females, while 11 of the teachers in the comparison group were males and four were females.

A total of 83 classes were randomly selected for data collection. These classes represented approximately 7,000 elementary school students in third, fourth, and fifth grades. Although the teachers taught to all students in their classes, data used in the study were collected from students whose parent or guardian permitted their participation in the study. Parental / guardian permission was received before the data collection began.The lessons were randomly selected to provide data for this investigation. Demographic information indicated that the students in these lessons primarily consisted of minority children and both genders were equally represented.

Teacher Training.

As part of the curriculum intervention, teachers from both *Be Active Kids!*© and Comparison curriculum received a three-day instructional in-service training during the summer and two half-day in-service workshops during the semester. Those in the *Be Active Kids!*© condition received specific training on the goal of the curriculum, its unique 5-E based instructional approach, and learning assessment procedure. The teachers were also provided opportunities in the summer training session to teach the lessons and receive feedback from the researchers and fellow teachers. The teachers from the comparison group were provided in-service training in the same format and time allotment. But their training was focused on the comparison curriculum instead of the *Be Active Kids!*© curriculum. Throughout the study, teachers from both curriculum conditions received similar amount of visitation from the researchers and research assistants. Their questions and concerns were addressed in a swift and effective manner.

Variables, Measures, and Psychometric Properties

Student Learning

Learning was assessed using knowledge test. Students in both groups completed a grade-appropriate knowledge test of nine questions prior to and after the "Dr. Love's Healthy Heart" module. The questions were selected from a pool of more than 70 that were validated for use with the *Be Active Kids!*© curriculum. The content validity of the questions was determined by a group of expert physical educators and science educators ($n = 7$). During validation, they rated each question on a 5-point scale on its knowledge accuracy (1 = inaccurate, 5 = accurate) and language appropriateness (third grade literacy level; 1 = inappropriate, 5 = appropriate) for the grade the question was designed for. Questions with average ratings lower than 5 were revised until they received an average score of 5. The criterion-related validity was determined by computing the index of difficulty and index of discrimination for each question. The index of difficulty was computed using the following formula:

Difficulty Index = [(Tc + Cc) / (Tn + Cn)] x 100%

Where: Tc - correct responses from the experimental schools
Cc - correct responses from the comparison schools
Tn - total number of respondents from the experimental schools
Cc - total number of respondents from the comparison schools

The ideal index of difficulty for maximal criterion-related validity is 50%. Therefore, question with a difficulty index between 40%-45% and between 55%-60% were deemed "good" or "usable." Questions between 45% and 55% were determined "excellent" and "must-use." Questions out of these ranges were eliminated from the test bank.

The index of discrimination was computed using the following equation:

Discrimination Index = [(Tc + Cc) / Tn] x 100%

The ideal index of discrimination should be above 40%. Thus, questions between 40% - 60% were classified as "good" or "usable." Those above 60% were "excellent." A total of 27 knowledge assessment questions (9 for each grade) were used for knowledge test. They were all deemed as "good" or "excellent" for their respective grade level. Table 1 on next page provides sample questions used in the assessment.

Learning Process Outcome

Student process outcome was measured using RT3® accelerometer motion sensors. The accelerometer is capable of recording three dimensional human movement and converting the movement into energy consumption in calories. For this study, we used total and activity caloric expenditures and composite physical activity counts to represent learner physical movement process outcome. The total and activity caloric expenditures were measured in age-adjusted metabolic equivalent (MET) unit. One MET represents the average, seated, resting energy cost of an adult and is set at 3.5 mL/kg^{-1}/min. of oxygen, or 1 kcal/kg^{-1}/hr^{-1} (Plowman and Smith, 1997). Physical activity counts are recorded in three-dimensions in an accelerometer and the combined amount of physical activity is represented in vector magnitude (VM) activity counts (Welk, 2002). In other words, VM represents the activity amount aggregated from all three dimensions. The accelerometer is about the size of a small pager. Each must be programmed for the specific user from whom the data are recorded. Demographic information used for programming the device includes gender, age, height, and weight. The information must be entered into the device during the programming prior to data collection to allow the device to adjust the recordings based on the demographic information of the user.

Table 1. Sample Questions in the Knowledge Test

3th Grade Question	If you want your heart to beat faster, you should increase your
Answer Choices	*Frequency intensity muscle strength*
4th Grade Question	After exercising, you can bring your heart rate back to its pre-activity level by
Answer Choices	*playing soccer jumping rope walking slowly*
5th Grade Question	I breathe harder during exercise because my body needs more
Answer Choices	*blood food oxygen*

Situational Interest

The Situational Interest Scale (Chen et al, 1999) was originally developed for middle school physical education students. It was revised for this study. The number of items was reduced from 24 to 18 and measurement scale was rescaled to a 4-point verbatim descriptor scale instead of the original 5-point (not at all true – very true) scale. The verbatim descriptors were validated for content consistency and language appropriateness with the same group of expert teachers using the same procedure and criteria. Revisions were made according to the results of the content validation. After the content validation, the revised scale was piloted with a sample of third grade non-participant students ($n = 64$) to further examine the appropriateness for reading levels. The students were instructed to indicate words and expressions that they did not understand, rather than rating the scale. Their feedback was incorporated in the final revision of the scale. Finally, with a confirmatory factor analytical approach, the construct validity of the scale was determined to be consistent with its original theoretical structure (Sun, Chen, Ennis, Martin, and Shen, 2005). Loadings for the five dimensions of situational interest, novelty, challenge, attention demand, exploration, and instant enjoyment, ranged from .78 to .99 and various model-data fit indices indicated an excellent fit (Sun et al., 2005). Sample items of the scale can be found in Table 2.

Data Collection

Learning

Validated knowledge tests were administered to the students prior to and after the curriculum intervention as part of instruction. The tests were designed using a computerized format for scanning. In responding to each question, students were instructed to blacken the small box associated with the answer they thought to be correct. They were instructed to work independently and honestly.

Table 2. Sample items from Knowledge Test and Situational Interest Scale

Source	Item and Scale
Novelty	My PE classes in the past two weeks are
	Very unique (4) Somewhat unique (3) Rather common (2) Very common (1)
Challenge	The thinking we did in my PE classes is
	Very complex (4) Somewhat complex (3) Rather simple (2) Very simple (1)
Attention Demand	My PE classes in the past two weeks make me
	Very attentive (4) Somewhat attentive (3) Little attentive (2) Not attentive at all (1)
Exploration Intention	I do experiments in my PE classes
	Almost everyday (4) On most days (3) A few days (2) Not once (1)
Instant Enjoyment	My PE classes in the past two weeks are
	Very exciting (4) Somewhat exciting (3) Rather dull (2) Very dull (1)
Total Interest	My PE classes are
	Very fun (4) Somewhat fun (3) Rather boring (2) Very boring (1)

The participating teachers administered the tests to their students. The testing procedure followed a well-paced protocol that was developed according to students' age and their reading levels. The protocol was piloted with a small group of students who were not participants of the study prior to the study and a formal procedure was developed to minimize factors affecting reliability of the data. The teachers received training on the protocol and practiced it during their in-service training for the study. During the tests they first instructed students to print their names, classes, and other necessary identification information. Afterwards, they read aloud the questions and answer choices one by one to the students to help them focus on the question. The teachers also answered students' questions for clarification purposes. In general the knowledge testing took about 30 minutes to complete.

Learning Process Outcome

Accelerometer data were collected from 83 30-minute physical education lessons randomly selected from *Be Active Kids!*© ($n = 42$) and Comparison ($n = 41$) curriculum conditions. From each lesson, three boys and three girls with various body sizes were selected as the representatives of the class to wear the accelerometers. Prior to data collection, the researchers measured the selected students' body height and body weight and programmed the accelerometer for each individual student. Data collection was conducted in lessons between pre-test and post-test. The researchers randomly selected lessons and went to the lessons unannounced to the teachers. Data from the *Be Active Kids!*© and Comparison schools were collected in parallel, almost simultaneously fashion to control for weather and other environmentally or administratively induced influences on the lessons in both curriculum conditions (e.g., district - wide cancellation of physical education classes due to state standardized tests for school accountability). That is, the researchers collected the data from matched *Be Active Kids!*©and Comparison schools during almost the same time of the day (morning or afternoon), on the same day or immediate alternate days next to each other.

The researchers were responsible for putting on and taking off the accelerometers. The process of attaching or detaching the device took about less than two minutes. Therefore, the students' participation in class activities was unlikely to be affected. Recorded caloric consumption data (in MET) and physical activity counts (in VM counts) were downloaded into laptop computers immediately after the lesson was over by the researchers on site. Real time was recorded in the device and downloaded to preserve lesson length integrity of the data.

Situational Interest

The Situational Interest Scale was administered to students in classrooms by trained teachers. The teachers read aloud each items and its choice descriptors to the students. They also repeatedly reminded students there were no right or wrong answers or choices and their responses to the items would in no way affect their grades in physical education and in any other school subjects. When asked, the teachers explained the meaning of the descriptors to the students, but did not advise students which one to choose. Students were allowed to change their minds during the process and advised to do so to ensure that their responses truly reflected their perception of interest of the content. During the process, the teachers repeatedly reminded the students to frame their responses based on the physical education they experienced in the past two weeks to ensure students' responses reflecting their thoughts about the curriculum they recently experienced. In addition, the teachers instructed students to complete the scale independently. The teachers made it very clear to students that talking or discussing was prohibited during the process.

Data Reducation and Analysis

Unit of Analysis and Data Reduction

Because the curriculum treatment was conducted at the teacher level, therefore students received the treatment in their intact classes. It is likely, in this research context, that students' individual responses are likely to be contaminated by their inevitable interaction with other students and the teacher, intra-correlation (auto correlation) among individual responses is likely to occur within the responses from a class. When inference statistical analysis is conducted on the data, a greater Type I error will be concealed because of using the elevated sample size (and the degree of freedom) from the individual level instead of that from the number of classes. Thus, the trustworthiness of the results will be jeopardized because of the interaction within a class (Scariano and Davenport, 1987; Silverman, and Solmon, 1998). To prevent erroneous results and subsequent erroneous interpretation of the data, we reduced all data at class level and used class means in data analysis.

Knowledge gain scores were generated using regression residual gain approach where students' pre-test scores were regressed on their post-test scores. Standardized residual gain scores were then generated for each student to represent his/her knowledge gain from the pre-test to the post-test to control for potential ceiling effect of the test on knowledge gain (Borg and Gall, 1989). The aggregated average knowledge gain scores of the participants in a class were used to represent their class in data analysis

We chose to use the vector magnitude activity counts (VM counts) rather than total calorie and activity calorie consumption (METs) to represent learning process outcome. The decision was based on (a) a moderately high correlation between VM counts and total calorie and activity calorie consumption, $r = .56$ and $.59$, respectively and (b) compared with calorie consumptions, VM is a direct measure of physical movement resulting directly from students' participation in learning tasks. Calorie consumptions, although accurate and valid, can be an indicator reflecting other physiological influences on the body not necessarily resulting directly from the participation, such as students' original lung capacity and oxygenating efficiency. Thus, using VM would allow a straightforward interpretation of the relationship between the variables we were examining.

In data reduction, each student's total VM counts during the 30 minute lesson were divided by 30 to provide his/her average VM counts by minute. The six individual students' average VM counts/per minute were then summed and divided by six. The aggregated average VM counts/per minute were then used to represent the VM counts/per minute for the entire class (approximately 25-30 students) in the subsequent analysis. Similarly, individual students' responses to the Situational Interest Scale were averaged and aggregated at the class level by the five dimensional sources (Novelty, Challenge, Attention Demand, Exploration Intention, and Instant Enjoyment) and total interest.

Data Analysis

Knowledge gain comparison between the *Be Active Kids!*© and Comparison curriculum condition were conducted using independent *t*-test. The analysis was performed separately for the 3rd, 4th, and 5th grades. Because the curricular experiences in one grade level was independent from that in another, the independent observation assumption for the *t*-test was not violated. Therefore the Bonferroni technique was not needed to adjust the *t*-test results. The *t*-test was also used in analyzing the means of VM counts from the two curriculum conditions. Between-curriculum comparison on situational interest and its dimensional source measures was performed using MANOVA because high correlations were found previously among the variables (Chen et al., 2001). Correlation analysis and two separate multiple regression analyses were conducted to determine the predictive function of situational interest and its dimensional sources on student knowledge gain and learning process outcome. In the analyses, knowledge gain scores and VM counts were used as the dependent variables and situational interest and its dimensional sources as predictors. In all analyses, statistical assumptions were tested. Appropriate approaches were adopted to adjust the results whenever a violation of assumptions was determined.

RESULTS

Curriculum Effect

Figure 1 and 2 describe knowledge gain and VM counts between the two curriculum conditions. Table 3 reports the results of independent *t*-test on the mean differences of knowledge gain and VM counts. The results showed that students in all grades in the *Be Active Kids!*© curriculum condition outperformed their counterparts in the Comparison condition in knowledge gain. In VM counts, there were no statistically significant differences between the two curriculum conditions.

☒ Target ☐ Comparison

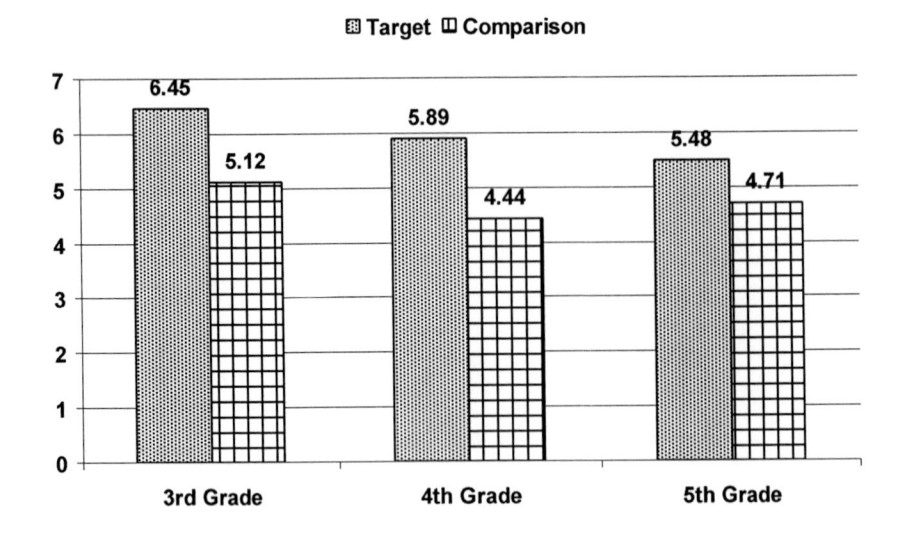

[Bar chart showing knowledge gain scores:
- 3rd Grade: Target 6.45, Comparison 5.12
- 4th Grade: Target 5.89, Comparison 4.44
- 5th Grade: Target 5.48, Comparison 4.71]

Figure 1. Knowledge Gain Scores between Curriculum Conditions by Grades

☒ Target ☐ Comparison

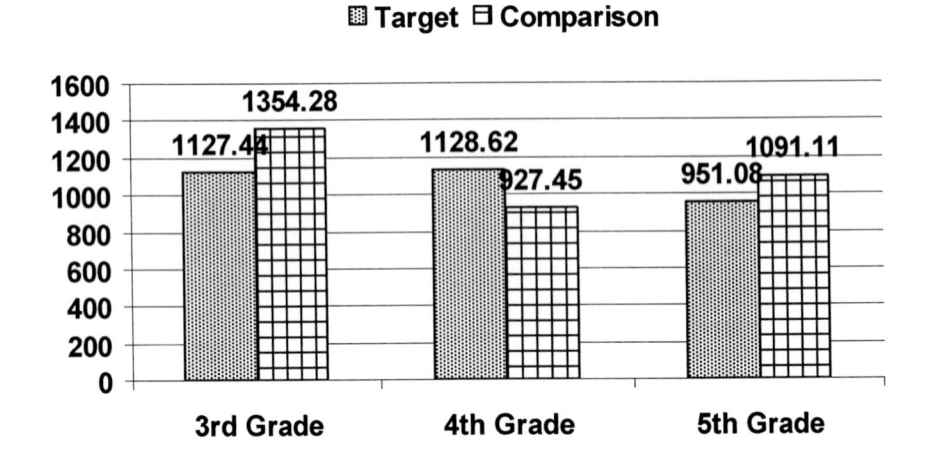

[Bar chart showing VM counts:
- 3rd Grade: Target 1127.44, Comparison 1354.28
- 4th Grade: Target 1128.62, Comparison 927.45
- 5th Grade: Target 951.08, Comparison 1091.11]

Figure 2. VM Counts between Curriculum Conditions by Grades

Figure 3 depicts the differences in situational interest and its dimensions between the two curriculum conditions. Because the focus of the study is on the comparison of curriculum effect on the variables, rather than examining grade or age impact, to simplify the comparison, grade was not used as a block variable in the analysis of situational interest and its dimensional sources. MANOVA revealed that there was a statistically significant difference between the two curriculum groups. A follow-up univariate analysis showed that the differences lay in the dimensions of Attention Demand ($F_{df=1}$ = 5.18, p = .025) and Exploration Intention ($F_{df=1}$ = 22.85, p = .001) between the *Be Active Kids!*© (M = 5.10, SD = 1.75; M = 6.48, SD = 2.20) and Comparison (M = 4.49, SD = 1.24; M = 5.19, SD = 1.33) conditions, respectively.

Table 3. Independent t-test Results for Knowledge Gain and VM Counts

	Levene's Equal Variance Test (F/p)	t Value	df	p^a
Knowledge Gain				
3rd Grade	1.78 / .19	11.04	24.00	.001
4th Grade	.20 / .66	11.09	27.00	.001
5th Grade	8.56 / .01	9.27[b]	14.08	.001
VM Counts				
3rd Grade	2.73 / .11	-.90	24.00	.13
4th Grade	.15 / .70	2.03	27.00	.15
5th Grade	.23 / .64	-1.37	26.00	.31

a Two-tailed
b Adjusted for violation of equal variance assumption

▧ Target ⊞ Comparison

	Attention	Challenge	Novelty	Exploration	Enjoyment	Interest
Target	4.84	6.74	6.55	6.76	4.84	4.77
Comparison	4.32	7.09	5.39	5.19	4.58	4.76

Figure 3. Situational Interest and Dimensional Sources between Curriculum Conditions

Prediction Function of Situational Interest

As reported in Table 4, meaningful correlation coefficients were found between knowledge gain and situational interest and its dimensional sources for the *Be Active Kids!*© curriculum condition, while none was meaningful for the Comparison curriculum. In the multiple regression analyses, both curriculum conditions were dummy - coded and used as a predictor (*Be Active Kids!*© coded 1 and Comparison 2). The codes were entered into the multiple regression analyses along with situational interest and its dimensional sources in a step-wise procedure.

Table 4. Correlation Coefficients of Situational Interest and Sources with Knowledge Gain by Target and Comparison Groups

	Attention	Challenge	Exploration	Enjoyment	Novelty	Total Interest
Target	.35**	.28*	.29*	.56**	.60**	.83**
Comparison	-.08	-.12	-.10	.11	.12	.14

* $p < .05$; ** $p < .01$

Multiple regression analyses yielded two distinctive equations with knowledge gain and VM to be separate dependent variables and situational interest, its dimensional sources, and the curriculum condition to be the predictors. Results reported in Table 5 show that knowledge gain requires both content specificity ($\beta = -.24$ weighing toward the *Be Active Kids!*© curriculum) and motivators associated with the content domain (situational interest and its dimensional sources in physical education) to predict. In contrast, VM counts can be predicted by a sole motivator, the Instant Enjoyment dimension. The results seem to suggest that students can increase their physical activity levels during physical education as long as the classes provide them with enjoyable experiences. *Learning* health-related scientific knowledge in physical education, however, requires more than simply providing an enjoyable environment. Providing an enjoyable and interesting experience situated within the realm of a viable curriculum seems to be crucial for learning to occur.

Table 5. Regression Analyses Results

Dependent Variable	Valid Predictor	R^2	R^2 change	β
Knowledge Gain				
	Curriculum	.28	.28	-.24
	Interest	.44	.16	.40
	Challenge	.50	.06	-.16
	Attention	.52	.02	.19
	Enjoyment	.55	.03	.23
VM Counts				
	Enjoyment	.37		.37

DISCUSSION

The primary purpose of this study was to examine the extent to which situational interest, as a motivator, predicted for student learning in the knowledge domain of health-science-based physical education in elementary schools. We specifically were interested in investigating the role of situational interest in knowledge acquisition and the extent to which this role functioned in a new, health-science centered curriculum and the traditional curriculum. To accomplish the purposes we used a randomized, controlled experimental design and carefully collected and analyzed the data. The findings suggest that optimal learning occurs when motivators (situational interest in this case) function with the presence of a well crafted curriculum. Without a well designed curriculum, situational interest, with its multi-dimensional sources, can only contribute to engaging students in the activities that may not enhance knowledge acquisition.

Situational Interest as a Curriculum Component

Motivation has been conceptualized from a dispositional perspective in that it is considered a force, drive, or desire within a person. In educational research, motivation is often studied independent from the content characteristics, thus, is rarely taken into account in curriculum inquiry (Burke, 1995). For instance, several motivation constructs have been studied in such a manner, self-efficacy (Badura, 1977), achievement goal orientations (Nicholls, 1984), and self concept (Harter, 1981). Two constructs, however, are conceptualized in attempt to bridge the gap between motivation and content. One is the construct of expectancy beliefs - task values (Eccles, 1983) in which learner motivation is viewed as a function of learners' perceived success in relation to a particular learning task and the potential value of the task in their lives. Learners learn better when they see the relevance of successfully mastering the content to their lives either within or outside of the school.

The second motivation construct is interest, particularly situational interest. Conceptualized as the appealing effect of an activity or a learning task, situational interest comes to be only when the learner is interacting with the task from which prolonged attention, heightened inquiry intention, and intensified excitement or enjoyment result (Hidi, 1990; Iran-Nejad, 1987). Situational interest, as a motivator, has been considered particularly useful for educators. Because it is environmentally induced, educators can consciously design learning tasks that generate certain conditions or contextual stimuli to bring on learners' positive affective reactions to the learning process and the task (Hidi and Berndorff, 1998). When an individual does not have pre-existing individual interest, often in the case of learning in academics, situational interest becomes particularly useful because it is controllable by the teacher. Hidi and Harackiewicz (2000) argue that situational interest is an important motivator for all learners, especially for those academically unmotivated.

Individual interest, defined as an individual's personal preference for an activity, is based the individual's existing knowledge about the activity and values he/she perceive the activity has (Renninger, 2000). Research studies have consistently demonstrated that both children and adults with high individual interest in an activity will pay closer attention, persist for longer period of time, learn more, and enjoy more when engaging in the activity than those who do not have a high individual interest in it (Ainley, 1998; Renninger and Wozniak, 1985; Schiefele, 1996).

Although both types of interest have been found to have positive impact on learning and achievement repeatedly (Hoffmann, Krapp, Renninger, and Baumert, 1998), their roles in the learning process are very different. Based on Alexander and her colleagues' work (1995, in press), we developed a hypothetical model to help visualize the interactive relationship between content, knowledge acquisition, and interest. As can be seen in Figure 4, the role of situational interest and individual interest changes with learner's knowledge growth from the acclimation learning stage to the competence and, ultimately, to the proficiency learning stage. It is clear in the hypothetical model that the content/curriculum and interest must work together to provide the most optimal learning experiences to enhance knowledge acquisition.

Our data (Figure 3) showed that students in both *Be Active Kids!*© and Comparison curriculum responded similarly in terms of situational interest in their physical education lessons in most dimensions but two. But the students in the *Be Active Kids!*© curriculum apparently gained more health-related knowledge about physical activity than those in the Comparison curriculum condition (see Figure 1 and Table 3). In addition, students' physical activity levels in both curriculum conditions did not differ with statistical significance, indicating that all students were active at a similar level (see Figure 2 and Table 3). Taken these data together, we can conclude that the role of curriculum or the content is crucial in determining students' knowledge acquisition in physical education. Without learnable content, students in physical education might still be able to enjoy themselves or the activity they are provided with and be physically active to receive health benefits. They will not, however, be able to acquire crucial knowledge about physical activity. Without a learning orientation, a physical education class will become a "happy, busy, good" experience (Placek, 1983) that might differ little from an organized playground experience.

Although situational interest and most of its dimensional sources did not differ between the two curriculum conditions, students did respond differently with statistical significance in terms of their perceptions of novelty and exploration opportunities the curricula provided (see Figure 3). Students in the *Be Active Kids!*© curriculum were more likely to think their curriculum provided novel learning experiences and exploration opportunities than their counterparts in the Comparison curriculum. This result seems to suggest that the constructivist approach to curriculum and instruction the *Be Active Kids!*© curriculum has endorsed has provided students with relatively new learning materials and experiences and encouraged students' autonomous and active role in learning the content. The potential role of novelty was highlighted in its correlation with knowledge gain in the *Be Active Kids!*© curriculum condition (see Table 4). While no definitive relationship can be determined through a simple, bivariate correlation coefficient, the preliminary result certainly warrants strong empirical attention and should be further studied in the future.

The differences found in knowledge gain, novelty, and exploration intention dimension lend a support to the Model of Domain Learning. Students in the study were assumed to be at the acclimation learning stage where they were more likely to be motivated by situational motivators, such as situational interest. The integrated impact of situational interest, a strong learning oriented curriculum, and the utilization of a constructivist instructional approach has resulted greater knowledge gain for students in the *Be Active Kids!*© curriculum than those in the Comparison curriculum. Situational interest, as an important motivator, is an integral component in the learning process. Some of its dimensional sources, such as novelty and exploration intention, may make significant contribution along with the curriculum to students' knowledge gain.

Predictors of Learning Outcomes

It can be assumed that students in elementary schools are acclimation learners. As depicted in Figure 4, they are most likely to have little content knowledge and inaccurate self concept in physical and cognitive dimensions. They are most likely to be motivated by situational factors, especially situational interest; and their learning process outcome (e.g., participation behavior in class) may not change much. Previous research (Chen et al. 2002; Shen et al., 2003) has provided preliminary evidence suggesting that the role of situational interest in physical education lies in its contribution to enhanced student in-class physical activity level. In other words, situational interest leads to enhanced students' engagement in class activities. Little evidence, however, is available to suggest its contribution to (or predictability for) knowledge acquisition (Chen et al., 2002; Shen et al., 2003).

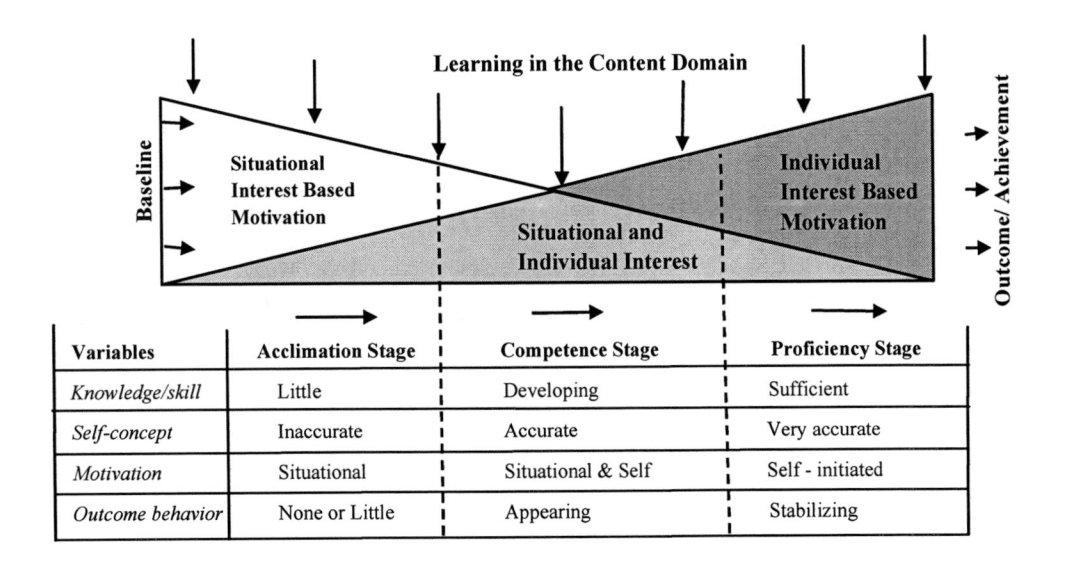

Variables	Acclimation Stage	Competence Stage	Proficiency Stage
Knowledge/skill	Little	Developing	Sufficient
Self-concept	Inaccurate	Accurate	Very accurate
Motivation	Situational	Situational & Self	Self - initiated
Outcome behavior	None or Little	Appearing	Stabilizing

Figure 4. The Model of Domain Learning

It was hypothesized for this study, based on theorizing the Model of Domain Learning, that if situational interest can raise students' attention, encourage active participation in learning, and provide instant, positive affective experiences to the learner, it should be a direct contributor to (or predictor for) knowledge gain. The multiple regression analyses were employed to examine this hypothesis. The results not only support the hypothesis, but also clarify the role of situational interest in both a strong learning oriented physical education curriculum and a traditional activity based curriculum.

The regression results in Table 5 clearly show that knowledge acquisition takes more than "fun" – often used in physical education as a synonym for situational interest. The curriculum factor accounts for 28% variance in students knowledge gain. The negative β coefficient suggests that the curriculum effect came from the *Be Active Kids!*© condition (coded 1) rather than the Comparison (coded 2). Situational interest and selected dimensional sources together account for the other 27% variance. This result on knowledge gain clearly indicates that the curriculum and situational interest are equally important to students' knowledge gain in physical education. It is worth pointing out that although Challenge, perceived level of difficulty, accounts for 6% variance, its negative β coefficient suggests that highly challenging or difficult tasks may not contribute much to knowledge gain.

The regression results have painted a much simpler picture for process outcome, in-class physical activity. Measured in physical activity counts, the process outcome may indicate how much health benefits students receive in a physical education lesson. The regression analyses identified a sole predictor, Instant Enjoyment, which accounts for 37% of variance of in-class physical activity. Thus, it can be concluded that adequate in-class physical activity can be achieved in both concept-based (*Be Active Kids!*©) and activity-based (Comparison) physical education.

Goodlad (1984) reported, based on a national data set, that physical education is the most likeable subject matter among K-12 students. They are more likely to report highest enjoyment in physical education than in any other subject matter. However, the students also consider physical education to be the least valued content area where little valuable knowledge is imparted to enhance their general learning experiences and contribute to their personal lives. It can be commonly observed that most physical education curricula are based on a collection of physical activities, mostly various sports, rather than a set of scientific concepts and principles that govern human physical movement for optimal performance and healthful living.

The regression results seem to suggest that, indeed, as long as physical education provides enjoyable experiences to students, they will be able to actively participate in physical activities planned by the teachers; even though these activities may not enhance their understanding of physical movement and health benefits of physical activity. To enhance students' knowledge about physical activity, the enjoyable and situationally interesting experiences must be incorporated in a strong learning oriented curriculum that provides viable knowledge intended to enhance students' cognitive understanding.

Implication for Constructivist Approach to Physical Education

The randomized, controlled experimental curriculum study clearly demonstrates the advantage of a constructivist approach to physical education curriculum. Researchers in physical education (e.g., Ennis et al., 1999; Kirk and Macdonald, 1998) have examined practical applications of constructivist learning theories in an effort to enhance the meaning and relevance of content to physical education students. Constructivist psychologists (Lave and Wenger, 1991; Vygotsky, 1978) have long suggested that students learn more deeply and remember the content materials longer when they learn through a series of active, hands-on experiences in which they apply existing knowledge and skills and seek new knowledge and skills to solve meaningful problems. Through this process, old knowledge and skills are consolidated and new knowledge and skills are acquired and meaningfully connected to and synchronized with existing knowledge and skills.

The the *Be Active Kids!*© curriculum was developed within the framework of the constructivism. At the curricular level, the curriculum provides a well defined scope with health-related knowledge components validated by kinesiological scientists. It is sequenced with a spiral curricular organization that allows important concepts and principles be learned and reviewed many times within and across grade levels. At the instructional level, the five-E approach provides students with numerous hands-on experiences to engage in both cognitive tasks and physical movement. Cognitively, students are expected to *predict* their physiological responses to certain types of exercise or physical activity, *hypothesize* what might happen as a result of physical activity, document and *calculate* information gathered during physical activity, and finally *evaluate* the information to reach conclusions that may or may not support their hypotheses. Physically, moving in the gymnasium is no long for moving's sake or "fun" only. Through physical movement, students *experiment* various physical activity patterns (e.g., aerobic vs. anaerobic), *generate* data needed for hypothesis examination (e.g., heart rate, breathing frequency, number of games played), and *verify* information gathered for evaluation. In this learning environment, both cognitive and physical tasks provide unique learning experiences to help students accomplish a goal that is to effectively construct scientific knowledge about physical activity and its health benefits to human body.

Consistent with the Model of Domain Learning (Figure 4), the constructivist approach facilitates student learning by providing situationally interesting tasks or problems that invite students to put forth their intellectual and physical effort. In this learning context students are most likely to construct their understanding of subject matter and their interests simultaneously (Newburg and Sims, 1996). With knowledge and individual interest growth, they will become competent learners who are motivated by both situational and individual interests and become active knowledge/information seekers (Alexander et al., 1995). They learn to value the knowledge learned, not because they are told that it is good for them but because they have understood the meaningfulness of the knowledge in a way that is immediately relevant in their current lives (Stinson, 1993; Sylvester, 1994).

It can be commonly observed that a curriculum can emphasize two types of goals. Competence-based goals focus on helping the learner acquire knowledge and skills of the content and develop their competence in the knowledge domain. Non-competence goals, however, aim at providing positive affective experiences to students for them to relate the learning process with positive affects. In a physical education curriculum, competence-based learning goals are often coupled and implemented with a strong influence of non-competence goals such as having fun and enjoyment during learning. This combination creates a particular complicated instructional climate in physical education where students are likely to engage in class activities not for knowledge acquisition and competence development, but for enjoyment.

The findings from this study have clearly demonstrated that the *Be Active Kids!*© curriculum with well balanced emphasis on both competence (knowledge acquisition) and non-competence (situationally interesting) goals leads students to greater knowledge acquisition than the traditional curriculum that has clear non-competence goals but ambiguous competence goals for knowledge acquisition. It can be speculated that, at times, non-competence goals can have strong overriding effect over competence-based goals. In such a curriculum context, students can have enjoyable experiences and positive emotions about physical education, but learn very little. The misconception of the value of physical education, as Goodlad (1984) observed, may result from this curriculum context where non-competence goals dominate the learning experience. The competence-based goals of physical education are overlooked or misunderstood by both students and teachers.

CONCLUSION

This randomized, controlled curriculum experiment research was designed to examine the predictability of situational interest for students' knowledge acquisition in the domain of health-science-based elementary school physical education. Specific research questions included (a) comparing differences in knowledge acquisition and situational interest between the *Be Active Kids!*© curriculum and the traditional curriculum and (b) examining predictability of situational interest for scientific knowledge acquisition in physical education. The Model of Domain Learning was used to guide the study and interpret the findings. The results have revealed that knowledge gain relies on a learning environment where both knowledge acquisition and positive affective experiences are well balanced. In this study, the *Be Active Kids!*© curriculum has provided profound knowledge for students to learn *and* created a situationally interesting environment that has been always appreciated by K-12 physical education students (Goodlad, 1984). In short, the curriculum is crucial in that it determines the knowledge components to be learned and specifies clearly defined learning objectives to achieve. Situational interest, along with its dimensional sources, serves as the primary motivator that keeps students' fondness of physical education, which motivates them to remain actively engaged in the learning tasks.

The findings indicate that learning in physical education takes more than "fun." For students to effectively learn health-related scientific knowledge about physical activity, educators should provide, first and foremost, a meaningful curriculum with the constructivist approach to instruction to facilitate effective knowledge acquisition. Cognitive intensity is equally, if not more, important as physical intensity in a learning oriented physical education curriculum. The students in both curriculum conditions spent similar physical effort during their physical education classes. But those in the *Be Active Kids!*© curriculum, which is cognitive-intensive, acquired more knowledge than their counterparts in the Comparison curriculum. Situational interest, which could be labeled "Fun" in most physical education classes, apparently is a necessary but not sufficient motivator for knowledge acquisition. For situational interest to function as an effective motivator for learning, it must be an integral component of an effective curriculum. Thus, situational interest should be taken into account when designing learning tasks to enhance students' knowledge acquisition in physical education.

REFERENCES

Ainley, M. D. (1998). Interest in learning in the disposition of curiosity in secondary students: Investigating process and context. In L. Hoffmann, A. Krapp, K. Renninger, and J. Baumert (Eds.), *Interest and Learning* (p. 257-266). Keil, Germany: Institute for Science Education at the University of Kiel.

Alexander, P. A. (in press). *Psychology in learning and teaching.* Columbus, OH: Prentice-Hall.

Alexander, P. A., Jetton, T. L., and Kulikowich, J. M. (1995). Interrelationship of knowledge, interest, and recall: Assessing a model of domain learning. *Journal of Educational Psychology, 87*, 559-575.

Arnold, P. J. (1979). *Meaning in movement: Sport and Physical education*. London: Heinemann.

Bandura, A. (1977). Self-efficacy: Toward a unifying theory of behavior change. *Psychological Review, 84*, 191-215.

Borg, W. R., and Gall, M. D. (1989). *Educational Research* (5th ed.). White Plains: NY: Longman.

Bruner, J. S. (1957). Going beyond the information given. In J. S. Bruner, E. Brunswik, L. Festinger, F. Heider, K. Muenzinger, C. Osgood, and D. Rapaport, *Contemporary approaches to cognition* (pp. 41-69). Cambridge, MA: Harvard University Press.

Burke, D. J. (1995). Connecting content and motivation: Education's missing link. *Peabody Journal of Education, 70*, 66-81.

Chen, A. (1996). Student interest in activities in a secondary physical education curriculum: An analysis of student subjectivity. *Research Quarterly for Exercise and Sport, 67*, 424-432.

Chen, A., and Darst, P. W. (2001). Situational interest in physical education: A function of learning task design. *Research Quarterly for Exercise and Sport, 72*, 150-164.

Chen, A., and Darst, P. W. (2002). Individual and situational interest: The role of gender and skill. *Contemporary Educational Psychology, 27*, 250-269.

Chen, A., Darst, P. W., and Pangrazi, R. P. (1999). What constitutes situational interest? Validating a construct in physical education. *Measurement in Physical Education and Exercise Science, 3*, 157-180.

Chen, A., Darst, P. W., and Pangrazi, R. P. (2001). An examination of situational interest and its sources in physical education. *British Journal of Educational Psychology, 71*, 383-400.

Chen, A., Shen, B., Scrabis, K., and Tolley, C. (2002, April). *Achievement Goals, Interests, and Learning Outcomes: A Study on Motivated Learning in Physical Education*. Paper presented at Annual meeting of the American Educational Research Association, New Orleans, LA.

Corbin, C. B. (2002). Physical activity for everyone: What every physical educator should know about promoting lifelong physical activity. *Journal of Teaching in Physical Education, 21*, 128-144.

Eccles, J. (1983). Expectancies, values and academic behaviors. In J. T. Spence (Ed.), *Achievement and achievement motives: Psychological and sociological approaches* (pp. 75-146). San Francisco: W. H. Freeman.

Ennis, C.D., Solmon, M.A., Satina, B., Loftus, S.J., Mensch, J. and McCauley, M.T. (1999). Creating a sense of family in urban schools using the "Sport for Peace" curriculum. *Research Quarterly for Exercise and Sport, 70*, 273-285.

Farnham-Diggory, S. (1977). The cognitive point of view. In D. J. Treffinger, J. K. Davis, and R. E. Ripple (Eds.), *Handbook of teaching educational psychology*. New York: Academic Press.

Goodlad, J. I. (1984). *A place called school*. New York: McGraw-Hill.

Griffin, L. L., and Placek, J. H. (2001). The understanding and development of learners' domain-specific knowledge: Introduction. *Journal of Teaching in Physical Education, 20*, 299-300.

Harter, S. (1981). A new self-report scale of intrinsic versus extrinsic orientation in the classroom: Motivational and informational components. *Developmental Psychology, 17*, 300-312.

Hidi, S. (1990). Interest and its contribution as a mental resource for learning. *Review of Educational Research, 60,* 549-571.

Hidi, S., and Berndorff, D. (1998). Situational interest and learning. In L. Hoffmann, A. Krapp, K. A. Renninger, and J. Baumert (Eds.) *Interest and Learning* (p. 74-90). Keil, Germany: Institute for Science Education at the University of Kiel.

Hoffmann, L., Krapp, A., Renninger, K. A., and Baumert, J. (Eds.) (1998). *Interest and Learning.* Keil, Germany: Institute for Science Education at the University of Kiel.

Iran-Nejad, A. (1987). Cognitive and affective causes of interest and liking. *Journal of Educational Psychology, 7,* 120-130.

Kirk, D., and Macdonald, D. (1998). Situated learning in physical education. *Journal of Teaching in Physical Education, 17,* 376-387.

Krapp, A., Hidi, S., and Renninger, K. A. (1992). Interest, learning, and development. In K. A. Renninger, S. Hidi, and A. Krapp (Eds.), *The role of interest in learning and development* (pp. 1-26). Hillsdale, NJ: LEA.

Lave, J., and Wenger, E. (1991). *Situated learning: Legitimate peripheral participation.* New York: Cambridge University Press.

Mitchell, M. (1993). Situational interest: Its multifaceted structure in the secondary school mathematics classroom. *Journal of Educational Psychology, 85,* 424-436.

National Association for Sport and Physical Education [NASPE] (2004). *Moving into the future: National standards for physical education* (2nd ed.). Reston, VA: Author.

Newburg, N.A., and Sims, R.A. (1996) Contexts that promote success for inner-city students. *Urban Education, 31,* 149-176.

Nicholls, J. G. (1984). Achievement motivation: Conceptions of ability, subjective experience, task choice, and performance. *Psychological Review, 91,* 328-346.

Pintrich, P. R., and Schunk, D. H. (2002). *Motivation in education: Theory, research and applications* (2nd ed.). Englewood Cliffs, NJ: Prentice-Hall.

Placek, J. H. (1983). Conceptions of success in teaching: Busy, happy, good? In T. Templin and J. Olson (Eds.), *Teaching in physical education* (pp. 46-56). Champaign, IL: Human Kinetics.

Plowman, S. A., and Smith, D. L. (1997). *Exercise physiology for health, fitness, and performance.* Boston: Allyn and Bacon.

Renninger, K. A. (2000). Individual interest and its implications for understanding intrinsic motivation. In C. Sansone and J. M. Harackiewicz (Eds.), *Intrinsic and extrinsic motivation: The search for optimal motivation and performance* (pp. 373-404). San Diego, CA: Academic Press.

Renninger, K. A., and Wozniak, R. H. (1985). Effect of interest on attention shift, recognition, and recall in young children. *Developmental Psychology, 21,* 624-632.

Rink, J. E. (2001). Investigating the assumptions of pedagogy. *Journal of Teaching in Physical Education, 20,* 112-128.

Scariano, S., and Davenport, J. (1987). The effects of violations of independence assumptions in the one-way ANOVA. *The American Statistician, 41,* 123-129.

Schiefele, U. (1996). Topic interest, text representation, and quality of experience. *Contemporary Educational Psychology, 12,* 3-18.

Schiefele, U. (1998). Individual interest and learning: What we know and what we don't know. In L. Hoffmann, A. Krapp, K. A. Renninger, and J. Baumert (Eds.) *Interest and*

Learning (p. 91-104). Keil, Germany: Institute for Science Education at the University of Kiel.

Schmidt, R. A., and T. Lee (1998). *Motor control and learning: A behavioral emphasis* (3rd ed.). Champaign, IL: Human Kinetics.

Shen, B., Chen, A., Tolley, H., and Scrabis, K. A. (2003). Gender and Interest-Based Motivation in Learning Dance. *Journal of Teaching in Physical Education, 22,* 396-409.

Shuell, T. J. (1986). Cognitive conceptions of learning. *Review of Educational Research, 56,* 411-436.

Silverman, S., and Solmon, M. (1998). The unit of analysis in field research: Issues and approaches to design and data analysis. *Journal of Teaching in Physical Education, 17,* 270-284.

Skinner, B. F. (1953). Science and human behavior. New York: Free Press.

Stevenson, H. (1983). How children learn-the quest for a theory. In P. H. Mussen (Ed.), *Handbook of child psychology: Vol. I. History, theory, and methods* (4th ed., pp. 213-236). New York: Wiley.

Stinson, S.W. (1993) Meaning and value: Reflections on what students say about school. *Journal of Curriculum and Supervision, 8,* 216-238.

Sun, H., Chen, A., Ennis, C. D., Martin, R., and Shen, B. (2005, April). *Conception of "Fun": Validating sources of situational interest in elementary school physical education.* Paper presented at 2005 annual meeting of American Educational Research Association, Montreal, Canada.

Sylvester, P.S. (1994). Elementary school curricula and urban transformation. *Harvard Educational Review, 64,* 309-331.

Thorndike, E. L. (1913). *Educational psychology: Vol. 2.* The psychology of learning. New York: Teachers College.

Vygotsky, L.S. (1978) *Mind in society: The development of higher psychological process.* Cambridge, MA: Harvard University Press.

Welk, G. J. (2002). Use of accelerometry-based activity monitors to assess physical activity. In G. J. Welk (Ed.), *Physical activity assessments for health-related research* (pp. 125-142). Champaign, IL: Human Kinetics.

INDEX

A

abstraction, 98, 99, 167, 174, 175
academic achievement, 66, 69, 72, 74, 213
academic difficulties, 77
academic motivation, 81
academic performance, 18, 77, 82, 84, 140
academics, 253
access, viii, 36, 44, 49, 51, 54, 58, 61, 63, 111, 139, 148
accountability, viii, 49, 59, 62, 247
accounting, 145
accuracy, 62, 121, 149, 150, 245
achievement, viii, xi, 2, 6, 9, 10, 12, 13, 14, 17, 19, 27, 28, 32, 34, 49, 65, 67, 68, 69, 74, 75, 76, 77, 78, 80, 81, 82, 83, 88, 106, 107, 108, 109, 113, 116, 192, 196, 213, 236, 238, 240, 241, 253, 259
achievement test, 88, 241
acquisition of knowledge, vii, xi, 1, 2, 8, 12, 22, 23, 24, 25, 26, 27, 28, 29, 123, 137, 235, 241
action research, 64, 219, 225, 229
activities, ix, x, xi, 4, 5, 10, 31, 36, 68, 69, 73, 74, 79, 81, 86, 89, 92, 93, 94, 98, 99, 100, 101, 102, 104, 105, 109, 110, 113, 165, 166, 167, 168, 170, 172, 173, 174, 179, 183, 184, 185, 194, 197, 206, 209, 217, 218, 219, 220, 221, 222, 223, 224, 225, 226, 227, 228, 229, 230, 231, 235, 238, 240, 243, 248, 253, 255, 256, 257, 259
activity level, xi, 38, 236, 246, 254
adaptation, 14, 183
adjustment, 22, 23, 28, 84
administration, 42, 45, 47, 155
adolescence, 188, 236
adolescents, 214, 239
adulthood, 236
adults, 14, 39, 40, 52, 141, 151, 187, 218, 220, 221, 226, 253
advances, 3, 67, 86, 160

advertising, 62
affective experience, 255, 257, 258
affective reactions, 253
age, 3, 13, 46, 101, 121, 124, 125, 128, 131, 142, 147, 148, 149, 150, 152, 155, 161, 188, 196, 228, 245, 247, 250
age-related, 46
aging, 40, 43, 45
aid, 62, 102, 131, 136
alternative(s), 5, 13, 16, 33, 34, 62, 91, 92, 98, 138, 187, 197, 224, 229
American Educational Research Association, 259, 261
amnesia, 39, 40, 42
amygdala, 41, 42, 46, 47
analysis of variance, 157
anger, 206
ANOVA, 126, 134, 135, 197, 201, 203, 204, 260
anthropology, 169
anxiety, 38, 67, 68, 75, 80, 83, 218
appreciation, 232
argument, 4, 91, 123, 242
arithmetic, 178, 179
assessment, viii, x, 29, 30, 32, 49, 50, 51, 54, 62, 76, 79, 83, 85, 86, 91, 101, 103, 104, 105, 106, 107, 108, 109, 110, 112, 116, 117, 133, 189, 217, 218, 220, 228, 243, 244, 245
assessment techniques, 109
assignment, 54, 55, 60, 62, 126, 180, 212
association, ix, 5, 102, 148, 154, 160, 175, 185, 191, 192, 193, 207, 208, 213, 216, 237, 239, 242
attention, 35, 36, 40, 43, 46, 68, 78, 87, 89, 91, 99, 106, 151, 177, 188, 192, 209, 210, 220, 221, 222, 225, 229, 230, 239, 240, 246, 253, 254, 255, 260
attitudes, 75, 76, 80, 81, 82, 83, 86, 87, 192, 213, 215, 216
attribution, 9, 34
attribution theory, 34

Australia, 193, 208, 209, 215, 216, 233
authenticity, 108, 110
authority, 198
automatization, 104
autonomy, viii, 65, 68, 69, 70, 71, 72, 77, 80, 83, 84
avoidance, 44, 46, 70, 71, 72, 74, 75, 76, 77, 79, 80, 83
awareness, viii, ix, 10, 51, 52, 54, 85, 86, 91, 92, 93, 94, 96, 97, 99, 102, 103, 104, 105, 106, 107, 108, 109, 112, 113, 114, 116, 117, 138, 139, 145, 146, 153, 154, 155, 156, 157, 158, 159, 162, 232

B

basic needs, 68
basic research, 31
behavior(s), ix, 13, 29, 35, 37, 43, 44, 65, 67, 68, 69, 72, 73, 74, 75, 76, 77, 78, 80, 81, 82, 83, 92, 95, 103, 113, 120, 122, 125, 126, 129, 131, 132, 134, 139, 169, 179, 191, 192, 193, 194, 195, 196, 197, 198, 201, 202, 203, 204, 205, 207, 208, 209, 210, 211, 212, 213, 214, 215, 216, 231, 237, 238, 241, 255, 259,
behavioral change, 79
behavioral sciences, 112
beneficial effect, 37, 41, 139
benefits, xi, 29, 36, 75, 76, 77, 99, 113, 127, 139, 141, 235, 239, 241, 242, 254, 256, 257
bias, 38, 113, 210, 243
binary decision, 170
biology, 99, 169, 193, 215, 216
body, xi, 185, 187, 209, 220, 221, 225, 235, 236, 246, 247, 249, 257
body weight, 247
boys, 125, 128, 173, 198, 241, 247
brain, viii, 5, 41, 46, 47, 49, 51, 53, 59, 161, 183
brainstorming, 102

C

Canadian, 44
candidates, 50, 59, 60
case study, 160, 167, 183, 187, 215
categorization, 141
causal attribution, 142
causality, 67, 82, 141
central executive, 146, 151, 152, 157, 158, 159
character, ix, 11, 26, 165, 222
childhood, 138, 166, 188, 218, 219, 229, 233, 236
children, vii, ix, x, xi, 3, 4, 6, 10, 33, 50, 52, 63, 66, 69, 70, 71, 75, 81, 84, 88, 89, 90, 99, 101, 109, 115, 119, 120, 121, 122, 123, 124, 125, 126, 127, 128, 129, 130, 131, 132, 133, 134, 135, 136, 137, 138, 139, 140, 141, 142, 143, 147, 148, 149, 150, 151, 153, 154, 155, 156, 157, 158, 159, 160, 161, 162, 163, 170, 184, 186, 193, 198, 214, 215, 217, 218, 219, 220, 221, 222, 223, 224, 225, 226, 227, 228, 229, 230, 232, 236, 237, 241, 244, 253, 260, 261
class teaching, 222, 226
classes, x, xi, 60, 106, 191, 192, 193, 194, 195, 196, 197, 198, 201, 203, 204, 205, 206, 207, 208, 209, 210, 211, 212, 213, 214, 215, 235, 241, 244, 247, 248, 252, 258
classroom(s), viii, ix, x, 50, 51, 58, 59, 61, 62, 63, 64, 65, 66, 68, 76, 78, 79, 80, 81, 82, 83, 86, 109, 113, 115, 139, 145, 149, 166, 168, 170, 183, 189, 191, 192, 193, 194, 195, 197, 198, 202, 204, 205, 206, 209, 210, 211, 212, 214, 215, 216, 217, 219, 220, 223, 224, 225, 227, 228, 229, 230, 231, 232, 239, 244, 248, 259, 260
classroom culture, 219
classroom environment, 59, 194, 214, 215
classroom events, 225
classroom management, 223, 229
classroom settings, 225, 229
classroom teachers, x, 192
coding, 129, 132, 146, 147, 151, 163
cognition, ix, 2, 30, 31, 33, 53, 73, 69, 81, 82, 84, 92, 93, 99, 109, 111, 112, 114, 141, 165, 166, 167, 168, 169, 170, 172, 173, 174, 177, 181, 182, 183, 184, 185, 186, 187, 189, 237, 259
cognitive ability(ies), viii, 4, 7, 24, 85, 86, 92, 121, 122, 128, 129
cognitive activity, 86, 87, 92, 168, 170, 172, 173, 175, 176, 178, 181, 183, 184, 186
cognitive capacities, 186
cognitive development, ix, 79, 108, 109, 111, 121, 140, 142, 165, 169, 170, 183, 226
cognitive dimension, 238, 239, 255
cognitive dissonance, 221
cognitive functioning, 46, 146, 239
cognitive impairment, 47
cognitive involvement, 229, 239
cognitive level, 106
cognitive load, 102
cognitive map, 87
cognitive performance, 7, 143, 169
cognitive perspective, 84, 237, 238
cognitive process(es), 7, 26, 53, 91, 92, 109, 141, 142, 169, 170, 173, 184, 186, 237
cognitive processing, 141
cognitive profile, 146
cognitive psychology, 31, 66, 86, 113, 189
cognitive science, 2, 86, 168

cognitive system, 169, 179
cognitive tasks, 94, 257
cognitive tool, 102, 103, 109, 113, 114
coherence, 15, 18, 19, 25, 30, 179, 180
cohesiveness, ix, 119, 121, 122, 124, 126, 127, 132, 135, 136, 138
collaboration, 100, 141, 142, 219, 225, 226, 229, 232
college students, vii, viii, 1, 13, 14, 65, 81, 82, 84, 98, 99, 128
commitments, 2, 107, 188
communication, ix, 111, 140, 180, 182, 183, 184, 191, 192, 193, 194, 195, 196, 197, 198, 201, 202, 203, 204, 207, 208, 209, 210, 211, 212, 213, 216, 229
community(ies), vii, 29, 187, 197, 218, 224
competence, vii, 1, 2, 3, 4, 5, 6, 7, 8, 9, 10, 11, 12, 14, 21, 22, 23, 25, 26, 27, 28, 29, 68, 69, 75, 76, 78, 79, 109, 140, 166, 189, 218, 239, 254, 257
competency, 103, 238
complexity, ix, 7, 11, 26, 30, 124, 140, 147, 152, 163, 165, 166, 170, 171, 173, 174, 176, 177, 178, 180, 181, 182, 183, 184, 185, 186, 187
components, vii, viii, 1, 2, 6, 8, 9, 10, 11, 22, 23, 27, 74, 81, 82, 85, 86, 92, 94, 96, 98, 102, 104, 151, 152, 153, 154, 155, 156, 158, 160, 200, 239, 240, 256, 258, 259
composition, 14, 98, 102, 110, 114, 158, 197
comprehension, 5, 87, 88, 89, 90, 91, 94, 95, 97, 98, 100, 102, 103, 107, 110, 111, 112, 113, 114, 115, 129, 130, 132, 133, 134, 149, 151, 154, 160, 161, 162, 163
compulsion, 67
computer(s), 15, 90, 99, 101, 102, 114, 188, 194, 248
computer technology, 114
computing, 245
concept, 33, 62, 66, 67, 70, 80, 88, 91, 108, 175, 184, 211, 228, 253, 255, 256
conceptions, 33, 34, 88, 184, 261
conditioning, 44, 46
conduct, 38, 167
confidence, 63, 89, 100, 202, 225
conflict, 34, 77
conformity, 33
confusion, 5, 55, 93, 229
consciousness, 93, 99, 168, 188
consequence(s), 5, 29, 31, 80, 89, 139, 140, 141, 157, 215
construct validity, 83, 246
construction, 16, 59, 87, 90, 94, 123, 138, 154, 166, 170, 183, 184, 185, 189, 215, 238
constructivist learning, 192, 256
consulting, 93
consumption, 245, 248, 249

content, 8, 10, 12, 13, 31, 73, 77, 78, 79, 88, 93, 98, 106, 124, 143, 196, 204, 221, 228, 238, 239, 240, 242, 243, 245, 246, 248, 252, 253, 254, 255, 256, 257, 259
context(s), vii, viii, x, 1, 3, 8, 9, 10, 12, 21, 24, 28, 29, 35, 36, 37, 38, 40, 41, 43, 45, 46, 47, 67, 68, 77, 79, 82, 90, 98, 99, 105, 107, 108, 109, 116, 120, 124, 139, 143, 169, 173, 175, 177, 178, 179, 180, 183, 188, 193, 195, 197, 198, 201, 211, 213, 217, 219, 220, 227, 228, 230, 231, 243, 248, 257, 258
contingency, 68
continuity, 4
contribution, 163
control, ix, 2, 5, 29, 37, 57, 65, 80, 82, 91, 92, 93, 95, 98, 99, 106, 107, 112, 115, 116, 117, 145, 146, 148, 152, 153, 155, 156, 157, 158, 159, 203, 206, 210, 215, 237, 241, 243, 247, 248, 261
control group, ix, 5, 106, 116, 117, 145, 146, 148, 152, 155, 156, 157, 158
conviction, 72
cooperation, 29
cooperative learning, 10
coping, 68, 69, 84, 90
coping strategies, 69
core, 12, 131, 133, 149
correlation, vii, x, 1, 3, 5, 6, 15, 17, 18, 23, 24, 25, 32, 60, 70, 117, 134, 136, 141, 149, 191, 192, 194, 200, 201, 207, 209, 211, 241, 248, 249, 251, 254
correlation analysis, vii, 1, 17
correlation coefficient(s), 17, 70, 211, 251, 254
cortex, 41, 45, 46
costs, 78
coupling, 168, 169, 180
course work, 74
creativity, 30, 33
credibility, 7
credit, 89, 121, 126, 239
criterion, 16, 18, 20, 21, 23, 38, 245
critical thinking, 113, 226
criticism, 109, 154
cues, 37, 38, 45, 47, 73, 129
cultural norms, 228
cultural values, 193
culture(s), 33, 64, 188, 193, 194, 195, 197, 198, 213, 214, 219
curiosity, 35, 36, 44, 105, 218, 226, 258
curriculum, xi, 62, 114, 128, 129, 130, 131, 132, 133, 134, 136, 137, 138, 139, 166, 172, 183, 187, 192, 213, 215, 229, 230, 231, 235, 236, 237, 242, 243, 244, 245, 246, 247, 248, 249, 250, 251, 252, 253, 254, 255, 256, 257, 258, 259

curriculum development, 187

D

damage, 41, 46
data collection, 172, 194, 209, 211, 225, 244, 246, 247
data set, 256
Deci, 67, 68, 70, 71, 73, 77, 80, 82, 83
decision, 30, 89, 113, 170, 232, 240, 249
decision making, 30, 89, 232
decision making process, 89
deductive reasoning, 67
defensive strategies, 68
deficit, 36, 42, 44, 154, 156, 157, 158, 159, 161, 163
definition, 21, 26, 38, 67, 79, 93, 120, 123, 146, 159, 182, 241
demand, 13, 17, 18, 19, 20, 22, 23, 24, 27, 51, 152, 153, 212, 240, 242, 243, 246
demographics, 243, 244
Department of Health and Human Services, 85
dependent, 36, 41, 46, 47, 66, 72, 77, 128, 131, 136, 137, 150, 153, 168, 194, 236, 243, 249, 252
dependent variable(s), 72, 153, 194, 249, 252
deprivation, 41, 44, 45
desire, 67, 229, 253
detachment, 107
developed countries, x, 191, 193
developing countries, 193
development, vii, viii, ix, xi, 1, 2, 5, 6, 8, 9, 11, 12, 14, 16, 25, 26, 27, 28, 29, 30, 39, 46, 52, 66, 69, 79, 80, 81, 84, 85, 86, 91, 100, 101, 102, 103, 104, 108, 109, 110, 111, 112, 113, 114, 115, 119, 121, 136, 139, 140, 141, 142, 143, 154, 161, 162, 165, 166, 168, 169, 170, 175, 177, 182, 183, 184, 187, 188, 189, 190, 205, 214, 216, 218, 219, 221, 225, 226, 227, 229, 231, 232, 233, 239, 257, 259, 260, 261
developmental dyslexia, 153
deviation, 202, 203
dialogue, 214
differences, x, xi, 3, 4, 5, 7, 10, 36, 40, 41, 43, 44, 46, 47, 50, 59, 60, 77, 81, 82, 84, 88, 94, 117, 121, 122, 130, 136, 140, 141, 142, 143, 145, 149, 152, 153, 154, 156, 157, 158, 159, 161, 162, 175, 178, 184, 185, 191, 195, 202, 203, 204, 210, 211, 212, 216, 236, 240, 249, 250, 254, 258
differentiation, 174, 178, 183, 187
dimensionality, 240
dimensions, xi, 25, 74, 76, 132, 192, 193, 194, 195, 197, 204, 205, 209, 210, 211, 215, 236, 240, 245, 246, 250, 254
direct measure, 249

direct observation, x, 191
directives, 227
disability(ies), 148, 151, 155, 161
discipline, 192, 206
discourse, 90, 174, 175, 180, 215, 218, 227
discrimination, 44, 46, 153, 245
discrimination learning, 46
disposition, 236, 239, 258
dissociation, 155, 158
diversity, 59, 135, 197, 214, 215
divorce, 114
domain-specificity, 34
dominance, x, 191
drive, 60, 91, 105, 237, 253
drug, 37, 42, 44
durability, 99
duration, 147, 159, 163
dyslexia, 153, 160

E

education, vi, x, xi, 12, 14, 31, 32, 33, 34, 51, 52, 64, 81, 82, 83, 99, 100, 110, 112, 113, 114, 139, 142, 143, 166, 167, 169, 175, 183, 186, 187, 189, 190, 196, 212, 213, 214, 215, 216, 217, 218, 219, 232, 233, 235, 236, 237, 238, 239, 240, 241, 242, 243, 244, 246, 247, 248, 252, 254, 255, 256, 257, 258, 259, 260, 261
educational psychology, 259
educational research, 49, 239, 253
educational settings, 49, 79
educational system, 110, 210, 231
efficiency, 93, 124, 146, 155, 156, 179, 249
ego, 71, 75, 80, 82, 83
elementary (primary) school, 10, 70, 120, 121, 124, 125, 142, 242, 243, 244, 252, 255, 258, 261
e-mail, 56, 184
emergence, 141, 180, 189
emotionality, 10
emotions, 34, 65, 73
empathy, 227
empirical studies, 5, 8
employment, 44
encoding, 37, 47, 122, 131, 138, 142, 148, 184, 185
English, ix, 83, 145, 146, 149, 150, 151, 152, 155, 156, 157, 158, 161, 196
English language proficiency, 196
environment, ix, x, 3, 5, 10, 12, 18, 20, 21, 22, 23, 24, 28, 36, 43, 47, 50, 90, 168, 169, 187, 191, 192, 193, 194, 208, 214, 215, 216, 217, 218, 220, 221, 224, 229, 233, 237, 239, 240, 252, 258
environmental factors, 2, 5
environmental stimuli, 37

episodic memory, 47, 141
episodic memory tasks, 141
equilibrium, 166
equipment, 15
equity, ix, 85, 86, 198, 210
ethnicity, 193
evaluation, x, 12, 13, 14, 15, 16, 17, 25, 32, 78, 82, 87, 93, 110, 132, 157, 177, 215, 217, 220, 222, 223, 224, 225, 227, 228, 243, 257
everyday life, 2, 33, 100, 188
evidence, x, 3, 4, 5, 31, 37, 42, 58, 69, 77, 78, 96, 108, 109, 110, 112, 148, 154, 155, 159, 162, 166, 173, 175, 180, 184, 187, 217, 218, 228, 230, 231, 241, 255
exclusion, 38, 40
excuse, 73, 78
execution, 3, 4, 5, 9, 13, 27, 78, 124, 128, 138, 139
executive processes, 153
exercise, x, xi, 29, 95, 191, 195, 206, 229, 236, 242, 246, 257
expectations, 28, 54, 67, 69
expenditures, 245
experiment, 38, 39, 40, 147, 150, 152, 155, 156, 157, 158, 159, 187, 188, 243, 244, 257, 258
experimental condition, 38
experimental design, 242, 253
expert teacher, 246
expertise, 2, 3, 5, 6, 7, 8, 9, 10, 11, 26, 27, 29, 30, 31, 32, 33, 34, 114, 120, 122, 140, 141, 142, 143, 185, 228, 231, 236
experts, 3, 6, 7, 27, 104, 111, 120, 122, 185, 211
exploitation, 169
expression, 44, 116, 187, 206, 225
extrinsic motivation, 67, 68, 81, 83, 260
extrinsic rewards, 3

F

facial expression, 206, 225
factor analysis(es), 33, 200, 201, 209, 240
factors, vii, x, 1, 2, 3, 4, 5, 8, 9, 10, 11, 13, 27, 33, 35, 69, 75, 81, 92, 95, 120, 122, 127, 145, 191, 198, 200, 202, 203, 204, 205, 208, 209, 212, 213, 214, 215, 236, 239, 247, 255
failure, 4, 37, 50, 56, 67, 68, 74, 78, 80, 93, 97, 100, 228
family(ies), 3, 6, 52, 128, 129, 131, 132, 137, 175, 176, 259
fear, 45, 46, 68, 78
feedback, 3, 10, 29, 78, 188, 219, 221, 228, 231, 232, 244, 246
feelings, 67, 69, 74, 77

female(s), x, 41, 42, 191, 195, 196, 197, 203, 205, 206, 210, 213, 216, 244
flexibility, 98, 187, 189
focusing, ix, 67, 74, 90, 91, 99, 104, 108, 145, 146, 166, 182, 242
food, 41, 60, 246
forecasting, 18
foreign language, ix, 145, 146, 149, 150, 151, 152, 153, 155, 156, 158, 159, 160, 161, 162, 163
forgetting, 37, 40, 43, 44, 46, 93
framework, viii, ix, 18, 75, 85, 86, 87, 102, 109, 115, 123, 143, 145, 146, 152, 170, 172, 179, 182, 183, 184, 187, 237, 239, 240, 256
framing, 223, 230
free recall, 121, 143, 212
free-choice, 83
freedom, 22, 195, 208, 248
frequency, 75, 153, 232, 241, 246, 257
friends, 224
frontal cortex, 41

G

gender, 107, 152, 155, 193, 195, 198, 202, 203, 204, 206, 210, 214, 216, 246, 259
gender differences, 195, 202, 203, 204, 210
gender effects, 214
gender equity, 198, 210
general intelligence, 154
generalization, 175, 194
generation(s), xi, 121, 140, 231, 235
genetics, 5
gestures, 186, 189
gifted, 33, 120, 121, 139, 140, 141, 142, 143
girls, 125, 128, 198, 210, 241, 247
goals, viii, 27, 50, 52, 65, 67, 68, 69, 70, 72, 73, 74, 75, 76, 77, 78, 79, 80, 81, 82, 83, 92, 93, 94, 98, 108, 109, 124, 192, 238, 257
government, 195, 196, 198, 212, 213, 215, 232
grades, 250
gradings, viii, 9, 11, 35, 37, 38, 39, 40, 41, 43, 66, 68, 69, 73, 74, 79, 86, 87, 89, 100, 107, 119, 121, 123, 124, 128, 131, 132, 137, 138, 146, 147, 152, 153, 157, 166, 168, 169, 172, 175, 176, 184, 185, 186, 212, 230, 239, 240, 247, 255, 256, 257
graduate students, 12
grants, 3, 7, 10, 139
group activities, 172, 222
group membership, 128
group size, 221
group work, 58, 62, 226, 227, 230
grouping, 62, 128, 131, 139, 195, 230

groups, vii, ix, 5, 32, 107, 115, 116, 117, 121, 122, 125, 128, 130, 131, 132, 133, 134, 135, 139, 145, 146, 148, 150, 152, 154, 155, 156, 157, 159, 172, 204, 205, 207, 210, 212, 222, 226, 245, 250
growth, 47, 123, 141, 142, 143, 188, 232, 238, 253, 257
growth and development, 141, 143
guessing, 177
guidelines, 89, 230
guilt, 67

H

habituation, 36, 40
happiness, 206
health, xi, 32, 34, 235, 237, 238, 239, 241, 242, 243, 252, 254, 256, 258, 260, 261
heuristic, 98, 171
high school, vii, viii, 13, 60, 65, 76, 96, 149, 163, 189, 216, 239
higher education, 32
higher quality, 71
hippocampus, 41, 45, 46, 47
history, 5, 62, 108, 168, 175, 261
homework, 55
homogeneity, 20
Hong Kong, vi, x, 217, 218, 219, 232, 233
hormones, 45
housing, 41, 44
human behavior, 80, 261
human experience, 190
human motivation, 9
human subjects, 40
hypothesis, 3, 5, 7, 26, 28, 29, 70, 103, 138, 147, 149, 150, 151, 152, 153, 155, 163, 255, 257

I

ideas, x, 3, 7, 56, 58, 59, 86, 89, 91, 95, 98, 102, 105, 183, 187, 217, 218, 219, 229, 231, 239
identification, vii, 1, 24, 51, 122, 125, 247
identity, 154
idiosyncratic, 90
imagery, 161, 183
imagination, 58, 224
implementation, x, 13, 42, 43, 217, 219, 220
impulsive, 105
inclusion, 22, 125
independence, 20, 21, 25, 26, 194, 200, 260
independent variable, 72, 194
indicators, 15, 117, 194, 212, 243
indirect effect, 21, 23, 24

individual differences, 4, 5, 10, 29, 76, 81, 82, 83, 84, 109, 124, 133, 139, 140, 143, 145, 155, 161, 163
individual students, 50, 79, 169, 170, 183, 194, 205, 208, 249
infants, 40, 46
inferences, 7, 26, 87, 94, 95, 108, 248
influence, v, viii, x, 7, 9, 10, 11, 12, 21, 25, 26, 27, 28, 37, 45, 65, 66, 69, 72, 75, 83, 87, 91, 95, 101, 104, 110, 119, 135, 136, 138, 142, 143, 146, 150, 158, 159, 166, 191, 192, 198, 215, 232, 237, 239, 257
information processing, 29, 86, 91, 121, 138, 161
initiation, x, 217, 220
innovations, 219
insight, 33, 95, 141
institutions, vii, 193, 197, 213
instructional methods, 10, 12, 28
instructional practice, 86, 232
instruments, 12, 196, 198
integration, 5, 67, 88, 117
integrity, 248
intelligence, vii, 1, 2, 4, 7, 8, 9, 12, 13, 17, 18, 19, 20, 21, 22, 23, 24, 25, 26, 29, 30, 31, 32, 33, 51, 111, 112, 119, 120, 122, 124, 125, 128, 133, 139, 141, 143, 148, 149, 151, 152, 154, 155
intelligence tests, 4
intensity, 45, 241, 246, 258
intentions, 68, 75, 168
interaction, x, 3, 7, 10, 14, 28, 33, 36, 43, 59, 74, 94, 103, 123, 126, 127, 128, 134, 135, 140, 153, 156, 157, 180, 184, 189, 191, 216, 229, 230, 236, 237, 240, 248
interest, vi, xi, 4, 5, 25, 78, 79, 80, 89, 105, 146, 212, 218, 219, 221, 225, 235, 236, 237, 239, 240, 241, 242, 246, 248, 249, 250, 251, 252, 253, 254, 255, 257, 258, 259, 260, 261
internal consistency, x, 13, 16, 191, 194, 200
internal locus of control, 68
internal mechanisms, 9
internalization, 67, 82, 103, 104, 108, 230
internalizing, viii, 85, 86, 104, 237
interpersonal conflict, 34
interpersonal processes, 109
interpersonal relations, 214
interpretation, 55, 58, 59, 88, 90, 109, 152, 157, 168, 169, 215, 229, 237, 248, 249
interpreting, 30, 53, 225
interrelations, 8, 128
intervention(s), viii, xi, 65, 83, 96, 99, 100, 106, 107, 115, 116, 117, 160, 161, 212, 230, 235, 242, 244, 246
intervention strategies, 160

interview, 84, 110, 173, 174, 175, 178, 180, 183, 192
intrinsic motivation, 67, 68, 70, 72, 75, 78, 80, 83, 260
intuition, 184
IQ, v, ix, 32, 88, 119, 121, 122, 124, 125, 126, 127, 128, 131, 133, 134, 135, 136, 137, 138, 140, 143
IQ scores, 125, 133, 137, 138
issues, 12, 43, 79, 89, 105, 108, 110, 111, 114, 176

J

Japanese, viii, 65, 69, 70, 71, 72, 75, 76, 81, 83, 84, 151
judgment, 69, 87
junior high school, viii, 65, 76, 96
justification, 91, 100

K

kindergarten children, 128, 232
knowledge, vii, viii, ix, xi, 1, 2, 3, 4, 6, 7, 8, 9, 10, 11, 12, 15, 17, 18, 20, 21, 24, 25, 26, 27, 28, 29, 30, 31, 32, 50, 51, 55, 56, 60, 63, 65, 66, 67, 72, 73, 77, 79, 85, 86, 87, 88, 89, 90, 91, 92, 93, 94, 95, 97, 98, 100, 102, 104, 105, 106, 108, 109, 110, 111, 112, 113, 114, 115, 119, 120, 122, 123, 124, 126, 127, 128, 129, 130, 131, 132, 133, 134, 135, 136, 137, 138, 139, 140, 141, 142, 143, 147, 150, 151, 160, 166, 167, 179, 185, 188, 189, 190, 192, 212, 214, 215, 218, 219, 220, 224, 225, 226, 228, 229, 230, 231, 235, 236, 237, 238, 239, 241, 242, 243, 245, 246, 247, 248, 249, 251, 252, 253, 254, 255, 256, 257, 258
knowledge acquisition, ix, xi, 2, 18, 20, 25, 27, 31, 79, 110, 111, 119, 120, 123, 124, 128, 132, 133, 134, 137, 138, 139, 235, 237, 242, 252, 253, 254, 255, 257, 258

L

labeling, 121
language, ix, 52, 59, 60, 101, 115, 143, 145, 146, 147, 148, 149, 150, 151, 152, 153, 155, 156, 157, 158, 159, 160, 161, 162, 163, 167, 179, 187, 189, 193, 196, 197, 209, 215, 220, 221, 225, 229, 245, 246
language processing, 160
language proficiency, 151, 152
language skills, 149
Latin America, 54, 97, 175, 180
laws, 31
LEA, 31, 32, 33, 34, 260

leadership, 54, 64, 97, 175, 180, 214
learners, 51, 52, 53, 55, 58, 61, 64, 86, 87, 88, 89, 98, 99, 100, 101, 103, 104, 105, 106, 107, 108, 109, 120, 145, 186, 188, 236, 237, 239, 240, 241, 242, 253, 255, 257
learning, iv, vii, viii, ix, x, xi, 1, 2, 3, 6, 7, 8, 9, 10, 12, 14, 15, 16, 17, 18, 19, 20, 22, 23, 24, 25, 26, 27, 28, 29, 30, 31, 32, 34, 35, 37, 38, 40, 42, 44, 45, 46, 49, 50, 51, 52, 53, 54, 55, 58, 59, 60, 61, 62, 63, 64, 65, 66, 67, 69, 70, 71, 72, 73, 74, 77, 78, 79, 80, 81, 82, 83, 84, 85, 86, 87, 89, 90, 91, 92, 93, 94, 95, 96, 97, 98, 99, 100, 101, 103, 104, 108, 109, 110, 111, 112, 113, 114, 115, 117, 120, 121, 124, 128, 138, 140, 141, 142, 143, 145, 146, 147, 148, 149, 150, 151, 152, 153, 154, 155, 158, 160, 161, 162, 163, 165, 166, 167, 168, 169, 172, 173, 175, 176, 180, 182, 183, 184, 186, 187, 188, 189, 191, 192, 193, 196, 198, 200, 204, 205, 208, 212, 213, 214, 215, 216, 217, 218, 219, 220, 221, 223, 224, 225, 226, 227, 228, 229, 230, 231, 232, 233, 235, 236, 237, 238, 239, 240, 241, 242, 243, 244, 249, 252, 253, 254, 255, 256, 257, 258, 259, 260, 261
learning activity, x, 217, 220
learning and memory, 35, 37, 38, 40, 42, 44, 138
learning behavior, 53, 239, 241
learning difficulties, 121, 151, 152, 161, 226
learning environment, vii, ix, x, 2, 8, 10, 12, 14, 18, 19, 20, 22, 23, 24, 25, 28, 63, 101, 114, 115, 167, 191, 192, 193, 200, 208, 214, 215, 216, 217, 218, 220, 223, 229, 230, 257, 258
learning outcomes, 79, 192, 241
learning process, viii, 14, 15, 18, 25, 32, 52, 53, 54, 65, 72, 74, 78, 79, 149, 173, 198, 218, 227, 230, 236, 237, 239, 241, 242, 243, 249, 253, 254, 255, 257
learning skills, 2, 3, 8, 9, 26, 27
learning styles, 14, 17, 28, 29, 51, 212
learning task, 15, 52, 54, 61, 67, 79, 92, 224, 225, 230, 240, 242, 249, 253, 258, 259
legislation, 49, 51
lesson plan, x, 60, 61, 217, 219, 220, 221, 225, 229
liberalization, 54, 97, 175, 180
life course, 141
life expectancy, 54, 97, 175, 180
life experiences, 99
lifestyle, xi, 235, 236, 237
limitation, 54, 97, 175, 180
linguistics, 169
listening, 89, 90, 149, 151, 156
literacy, 54, 97, 110, 112, 150, 154, 161, 175, 180, 197, 245

literature, x, 36, 68, 74, 77, 120, 123, 137, 192, 195, 208, 212, 216, 217, 218
lobbying, 54, 97, 175, 180
location, 42, 125, 159, 175, 180, 193
long term memory, 86, 150
longitudinal study, 149, 150, 161, 162
long-term retention, 77
love, 53, 55, 58
lying, 7, 70, 72

M

magnetic resonance, 5
maladaptive, 68, 75
male(s), x, 41, 42, 44, 191, 195, 196, 197, 203, 205, 206, 210, 213, 244
management, 109, 223, 229
manipulation, 153, 157, 158, 159, 177, 187
MANOVA, 240, 249, 250
manufacturing, 106
mastery, 68, 70, 71, 74, 75, 76, 77, 78, 79, 109
matching, 38, 227
mathematics, 6, 98, 111, 114, 122, 166, 188, 214, 215, 227, 240, 260
mathematics education, 166
maturation, 101
measurement, 15, 16, 25, 32, 33, 39, 149, 246
measures, viii, 13, 15, 17, 18, 38, 43, 49, 50, 51, 62, 72, 76, 100, 129, 133, 134, 137, 141, 143, 150, 151, 153, 154, 157, 159, 175, 241, 243, 249
media, 90
mediation, 136
memorizing, 73, 100
memory, viii, ix, 2, 3, 4, 5, 6, 7, 30, 35, 36, 37, 39, 40, 41, 42, 43, 44, 45, 46, 47, 94, 110, 111, 112, 119, 120, 121, 122, 123, 124, 125, 128, 129, 130, 131, 132, 137, 138, 139, 140, 141, 143, 145, 146, 147, 148, 149, 150, 151, 152, 153, 154, 155, 156, 157, 158, 159, 160, 161, 162, 163, 239
memory capacity, 156
memory performance, 122, 128, 132, 137, 140, 141, 143, 148, 150, 151, 156, 157, 158, 159, 163
memory processes, 154
mental actions, 238
mental age, 101
mental development, 101
mental health, 34
mental processes, 53, 101, 237
mental retardation, 121, 141
mentor, 60, 101
meta-analysis, 113
metacognition, 51, 52, 53, 67, 91, 92, 93, 95, 99, 100, 111, 112, 113, 114, 139

metacognitive knowledge, 92, 93, 94, 99, 120, 122, 139
methodology, ix, 26, 152, 158, 165, 183
miscommunication, 179
misconceptions, 185
misunderstanding, 229
mnemonic processes, 41
modeling, 2, 73, 86, 95, 96, 98, 102, 183, 187, 189, 225, 231, 232
models, v, vii, x, xi, 1, 2, 6, 7, 9, 13, 23, 25, 26, 28, 62, 66, 76, 91, 94, 95, 98, 99, 112, 115, 152, 166, 169, 180, 184, 190, 217, 219, 230, 235, 236, 254, 255, 257, 258
monitoring, 93, 94, 95, 98, 99, 109, 110, 111, 112, 113, 114, 123, 218
mood, 37, 45
motivation, vii, viii, xi, 1, 2, 3, 4, 5, 6, 8, 9, 11, 12, 13, 14, 16, 17, 19, 20, 21, 23, 24, 25, 27, 30, 32, 34, 36, 65, 66, 67, 68, 69, 70, 71, 72, 74, 78, 79, 80, 81, 82, 83, 84, 99, 113, 115, 145, 160, 180, 215, 235, 236, 237, 238, 239, 240, 241, 242, 253, 259, 260
motives, 14, 17, 74, 83, 168, 259
motor skills, 238, 241
movement, 126, 177, 185, 219, 222, 224, 238, 239, 241, 243, 245, 249, 256, 257, 259
multidimensional, 32, 100, 110
multimedia, 112
multiple regression, vii, 1, 17, 18, 20, 21, 24, 25, 249, 252, 255
multiple regression analyses, 18, 20, 21, 24, 25, 249, 252, 255
multivariate distribution, 20
music, 5, 59, 62, 219, 221, 224, 225
musicians, 3

N

narratives, 231
National Institutes of Health, 85
National Research Council, 115
needs, 50, 55, 58, 59, 64, 68, 74, 77, 78, 82, 151, 187, 193, 213, 228, 246
negative attitudes, 75
negative outcomes, 77
negative relation, 5, 77
negotiating, 109
negotiation, 98, 141, 226
networks, 32, 87, 186, 188, 189
neural networks, 186, 188, 189
neurotransmitter, 41
newspapers, 90
nicotine, 42, 43, 45

No Child Left Behind, 49, 51, 52
noise, 155, 206
non-verbal, x, 151, 152, 155, 191, 192, 194, 196, 203, 204, 206, 207, 209, 210, 213
North America, 83, 193
novel stimuli, 47
novelty, 35, 36, 38, 40, 41, 43, 44, 47, 121, 240, 246, 254
novelty seeking, 44

O

obesity, 236
objectives, 17, 104, 219, 258
obligation, 107
observable behavior, 241
observations, 108, 172, 173, 180, 192, 193, 195, 197, 207, 206, 210, 211, 212, 213
olfaction, 44
openness, 225
optimal performance, 256
orchestration, 109
organization, vii, ix, 1, 4, 6, 7, 8, 9, 15, 20, 21, 23, 24, 25, 26, 27, 28, 32, 34, 46, 80, 86, 119, 121, 128, 131, 132, 135, 136, 138, 142, 146, 256
original training, 36
overload, 13, 17, 19
ownership, 192, 212, 218

P

parents, 6, 62, 198, 237
parietal cortex, 47
participation, xi, 2, 189, 221, 222, 223, 225, 227, 229, 230, 235, 236, 243, 244, 248, 249, 255, 260
partnership, 52, 103
passive, ix, 46, 66, 72, 145, 146, 152, 161, 222, 238
path model, 72, 76, 151
pathways, 81
pedagogy, x, 58, 59, 89, 214, 217, 220, 223, 228, 230, 233, 260
peers, 100, 101, 102, 120, 121, 134, 136, 172, 173, 174, 192, 218, 221, 225, 230
perceived control, 83
perceived self-efficacy, 72, 73
perception(s), ix, 10, 11, 14, 20, 21, 23, 24, 25, 28, 68, 72, 75, 76, 77, 78, 83, 84, 99, 168, 169, 182, 183, 187, 191, 194, 195, 197, 202, 203, 204, 205, 207, 208, 209, 210, 211, 212, 213, 215, 216, 239, 248, 254
performance, viii, ix, 2, 3, 4, 5, 7, 8, 9, 10, 11, 12, 13, 15, 16, 18, 19, 20, 21, 23, 24, 25, 27, 29, 30, 31, 33, 35, 36, 37, 40, 44, 45, 49, 52, 59, 67, 68, 69, 71, 73, 74, 75, 76, 77, 78, 80, 81, 82, 83, 84, 85, 86, 87, 91, 99, 101, 102, 103, 105, 106, 107, 108, 109, 110, 112, 116, 117, 119, 120, 121, 122, 124, 127, 128, 132, 133, 134, 135, 136, 137, 138, 139, 140, 141, 143, 146, 148, 149, 150, 151, 152, 153, 154, 156, 157, 158, 159, 163, 170, 172, 185, 238, 241, 243, 256, 260
personal goals, 67
personal learning, viii, 49, 54, 59, 61
personality, 4, 5, 9, 51, 80, 188
personality measures, 51
pessimism, 80
philosophy, 169, 219
phonemes, 147, 153, 158
phonological form, 147
phonology, 158
physical activity, xi, 167, 175, 176, 184, 185, 235, 236, 238, 240, 241, 242, 243, 245, 248, 252, 254, 255, 256, 257, 258, 259, 261
physical education, xi, 235, 236, 237, 238, 239, 240, 241, 242, 243, 244, 246, 247, 248, 252, 254, 255, 256, 257, 258, 259, 260, 261
physical environment, x, 217
physical fitness, 238
physics, 30, 99, 111, 166, 168, 169, 170, 189
placebo, 106, 107, 116
planning, x, 60, 93, 98, 102, 103, 123, 217, 218, 219, 220, 225, 228, 229, 230
policy makers, 80
policy(ies), 80, 110
poor, 69, 75, 87, 88, 94, 112, 122, 135, 136, 140, 143, 148, 154, 156, 159, 161, 197
poor performance, 75, 159
population, 195, 196, 197
positive correlation, 17, 18, 72, 212, 241
positive emotions, 257
positive reinforcement, 238
positive relation, 18, 77
positive relationship, 77
post-hoc analysis, 201
poverty, 243
power, 16, 29, 112, 116, 155, 214
practical knowledge, 225, 231
predictability, xi, 235, 237, 241, 255, 258
prediction, 18, 21, 25, 150
predictors, xi, 23, 149, 153, 236, 249, 252
preference, 15, 18, 19, 20, 28, 37, 38, 41, 43, 44, 82, 206, 236, 239, 253
prefrontal cortex, 47
preschool children, 142, 184
pressure, 68, 74

prior knowledge, viii, 32, 85, 86, 87, 88, 89, 97, 103, 104, 105, 106, 107, 108, 113, 115, 117, 143, 213, 218, 227, 229
probability, 22, 54, 147
problem solving, 33, 75, 79, 81, 93, 98, 99, 100, 102, 110, 111, 112, 113, 114, 121, 140, 141, 142, 169, 189, 243
problem-solving strategies, 99, 141, 142
problem-solving task, 100
procedural knowledge, 2, 7, 26, 93, 227
procedures, viii, 12, 16, 17, 35, 36, 40, 43, 79, 87, 98, 99, 177
production, 129, 130, 132, 133, 134, 141, 219, 231
professional development, 231, 233
professions, 233
program(s), x, 15, 16, 17, 51, 55, 96, 98, 99, 102, 139, 157, 192, 201, 212
programming, 242, 246
psychiatrist, 180
psychological development, 111
psychological processes, 115, 162
psychology of learning, 261
pupil, 109, 219, 225

Q

qualifications, x, 21, 191
qualitative differences, 4, 7
questioning, 93, 95, 96, 153, 192, 219, 226, 227
quizzes, 55

R

random assignment, 212
range, vii, 1, 109, 116, 125, 126, 128, 144, 150, 200, 201, 206, 211, 229, 243
rating scale, 233
ratings, 144, 240, 245
reading, viii, 50, 55, 56, 61, 62, 85, 86, 87, 89, 90, 91, 93, 94, 95, 96, 97, 98, 99, 100, 102, 103, 104, 105, 106, 107, 108, 110, 111, 112, 113, 114, 115, 116, 117, 122, 141, 146, 149, 151, 154, 160, 161, 162, 163, 180, 221, 222, 228, 246, 247
reading comprehension, 87, 89, 90, 91, 94, 95, 98, 100, 102, 103, 110, 111, 112, 113, 114, 115, 149, 151, 163
reading comprehension test, 113
reading difficulties, 115
reality, 55, 100, 113, 219
reasoning, 6, 8, 87, 91, 114, 143, 146, 169, 178, 180, 183, 189, 190, 232

recall, ix, 45, 80, 92, 110, 113, 119, 121, 122, 124, 125, 126, 127, 128, 131, 132, 133, 134, 135, 136, 137, 138, 140, 141, 142, 147, 148, 150, 152, 156, 157, 163, 186, 205, 210, 258, 260
recalling, 121, 151, 157
recognition, 5, 36, 37, 39, 40, 41, 42, 43, 44, 45, 46, 47, 93, 168, 260
reconstruction, 91, 180
recovery, 42
recruiting, 108
reflection, 29, 92, 121, 220, 229, 231
reflective practice, 52, 231
regression, xi, 6, 17, 18, 20, 21, 23, 208, 211, 236, 241, 248, 252, 255, 256
regression analyses, 20, 21, 249, 252, 255, 256
regression method, 17, 18
regulation(s), 58, 66, 67, 68, 70, 71, 73, 74, 77, 78, 80, 83, 84, 99, 109, 113, 139
reinforcement, 36, 82, 108, 192, 230, 237
relational, 17
relationship(s), viii, ix, 65, 70, 71, 72, 74, 75, 76, 77, 78, 90, 93, 98, 136, 145, 146, 147, 149, 150, 151, 153, 154, 155, 162, 166, 167, 170, 173, 186, 194, 207, 211, 215, 216, 220, 226, 241, 249, 253, 254
relevance, 20, 55, 56, 152, 192, 212, 253, 256
reliability, x, 13, 14, 15, 16, 29, 132, 191, 194, 195, 198, 200, 208, 209, 211, 247
religion, 193
remembering, 40, 93, 98, 111, 143
repair, 94, 95, 226
replication, 141
report, viii, 53, 55, 65, 69, 114, 131, 208, 210, 212, 217, 218, 219, 242, 256, 259
research, iv, vii, viii, ix, x, 5, 7, 9, 12, 13, 14, 15, 17, 20, 27, 28, 29, 31, 32, 35, 36, 40, 43, 53, 56, 62, 65, 66, 67, 68, 74, 76, 79, 80, 82, 83, 86, 95, 98, 99, 100, 106, 107, 109, 110, 111, 113, 114, 115, 117, 120, 121, 123, 126, 135, 137, 138, 139, 140, 145, 146, 147, 148, 151, 155, 158, 160, 161, 165, 166, 167, 168, 169, 172, 175, 177, 179, 183, 184, 186, 187, 191, 193, 194, 195, 208, 211, 213, 214, 215, 219, 229, 231, 232, 239, 240, 241, 242, 244, 248, 255, 258, 260, 261
resources, 56, 57, 63, 64
responding, 53, 54, 68, 225, 247
response, 12, 50, 51, 59, 105, 107, 110, 113, 124, 160, 167, 169, 180, 181, 197, 205, 206, 237, 238
response format, 197
responsibility, iv, viii, 49, 50, 52, 53, 73, 95, 99, 107, 109, 142, 220, 224, 226, 231
restructuring, 30, 91
retention, 36, 37, 38, 40, 41, 42, 45, 46, 87, 162
retention interval, 37, 40, 41, 42

retina, 168
retrieval, iv, 37, 47, 90, 131, 160
reward(s), 2, 44, 83, 215
risk(s), 56, 57, 163, 225
Ryan, Jack, 67, 68, 70, 71, 73, 74, 75, 76, 80, 82, 83, 151, 162, 192

S

sample, 171, 172, 196, 246, 247
satisfaction, 6, 67, 72, 73, 78, 222
schema, 53, 87, 89, 90, 97, 105, 106, 108, 110
schizophrenia, 34
scholastic achievement, 149, 151
school, vii, ix, x, xi, 3, 10, 13, 27, 30, 34, 50, 52, 60, 62, 63, 68, 70, 73, 86, 90, 99, 100, 106, 107, 110, 113, 120, 121, 123, 124, 125, 129, 141, 142, 149, 162, 163, 165, 166, 175, 184, 189, 191, 192, 194, 195, 196, 198, 200, 201, 202, 204, 207, 208, 209, 211, 212, 213, 214, 215, 216, 217, 219, 225, 228, 232, 233, 235, 236, 237, 238, 239, 240, 241, 242, 243, 244, 245, 246, 247, 248, 252, 253, 255, 258, 259, 260, 261
school achievement, 30, 34, 149
school enrollment, 243
schooling, 111, 115, 233, 238
science, ix, xi, 2, 34, 62, 82, 86, 165, 166, 167, 168, 169, 170, 172, 175, 182, 183, 184, 185, 187, 189, 190, 191, 193, 194, 195, 196, 198, 203, 204, 205, 206, 207, 208, 209, 210, 211, 212, 213, 214, 215, 216, 235, 237, 242, 243, 245, 252, 258
scientific knowledge, 166, 237, 242, 243, 252, 257, 258
scores, xi, 13, 20, 41, 49, 54, 58, 59, 60, 70, 72, 88, 117, 126, 130, 131, 132, 133, 134, 135, 136, 138, 149, 197, 200, 236, 241, 243, 248, 249
second language (ESL), ix, 145, 146, 149, 150, 151, 152, 161, 162
secondary education, 13
secondary schools, 196, 215, 216, 239
secondary students, ix, 191, 192, 194, 195, 197, 209, 211, 215, 258
selection, 12, 89, 121, 230
selective attention, 142
self esteem, 218
self-awareness, 82
self-confidence, 69, 74
self-control, 99
self-efficacy, viii, 2, 9, 12, 27, 65, 67, 69, 72, 73, 74, 78, 79, 83, 84, 253
self-esteem, 70, 78, 83
self-expression, 238
self-improvement, 78

self-monitoring, 94
self-perceptions, 83, 99
self-presentation, 69
self-regulation, 66, 67, 74, 79, 82, 83, 84, 92, 93, 94, 110, 140
self-worth, 67
semantic information, 140
semantic memory, 34
sensations, 168
sensitivity, 146, 148, 153, 154, 155, 156, 157, 158, 162
sentence comprehension, 152
separation, 14
series, 12, 28, 34, 36, 37, 96, 98, 156, 173, 200, 219, 224, 238, 239, 256
Sessions, Peter, 132, 133, 134
sex differences, 41, 45, 210, 214
sharing, x, 52, 217, 219, 220, 225, 228, 230, 231
short term memory, 146, 150, 159, 160, 161, 162, 163
situation, vii, viii, 1, 10, 12, 24, 51, 53, 54, 55, 63, 65, 69, 72, 73, 87, 92, 94, 97, 102, 120, 142, 149, 166, 167, 168, 170, 173, 174, 177, 178, 179, 180, 181, 182, 184, 186, 187, 193, 197, 204, 206, 212
skill acquisition, 4, 29, 34, 236, 239, 242
skills, vii, ix, xi, 1, 2, 3, 4, 5, 6, 7, 8, 9, 26, 27, 28, 29, 32, 34, 50, 51, 65, 67, 76, 77, 86, 87, 88, 92, 94, 97, 98, 99, 100, 102, 103, 108, 110, 113, 123, 140, 145, 146, 148, 149, 150, 153, 154, 162, 215, 226, 229, 233, 235, 237, 238, 239, 241, 256, 257
social behavior, 238
social class, 193
social context, 115, 193, 198, 233
social development, vii
social environment, 215, 218
social interaction, 238
social roles, 195
social structure, 141
social support, 101
specialization, 5, 8, 12
specific knowledge, 4, 7, 26, 98, 123, 124, 128, 134, 137, 139, 141, 143, 163, 236, 259
speech, 154, 220, 225
speech perception, 154
speed, 29, 34, 121, 122, 124, 127, 141, 142, 153, 154
sports, 31, 33, 236, 243, 256
SPSS, 17, 200, 201
stabilization, 189
staff, 213, 231
staff development, 213
stages, vii, viii, 1, 4, 8, 85, 86, 104, 134, 137, 150, 169, 188, 237, 239, 240

standard deviation, 17, 99, 116, 126, 127, 202, 203, 210, 212
standardization, 49, 50
standardized testing, 54, 63
standards, 77, 231, 232, 243, 260
statistics, 17, 22, 239
stimuli, 35, 36, 37, 40, 42, 43, 45, 87, 125, 147, 148, 150, 156, 159, 168, 227, 238, 253
STM, 153, 161
storage, 148, 150, 156
strategies, vii, viii, ix, xi, 1, 8, 9, 10, 14, 16, 17, 27, 28, 49, 50, 51, 52, 54, 63, 64, 65, 66, 67, 68, 69, 70, 71, 72, 73, 74, 78, 79, 80, 81, 82, 83, 84, 86, 90, 92, 93, 94, 95, 96, 98, 99, 100, 101, 102, 104, 107, 110, 114, 115, 116, 117, 119, 120, 121, 122, 123, 124, 128, 131, 134, 135, 136, 137, 138, 139, 140, 141, 142, 143, 160, 193, 216, 218, 220, 221, 225, 230, 237, 238
strategy use, ix, 14, 66, 69, 81, 84, 119, 120, 121, 122, 123, 124, 126, 127, 128, 131, 136, 137, 138, 139, 140, 141, 142
stress, 41, 42, 44, 45, 46, 54, 68, 69, 72, 232
structural equation modeling, 32, 72
structural knowledge, 32
structuring, 185
student achievement, 49, 108
student motivation, 79, 82, 239
students, vii, viii, ix, x, xi, 1, 11, 12, 13, 14, 15, 16, 17, 20, 24, 28, 29, 49, 50, 51, 52, 53, 54, 55, 58, 59, 60, 61, 62, 63, 65, 66, 68, 69, 72, 73, 74, 76, 77, 78, 79, 80, 81, 82, 83, 84, 85, 86, 89, 90, 91, 92, 95, 96, 98, 99, 100, 101, 102, 103, 106, 107, 108, 109, 111, 112, 117, 123, 128, 139, 140, 141, 143, 145, 146, 149, 151, 152, 155, 163, 165, 166, 167, 168, 169, 170, 172, 173, 175, 176, 177, 178, 179, 180, 181, 182, 183, 184, 185, 186, 189, 191, 192, 193, 194, 196, 197, 198, 200, 202, 203, 204, 205, 206, 207, 208, 209, 210, 211, 212, 213, 214, 216, 227, 231, 235, 236, 240, 241, 242, 243, 244, 246, 247, 248, 249, 250, 252, 253, 254, 255, 256, 257, 258, 260, 261
students' ideas, 205
students' understanding, 189, 205
study, viii, ix, xi, 2, 9, 13, 14, 15, 16, 17, 18, 20, 22, 23, 24, 25, 27, 28, 30, 31, 32, 35, 36, 38, 40, 60, 65, 68, 69, 72, 75, 76, 78, 80, 99, 106, 107, 108, 113, 117, 121, 124, 125, 126, 128, 131, 132, 133, 134, 137, 138, 140, 147, 148, 149, 150, 151, 152, 154, 155, 156, 159, 160, 161, 162, 163, 165, 167, 172, 176, 177, 180, 181, 183, 184, 185, 186, 187, 188, 191, 192, 193, 194, 195, 196, 198, 200, 202, 207, 208, 209, 210, 211, 212, 213, 214, 215, 217, 218, 219, 223, 227, 228, 229, 231, 232, 235, 237, 240, 242, 244, 245, 246, 247, 250, 252, 254, 255, 256, 257, 258
subjective experience, 81, 260

T

Taiwan, 193, 194, 208, 209, 211, 216
target behavior, 73
task demands, 124
teacher instruction, 172
teacher training, 213
teachers, viii, ix, x, xi, 49, 50, 51, 52, 53, 55, 59, 60, 61, 62, 63, 66, 80, 89, 90, 95, 99, 104, 109, 111, 139, 165, 167, 169, 182, 183, 186, 191, 192, 193, 194, 198, 203, 204, 205, 206, 207, 209, 210, 211, 212, 213, 214, 217, 218, 219, 220, 221, 222, 223, 224, 225, 226, 227, 228, 229, 230, 231, 232, 233, 235, 237, 240, 242, 243, 244, 247, 248, 256, 257
teaching, ix, x, 12, 14, 17, 18, 28, 29, 33, 50, 51, 52, 59, 60, 62, 64, 66, 67, 79, 82, 83, 86, 89, 98, 100, 109, 110, 113, 115, 136, 143, 161, 165, 187, 193, 197, 198, 203, 204, 206, 207, 210, 212, 213, 214, 215, 216, 217, 218, 219, 220, 221, 225, 226, 228, 230, 231, 232, 233, 240, 243, 258, 259, 260
teaching experience, 228
teaching strategies, 187, 230, 231
team members, 219
technology, 102, 114, 215, 216
tertiary education, 197
test items, 101, 196, 199
test scores, 49, 77, 243, 248
The Let Me Learn Process® Learning Connections Inventory©, viii, 49
theoretical assumptions, 2
theory, viii, ix, xi, 2, 3, 4, 5, 6, 7, 9, 10, 11, 14, 26, 28, 29, 30, 31, 32, 34, 46, 51, 62, 67, 68, 69, 72, 79, 81, 82, 85, 86, 87, 89, 90, 97, 101, 102, 104, 108, 109, 112, 113, 119, 120, 140, 143, 162, 165, 170, 189, 190, 194, 218, 232, 233, 235, 259, 261
thinking, 2, 3, 6, 7, 26, 27, 31, 32, 51, 53, 91, 94, 96, 99, 100, 102, 103, 105, 108, 109, 111, 113, 140, 143, 167, 188, 190, 205, 210, 211, 213, 220, 226, 228, 239, 247
threat(s), 68, 70, 75, 76, 77, 78, 80
time, viii, ix, 3, 4, 7, 10, 16, 26, 33, 35, 36, 37, 38, 40, 41, 42, 43, 50, 51, 52, 54, 55, 56, 57, 58, 59, 78, 90, 98, 101, 102, 107, 115, 119, 120, 124, 131, 133, 134, 137, 138, 139, 147, 161, 165, 166, 167, 170, 172, 173, 179, 181, 182, 183, 186, 192, 205, 212, 215, 221, 222, 224, 226, 227, 230, 236, 241, 244, 248, 253
time periods, 107
timing, 161

torture, 62
training, vii, x, 1, 3, 8, 32, 35, 36, 37, 38, 40, 42, 43, 45, 88, 99, 111, 123, 131, 140, 162, 184, 185, 186, 192, 213, 218, 244, 247
training programs, x, 192
transformation, 184, 231, 261
translation, 150, 218
treatment(s), 33, 37, 40, 99, 107, 116, 117, 197, 248
trial, 42, 45, 93, 125, 126, 129, 130, 131, 132, 135, 177
triangulation, x, 217, 220
trust, 206, 208
trustworthiness, 248
Type I error, 248

U

uncertainty, 69, 187, 189
unconscious, 27, 91
United Kingdom (UK), 160, 161, 162
United Nations (UN), 178
United States (US), 31, 60, 160, 236, 242
units of analysis, 194, 200, 201, 207, 208, 209
university education, 14
university students, 79, 146

V

validation, 13, 14, 15, 25, 28, 55, 84, 241, 245, 246
validity, x, 13, 14, 15, 25, 29, 30, 83, 169, 191, 194, 195, 198, 200, 201, 209, 211, 245
values, x, 13, 15, 20, 21, 23, 67, 68, 72, 81, 87, 117, 173, 191, 193, 194, 199, 200, 201, 202, 203, 204, 207, 208, 209, 210, 211, 212, 219, 239, 253, 259
variable(s), 4, 6, 10, 12, 17, 18, 20, 21, 23, 127, 133, 141, 153, 209, 241, 245, 250, 252
variance, 14, 17, 18, 20, 21, 24, 149, 192, 194, 199, 200, 201, 207, 208, 209, 211, 251, 255, 256
variation, 25, 37, 43, 166, 177, 180, 181, 184, 201

varimax rotation, 200
verbal justifications, 130
verbal persuasion, 86
vision, 16, 218, 219
visual stimuli, 40
vocabulary, 52, 121, 146, 147, 149, 150, 151, 153, 154, 155, 160, 161, 162, 163, 231
voice, 56, 172, 220, 221, 223, 225, 227
voice mail, 56

W

wait-time, 205
waking, 54
warrants, 254
water, 129, 197
weapons, 125
word recognition, 150
words, 6, 52, 54, 57, 59, 60, 90, 94, 97, 101, 102, 106, 125, 131, 145, 146, 147, 148, 149, 150, 151, 152, 153, 155, 156, 157, 158, 159, 163, 179, 180, 181, 195, 216, 222, 238, 246, 255
work, vii, viii, 1, 4, 8, 9, 12, 13, 14, 16, 17, 18, 19, 20, 22, 23, 24, 25, 26, 27, 28, 36, 49, 50, 52, 53, 54, 55, 56, 58, 59, 61, 62, 70, 71, 77, 89, 99, 100, 105, 108, 116, 166, 168, 169, 176, 177, 183, 184, 185, 187, 188, 193, 205, 206, 211, 216, 219, 220, 222, 223, 226, 227, 228, 230, 237, 247, 253
workers, 55, 197
working memory, ix, 4, 105, 135, 145, 146, 147, 148, 151, 152, 153, 155, 156, 158, 159, 160, 161, 162, 163
writing, 55, 59, 61, 62, 84, 98, 99, 102, 103, 114, 115, 142, 146, 154, 220, 225, 230
writing process, 102

Y

young adults, 39